WATERWORLDS

Ethnography, Theory, Experiment

Series Editors:
Martin Holbraad, *Department of Anthropology, University College London*
Morten Axel Pedersen, *Department of Anthropology, University of Copenhagen*
Rane Willerslev, *Museum of Cultural History, University of Oslo*

In recent years, ethnography has been increasingly recognized as a core method for generating qualitative data within the social sciences and humanities. This series explores a more radical, methodological potential of ethnography: its role as an arena of theoretical experimentation. It includes volumes that call for a rethinking of the relationship between ethnography and theory in order to question, and experimentally transform, existing understandings of the contemporary world.

Volume 1
AN ANTHROPOLOGICAL TROMPE L'OEIL FOR A COMMON WORLD
AN ESSAY ON THE ECONOMY OF KNOWLEDGE
By Alberto Corsín Jiménez

Volume 2
FIGURATIONS OF THE FUTURE
FORMS AND TEMPORALITIES OF LEFT RADICAL POLITICS
IN NORTHERN EUROPE
By Stine Krøijer

Volume 3
WATERWORLDS
ANTHROPOLOGY IN FLUID ENVIRONMENTS
Edited by Kirsten Hastrup and Frida Hastrup

Volume 4
VIOLENT BECOMINGS
STATE FORMATION, SOCIALITY, AND POWER IN MOZAMBIQUE
Bjørn Enge Bertelsen

Volume 5
VITAL DIPLOMACY
THE RITUAL ON A DAMMED RIVER IN AMAZONIA
Chloe Nahum-Claudel

WATERWORLDS
Anthropology in Fluid Environments

Edited by
Kirsten Hastrup and Frida Hastrup

berghahn
NEW YORK • OXFORD
www.berghahnbooks.com

First published in 2016 by
Berghahn Books
www.berghahnbooks.com

© 2016, 2017 Kirsten Hastrup and Frida Hastrup
First paperback edition published in 2017

All rights reserved.
Except for the quotation of short passages for the purposes
of criticism and review, no part of this book may be reproduced
in any form or by any means, electronic or mechanical,
including photocopying, recording, or any information
storage and retrieval system now known or to be invented,
without written permission of the publisher.

Library of Congress Cataloging-in-Publication Data

Names: Hastrup, Kirsten. | Hastrup, Frida.
Title: Anthropology in fluid environments / edited by Kirsten Hastrup and
  Frida Hastrup.
Description: New York : Berghahn Books, 2016. | Series: Ethnography, theory,
  experiment ; v. 3 | Includes bibliographical references and index.
Identifiers: LCCN 2015007892| ISBN 9781782389460 (hardback : alk. paper) |
  ISBN 978-1-78533-735-2 (paperback) | ISBN 9781782389477 (ebook)
Subjects: LCSH: Water—Social aspects. | Water use—Social aspects. | Water
  and civilization. | Human ecology.
Classification: LCC GB665 .A6 2015 | DDC 333.91—dc23
LC record available at http://lccn.loc.gov/2015007892

British Library Cataloguing in Publication Data

A catalogue record for this book is available from the British Library

ISBN 978-1-78238-946-0 (hardback)
ISBN 978-1-78533-735-2 (paperback)
ISBN 978-1-78238-947-7 (ebook)

CONTENTS

List of Illustrations		vii
Preface and Acknowledgements		x
Introduction.	Waterworlds at Large *Kirsten Hastrup and Frida Hastrup*	1
Chapter 1.	East Anglian Fenland: Water, the Work of Imagination, and the Creation of Value *Richard D.G. Irvine*	23
Chapter 2.	Fluid Entitlements: Constructing and Contesting Water Allocations in Burkina Faso, West Africa *Ben Orlove, Carla Roncoli and Brian Dowd-Uribe*	46
Chapter 3.	Raining in the Andes: Disrupted Seasonal and Hydrological Cycles *Astrid B. Stensrud*	75
Chapter 4.	Respect and Passion in a Lagoon in the South Pacific *Cecilie Rubow*	93
Chapter 5.	West African Waterworlds: Narratives of Absence versus Narratives of Excess *Mette Fog Olwig and Laura Vang Rasmussen*	110

Chapter 6.	To the Lighthouse: Making a Liveable World by the Bay of Bengal *Frida Hastrup*	129
Chapter 7.	Enacting Groundwaters in Tarawa, Kiribati: Searching for Facts and Articulating Concerns *Maria Louise Bønnelykke Robertson*	141
Chapter 8.	Mapping Urban Waters: Grounds and Figures on an Ethnographic Water Path *Astrid Oberborbeck Andersen*	162
Chapter 9.	Water Literacy in the Sahel: Understanding Rain and Groundwater *Anette Reenberg*	184
Chapter 10.	Deep Time and Shallow Waters: Configurations of an Irrigation Channel in the Andes *Mattias Borg Rasmussen*	203
Chapter 11.	Moral Valves and Fluid Properties: Water Regulation Mechanisms in the *Bâdia* of South-Eastern Mauritania *Christian Vium*	219
Chapter 12.	Reflecting Nature: Water Beings in History and Imagination *Veronica Strang*	247
Chapter 13.	The North Water: Life on the Ice Edge in the High Arctic *Kirsten Hastrup*	279
Notes on Contributors		300
Index		304

LIST OF ILLUSTRATIONS

3.1 Average yearly precipitation in Chivay, 1973–1982 and 2008–2011. 84

8.1 The hydraulic scheme and system of distribution of water by AUTODEMA, the operator of the major hydraulic system. Produced by AUTODEMA and printed with permission. 172

8.2 Plan of the SEDAPAR system of distribution of drinking water. Printed with permission. 173

8.3–8.6 The multilayered map of Arequipa, made with the architect in SEDAPAR, January 2012. Printed with permission. 179

8.3 Natural flows of water. 179

8.4 Natural flows and irrigation canals. 179

8.5 Potable water, wastewater, irrigation canals and natural flows. 179

8.6 Potable water, wastewater, irrigation canals and natural flows, and a ground plan of buildings. 179

9.1 The dam at Touro, northern Burkina Faso, following the storm in 2006, shortly after the construction. Photo by Anette Reenberg. 192

9.2 Small-scale irrigation in Niger. Motor pumps provide water for agriculture in the cuvettes. Photo by Anette Reenberg. 197

11.1 Morning view of the eastern fringes of the city Oualata, with the well *Ain al-Argoub* surrounded by animals in the dry riverbed (*oued*). Photo by Christian Vium. 220

11.2 Nomadic herders pulling water at the well *Ain al-Argoub* on the eastern fringes of the city Oualata. Photo by Christian Vium. 222

11.3 Médé, a herder from the Hamonat tribal faction, portrayed as he waits for water at the well Ain al-Argoub outside Oualata. Photo by Christian Vium. 228

12.1 The Worm around Penshaw Hill. Drawing by Danny Parkinson. 248

12.2 Sir John Lambton slew the worm. Image originally created by John Dickson Batten. 249

12.3 Bark painting from western Arnhem Land, Australia. The Rainbow Serpent Ngalyod giving birth to Aboriginal people. Artist, Billinyara Nabegeyo. 251

12.4 Cloud Dragon screen in Kennin-Ji, twelfth-century Zen Temple (Kyoto). Photo by Veronica Strang. 252

12.5 A configuration of early human–environmental relationships. 254

12.6 A more hierarchical and human-centred configuration of relations with water and 'nature'. 256

12.7 Hercules slaying the Lernean hydra, c.525 B.C.E. Collection of the J. Paul Getty Museum, Malibu, California. Digital image courtesy of the Getty Museum's Open Content Program. 257

12.8 Stone marker from Coventina's Well. Photo by author. 259

12.9 Illumination from the beginning of St Matthew's Gospel in a Bible bequeathed by William of St Carilef. Image courtesy of Durham Cathedral Library. 261

12.10 Russian icon of St George and the dragon, c.1450. Image courtesy of National Museum, Stockholm. 263

12.11 Church carving: crusaders slaying 'infidels', Acca, Israel. Photo by author. 265

12.12 A contemporary configuration of human–environmental relations. 268

12.13 The Bishop of Durham, Justin Welby, being presented with the Conyers Falchion in 2011. Photo by Keith Blundy | aegiesPR. 269

12.14 The newly appointed Bishop of Durham, Paul Butler, being presented with the falchion in Croft-on-Tees in 2014. Photo by Keith Blundy | aegiesPR. 270

12.15 The falchion presented to each new Bishop of Durham. Photo by author. 270

PREFACE AND ACKNOWLEDGEMENTS

This book springs out of a collaborative anthropological research project called Waterworlds that was established in 2009 around three major water-related challenges: the melting ice, the rising seas, and the drying lands. Wherever the project participants worked – and many of them have contributed to this volume – water was somehow in focus, either because it took a new form, such as ice turning to water, or because there was too little or too much of it, or because it became too violent. As a whole, the ethnographic work of Waterworlds showed water and social life to be fundamentally co-constituted.

The relationship between human life and the planet of which it is part has changed dramatically over the past couple of centuries. The human footprint is everywhere, and people all over the world experience an increasing volatility in the surrounding landscapes. Well-established boundaries are perforated as global changes affect local resources. In the process, the very notion of locality is destabilized. This poses a new challenge to anthropology, always committed to the 'local', but now faced with inevitably fluid boundaries. Part of the fluidity presently experienced springs out of unpredictable and unbounded waters, in focus here. However, the larger vision of this book is to meet the general anthropological challenge of establishing an analytical object amidst unbounded ethnographic fields.

We would like to acknowledge the ERC Advanced Grant (2009–2014), which allowed us to pursue this general challenge by working in regions that are wide apart, and to theorize across different waterworlds. Thanks are also owed to our editor, Molly Mosher of Berghahn Books, for her professionalism and patience, and to the two anonymous reviewers for their constructive and much appreciated comments.

January 2015
Kirsten Hastrup and Frida Hastrup

Introduction
Waterworlds At Large

Kirsten Hastrup and Frida Hastrup

The present times are promising in anthropology, ready and able to cast its moorings in received notions of culture and society that reflect a basically sedentary view of the analytical object. Instead, there is a general acknowledgement of unstable worlds, marked by unstable boundaries, migrating people, shifting resource bases and new global technologies, as well as multiplying flows of things, images and knowledge. In this book we focus on the part played by water in the making and unmaking of fluid worlds. Through diverse ethnographies of 'waterworlds' we explore social life as configured by water in one form or another, and show how this allows for an acknowledgement of the anthropological object as unbounded and premised on a unity of nature and society.

Possibly, not everybody would agree with the promise of a situation that seems to create ever more messiness in the discipline of anthropology, both in terminology and purpose. There is much to be said, though, for a creative '*un*-disciplining', if it is then better able to respond to the historical situation of fast-flowing images and ideas across the world and to the pressing global ecological crisis. Now is a moment when we cannot conceive of the Earth regardless of human whims and social forms. The term 'anthropocene' has been coined for a proposed new era to succeed the Holocene, the latter being the period following the last glacial period up until the present, as identified by geological measures (Crutzen 2002; Ehkers and Kraft 2006). In the anthropocene, the imprint of human activities on the Earth's ecosystems is seen around the globe and deeply affects its future; this unprecedented human impact on the planet is part of the definition of the term. Partly owing to the rapid population increase, and partly to the development of earth-shattering technologies and extractive industries, over the past century humans have disturbed the globe to a degree that it is no longer possible to speak of a self-generating *natural* world. Although still subject to debate in the natural sciences – mainly geology, from where the notion springs – it seems appropriate to co-opt the notion of the anthropocene to anthropology, where nature and social life have by now been recognized as intertwined (K. Hastrup 2013b).

In this volume, we suggest that the promise of anthropology is closely linked with what we would like to call 'the anthropocene moment'. This moment is marked by an awareness of the future of the Earth being inexorably linked to human history and to the human capacity for reflection, and for remaking or destroying the world. In the chapters that follow, we shall see multiple instances of formative, reflexive powers in places where basic environmental conditions are changing, and fluidity on all accounts is the order of the day. The notion of the anthropocene thus sets the scene for the book not simply as a description of an environmental and climatic revolution, but for an anthropology that recognizes the need to join forces across disciplines, parts of the world, knowledge domains, professionals and so-called lay people in analysing and grappling with what is to become of the Earth. The very object of study – world-making projects in fluid environments – is necessarily a result of empirical and analytical concern for a shared globe, to which ideas of settled and natural entities no longer apply.

The book does not offer tales of destruction or despair, although this may sometimes lurk in the ethnographies. With the cases presented below, the book shows how humans are not only part of the problem, but also part of the solution to the uncertainties of our common future. In the anthropocene moment, where else would we look for inventive and even interventionist action of redress? In this era there is no given anthropological object, but multiple and composite objects emerging out of particular reflexive or analytical processes, in which humans always engage. In other words, anthropology finds itself at a moment in time when the field is literally wide open, and where new certainties have not yet sedimented. Evidently, people live in actual places, whether they see themselves as stationary or mobile, and anthropological fieldwork is likewise conducted in specific places. Even if both social life and anthropological knowledge are therefore 'located', they are never entirely 'local', nor well bounded (Turnbull 2003). Whatever anthropologists are studying, it bends and stretches in both space and time according to the interests of the interlocutors and of the fieldworkers, and it may incorporate diverse people, other species, deep geological times, historical precursors, drifting ideas, winds and weather, as well as diverse kinds of knowledge – all of them contributing to the make-up of the world. From an anthropological perspective, unspecified relations become temporarily specified, and a world emerges as a set of connected relations. Such processes of 'worlding' are the central tenet of this book (cf. Tsing 2010).

As an entry into an anthropocene anthropology that explores and indeed productively engages with the unbounded quality of ethnographic knowledge, the chapters below focus on the role of water in worlding exercises across the globe. In the course of the inquiries, the power of water to make or unmake social worlds is explored, as people refashion their lives according to their understandings of water's course and force, and their views of the future. It becomes clear that the worlds we are talking about here are emergent and an outcome of analysis, carried out by all people acting upon some sort of anticipation (K. Hastrup 2013a).

By using the notion of 'worlding' and focusing on 'waterworlds', we thus experiment with a strategic perspective, allowing the chapters to speak to each other, and testifying to the mingling of empirical matter and analytical ambition. At the anthropocene moment in anthropology there is no epistemological distance between the 'real' world of people 'out there' and the world presented in the ethnographic cases. Both emerge in 'the ethnographic moment' (Strathern 1999). The focus on water highlights the need for rethinking the anthropological object in a fluid environment, by default connecting everybody across the globe in the anthropocene, and making things, living beings and places change according to analytical perspective.

Liquid Worlds

When the gigantic steamer *Titanic* hit an iceberg in April 1912, and the captain realized the imminent danger, he used new technology to try to alert other ships in the area. Some ships received the call for help, but were too far away to be of any use, while some closer ones did not have any wireless equipment with which to receive the signal from Titanic; and on board the closest ship, only 19 miles away, the wireless operator had closed down for the night ten minutes before the alarm. *Titanic* went down with the loss of over fifteen hundred passengers and crew.

Before *Titanic* disappeared its alarm signal had been picked up by a wireless station in Newfoundland. 'Shortly after that hundreds of wireless instruments along the Atlantic coast began to transmit, and the airways became jumbled in the confusion. The *Titanic*'s wireless had a range of only 1,500 miles, so signals to Europe had to go first to New York and then across the ocean by cable; still, by early morning, the entire world was privy to news of the disaster' (Kern 1983: 66). The globe became united in disaster by way of the wireless, possibly for the first time; such magical power of technology did not pass unnoticed – even though, obviously, for most people on board *Titanic* the 'magic' still had its limitations. Stephen Kern quotes an entry in the *New York Times* on 21 April 1912:

> Night and day all year round the millions upon the earth and the thousands upon the sea now reach out and grasp the thin air and use it as a thing more potent for human aid than any strand of wire or cable that was ever spun or woven. Last week 745 [sic] human lives were saved from perishing by the wireless. But for the almost magic use of the air the *Titanic* tragedy would have been shrouded in the secrecy that not so long ago was the power of the sea. (*New York Times*, quoted by Kern 1983: 67)

Other secrets were also unveiled, notably – in our context – the secrets of human life in far away places. People had always been travelling, and exploration of the continents and their inhabitants had taken off and multiplied since the Enlightenment. In the nineteenth century, European explorers had gone out of their way to map new lands – not to say that they had gone out of their minds (Fabian 2002). But their plights remained unknown until they were back, if they made it. Around 1900, one not only had ethnographic pictures brought home from the field by anthropologists, but one also had instantaneous news of calamities that had hit somewhere. Distance was minimized.

The fate of *Titanic* of course also installed a sense of collective dread in people – a feeling that the excessive size and volume of the steamer had been too daring. But it was the First World War that for a time arrested the uniform modernist belief in technology's unquestioned contribution to human progress; the technologies of war surpassed any imagination. Today, a hundred years later, we have a parallel issue with late modern technologies, harnessed by industry and placed all over the globe, distributing risk (Beck 1998). The major issue is the fact of global warming due to CO_2 emissions, not least from the use of fossil fuels, and visible for instance in the darkening peaks of glaciers (Orlove, Wiegandt and Luckman 2008). This reminds us about the anthropogenic nature of the current changes, and once again, a certain sense of dread glues to technologies that have united the globe into one world, because their effects seep into every corner, unseen and unmanageable.

Zygmunt Bauman (2006) has analysed the uncertainties related to living in such 'liquid modernity', where customary cause-and-effect sequences are falling apart, and unknowable dangers seem to lurk around the corner. The result, according to Bauman, is a 'liquid fear' that is part and parcel of life in the early twenty-first century, not least relating to the invisible pollution and the unknown terrorist who may be in our midst. The threats may be everywhere or nowhere, and they seep into our lives and affect our actions without our really noticing it, and without improving our means to avert them. Like the violence of which Veena Das has written, the liquid fear descends into the ordinary (Das 2007). The electronic media are very much part of our sense of dread, as news about secret encroachments upon people's privacy multiply. The magic of the wireless has become black.

Interestingly, Bauman also recalls *Titanic*, but as an imagery rather than a real death-bound steamer. He cites a film critic, who had pondered over the extraordinary triumph of the film *Titanic* from 1997, and suggested the following:

> Titanic is us, our triumphalist, self-congratulating, blind, hypocritical society, merciless towards its poor – a society in which everything is predicted except the means of predicting. ... (W)e all guess that there is an iceberg waiting for us, hidden somewhere in the misty future, which we will hit and then go down to the sounds of music. (Jacques Attali, quoted in Bauman 2006: 12)

Bauman adds that in retrospect – after 9/11 (2001), the Asian tsunami (2004) and Hurricane Katrina (2005) – the suggestion seems downright prophetic. The iceberg is a token of all the unknowns that may hit us while we are travelling through life, trying to overcome our fear of moving. It is not the intention here to dwell on disasters as such; after all they are soon difficult to single out from the everyday (F. Hastrup 2011a), but to suggest that in a world where everybody is potentially privy to what happens in any corner of it, the free-floating images of all sorts of calamity affect our ways of thinking and relating to the present. They are part and parcel of the liquid times, of which Bauman speaks (2007). At a mundane level, the liquidity of the present relates to social forms, political institutions, access to the labour market, and to an individualization of responsibility. It has shifted allegiances around in a way that undermines the modern social imaginary, as envisaged by Charles Taylor (2005), and founded upon the nation-state.

> The virtue proclaimed to serve the individual's interests best is not *conformity* to rules ... but flexibility: a readiness to change tactics and style at

short notice, to abandon commitments and loyalties without regret – and to pursue opportunities according to their current availability, rather than following one's own established preferences. (Bauman 2007: 4)

As implied in the notion of liquid times, living with uncertainty and not least with an unknown and largely unknowable future is not a matter of finding new and more sophisticated technological solutions, but mainly of renegotiating the idea of society and of subjectivity. Focusing on water in diverse forms, as the following chapters do, takes us towards a clearer vision of the ways in which the anthropological object takes shape in the course of analysing the unbounded liquid worlds.

When suggesting the term 'waterworlds' for these, we are not speaking of 'modern water', harnessed in hydrology, abstracted from the ecological and social relations that surround it, and converted into a scientific, measurable entity (Linton 2006). The water in the present book is part and parcel of the lived world; it is social by nature. According to Veronica Strang (2005), water is at the heart of human life, sensory experience and cultural meaning. We do not claim primacy of water in all worlding processes, save for noting that all life depends on water. In the chapters that follow, water is a perspective chosen to focus ethnographic attention on comparable themes, and to show how liquid fears are curbed in practice. In a recent special issue of *Social Studies of Science* (2012), the editors note:

> Water flows through our lives. It quenches thirst, sustains crops, generates power, cools industry, carries ships, disposes waste, and maintains ecosystems. Where the flow of water is reliable, clean and plentiful, it fosters growth; where the flow is too much, too little, or too dirty, it wreaks havoc. The use and management of the world's fresh water has therefore become a key contemporary issue: a topic of intense political debate and popular concern, and a focus of considerable scholarship within the social sciences. (Barnes and Alatout 2012: 483)

What we would like to do here is to explore this general power of water through concrete ethnographic analyses in which water and humans co-configure social worlds and values (K. Hastrup 2013e). Ben Orlove and Steve Caton have pointed out that the specific anthropological contribution to the study of waterworlds lies with 'seeing water not only as a resource, but also as a substance that connects many realms of social life' (Orlove and Caton 2010: 401); yet here water remains outside of what it connects, it seems. While categories are necessary for communication, the very fluidity of environments should not be dammed too early in a quest for managing water and putting it to work for humans (cf. Kaika 2006). Water has become acknowledged as an in-between category, permeating anthropological discussion in new ways and linking the two pillars upon which modern science developed: nature and culture. Stefan Helmreich writes:

> Water oscillates between natural and cultural substance, its putative materiality masking the fact that its fluidity is a rhetorical effect of how we think about 'nature' and 'culture' in the first place. Water as nature appears as both potentiality of form and uncontainable flux; it moves faster than culture, with culture often imagined in a land-based idiom grounded in the culture concept's origins in European practices and theories of agriculture and cultivation (Williams 1976). Water as nature appears as that flowing substance that culture may be mobilized to channel – think of canal locks, dams, and irrigation networks. Water as culture, meanwhile, can materialize as a medium of pleasure, sustenance, travel, poison and disaster. (Helmreich 2011: 132)

It is an intriguing proposition that nature 'moves faster' than culture. But why is that so, and how may it be measured? Another question is how water may 'oscillate' between nature and culture; this probably has less to do with water than with the human mind, seeking to understand the world in such a dualistic manner. Even while trying to dissolve the opposition between nature and culture, it resurfaces in statements that seem convincing at first sight, until one realizes that the argument is still steeped in a dualistic worldview that waterworlds explode.

We agree that it is difficult to keep things afloat, and we acknowledge the objectifying power of language. Yet, at this moment – that we have called 'the anthropocene moment in anthropology' – we should at least attempt to keep the doors open to a new and productive sense of liquidity that may surface ethnographically. We need to engage in more critical description, of the kind suggested by Anna Tsing, which is 'critical, because it asks urgent questions; and description, because it extends and disciplines curiosity about life' (Tsing 2013: 28). Such critical description may, at least for a while, allow us to explore the various socialities that are at play in the world.

Interdisciplinary Encounters

There is ample reason to extend the notion of sociality to non-human life forms, as suggested by Tsing (2013). This implies that neither species nor scholarly disciplines act in isolation. One might claim that whatever the object of interest may be, fieldwork – often seen as the constitutive method of anthropology – is inherently interdisciplinary, if for no other reason than because it plays out as social encounters across different perspectives. What is interesting, though, is that dialogue across disciplines and differences was also an early hallmark of the emergent anthropology in late nineteenth century.

A premium example of this is Alfred C. Haddon's Torres Straits Expedition in 1898–99. His work has been seen as a watershed in British anthropology – a nascent form of modern systematic and scientific fieldwork (Stocking 1983: 83–84; Edwards 1997: 14). Haddon was a zoologist, and he is credited with having imported the term fieldwork into anthropology from zoology (Herle and Rouse 1998: 17). Certainly, this was a decisive moment. In the preface to the first publication from the expedition, Haddon wrote:

> During the years 1888–89 I spent some eight months in Torres Straits, investigating the marine zoology of that district, and having become interested in the natives I devoted my spare time to recording many of their present and past customs and beliefs. Some of the results of these studies have already been published. Later I proposed to publish a Memoir on the Ethnography of the Islands of Torres Straits, but on going over the material I found that it was too deficient to make into a satisfactory monograph. I then determined to go once more to Torres Straits in order to collect more data, with a view to making, with the aid of colleagues, as complete a study of the people as was practicable. (Haddon 1901: v)

Wherever Haddon had made his zoological observations, people had told him that their culture was disappearing, and he engaged in downright salvage anthropology.

> In many islands the natives are fast dying out, and in more they have become so modified by contact ... no one can deny that it is our bounden duty to record the physical characteristics, the handicrafts, the psychology, ceremonial observances and religious beliefs of vanishing peoples; this also is a work which in many cases can alone be accomplished by the present generation ... The history of these things once gone can never be recovered. (Haddon 1897: 306; quoted in Edwards 1997: 14)

What emerges here is the death of traditional cultures due to the seeping in of foreign ways of world-making.

Haddon went on to assemble a team that was to set the tone of anthropology at Cambridge for generations to come, notably W.H.R. Rivers, C.G. Seligman, W. MacDougall and C.S. Myers. Between them they covered a wide range of disciplines, among which psychology stood out strongly (Kuper 1990). Also Haddon's own field, zoology, left a strong mark upon the findings. It has even been suggested that

> Haddon's success in his first ethnographic research, and in the subsequent development of his career as an ethnologist, was due to his particular way of looking at the anthropological field with the eyes of a biologist. The apparent conversion of Haddon from zoology to ethnology was nothing but the transference of a great part of the techniques, instruments, theories, models and points of view of biology to the study of anthropology. (Roldán 1992: 23)

This is an interesting point, bearing the mark of its own time; for Haddon the world was seen through many species – a theme that is recurring today.

Haddon's team was very well equipped with technological instruments as befitted modern science, notably camera and cinematographe, underscoring the fact of vision being the central question of the expedition, and producing ethnography of 'high visual quality' (Grimshaw 2001: 20). Rivers literally studied the native's eyesight and colour vision to an astonishing degree of detail. Here is how he presents his work:

> We were able during our four months' stay in Murray Island to cover a fairly wide field in our work. The subjects, which we investigated, included visual acuity and sensibility to light difference; colour vision, including testing for colour blindness, colour nomenclature, the thresholds for different colours, after-images, contrast, and the colour vision of the peripheral retina; binocular vision; line-dividing; visual illusions, some of which were investigated quantitatively; acuity and range of hearing; discrimination of tone difference; rhythm; smell and taste; tactile acuity and localization; sensibility to pain; temperature spots; discrimination of weight and illusions of weight; reaction-time, including auditory and visual simple reaction-time and choice-time; estimation of intervals of time; memory; mental fatigue and practice; muscular power and motor accuracy; drawing and writing; blood-pressure changes under various conditions, etc. (Rivers 1901: 1–2)

The complete picture of the people in Torres Straits, to which Haddon aspired, was not only a metaphor. It was part of a scientific strategy of close-up observation and objective documentation of human life in all its width; it was a (modern) way of *performing* science (Edwards 1998). Through such performances, the modern ethnographic subjects emerged (K. Hastrup 2013c).

Today, anthropology has left behind the modernist notions of objectivity and straightforward documentation. If, in Haddon's time, cultures seemed threatened and rescue operations necessary, today we live with enormous environmental challenges calling on all resources if the world is to change its course. We thus still need to explore the diversity of life, not to preserve it in a congealed form but to learn from its inherent malleability, whether or not this is seen as a threat to or a precondition of survival. In the early twenty-first century, the world again seems uncertain and full of openings and perils, owing both to new technologies and to flows of consciousness. We are no longer talking about James Joyce's individual protagonist's stream of consciousness, but about new, global flows of images, resources, knowledge, sensations, fears, and economic values, coming from and going to nowhere in particular, but shared by all. Globalization runs its own course, *not* by design but by accident – not one single accident, but many – propelling the world in many directions at one and the same time. People, materials and ideas have been set afloat in unprecedented ways, and anthropology must follow suit, being still committed to study social life, wherever and however it unfolds, and whether in a world in crisis or not. And once again, it is acknowledged that no single anthropologist – or scientific discipline – can cover it all, but anthropology may nevertheless contribute a unique perspective on the world in which each and every one of us lives – albeit in different ways.

Haddon the zoologist already drew parallels about human and other species and their being steeped in complex relations. We also know very well that our forebears in later (modern) anthropology paid much heed to the relationship between people and their gardens (Malinowski) or between people and their cattle (Evans-Pritchard), just to allude to a few masterpieces of anthropology in the previous century (cf. K. Hastrup 2013d). Yet, the present moment allows or indeed forces us to dispense with the 'between', and to dive directly into the consistent fluidity of everything social.

Recently, such a proposition has been made on ethnographic grounds in the book *Saltwater Sociality* by Katarina Schneider (2012), suggesting how movement is the dominant trope of relationality in the Melanesian island community she studied. The islanders insisted on 'the inherent indeterminacy of movements, human and non-human alike, "at sea"' (ibid.: 15). Their fishing life, and their dependence on the sea, formatted all of their social relations in terms of movements, being the essential 'objects' of social life (ibid.: 21). While evidently presenting a particular ethnographic case, Schneider reminds us that fluidity itself may form a base for sociality, if (at first sight) a non-solid one.

From the ethnographic present in Melanesia we may move on to taking a larger view of the Pacific, where the dynamics of the past millennium have been discussed by Patrick Nunn (2007), convincingly combining knowledge from diverse disciplines. While the periodization of climate is subject to debate, there seems to be some agreement about two distinguishable periods during the last millennium, the Medieval Warm Period and the Little Ice Age. The first of these periods peaked around AD 1000–1100; the second reached its low point in the seventeenth century. In Europe, the historical records demonstrate the social implications of this. Among them is a tendency in the warm period for expansion, such as the Viking expansion in the North Atlantic, and for the development of new social forms; in contrast, the Little Ice Age was a time of contraction, with periods of hunger and a breakdown of social forms. This seems to be a general pattern also for earlier periods, and across the globe, including the Pacific.

The Pacific Basin is a geographical region in the classical sense, Nunn suggests, but it is in many ways a knowledge void (Nunn 2007: 18). 'The common perception of many people, accustomed to flying over the Pacific, is of this third of the Earth as empty' (ibid.). Nunn then goes on to show how it is possible to establish the effects of the two climatic periods mentioned above, also for the Pacific, and to link them with the migrations across the ocean and successive settlements on the various islands. Moving east and south from the originally colonized area closest to New Guinea, it was in the Medieval Warm Period that the navigators finally reached the farthest shores – probably in intentional search for new lands (ibid.: 31–32). In a more synoptic work, Nunn and his associates have shown how in the region as a whole, the warm and the cold periods are reflected in 'periods of plenty and periods of less' in the Pacific (Nunn et al. 2007). The main message from Nunn's work is that the ocean and the climate it fosters are not just one stable thing, but a dynamic partner in navigational and social opportunities and setbacks.

The Pacific shows how nature becomes infrastructure, once people move in and about (cf. Carse 2012). This idea is further sustained when we look at the European colonization of the Pacific, one expedition after another 'discovering' what was already appropriated and engaging in new transcultural histories of exchange – and extensive entanglement of objects that were to affect the imageries at both ends of the voyage (Thomas 1991). It is by its facilitating oceanic transport and global connections – in prehistory as well as in colonial times – that the ocean presents itself as infrastructure, a non-solid yet consistent carrier of sociality, emerging in the process of movement and connectivity, and calling for hybrid geographies, in the terms of Sarah Whatmore (2002). In her work, hybridity points to the thinking and practising of space by humans and others as part of the space to be charted. This is an open-ended task – in contrast to the geometric habits of earlier geographers – displacing the idea of a universal design and emphasizing the multiplicity of space-times generated by heterogeneous movements. 'The spatial vernacular of such geographies is fluid, not flat, unsettling the coordinates of distance and proximity; local and global; inside and outside' (Whatmore 2002: 6). Furthermore, it calls for a relational ethics that may embrace the inter-subjectivity of radically different kinds of subjects (ibid.: 159), and nurture interdisciplinary encounters.

Unbounded Socialities

Tsing has suggested a notion of a more-than-human sociality as a way of describing worlds made up of both humans and non-humans, the more pressing now that we are beginning to imagine and experience the implications of the anthropocene (Tsing 2013). With humans everywhere, we need to know more about their interrelationship with beings and things other than human, such as the mushrooms and forests that feature in her own work. She thus directs us towards the co-constitution of human and non-human agents, which in her case are living species. She then asks the question:

> What about things that are not alive? Aren't they social too? I cannot think of a good reason to argue that non-vital things are not social. After all, they are constituted in relations with others. They react; they are transformed. There is no reason not to extend social theory to rocks and rivers. Eduardo Kohn (n.d.) has a useful way of guiding us here: he argues that living things include futures in what they do in the present. The yet-to-come is part of the way living things react; we offer our living designs in regard to potential futures. This is not the case with rocks or other non-vital things. I think this makes a difference, not to the definition of sociality, but to the kinds of critical descriptions upon which analysts may embark. Critical description of living things maps those designs, intentional or unintentional, that gesture toward the future, making worlds for the yet-to-come as well as for the present. (Tsing 2013: 28–29)

Tsing's own critical description uncovers the sociality of living things in forests in which a particular mushroom thrives in the wake of a long history of human intervention in the forest. We would like to suggest that non-living things might likewise be seen to include their own future. One could easily think of the long history of the Pacific, responding to and part of the Earth's slow rhythm, oscillating between colder and warmer periods. Is there no future inhering in such movement? Would water be non-living on the definition offered?

The point of posing such rhetorical questions is to emphasize that whatever we are defining or un-defining as living, we humans are the definers. Tsing is aware of the fact that we can 'only know more-than-human socialities through human knowledge practices, including practices of living' (Tsing 2013: 34). This means that the onus of definition is always on the humans, and in our view this also applies to the definition of what it means to include one's future in present action. Our point here is that the 'more-than-human' is always seen in relation to 'human', remaining at the centre of its own knowledge practices, such as the suggestion of an anthropocene era, when weather and wind, water and sky are all part of the world where such practices take off – potentially enabling a joint future for humans and non-humans alike. We can thus add another meaning to the notion of the anthropocene moment, beside it describing human intervention as a 'geological' motor of disturbance: it also implies a call for a reconsideration of the ways in which analysis is generative of particular objects in the fluid more-than-human sociality.

What is transpiring in the anthropocene moment is the volatile nature of natures, human and non-human, and the limitation of knowledge practices that rest on modern assumptions of solid categories and scientific boundaries. There is a need to redefine the conversation across disciplines that were defined as singular. Given the entanglements of objects and the more-than-human socialities that anthropologists encounter in their fluid fields, they also have to think about theory in a new way. It is not something raised above the world, but very much part of its making. In liquid times, theorizing is perforce less 'disciplined' than before – it is in a sense an ethnographic fact (F. Hastrup 2011b).

A fine example of such unbounded fields of theorization is provided by Helmreich who studied the *Alien Ocean* (2009), by diving into the microbial seas and the world of marine biologists. In the process, he encountered global networks of science, of capitalism and of activism that showed how deeply even the vast oceans are now integrated in global processes that we normally talk about as if they belong exclusively to the land masses and their inhabitants. Thus Helmreich's study expands the 'liquid times' still deeper than Bauman's, the latter neglecting the sociality beyond the human.

Helmreich was also moved towards recognition of the need to rethink theory. 'In *Alien Ocean*, I read anthropological and oceanographic material and theories through one another. In this process, I treat theories – whether in anthropology or marine biology – both as tools for explaining worlds and as phenomena in the world to be examined. I think of such tacking back and forth as working *athwart theory*' (Helmreich 2009: 23). This is different from simply being interdisciplinary, or being 'against theory'. It is a strategy that sits well also with the present pursuit. It becomes even clearer if we let Helmreich himself elaborate:

> Working athwart theory asks not for isomorphism of direct representation, nor for the second order objectivity of triangulation, but rather for an

> empirical itinerary of associations and relations, a travelogue which, to draw on the natural meaning of *athwart*, moves sidewise, tracing the contingent, drifting and bobbing, real-time, and often unexpected connection of which social action is constituted, which mixes up things and their descriptions. Such an approach operates through not taking for granted a context within which a text or event will sit but rather creating and inhabiting contexts along the way. (Helmreich 2009: 23–24)

Such sidewise movement of theoretical work is appropriate for anthropological work in fluid environments, and with the inherent necessity for a theory of nonscalability, which 'recalls attention to the wild diversity of life on the earth' (Tsing 2012: 505). Modernity and colonialism were bound up with an idea of scalability; that is, 'the ability to expand – and expand, and expand – without rethinking basic elements' (ibid.). This is easily recognized in the history European expansion through plantations designed for colonial extraction, while excluding biological and cultural diversity.

> Modernity is, among other things, the triumph of technical prowess over nature. This triumph requires that nature be cleansed of transformative social relations; otherwise it cannot be the raw material of techne. The plantation shows how: one must create terra nullius, nature without entangling claims. Native entanglements, human and not human, must be extinguished; remaking the landscape is a way to get rid of them. (Tsing 2012: 513)

Ethnographic practice may enlighten us on the nonscalable worlds and the messy geographies that they entail. The practice centres on a heteroglot conversation that gradually creates understanding across diverse perspectives, and allows the anthropologist to move beyond preconceived notions. It is a challenge because 'the anthropologist's contexts and levels of analysis are themselves often at once both part and yet not part of the phenomena s/he hopes to organize with them. Because of the cross-cutting nature of the perspectives they set, one can always be swallowed by another' (Strathern 2004: 75).

This view of ethnographic practice manifests a radical break with the outlook of Haddon and his crew in the pioneering years of fieldwork. His was a modernist quest for solid, objective knowledge in the vein of the natural sciences. In some areas of research such quest is still pursued, arguably for the global good. David Turnbull has analysed how Western interests in finding a cure for malaria had actually overlooked the local specificities of the disease and the salient differences of the affected populations, such as, for example, the highlanders in Papua New Guinea. His analysis suggests 'that the kinds of epistemological, moral and ontological disciplining of people, practices and places that characterise the ways in which the knowledge space of Western laboratory science is extended are inappropriate in the disordered, complex world of tropical disease' (Turnbull 2003: 177). In this case, where Western medical industries have vested interests, nobody seems ready to leave a standard paradigm of a unified category of disease.

Another case is presented in Turnbull's analysis of turbulence research, being a contrastive example to the malaria case. With the study of turbulence we get near to our own interest in fluid environments and the question of how to keep things open, even while seeking general knowledge of sorts. On entering the field of turbulence research, Turnbull realized that there was no agreement on either the phenomenon or how to deal with it.

> Yet despite the lack of consensus there is sufficient coherence for the practitioners to act as if here is a field of turbulence research. Coherence in this case does not derive from a unifying paradigm or the adoption of an agreed set of instruments or methods. It derives from a very loose recognition that the phenomenon at issue is turbulence, even though its nature cannot be specified and even though it occurs in a very diverse set of flow situations from blood vessels to aircraft wings to the earth's atmosphere. But equally important, coherence results from the work of the researchers in the field trying to establish equivalences and connections in problem solving while also struggling for authority. (Turnbull 2003: 190)

In fluid environments, the anthropological object of interest seems as inherently indeterminate as turbulence; but here, too, the practitioners seem to drift towards a consensus about the need to establish equivalences that highlight their shared concerns.

Given that it is 'people' – like Bauman, Helmreich, Tsing and ourselves – who decide what is worth analysing and what is not, the continuous process of conversation between anthropologists and others is as important as ever. We need to share at least a loose recognition of the malleability of social life, and work to establish connections. Because we are living in a world of non-solids, we rely on the surplus of experience and ethnographic knowledge that will allow us the necessary analytical flexibility – flexibility being defined by Gregory Bateson as 'uncommitted potential for change' (Bateson 1972: 497).

Haddon exemplified such potential, when he first took anthropology to the field. Remarkably, apart from the legacy of fieldwork itself, the '[e]xpedition's results failed notably to mark subsequent work in anthropology [or] in psychology. Its conclusions were rarely incorporated into these disciplines, students were infrequently exposed to its results in any detail, and its role in theory-building was minimal' (Herle and

Rouse 1998: 19). Part of the explanation was slow publication, not least on the part of Haddon himself – his own contribution only appeared in 1935, yet it was still 'Report no. One'! It was generously reviewed as a masterpiece (Ashley-Montagu 1937), yet the fact is it was already archaic when it appeared (Urry 1998: 232).

What is possibly more significant, if we want to understand why this pioneering effort never fulfilled its promise, was an inherent tension between the vision of solid, modern laboratory work, exemplified in the long list of Rivers' experimental work with the people in Torres Strait quoted above, and the ever evanescent real-life situations. Rivers wrote: 'Each man who came for a morning's work received a stick of tobacco at the end of the morning and the children received sweets. It is perhaps well to mention that most of our observations on adults were made under the influence of tobacco' (Rivers 1901: 5). Tobacco or not, Rivers could only conclude that, from a scientific perspective, there was no major difference between the islanders and people from so-called more civilized regions. He thus discarded the notion of the islanders being at a different evolutionary stage.

At the same time he had a keen eye for the complexity of their linguistic and cultural situation, and discovered – by implication, if not by design – that even in their isolation they were steeped in a wide network of migrating social forms (Urry 1998: 224). Once out of the Torres Straits laboratory, Rivers went to pursue a study of the Todas in the Nilgiri Hills of southern India. This work deserves specific mention here, because in the Nilgiri Hills he came across another feature of the epoch, seeing the construction of 'observatories of modernity', combining scientific pursuit and colonial interest in making reliable global standards and universal values (Schaffer 2007). These observatories were most often set in colonial hill stations and soon became central institutions.

> There, seemingly reliable data might be gathered by the application of unrivalled hardware to pristine phenomena in a state of nature. Yet they were highly marginal, isolated from the centres of their sciences and often deliberately cut off from support or intimacy. This ambiguous geography helps us [to] understand how hill-stations like these worked as observatories of modernity a century ago. (Schaffer 2007: 21)

In such a setting Rivers studied the Todas, an enigmatic pastoral people, and his work soon became part of the wider colonial work of organizing the motley cast of races and groups, that soon would solidify and emphasize differences – rather than the human unity, uncovered by science. Anthropology came out of the laboratory and into history.

This, we surmise, also holds at the present moment. We are not launching a new paradigm or setting up new standards for proper anthropology. We simply want to show how anthropology has moved, and how anthropological analysis is part and parcel of the ways in which we may understand the world. 'The field' nowadays extends in all directions in time and space, and combines a welter of different sources; so does 'the world' within which people live, and the major ambition of this volume is to demonstrate the power of anthropology as an *analogue* method that works by relating different features to one another in a continued world-making dialogue that cuts across boundaries of disciplines, concerns, social positions, places of origin and the like (cf. F. Hastrup 2014). In working with people, the anthropologist gains from and contributes to the combined analytical powers that make worlds.

The Present Volume

The dialogue between ethnographers and fields transpires from the chapters to follow, showing how worlds emerge in concrete encounters and events, and how water and other fluid features become vehicles for the imagination and the creation of value and place. No less important, they show how fluid environments necessitate a close attention to the non-solids of social worlds and of anthropological knowledge objects.

The volume is structured around the three highly interconnected themes described above, namely *liquid worlds, interdisciplinary encounters* and *unbounded socialities*. These form a guide for reading the chapters and are an organizing principle – though no more solid than the worlds the volume engages with.

As means of exploring *liquid worlds,* in Chapter 1 Richard Irvine takes us to the East Anglian fenland, and the history of swamping, draining and refashioning the landscape. In the process of digging up the history of the fenlands, Irvine unravels the social and moral significance of the balance between wet and dry through the ages. In Chapter 2, by Ben Orlove, Carla Roncoli and Brian Dowd-Uribe, the moral and political dimensions of fluid environments are taken a step further into a notion of fluid entitlements. On the strength of their extensive, combined studies in Burkina Faso and neighbouring countries, they provide a detailed analysis of particular disjunctures – between systems of governance and forms of knowledge – and reveal how the increasingly fluid entitlements to water demand that we rethink notions of citizenship. In Chapter 3, Astrid Bredholt Stensrud draws our attention towards rain in the Andes, where changing seasonal and hydrological cycles heavily affect the relations between human and other-than-human bodies. By focusing on knowledge practices and social performances, the chapter explores the ways in which the disrupted patterns of rain and seasonality affect the ways of remembering and predicting rain. In Chapter 4, Cecilie Rubow takes us to the Muri lagoon on Rarotonga in the Cook Islands, with a view to understanding how individuals relate to the place and comprehend the current threats to the shallow water. The chapter portrays three women and their concerns for the lagoon, which are seen to be both varied and belonging to different registers of thought. Together these perspectives lead the author to discuss the imaginative transcendence of the landscape. In Chapter 5, Mette Fog Olwig and Laura Vang Rasmussen discuss how and why the narrative of drought has been so predominant in the perception of the environmental situation in West Africa. In actual fact, and as highlighted through the authors' fieldwork in the region, flooding due to violent rain has caused considerable damage and called for humanitarian assistance. Yet, people in the region invariably point to desertification as the critical issue. The absence and the excess of water are both major challenges, and the authors suggest that the emerging climate change narrative may prove able to comprise both.

As for the *interdisciplinary encounters,* in Chapter 6, Frida Hastrup shows how a lighthouse built on a shore of the Bay of Bengal becomes a shared analytical resource for people who live by it, be they fishermen, state officials, experts in nanotechnology, or anthropologists. Across these different positions, the lighthouse serves to calibrate various actors' diverse expectations of shared life by the sea. In Chapter 7, Maria Louise Bønnelykke Robertson takes us to an atoll community in the South Pacific, where the fragility of the groundwater resource is an evermore pressing issue. The invisibility of the groundwater as a shared resource makes it open to various and often incompatible imaginations and enactments by people living in different places, incoming development practitioners, and concerned scientists. The fluid perceptions of both the quantity and quality of fresh water in the shallow lens between the surface of the soil and the salt water that seeps in from beneath show – in practice – how concerns permeate the sense of fact. In Chapter 8, Astrid Oberborbeck Andersen brings us to an urban context in Peru, where water is seen as simultaneously scarce and abundant. This paradox is explored with a view to the materiality of water, and to recent changes in precipitation and in water governance. By using detailed maps of waterways and hydraulic grids, the author shows how a systematic mapping of diverse connections makes water emerge as an object of knowledge in a multi-layered waterscape. The chapter makes a clear case for the merging of empirical and analytical matters. In Chapter 9, Anette Reenberg addresses how people in the Sahel region deal with uncertainty about water resources that are vital for their livelihood. On the basis of fieldwork in a region that has suffered both fluctuating rainfall and dwindling groundwater, she introduces the concept of water literacy as an indication of people's understanding and capacity for acting upon situations of strain. Water literacy is not an issue of schooling or possessing scientific knowledge but a capacity to assess the probabilities of rain, for instance, and to identify alternative strategies for manoeuvring.

As the first case of *unbounded socialities,* in Chapter 10 Mattias Borg Rasmussen explores a flow of water in the Peruvian highlands. He follows a particular irrigation channel from its sources in the high mountains down to the bottom of the valley, and discusses how the channel has come to embody different historical moments and turns, thus embodying both space and time. He shows how the different 'moments' of the channel also instantiate diverse political regimes and notions of peasant communities in the more recent history. The channel thus becomes a vehicle not only for irrigation water but also for social imaginaries. In Chapter 11, Christian Vium takes us to the desert of Mauritania and describes how the wells are not only nodal points in the pastoral economy but also in the social life of the nomads. The region is experiencing a major crisis in the access to water, which necessitates a strict adherence to age-old notions of collective property and notions of solidarity – in spite of an acknowledgement that some families have priority at the actual location. Property rights seem to subside to notions of honour and the obligation to share, causing the wells to function as valves that enable the regulation of pressure and flow of animals, people, morality and property. In Chapter 12, Veronica Strang explores another imaginative resource, that of Durham's Lambton Worm, a serpent emerging from the River Wear and featuring in ballads and stories from the Middle Ages onwards. Water serpents and other beings are brought to bear on the general discussion of different social relations to the natural world, and their historical development. The chapter presents a strong case for suggesting that the material properties of water continue to flow into and shape human imagination, all while they transform landscapes and generate or destroy life. In Chapter 13, Kirsten Hastrup takes us to the deep sea, more specifically to the North Water, a high Arctic 'oasis' – a patch of open water in the ice covered sea that allows life to flourish even in the most deep-frozen part of the North. Based on fieldwork in a hunting community in the region, she explores the implications of living on the edge between ice and sea, and between the animal and the human world. These years, the ice cover is decreasing and access to prey is becoming more difficult, landing the hunters with new challenges and new attempts at scaling their world. The general point is that one of the implications of a fluid environment is a distinct temporariness of social forms, and of their extension.

Between them, the chapters bear witness to the challenges of the present moment in anthropology, where the fluidity of socialities and frames for orientation marks the worlds of all. If water is not simply seen as a chemical substance, but takes shape within particular perspectives, it emerges as a fluid object in more senses than one, challenging anthropologists to foreground and engage with its mutable character and, more generally, to responsibly explore the generative role of analysis.

Acknowledgement

The authors wish to thank the two anonymous reviewers whose constructive comments to this Introduction contributed to its improvement.

References

Ashley-Montagu, M.F. 1937. 'Reports of the Cambridge Anthropological Expedition to the Torres Straits, Volume I: Review', *Isis* 27(2): 349–53.
Barnes, J., and S. Alatout. 2012. 'Water Worlds: Introduction to the special issue of *Social Studies of Science*', *Social Studies of Science* 42(4): 483–88.
Bateson, G. 1972. *Steps to an Ecology of Mind*. New York: Ballantine Books.
Bauman, Z. 2006. *Liquid Fear*. Cambridge: Polity Press.
———. 2007. *Liquid Times*. Cambridge: Polity Press.
Beck, U. 1998. *World Risk Society*. Cambridge: Polity Press.
Carse, A. 2012. 'Nature as Infrastructure: Making and Managing the Panama Canal Watershed', *Social Studies of Science* 42(4): 539–63.
Crutzen, P.J. 2002. 'Geology of Mankind: The Anthropocene', *Nature* 415: 25.
Das, V. 2007. *Life and Words: Violence and the Descent into the Ordinary*. Berkeley: University of California Press.
Edwards, E. 1997. 'Making Histories: The Torres Strait Expedition of 1898', *Pacific Studies* 20(4): 13–34.
———. 1998. 'Performing Science: Still Photography and the Torres Strait Expedition', in A. Herle and S. Rouse (eds), *Cambridge and the Torres Strait: Centenary Essays on the 1898 Anthropological Expedition*. Cambridge: Cambridge University Press, pp. 106–35.
Ehkers, E., and T. Kraft (eds). 2006. *Earth Systems Science in the Anthropocene*. New York: Springer Press.
Fabian, J. 2002. *Out of Our Minds: Reason and Madness in the Exploration of Central Africa*. Berkeley: University of California Press.
Grimshaw, A. 2001. *The Ethnographer's Eye: Ways of Seeing in Modern Anthropology*. Cambridge: Cambridge University Press.

Haddon, A.C. 1901. 'Preface'. *Reports of the Cambridge Anthropological Expedition to Torres Straits, Vol. II: Physiology and Psychology*. Cambridge: Cambridge University Press.

Hastrup, F. 2011a. *Weathering the World: Recovery in the Wake of the Tsunami in a Tamil Fishing Village*. Oxford: Berghahn Books.

———. 2011b. 'Shady Plantations: Theorizing Coastal Shelter in Tamil Nadu', *Anthropological Theory* 11(4): 425–39.

———. 2014. 'Analogue Analysis: Ethnographic Fieldwork as Inventive Conversation', *Ethnologia Europaea* 44(2): pp. 48–60.

Hastrup, K. 2013a. 'Anticipating Nature: The Productive Uncertainty of Climate Models', in K. Hastrup and M. Skrydstrup (eds), *The Social Life of Climate Change Models*. London and New York: Routledge, pp. 1–30.

———. 2013b. 'Introduction: Anthropology on the Edge', in K. Hastrup (ed.), *Anthropology and Nature*. London and New York: Routledge, pp. 1–26.

———. 2013c. 'Andaman Islanders and Polar Eskimos: Emergent Ethnographic Subjects c.1900', *Journal of the British Academy* 1: 1–28.

———. 2013d. 'Anthropological Contributions to the Study of Climate: Past, Present, Future', *WIREs Climate Change* 4(4).

———. 2013e. 'Water and the Configuration of Social Worlds: An Anthropological Perspective', *Journal of Water Resource and Protection* 5: 59–66.

Helmreich, S. 2009. *Alien Ocean: Anthropological Voyages in Microbial Seas*. Berkeley: University of California Press.

———. 2011. 'Nature/Culture/Seawater', *American Anthropologist* 113(1): 132–44.

Herle, A., and S. Rouse. 1998. 'Introduction: Cambridge and the Torres Strait', in A. Herle and S. Rouse (eds), *Cambridge and the Torres Strait: Centenary Essays on the 1898 Anthropological Expedition*. Cambridge: Cambridge University Press, pp. 1–22.

Kaika, M. 2006. 'Dams as Symbols of Modernization: The Urbanization of Nature between Geographical Imagination and Materiality', *Annals of the Association of American Geographers* 96(2): 276–301.

Kern, S. 1983. *The Culture of Space and Time: 1880–1918*. Cambridge, MA: Harvard University Press.

Kuper, A. 1990. 'Psychology and Anthropology: The British Experience', *History of the Human Sciences* 3(3): 397–413.

Linton, J. 2006. *What is Water? The History of a Modern Abstraction*. Vancouver: UBC Press.

Nunn, P. 2007. *Climate, Environment and Society in the Pacific during the Last Millennium*. Amsterdam: Elsevier.

Nunn. P., et al. 2007. 'Times of Plenty, Times of Less: Last-Millennium Societal Disruption in the Pacific Basin', *Human Ecology* 35: 385–401.

Orlove, B., and S. Caton. 2010. 'Water Sustainability: Anthropological Approaches and Prospects', *Annual Review of Anthropology* 39: 401–15.

Orlove, B., E. Wiegandt and B.H. Luckman (eds). 2008. *Darkening Peaks: Glacier Retreat, Science and Society*. Berkeley: University of California Press.

Rivers, W.H.R. 1901. *Reports of the Cambridge Anthropological Expeditions to Torres Straits. Vol. II: Physiology and Psychology*. Cambridge: Cambridge University Press.

Roldán, A.A. 1992. 'Looking at Anthropology from a Biological Point of View: A.C. Haddon's Metaphors on Anthropology', *History of the Human Sciences* 5(4): 21–32.

Schaffer, S. 2007. 'Astrophysics, Anthropology and Other Imperial Pursuits', in J. Edwards, P. Harvey and P. Wade (eds), *Anthropology and Science: Epistemologies in Practice*. Oxford and New York: Berg, pp. 19–38.

Schneider, K. 2012. *Saltwater Sociality: A Melanesian Island Ethnography*. Oxford: Berghahn Books.

Stocking Jr, G.W. 1983. 'The Ethnographer's Magic: Fieldwork in British Anthropology from Tylor to Malinowski', in G.W. Stocking Jr (ed.), *Observers Observed: Essays on Ethnographic Fieldwork* (History of Anthropology I). Madison: University of Wisconsin Press, pp. 70-120.

Strang, V. 2005. 'Common Senses: Water, Sensory Experience and the Generation of Meaning', *Journal of Material Culture* 10(1): 92–120.

Strathern, M. 1999. 'The Ethnographic Effect', in *Property, Substance, and Effect*. London: The Athlone Press, pp. 1–26.

———. 2004. *Partial Connections* (updated version). Walnut Creek, CA: AltaMira Press.

Taylor, C. 2005. *Modern Social Imaginaries*. Durham, NC: Duke University Press.

Thomas, N. 1991. *Entangled Objects: Exchange, Material Culture, and Colonialism in the Pacific*. Cambridge, MA: Harvard University Press.

Tsing, A.L. 2010. 'Worlding the Matsutake Diaspora: Or, Can Actor–Network Theory Experiment with Holism', in T. Otto and N. Bubandt (eds), *Experiments in Holism: Theory and Practice in Contemporary Anthropology*. Chichester: Wiley-Blackwell, pp. 47–66.

———. 2012. 'On Nonscalability: The Living World Is Not Amenable to Precision-Nested Scales', *Common Knowledge* 18(3): 505–24.

———. 2013. 'More-than-Human Sociality: A Call for Critical Description', in K. Hastrup (ed.), *Anthropology and Nature*. London and New York: Routledge, pp. 27–42.

Turnbull, D. 2003. *Masons, Tricksters and Cartographers*. London and New York: Routledge.

Urry, J. 1998. 'Making Sense of Diversity and Complexity: The Ethnological Context and Consequences of the Torres Strait Expedition and the Oceanic Phase in British Anthropology', in A. Herle and S. Rouse (eds), *Cambridge and the Torres Strait: Centenary Essays on the 1898 Anthropological Expedition*. Cambridge: Cambridge University Press, pp. 201–33.

Whatmore, S. 2002. *Hybrid Geographies: Natures, Cultures, Spaces*. London: Sage.

1

East Anglian Fenland

Water, the Work of Imagination, and the Creation of Value

Richard D.G. Irvine

Of Wet and Dry Landscapes

But what is a fen? Is it not a wetland, defined first and foremost by its waterlogged nature? Borrowing liberally from Motley's (1855) description of the lowlands of Holland and Belgium, Wheeler (1868: 3) characterizes the fens of East Anglia as historically consisting of 'wide morasses, in which oozy islands were interspersed among lagoons and shallows, a district partly below the level of the tides and subject to constant overflow from the rivers, and to frequent inundations from the sea'. This is a liquid, not a solid, description; even the islands ooze.

A common ecological definition is that a fen is a groundwater-fed wetland (Bedford and Godwin 2003) (as opposed to a bog, which is precipitation fed), though more specific definitions have focused on the chemical characteristics of the wetland, such as the suggestion made by Wheeler and Proctor (2000: 197) of a pH level cut-off point, with fen defined as a mire (that is to say, peat-forming wetland) with a pH value greater than 5.5. All the same, Wheeler and Proctor (ibid.: 188–89) recognize that such typologies are at the tail end of a long etymological history (see Haslam 2003: 2–7, for an extensive inventory of popular and scientific usages), and from the point of view of thinking about the human experience of the landscape (or waterscape), it becomes very tricky to disentangle ecological terminologies from local uses of the term 'fen'.

The East Anglian fenlands present a particular challenge to water-bound definitions. What is the fenland today? It is a flat, open, low-lying landscape, dedicated largely to arable farming. The exposed peat soil, when it is visible, is a vivid black. The land is level and apparently featureless – so level and featureless, in fact, that in the nineteenth century the landscape inspired Samuel Rowbotham's observational experiments (carried out on the Old Bedford River, a fenland drainage channel) designed to prove that the planet Earth was, indeed, flat (Rowbotham 1865). There are very few protrusions in the land, and with no apparent landmarks to capture the eye, the fields seem to stretch into the distance as far as the horizon. With so little in the way of raised contours or tree cover to break the wind, you feel exposed to the elements as you move across the land. At dry times of year, the wind picks up the peat surface soil, carrying it away in dark, thick, clouds – a phenomenon known locally as 'fen blow'. Today's fen, then, does not lend itself to liquid description, but is characterized by the drier properties of the land as arable farm; properties that arise from its past qualities as wetland, but which in the present require the *absence* of water. This absence is, as we shall see, the product of tremendous labour. We are talking about a wetland from which water has been excluded – drained, channelled, diverted, managed, though never fully banished.

The goal of this chapter is to trace this (partial) exclusion of water. More specifically, I will write about the disputes that surround this exclusion; this is an ethnography of fen as a contested landscape, where water's presence or absence (both real and imagined) shapes arguments over the region's identity, use, purpose and future. To this end, I will tell stories of three episodes of change and contestation: the politics of East Anglian drainage works during the mid seventeenth century; the militaristic struggle against water in the Fenland during the Second World War; and contemporary efforts to 're-wet' swathes of the landscape.

Civilizing the Swamp: Seventeenth-Century Drainage

Human attempts to impose some control over fenland water flow have a long history. Roman drainage and navigation channels had a transformative impact on the geography of some areas of the fens (Rippon 1999), and these Roman waterways continue to be visible, and in many cases usable, to this day (as will become apparent in the case studies I present later in this chapter). Following the Roman period, monastic houses were at the forefront of attempts to embank waterways and dig ditches, allowing additional drainage of land to increase yields on their estates (Darby 1940; Sayer 2009); difficulties encountered following the dissolution of the monasteries indicate the significance of their role in fenland drainage (Darby 1956: 5–11).

Given this longer history, why start an account of the drainage of the fens in the Early Modern period? Certainly, academic accounts, presentations in museums, local histories and narratives all refer to seventeenth-century drainage as *the* drainage of the fens. The definite article is misleading on a number of scores; not only does it exclude these earlier drainage efforts, it also obscures the fact that much of the work of drainage during the seventeenth century met with mixed success (as we shall see), and the visible landscape of the fens today owes a great deal to nineteenth- and twentieth-century drainage efforts. This is not, however, to belittle the importance of seventeenth-century drainage.

Such drainage was a major undertaking of venture capitalism; indeed, this is reflected in the fact that the term used for the investors in such drainage was 'Adventurers'. In 1631, thirteen of these Adventurers, mostly already landowners in the region, joined together under the leadership of Francis Russell, the Fourth Earl of Bedford, to form The Bedford Level Corporation. Each owned one or two shares in the corporation, with each share dependent on an initial investment of £500, to be used towards the drainage works. In return for this initial investment, each Adventurer was promised private ownership of four thousand acres of land per share. Their contract received the approval of King Charles I, who in return expected his own twelve thousand acres allotment of land. What is clear from this project, the largest and surely most significant drainage initiative at this time in England, is not only the enormous scope of its ambition, but also the economic and ecological impact of such an endeavour, transforming an enormous portion of peat wetland into drained land for agricultural purposes, and granting rights of private ownership over large portions of land that were previously designated as common (see Wells 1830 for a detailed historical account produced for the corporation itself; see also Darby 1956 for a comprehensive account of the economic history of drainage). Under the direction of the Dutch engineer Cornelius Vermuyden (see Harris 1953 for an account of Vermuyden's role), the corporation commenced the embankment of existing rivers, and the cutting of enormous channels to improve drainage and allow for more direct outfall to the North Sea, ranging in distance from two to twenty-one miles.

So this was a programmatic attempt to change what the fen was; to make a wet land a dry land (to a limited extent, at least; the first scheme still anticipated some seasonal flooding). But alongside the technical accomplishment of changing patterns of water flow, we must also consider the significance of the work of this period in changing the way people *think* about the fen and what it is. The fenland becomes a source of potential wealth, but only if the water can be excluded. It is, in this sense, a land of imagination. The petroleum geologist and oil company director Wallace Pratt, in his paper 'Toward a Philosophy of Oil-Finding' wrote:

> Where oil is first found, in the final analysis, is in the minds of men. The undiscovered oil field exists only as an idea in the mind of some oil-finder. When no man any longer believes more oil is left to be found, no more oil fields will be discovered, but so long as a single oil-finder remains with a mental vision of a new oil field to cherish, along with freedom and incentive to explore, just so long new oil fields may continue to be discovered. (Pratt 1952: 2236)

This remark has tremendous resonance as an illustration of the mindset of the 'Adventurer'. The quest to find new resources requires imagination: oil finding is not just about capital investment and technical expertise, but the vision that recognizes the potential to find wealth in places where that wealth had not previously been imagined. So too for the creation of new agricultural land and the 'black gold' of fenland peat soil (to adopt the term commonly used by today's fenland farmers). The creation of a new kind of agricultural land on this scale is first and foremost a discovery 'in the minds of men'.

The work of drainage is the work of imagination. A major drainage scheme of this sort requires the fens to be treated as a kind of *terra nullius,* indeed, as a blank space onto which desires can be projected. The Adventurers must imagine and re-imagine the fens: first, imagining them as a void; then, re-imagining them through the projection of a promised land onto this void. This is made quite apparent by the establishment of a parallel between the work of drainage and God's work of creation out of the void – William Dugdale, author of a *History of Imbanking and Drayning* commissioned by Lord Edward Gorges, an Adventurer with the Bedford Level Corporation, begins his account in this way: 'That works of Drayning are most antient and of divine institution, we have the testimony of Holy Scripture. In the beginning God said, let the waters be gathered together...' (Dugdale 1662: 1).

Dugdale's method of representation is instructive: we are left in no doubt that the pre-drainage fens are a chaotic space, where the elements themselves are disordered. 'What expectation of health can there be to the bodies of men, where there is no element of good? The Air being for the most part cloudy, gross, and full of rotten harrs; the Water putrid and muddy, yea full of loathsome vermin; the Earth spungy and boggy; and the Fire noisome by the stink of smoaky hassocks' (Dugdale 1662:

7). This is a depiction of fen as somehow before time, before civilization. As McLean (2007, 2011) has noted in his reflections on European peat bogs and fens, these swampy margins often come to be represented as a prehistoric unknown, untamed. It is 'black primordial goo' (2007: 61). Little wonder, then, that progress declares war on the swamp. McLean (2011: 602–3) gives an account of Mussolini's ill-fated Utopian resettlement of more than sixty thousand people on reclaimed land on the Pontine Marshes, while poets and artists – such as those McLean (2007) met in a sculptor's symposium in County Wicklow, Ireland – peer into the mud as though it were a window into the past and ask themselves what is down there. Pre-drainage fen is *primitive*; it is exactly this sense that we get from reading Dugdale. And being primitive, it is surely no good.

By contrast, drained fen is land that is 'improved', and the work is commended as a plan to 'enrich these countries by several new plantations, and divers ample privileges' (Dugdale 1662: 414). Given that Dugdale was writing to a commission, we might think of him as the producer of paid propaganda, but he was by no means alone in his vision of the creative power of drainage. Keegan (2008: 151–59) provides something of an inventory of poetry written in praise of the work of the Adventurers; she quotes, for example, a poem attributed to Samuel Fortrey, and found in another historical narrative of drainage published by Jonas Moore, surveyor for the Adventurers (Moore 1685):

> I sing of Flood muzled, and the Ocean tam'd,
> Luxurious Rivers govern'd, and reclam'd,
> Waters with Banks confin'd, as in a Gaol,
> Till kinder Sluices let them go on Bail;
> Streams curb'd with Dammes like Bridles, taught t'obey
> And run as strait, as if they saw their way.

In place of chaos, order; and in place of flood, progress. The result is envisioned as a fertile paradise of plenty: 'The Land of Promise, now in part enjoy'.

In this task of imagining the transformation of the fens, the work of projecting a 'before' and 'after' onto the apparent blank canvas of the fenland made ample use of the power of maps. As Willmoth (1998) has pointed out, in preparing his *History of Imbanking and Drayning* Dugdale sought sponsorship for the production of engraved plates, allowing the end result to be lavishly illustrated. Such illustration not only created the appearance that this was a work of antiquarian importance to be placed on a level with Dugdale's work on more conventional historical subjects, such as his history of English abbeys, *Monasticon Anglicanum*, but also ensured that the story of creation of land from waste had the maximum visual impact. Dugdale included within the volume a 'Mapp of the Great Level; Representing it as it lay Drowned'; here, it appears, Dugdale took a map that had been produced by William Hayward earlier in the century and, through shading those areas subject to flooding, created an image of the fens as a vast sea, so that 'the flooded state of the Fens appeared almost their sole characteristic' (Willmoth 1998: 283). Here, he was adopting a strategy used by other mapmakers of the time; in 1645 the Dutch mapmaker Joannes Blaeu also produced a similar map based on William Hayward's earlier map of the fens; 'Heavy shading was added to make the whole central area appear under water, and the new title, Regiones Inundatae – "flooded regions" – makes the propagandist nature of this particular enterprise very clear' (Willmoth 2009: 15). In this way, the fens could be simplified in their entirety as a wild, flooded zone, awaiting civilization. Maps of the fens after drainage, by contrast, imply a neat grid pattern of drainage ditches and allotted agricultural land. Jonas Moore's map of the Great Level, produced in 1658 and redrawn for inclusion in Dugdale's *History*, 'is an extremely impressive production, at a scale of about two inches to a mile. It has some of the characteristics we might now associate with an aerial survey, although it depicts an area where no kind of bird's-eye view could in practice be obtained' (Willmoth 2009: 18). Looking down on the fenlands from above, we see the achievement of the drainage as nobody on the ground could have seen it; as a perfectly ordered design.

What is perhaps most striking about seventeenth-century accounts of drainage, and what still clearly has a resonance to this day, is that the works are framed as a *moral* project. We have already seen Dugdale's claim that pre-drainage, the fen contained 'no element of good' (1662: 7); later he describes the land and its inhabitants thus: 'until of late years, a vast deep fen, affording little benefit to the realm, other than fish or fowl, with overmuch harbour to a rude, and almost barbarous sort of lazy beggarly people' (Dugdale 1662: 171). It is noteworthy than the inhabitants of the fen were singled out as lazy; indeed, sloth comes to be seen as a characteristic of the fenland environment itself, and drainage a remedy to this natural laziness: 'the river Ouse, formerly lazily loitering in its idle intercourses with other rivers, is now sent the nearest way (through a passage cut by admirable art) to do its errand to the German Ocean' (Fuller [1655] 1840: 149). The 'improvement' of the fens, then, is a project that replaces laziness with industry, to the benefit of land and people; to return to Samuel Fortrey's poem in Jonas Moore's narrative of drainage:

> When with the change of Elements, suddenly
> There shall a change of men and Manners be;
> Hearts, thick and tough as Hydes, shall feel Remorse,

And Souls of Sedge shall understand Discourse,
New hands shall learn to Work, forget to Steal,
New legs shall go to Church, new knees shall kneel.

Clearly this is not just a work of improvement; it is an inscription of the Protestant Work Ethic on the land and on the people. The Earth is given to humans for their use; 'labour in the service of impersonal social usefulness furthers the divine glory and is willed by God' (Weber 1930: 76) – and to waste land given by God through failing to add labour is surely a sign of immorality.

This moral justification for the project of the Adventurers rests on the idea that the fens were *waste*. Such an idea was to become central to the philosophy of property of Locke: 'Let anyone consider, what the difference is between an Acre of Land planted with Tobacco, or sugar, sown with Wheat or Barley; and an acre of the same land lying in common, without any husbandry upon it' (Locke [1689] 1960: 296). In this way, Locke makes the case for the creation of property in land. To add labour to land is to make it productive; and when the individual, who is proprietor of himself, mixes his labour with a resource in the commons, as is necessary for survival, it becomes his property. Were he not to do this, it would surely *go to waste*. Here, we see the same rationality that was put to work in the Adventurer's drainage of the East Anglian fens; adding the labour of drainage to the 'waste' of a wetland in order to make it productive, and in doing so creating private property. Later, Locke makes his point even more starkly: 'Land that is left wholly to Nature, that hath no improvement of pasturage, Tillage, or Planting is called, as indeed it is, wast' (ibid.: 297).

Locke attempts to drive his argument about the importance of labour and private property home with a contrast. 'There cannot be a clearer demonstration of anything, than several nations of the Americans who are rich in land and poor in all the Comforts of Life; whom nature having furnished as liberally as any other people, with the materials of plenty ... yet for want of improving it by labour, have not one hundredth part of the conveniences we enjoy' (Locke [1689] 1960: 296–97). With this parallel in mind, the drainage of the fens becomes a kind of internal colonialism (Evans 1997), with the 'rude, and almost barbarous' natives of the fens treated as the primitive inhabitants of a newly discovered land. Such an attitude is well illustrated by Fuller ([1655] 1840: 147) in his contemporaneous account of the arguments raised for and against drainage:

> *Argument:* Many thousands of poor people are maintained by fishing and fowling in the fens, which will all be at a loss of livelihood, if their barns be burnt, that is, if the fens be drained.

Answer: It is confest that many whose hands are becrampt with laziness, live (and only live, as never gaining any estates) by that employment. But such, if the fens were drained, would quit their idleness, and betake themselves to more lucrative manufactures.

But if those in favour of drainage made their case in moral terms, the same was true of those who raised their voices in opposition to the project. One of the best-known statements of opposition – largely because it was preserved by Dugdale and included in his history (1662: 392) – was the 'Powte's Complaint', a song in ten stanzas.[1]

> Behold the great design, which they do now determine,
> Will make our bodies pine, a prey to crows and vermine:
> For they do mean all Fens to drain, and waters overmaster,
> All will be dry, and we must die, 'cause Essex calves want pasture.

Here, the protest is that purely economic interests – envisaged as the use of land for the fattening of cattle – will result in the driving out and starvation of fen-dwellers. A pamphlet of around 1646, *The Anti-Projector; or the history of the fen project,* also presses for the welfare of those who rely on the fen for their livelihood. 'The Undertakers have alwaies vilified the fens, and have misinformed many Parliament men, that all the fens is a meer quagmire, and that it is a level hurtfully surrounded, and of little or no value: but those which live in the fens, and are neighbours to it, know the contrary'; the Anti-Projector sets out to correct this mistaken impression of the fenland economy, before concluding: 'Lastly, we have many thousand cottagers, which live on our fens, which otherwise must go a begging. So that if the undertakers take from us a third part of our fens, they destroy not only our pastures and corn ground, but also our poor, and utterly disable us to relieve them'. Produced during the English Civil War, the pamphlet welcomes the disruption those events had brought to drainage works, praising the 'divine providence' that had brought drainage temporarily to a halt as the result of 'the praiers of a numerous godly pretious people'. Given the Royal support given to drainage works, it may well be thought that the Parliamentarian cause would align with the interests of the author of the Anti-Projector; and indeed Oliver Cromwell, born on the edge of the fens, was hailed as a champion of the fenman's interests (Ravensdale 1974: 31). Nevertheless, the end of the English Civil War and the execution of King Charles I did not put a stop to programmes of improvement; and as Darby (1956: 64) points out, in 1649, the chief advocate of an act for the completion of the drainage work of the Earl of Bedford and the Adventurers was Cromwell himself.

In contrast to the representation of drainage as divine providence, opponents depicted the works as a perversion of the natural course of God's creation. Ravensdale (1974: 31) quotes a complaint made against the work of drainage at a Session of Sewers in Peterborough in 1622: 'fens were made fens and must ever continue such; to set yourself so stubbornly against God's will in this way surely arouses suspicion, thus the people think that the Undertakers will work by witchcraft'. So if the Adventurers claimed a biblical and Godly mandate for the work of drainage, they certainly did so in the face of opposition. As Camden (1610: 492), touching upon the drainage proposals in his topographical survey of the British Isles, states: 'many think it the wisest and best course ... Not to intermeddle at all with that which God hath ordained'.

Of course, perhaps the greatest argument against drainage came from the land itself. Drainage may have been a work of imagination, but as ideas come to be inscribed, they must take account of the material properties of the land; and the properties of peat fen were not fully understood at this time. It was not anticipated that as the land was drained, the surface of the peat fen would rapidly lower (Darby 1956: 104–13; Godwin 1978: 124–13). This shrinkage is a consequence partly of the contraction of the land caused by the loss of water during the drying process, but also of processes that follow the exposure of the formerly waterlogged peat to the air. 'As water is withdrawn from a body of peat and air fills the spaces in it, there begin swift chemical oxidations followed by bacterial and fungal attack and breakdown by animal organisms. The peat being essentially organic, the ultimate product of all these processes must, to a very large extent, be carbon dioxide that diffuses into the atmosphere' (Godwin 1978: 126). This is a process known as wastage. Following the Lockean rationality of property, we might understand the addition of labour as an attempt to create productive land where once there was waste; to cast the land as waste was a precondition of this work, but the wastage of the land was its unforeseen consequence. As a result, much of the drainage work rapidly became ineffective, and by the mid-1660s many owners were complaining that their lands were frequently flooded.

Drainage as Battlefield: The Fenland during the Second World War

Let us move on to the second episode of contestation: drainage during the Second World War. Our focus here will be on an area of land east of the River Cam in Cambridgeshire. The portions of fenland involved are known as Wicken Fen, Burwell Fen and Adventurers' Fen (the latter, of course, named after the Earl of Bedford's Adventurers), and are shaped by three artificial channels of Roman origin that converge as they carry water towards the River Cam: Wicken Lode, Burwell Lode and Reach Lode. Wicken Fen was and is a nature reserve, a site that has a long association with botanical and entomological study dating back to at least the 1820s (Cameron 2013). Burwell Fen and Adventurers' Fen were both areas that had histories of cultivation and resource extraction. Ennion (1949: 44) describes the history of peat digging and agriculture on Adventurers' Fen; the land had become drowned once again, and 'allowed to revert … to a condition which must have been very like fifteenth century fen'; as Bloom (1944: 122) notes of Burwell Fen, in those places where peat had been removed for fuel the land level had dropped particularly low, leading to near constant inundation.

Alan Bloom (1944) and Eric Ennion (1949) narrate two opposing sides of a tension over the use of these areas of land. For Bloom, immersed in the work of draining and cultivating the land, the story is one of victory. But for Ennion, a local General Practitioner and naturalist, the story is one of loss: 'The glimpse we had of what real fen was like will soon be forgotten … It is never likely to get flooded for more than a short time again' (1949: 43). He begins by conjuring up an image of the symbolic slaughter of the fen:

> The water from the ditches and the interlines, the moisture from the peat, bled in an endless trickle into the deep new drain. It hurried, brown and swirling under a scum of broken reed roots … out of the bounds which had held it for heaven knows how many years. When all was dry, men set the fen on fire. Spurts of flame began to flicker here and there and presently leapt up to redden the fringes of the great smoke cloud, which hung above them. An undergrowth of dried-out moss and litter nursed the flames along. Reed beds, sedges and sallows vanished in a whirl of flying ashes amid the crackle and the roar. I went down afterwards. There was a single gull wheeling over the dead black land and a wild duck trying to hide in two inches of water at the bottom of a drain. (Ennion 1949: ix)

His account is largely one of the birdlife and the insects for whom the wetland was a habitat, but it is also a description of the resources that the fen provided for those who dwelled there; eels, reeds for thatch, willow for wicker baskets and eel traps, and so on. In this way, he evokes the flora and fauna that he laments having given way to drainage and progress. 'The new aim was not to control the water but to banish it … It was the old, old cry: is not a fat sheep better than a goose, a stalled ox better than a dish of eels? That's what the Adventurers said in 1630, but the Bailiff of Bedford (the floods from the Bedfordshire watershed) came down and they failed' (Ennion 1949: 54).

Turning now to Bloom: the account of his arrival at the farm following his purchase in 1939 is marked with the pessimistic evaluation of local residents: 'No use farming against water' (Bloom 1944: 23). Like Ennion, they too know the power of the Bailiff of Bedford, yet Bloom is undaunted by the challenge. The context of the war provides an important backdrop to the story; in the middle of the interwar period, agriculture was a baby nobody wanted; but after 1936, as the aggressor powers stalked their prey while England hedged and parried, it was seen that home-grown food might become important again (ibid.: 39). Bloom's cultivation of sugar beet, for example, is able to provide a home-grown supply of sugar in place of a demand for sugar cane from across the now highly dangerous Atlantic; though it is worth noting that in marked contrast to Bloom's presentation about the patriotism of growing sugar beet, for Ennion, their appearance is somehow a betrayal of the land's identity: 'No crop is less in sympathy with an English landscape than this alien' (Ennion 1949: x).[2]

Bloom's book is a story of war, not just in the sense that the war creates an urgent need for cultivation to ensure Britain's food security, but also in the sense that Bloom sees himself at war with the water (as well as with the naysayers who would insist that the land can never be won back from the water). 'To my way of thinking, [the farm] had become a battlefield on which the forces of dereliction had paused in their encroachment on the farmed land. For years the advantage had lain with the wilderness. No man could farm against water, and water was the governing factor. But now the tables were being turned. The plough looked like going over to the offensive' (Bloom 1944: 74). The warlike character of the struggle is heightened by the involvement of the Royal Engineers, whose military expertise is called upon to train men to blow up the bog oaks that are an impediment to the cultivation of the land (ibid.: 152–53).

In this sense, Bloom is heir to the Adventurer's battle against waste and wilderness;[3] but we also see in these accounts the emergence of a new kind of moral struggle between agricultural and environmental conservation interests. As Einarsson (1993) has pointed out in an account of the politics of whaling in the Arctic, attention to conservation and environmental protection has often resulted in a blindness to the interests of human cultural survival; we see a similar tension in the portrayal of local resource users as 'invaders' and 'destroyers' of the mangrove forests in Tanzania, in contrast to local claims of long-term habitation and use of the mangrove (Beymer-Farris and Bassett 2012).

At the same time, it is clear that an emphasis on productivity, narrowly defined, can easily overpower environmental concerns (Argyrou 2005). It is therefore interesting to reflect on the culture conflict that emerges between Bloom and the naturalists of Wicken Fen: 'As a farmer and the owner of the adjoining land, I'd got to fight the National Trust, or rather, I supposed, the local governing Committee' (Bloom 1944: 75). With the support of the War Agricultural Committee, Bloom obtains the land at Adventurers' Fen to add to his land at Burwell Fen, and remarks that '[t]he National Trust had done the job of making a swamp very thoroughly' (ibid.: 91). His agricultural workers, as residents of Wicken, are said to be pleased to begin the work of drainage on former National Trust property; this area, which for Ennion consisted of 'glorious bird-haunted wastes of reed and water' (ibid.: x), 'had long been to them an annoying and useless background' (ibid.: 96).

The conflict is clearly illustrated by Bloom's encounter with a young former botany student who sees the drainage work as an act of destruction, and remarks that it will take years for the land to grow up again into its natural state.

> This floored me. In the welter of 'destruction' as he called it, the thought that Adventurers' Fen might ever be allowed to revert had scarcely entered my head … it was like showing a red rag to a bull for him to talk calmly about reversion as a foregone conclusion … I continued on my errand thoroughly riled. It was his general attitude that annoyed me. He was so coldly matter of fact, as if to him agriculture was a nuisance. As if food producing should play second fiddle to his own abstract and academic interests. (Bloom 1944: 150)

As Strang (2005) has shown in her ethnography of the Mitchell River Catchment in northern Queensland, agriculture-driven and environmental narratives may share the same core symbol and object of attention, and yet find themselves at cross purposes precisely because of attitudes towards production and the value of certain kinds of production; in the case she presents, water is a clear source of productivity, but what kind of productivity? Does a focus on agricultural yield exclude any consideration of non-human effects of water use? And does an attempt to shift focus away from agricultural yield demean the importance of the farmer's labour?

There are clear parallels between the moral issues at stake in the seventeenth-century story of drainage and protest, and this mid twentieth-century wartime episode. In both periods, labour is the moral force that asserts its will to remake the land; and in both periods this labour is open to the accusation that it lays the way for an alien intrusion. In the first section of this chapter, I showed how the Adventurers sought to portray undrained land as waste, and to be civilized through the moral virtue of work. Bloom is heir to this ethic, and yet finds himself accused of waste, a situation he clearly finds astonishing: 'it was staggering to find at such a time – in the midst of the nation's greatest peril – that anyone, or for that matter any body of men, should consider the reclamation of valuable food-producing land a waste of energy, a waste of money, and, moreover, should calmly contemplate relinquishing it once more to its fate when that immediate peril was past' (Bloom 1944: 151). What is productive and what is waste is clearly left unstable.

And still, at the heart of this debate, in both the seventeenth and the twentieth centuries, we hear that voice of warning: you cannot 'farm against water'. Water cannot be contained merely as a narrative in human moral arguments; it finds its own way. In the years following the wartime drainage, the fenland would once again be subject to extreme flooding throughout the Great Ouse river system. In March 1947, unexpectedly high tides coupled with a quick thaw after a long frost and very heavy snowfall meant that the fenland, with its low-lying nature, low river gradient and the exacerbating effects of peat shrinkage, was subject to extreme flooding (Wilson 1947), with great swathes of farmland inundated. Again, we are told farming 'went to war' against water, assisted by British troops and German prisoners of war; 'No praise is too high for the manner in which they went into the battle against the waters' (ibid.: 29). They would be called to do battle again in January–February 1953, as the east coast was once more affected by extremely heavy floods, causing major loss of life and agricultural land (Summers 1978). Human attempts to tame water meet resistance in the power of the water itself, leaving people to resume the labour of making inundated land productive once again: 'That production will suffer is inevitable; but the Fen folk, dour and undemonstrative, yet full of vigour and brave enterprise, will see to it that what vital food can be grown, will be grown this year on their re-claimed acres' (Wilson 1947: 28).

The Future Past: The Politics of Re-wetting Today

Our final episode begins with an archaeological excavation at Willingham Mere, on the southern fen edge[4] (Evans et al. 2011). The mere itself, now drained, is only visible at ground level as a stretch of white lake marl. The single trench was positioned in present-day farmland on the edge of the former lake, with the aim of gathering evidence about the early prehistoric fen environment; as was explained in the publicity material available at the excavation site, 'We are excavating the remains of prehistoric fen and mere deposits to search for preserved wood, plant and pollen remains, as well as the bones of fish, mammals and birds that would have lived at Willingham Mere thousands of years ago'.

The excavation, carried out as a collaboration between the Cambridge Archaeological Unit, Hanson Aggregates and the Royal Society for the Protection of Birds (RSPB), offers an interesting perspective on changing land use: not only do we see how inundation and drainage transformed the landscape of the past, but the excavation was being carried out ahead of gravel quarrying work by Hanson – and after Hanson have extracted gravel from the site, it is planned that it will become a wetland habitat and an RSPB nature reserve. An RSPB volunteer in attendance clearly saw this sequence of activity as a key attraction of the project. 'It's coming full circle, you've got this environment that used to be a wetland environment, it's been drained, but now it's going to be quarried and then returned to a wetland environment ... So that's what's interesting about what they're digging up – it's the past and it's the future'.

At the lower organic silt level, interpreted as Bronze Age, were large amounts of preserved wood fragments – the detritus of alder carr woodland; bird (apparently coot) and fish bones were also recovered. At the upper organic layer, interpreted as Iron Age, the bones of species including mallard and pike were recovered; in the layer of marl above this were freshwater mussel shells. From the point of view of the archaeological excavation, this provided evidence of environmental transformation to piece together with data from other nearby sites; a story over 3,500 years of woodland and inundation, the subsequent open water of the mere that existed following Roman damming activity, and recent drainage. From the point of view of the RSPB involvement, such discoveries also had the potential to speak about the present and the near-future. They were presented as counter-factual finds, enabling us to ask *what if* this area was a wetland environment today? The publicity material handed out on site not only included images of coot, but also of more exotic species found on nearby sites: 'Remains of the Giant Dalmatian pelican (which had a wing span of over 3 metres) have also been found nearby – today these are world endangered and no longer found in the UK'. As the RSPB volunteer put it, 'It's like Bronze Age birdwatching' – not only a downpayment on the birdwatching to be done at the RSPB reserve of the near-future, but also a way of imagining this future 're-wetting' as a return to an earlier state. 'Pond dipping' in the nearby drainage ditch also enabled the establishment of visual parallels between past and present; at the same time as ramshorn snail shells were being excavated from the lower organic silt, so too were present-day ramshorn snails being netted from the ditch.

Much like the seventeenth century, the twenty-first century is an era of transformative schemes projected onto the fenland landscape; only today, the schemes are those of 're-wetting', envisaged as a restoration of the pre-drainage environment (although given the nature of peat wastage, clearly re-wetting cannot imply the restoration of peat lands, other than in the very long term). In addition to the RSPB's schemes in collaboration with the Cambridge Archaeology Unit and Hanson Aggregates, and on an altogether grander scale, the 'Great Fen Project' aims to create a 3,700 hectare wetland south of Peterborough, while the National Trust aims to create a 5,300 hectare wetland, centred on its existing holdings at Wicken Fen, as part of its Wicken Vision; both projects have been purchasing land from existing landowners as and when it becomes available, and seeking agreements for the transfer of land in the future. Indeed, in presenting the future land use, visual depictions of the land under water in the past are used as ways of helping people to envisage the future. At the Wicken Fen education centre, Joannes Blaeu's propagandistic 1684 map Regiones Inundatae is displayed; only now it seems to be deployed as a way of showing how much wetland has been lost, rather than how much waste has been vanquished. Similarly, in presentations about the conservation work at the centre, Ennion's drawings of Adventurers' Fen prior to wartime drainage are shown as an example of what could happen if the land 'naturally rewilded itself ... let it go, see what it does'.[5] Whereas the projects of the seventeenth century saw the primordial muddy fen as waste, the great 'visions' of the twenty-first century have redefined the 'productive' act of drainage as an act of waste; habitat destruction on a massive scale, leaving only 'arable desert'.

So the water, once excluded, is now invited back on to former farmland. Scrapes and ponds have been excavated, with ditches widened, banks sculpted into shallow slopes, and a clay bund to retain water on the site (Friday and Chatfield 1997). Of course, given how strongly this appears to contradict the doctrine of improvement that drove the transformation of the fens for so long, it is not surprising that this development has met with hostility from some. As recalled by one of the RSPB volunteers at the Willingham Mere excavation: 'I was telling one of the visitors that the land would eventually become nature reserve. I thought he might be interested but he just shook his head and said, "What a waste, what a waste". For him it was farmland and he couldn't get his head around anything else. It's certainly not the first time I've heard something like that'.

If we consider the area around Wicken Fen, close to the scene of Bloom's labour and Ennion's lament, it is clear that a number of the landowners whose land falls within or adjacent to the Wicken Vision proposed 're-wetting' are disapproving of the initiative for a range of reasons. 'Who's it for, who's it for?', asked one landowner. 'People in the city, that's who it's for. And you think they're all going to cycle here? [Laughs] They're going to be coming in their cars of course, that's not very good for the green ... a green lung for Cambridge, that's what they're calling it – for Cambridge, not for us'. This critique of the 'Vision' points to an imbalance of power between the rural and the city, and the increasing sense of the rural as a space defined for and by urban dwellers. This is a key theme in contemporary Britain, given urban resettlement in rural areas and the refocus of rural space as a tourist destination (e.g. Murdoch and Pratt 1993; Neal 2009). Further to this, it suggests a hypocrisy at the heart of 're-wetting' as an environmental project, given that it will generate more traffic. 'They've got a windmill in there [a wind drainage pump], it doesn't work of course, just a relic. That's all farming is to them, a relic. And you know what they're so proud of? They've built their own windmill, not for pumping water out, but for sucking it in! It's a joke'. The idea of a wind-driven pump (installed by Wicken Fen in 2011) that would contribute to raising the water table rather than draining the land seemed an apt illustration of the structural inversion of priorities.

This idea that the re-wetting project somehow disregards the importance of farming also featured in conversations with a second landowner, a retired farmer particularly active in opposition to the Wicken Vision. I first met him in January 2011, following a Plough Sunday[6] service at Burwell. One of the readings at the service had been taken from Deuteronomy 8: 'a land with wheat and barley, vines and fig trees, pomegranates, olive oil and honey'. I was sitting there thinking, Pomegranates! That's about the only thing we can't grow here! This triggered a lengthy reflection by the landowner on the fertility of the land, and its continued richness in spite of peat wastage. He went on to express his scorn for 'turning the fen into some kind of theme park', listing some of the tourist and leisure activities organized by Wicken Fen. 'They don't seem to think that the fens still have a serious role to play'. In terms very similar to Bloom's, as seen above, agricultural productivity was justified as essential, given the continuing need for food security. Indeed, such work had a clear moral imperative; given global population growth, it is arguably immoral to expect people overseas to grow our food for us.

If those who oppose re-wetting can muster moral arguments for the importance of putting land to work for the sake of food security, the National Trust are able to muster their own moral argument in terms of the climatic impact of drainage, through a historical assessment of the damage already done; damage that advocates of re-wetting claim needs to be reversed. In 2008, the National Trust commissioned Haycock Associates to calculate the atmospheric impact of drainage in the Vision area over the preceding two hundred years. The total footprint of drainage in the area was said to equate to around 101,500,000 tonnes of carbon dioxide in the atmosphere. The importance of the fenland is thus asserted as part of an ethic of climate activism (albeit a somewhat retrospective ethic).

In the Beginning…

These stories, taken together, provide us with a history not only of land and water, but also of labour, productivity and value. But as with all histories, there is the awkward question of where to start. 'In the beginning God said, let the waters be gathered together…'; here, as we have seen, is the scriptural justification that Dugdale (1662: 1) gives for drainage being a Godly work. Drainage is an act of creation, making land anew. And so, if we are to start our history here, Fenland's Genesis comes as the waters are gathered away.

Yet it is never as simple as that. Even in the act of digging to drain the water and make productive land, other, deeper histories become visible. The land is rich in relics that prompt speculation about past environments (Irvine and Evans 2012). In this regard, archaeological investigations, such as those at the Willingham Mere excavation, are part of a common strand of fenlanders' digging into the past environment. We see, for example, the exposure of extinct river courses during the process of ditch digging,[7] as well as the discovery of beaver skulls and the remains of other creatures that speak of a different kind of habitat existing in the past. In particular, the continual nuisance of the bog oaks that prompted complaint from Bloom and needed to be blasted with wartime expertise are evidence of forested land becoming waterlogged, with the trees later falling and becoming preserved in the 'oozy' landscape of the fens. As Bloom remarks, reflecting on these encounters with the past, 'I doubt whether any story could be told beyond that of floods and drier periods alternating all through the centuries down to the time when men began to secure the means to subjugate, and apply those means' (Bloom 1944: 167). Here drainage is not a Genesis, but (so Bloom hopes) a final episode in a long struggle. Clearly, however, the 'Bailiff of Bedford' retains his power, given the subsequent 'evictions' brought about by post-war fen floods.

To start the creation story somewhat differently, we might turn to the words of John Locke ([1689] 1960: 301): 'In the beginning the world was America'.[8] Although the words appear as part of a reflection on the absence of money, the wider context relates to the unenclosed character of pre-colonial America; and as we have seen, Locke's treatment of America here is as waste: 'for I ask, whether in the wild woods and uncultivated waste of America, left to nature, without any improvement, tillage or husbandry, a thousand acres yield the needy and wretched inhabitants as many conveniences of life, as ten acres of equally fertile land do in Devonshire, where they are well cultivated?' ([1689] 1960: 294). As I have argued above, the fenlands are a clear illustration of Locke's philosophy of property; through the adding of labour to that which God has given man in common, solid, productive land is created where once there was muddy waste. The fens are illustrative of the idea that 'In the beginning the world was America', precisely because they embody the idea of a waste that needed to be conquered to become productive. Of course, as scholars reading Locke's Second Treatise of Government have critically pointed out (for example, Arniel 1996; Kehoe 2009), Locke's declaration of pre-colonial Americas as waste must be linked to his business interests, and in particular his investments in American lands and his profit from their enclosure. So too, we have seen that the declaration of the pre-drainage fens as waste – and more than that, as an immoral waste – was linked to the capital investment of the Adventurers.

Indeed, what we have seen from the stories above is that 'waste' is itself the subject of enormous contestation. We see the problem vividly if we consider the nature of waste in the fens in the context of Locke's famous caveat that in adding one's labour to a resource and those appropriating it, one should leave 'enough, and as good' for others (Locke [1689] 1960: 291). The history of fen drainage illustrates the difficulty of this imperative; to use is not just to *prevent* waste, but, because of the properties of peat, to *cause* waste. To increase the fens' productivity through drainage in the short term is to cause it to waste away in the long term. Far from leaving 'enough and as good', in the long term nothing of the peat is left. Furthermore, Locke's caveat is simply to assure no prejudice to any man; a judgement of value that excludes non-human benefit – from this perspective, to leave land for the dwelling of non-human flora and fauna is deemed waste (Irvine and Gorji 2013). Yet the interests of conservation and re-wetting are motivated by a 'non-anthropocentric climate ethic' (Nolt 2011) that finds value beyond the human scale. So if Locke's approach to property and waste seems fitting for the rationality of seventeenth-century adventurers, it is difficult to translate to the present-day context until we recognize that we are recasting unused space as a resource; we are producing value from non-use. Yet as Cameron (2013) has pointed out, this non-use is not without labour. The production of Wicken Fen as an unused space is made possible only through tremendous maintenance, and needs to be located within the context of a wider rural economy that seeks sources of value beyond agriculture; in particular, we have to bear in mind the Common Agricultural Policy's transformation of rural heritage and protection of the environment into an exploitable resource through its direct payment scheme (Gray 2000). The calculation of carbon release points to another source of value in non-use – the emerging market which allows us to treat non-released carbon as an alienable resource (Callon 2009).

To return, then, to the question that I started out from: what is a fen? The different answers that can be given to this question point to the contested histories of productivity and value that shape the region. To return to the claim made by Pratt (1952) – 'Where oil is first found, in the final analysis, is in the minds of men' – we might be tempted to make the same claim for fens, at least in so far as they are imagined and re-imagined as sources of waste or value. In this sense, the fen emerges through visions of the past and the future. Thus, we see histories of creation where once there was waste, and also stories of temporal return – a re-wetting that will return the land to a prior (primordial?) state.

Yet for all the contestation that surrounds fens, the land and the water possess their own power. As the excavation at Willingham Mere shows, this is a landscape with a long history of inundation; indeed as Sturt (2006) has pointed out, this is a landscape that five thousand years ago was subject to major marine transgression. In becoming aware of past deluges below the ordered surface, we see the places where there was once water and, given peat shrinkage, post-glacial rebound, and rising sea levels, where there may in the future be water again – and the water cares nothing for our models of value. The visions of the seventeenth century and of wartime drainage were severely compromised by subsequent flooding; those who project visions of twenty-first century conservation wetland for recreation may well find that water creates a future that they too had not envisaged. We may work to shape the fen through our own imagination; but re-wetting or no re-wetting, the Bailiff of Bedford may yet return of his own free will.

Acknowledgements

Research for this paper was carried out first as part of the AHRC funded network 'Climate Histories: Communicating Cultural Knowledge of Environmental Change' (grant number AH/H039236/1), and then later as part of the AHRC funded project, 'Pathways to understanding the changing climate: time and place in cultural learning about the environment' (grant number AH/K006282/1). I am enormously indebted to Barbara Bodenhorn, David Sneath, Chris Evans, and Libby Peachey for their support during my research and their advice on this paper. I am also grateful to Kirsten Hastrup and the Waterworlds team for their invitation to present this research.

Notes

1. 'Powte' was the old English word for the sea lamprey (Darby 1956: 55).
2. This is an important theme in arguments over the identity of the fen. The anti-drainage pamphlet *The Anti-Projector; or the history of the fen project* published c.1646 also disparages 'alien' crops: 'What is coleseed and rape, they are but Dutch commodities, and but trash and trumpery'.
3. It is surely significant, and worthy of further investigation, that many recollections of the floods of this time blend flood memories with wartime memories. When interviewing residents in the Whittlesey Mere area about flood memories, the role of the military and the presence of military amphibious vehicles assisting in flood rescues are important themes, and they are frequently connected with talk of the military struggle in the war and the associated hardships such as rationing.
4. The excavation took place from 31 May to 10 June 2011. I participated in the excavation as part of broader programme of ethnographic fieldwork carried out in the region from May to September of that year.
5. From a presentation given at a conference 'Desire for the Wild – Wild Desires?', held in Wicken Fen and at Pembroke College, Cambridge in April 2013, which had been organized by me and other colleagues. Throughout the first day of the conference, held in and around the nature reserve, the process of re-wetting was juxtaposed with the ecological impoverishment of the 'arable desert' that drainage had created.
6. 'Plough Sunday' is the first Sunday following the Epiphany. Traditionally the start of the agricultural year, the day would be marked by a special church service, with festivities continuing on the following day, 'Plough Monday'. Once a major festival in the Fenland area, these days still remain a focus for celebrations in some communities.
7. As Smith (1997) has noted, such discoveries during the process of agricultural labour were crucial in stimulating the development of fenland archaeology at the University of Cambridge.
8. Evans (1997) begins his article on Fenland histories with these words from Locke, and I am indebted to him for making such a suggestive connection.

References

Argyrou, V. 2005. *The Logic of Environmentalism: Anthropology, Ecology and Postcoloniality*. Oxford: Berghahn Books.
Arniel, B. 1996. *John Locke and America: The Defence of English Colonialism*. Oxford: Clarendon Press.

Bedford, B.L., and K.S. Godwin. 2003. 'Fens of the United States: Distribution, Characteristics, and Scientific Connection versus Legal Isolation', *Wetlands* 23(3): 608–29.
Beymer-Farris, B.A., and T.J. Bassett. 2012. 'The REDD Menace: Resurgent Protectionism in Tanzania's Mangrove Forests', *Global Environmental Change* 22(2): 332–41.
Bloom, A. 1944. *The Farm in the Fen*. London: Faber.
Callon, M. 2009. 'Civilizing Markets: Carbon Trading between in vitro and in vivo Experiments', *Accounting, Organisations and Society* 34(3/4): 535–48.
Camden, W. 1610. *Britain, Or A Chorographicall Description of the Most flourishing Kingdomes, England, Scotland, and Ireland, and the ilands adioyning*, trans. P. Holland. London: Georgii Bishop and Ioannis Norton.
Cameron, L. 2013. 'Resources of Hope: Wicken Fen Stories of Anthropogenic Nature', *Cambridge Anthropology* 31(1): 105–18.
Darby, H.C. 1940. *The Medieval Fenland*. Cambridge: Cambridge University Press.
———. 1956. *The Draining of the Fens, Second Edition*. Cambridge: Cambridge University Press.
Dugdale, W. 1662. *The History of Imbanking and Drayning of Divers Fenns and Marshes*. London: Alice Warren.
Einarsson, N. 1993. 'All Animals are Equal but Some are Cetaceans: Conservation and Culture Conflict', in K. Miltin (ed.), *Environmentalism: The View from Anthropology*. London: Routledge, pp. 71–82.
Ennion, E.A.R. 1949. *Adventurers Fen*, enlarged edition. London: Herbert Jenkins.
Evans, C. 1997. 'Sentimental Prehistories: The Construction of the Fenland Past', *Journal of European Archaeology* 5(2): 105–36.
Evans, C., et al. 2011. *Willingham Mere, 'Digging Environment' Project (31st May – 10th June)*. Cambridge: Cambridge Archaeological Unit, University of Cambridge.
Friday, L.E., and M.P. Chatfield. 1997. 'The Next 100 Years', in L. Friday (ed.), *Wicken Fen: The Making of a Wetland Nature Reserve*. Colchester: Harley, pp. 277–282.
Fuller, T. (1655) 1840. *The History of the University of Cambridge from the Conquest to the Year 1634*. Cambridge: J. and J.J. Deighton and T. Stevenson.
Godwin, H. 1978. *Fenland: Its Ancient Past and Uncertain Future*. Cambridge: Cambridge University Press.
Gray, J. 2000. 'The Common Agricultural Policy and the Re-invention of the Rural in the European Community', *Sociologia Ruralis* 40(1): 30–52.
Harris, L.E. 1953. *Vermuyden and the Fens: A Study of Sir Cornelius Vermuyden and the Great Level*. London: Cleaver-Hume.
Haslam, S.M. 2003. *Understanding Wetlands: Fen, Bog and Marsh*. London: Taylor and Francis.
Irvine, R.D.G., and C. Evans. 2012. 'Greenlands and Waterlands: Digging into Climate History in the East Anglian Fenlands', *Current Anthropology* 53(2): 237–39.
Irvine, R.D.G., and M. Gorji. 2013. 'John Clare in the Anthropocene', *Cambridge Anthropology* 31(1): 119–32.
Keegan, B. 2008. *British Labouring-Class Nature Poetry, 1730–1837*. Basingstoke: Palgrave Macmillan.

Kehoe, A.B. 2009. 'Deconstructing John Locke', in *Postcolonial Perspectives in Archaeology*, P. Bikoulis, D. Lacroix and M. Peuramaki-Brown (eds). Calgary: Chacmool Archaeological Association.

Locke, J. (1689) 1960. *Two Treatises of Government*, P. Laslett (ed.). Cambridge: Cambridge University Press.

McLean, S. 2007. '"To Dream Profoundly": Irish Boglands and the Imagination of Matter', *Irish Journal of Anthropology* 10(2): 61–68.

———. 2011. 'Black Goo: Forceful Encounters with Matter in Europe's Muddy Margins', *Cultural Anthropology* 26(4): 589–619.

Moore, J. 1685. *The History or Narrative of the Great Level of the Fenns, Called Bedford Level*. London: Moses Pitt.

Motley, J.L. 1855. *The Rise of the Dutch Republic*. New York: Harper and Brothers.

Murdoch, J., and A.C. Pratt. 1993. 'Rural Studies: Modernism, Postmodernism and the "Post-rural"', *Journal of Rural Studies* 9(4): 411–27.

Neal, S. 2009. *Rural Identities: Ethnicity and Community in the Contemporary English Countryside*. Farnham, Surrey: Ashgate.

Nolt, J. 2011. 'Nonanthropocentric Climate Ethics', *WIREs Climate Change* 2(5): 701–11.

Pratt, W.E. 1952. 'Toward a Philosophy of Oil-Finding', *Bulletin of the American Association of Petroleum Geologists* 36(12): 2231–36.

Ravensdale, J.R. 1974. *Liable to Floods: Village Landscape on the Edge of the Fens, A.D. 450–1850*. Cambridge: Cambridge University Press.

Rippon, S. 1999. 'Romano-British Reclamation of Coastal Wetlands', in H. Cook and T. Williamson (eds), *Water Management in the English Landscape: Field, Marsh and Meadow*. Edinburgh: Edinburgh University Press, pp. 101–21.

Rowbotham, S.B. 1865. *Zetetic Astronomy: Earth Not a Globe! An Experimental Inquiry into the True Figure of the Earth Proving it a Plane without Axial or Orbital Motion; and the only Material World in the Universe!* London: Simpkin, Marshall and Co.

Sayer, D. 2009. 'Medieval Waterways and Hydraulic Economics: Monasteries, Towns and the East Anglian Fen', *World Archaeology* 41(1): 134–50.

Smith, P.J. 1997. 'Grahame Clark's New Archaeology: The Fenland Research Committee and Cambridge Prehistory in the 1930s', *Antiquity* 71(271): 11–30.

Strang, V. 2005. 'Water Works: Agency and Creativity in the Mitchell River Catchment', *The Australian Journal of Anthropology* 16(3): 366–81.

Sturt, F. 2006. 'Local Knowledge is Required: A Rhythmanalytical Approach to the Late Mesolithic and Early Neolithic of the East Anglian Fenland, UK', *Journal of Marine Archaeology* 1(1): 119–39.

Summers, D. 1978. *The East Coast Floods*. Newton Abbot, Devon: David and Charles.

Weber, M. 1930. *The Protestant Ethic and the Spirit of Capitalism*, trans. T. Parsons. London: Allen and Unwin.

Wells, S. 1830. *The History of the Drainage of the Great Level of the Fens, called Bedford Level; with the Constitution and Laws of the Bedford Level Corporation*. London: R. Pheney.

Wheeler, B.D., and M.C.F. Proctor. 2000. 'Ecological Gradients, Subdivisions and Terminology of North-west European Mires', *Journal of Ecology* 88(2): 187–203.

Wheeler, W.H. 1868. *History of the Fens of South Lincolnshire: Being a Description of the Rivers Witham and Welland and their Estuary; and an Account of the Reclamation and Drainage of the Fens Adjacent Thereto.* Boston, Lincolnshire: J.M. Newcomb.

Willmoth, F. 1998. 'Dugdale's History of Imbanking and Drayning: A "Royalist" Antiquarian in the Sixteen-Fifties', *Historical Research* 71(176): 281–302.

———. 2009. 'Fens Maps and Moore's Mapp of the Great Levell', in S. Oosthuizen and F. Willmoth (eds), *Drowned and Drained: Exploring Fenland Records and Landscape.* Cambridge: University of Cambridge Institute of Continuing Education, pp. 13–20.

Wilson, F.W. 1947. *The Battle of the Banks: The Story of the Fen Floods around Ely.* Ely: The Rotary Club of Ely.

2

Fluid Entitlements

Constructing and Contesting Water Allocations in Burkina Faso, West Africa

Ben Orlove, Carla Roncoli and Brian Dowd-Uribe

Introduction

Water has emerged as a topic of interest in several areas within anthropology, including environmental anthropology, political anthropology, and science and technology studies; it is also central to sustainable development at large. The Upper Comoé watershed in Burkina Faso, West Africa illustrates the complementarity of these different foci.[1] In this region, a large sugar-cane plantation manages reservoirs for its own use and for other groups downstream, including a regional town, an irrigated perimeter cultivated by a rice-producing cooperative and a number of small-scale vegetable growers, organized into committees. There has been a history of disputes about water, particularly between the plantation (which benefits from its political position as the most powerful actor in the region and from its physical position upstream of the other users) and the poorer rice and vegetable farmers. In the 1990s and early 2000s, these disputes played out in the context of clientelistic politics. In recent years, the patterns of conflict have been altered by the introduction of a new system of integrated water resource management, which has as its goals the decentralization of water governance, participatory water planning and incorporation of climate forecasts, and as its means the establishment of committees, with the authority to discuss questions related to water and to prepare plans for water management. The issues of changing resource use, shifts in governance and new technologies associated with different areas within anthropology, are thus all present in the region.

Despite — or perhaps because of — this new system of management, the Comoé watershed continues to be the site of conflict, both between water users and between systems of governance of water. An examination of specific instances of conflict shows that different frameworks are in play for valuing water and for assigning rights to water, and that the different cultural and technological systems of water measurement and water management are not easily combined. This case points to the possibility of expanding the understanding of water politics beyond issues of usage allocation to broader concerns about control and the recognition of claims to entitlement.

The case provides an opportunity to examine water entitlements. Many social scientists associate the concept of entitlement with the writings of the economist Amartya Sen, who defined entitlements as the legitimate claims of individuals in a given society to goods. He states: 'Entitlement refers to the set of alternative commodity bundles that a person can command in a society using the totality of rights and opportunities that he or she faces' (Sen 1984: 497). He noted several types of entitlements, distinguishing the different forms that grant access to commodities, such as trade and production (both of which may include one's own labour), inheritance and transfer. Sen used the notion of entitlement to explain that major world famines were due not to a lack of food, but to a failure of entitlement systems to grant access to food to all members of society (Sen 1981). This work provided the foundation for his more general examination of welfare economics, for which he was awarded the Nobel Prize in Economics in 1998.

It is worth noting the word 'title', which lies at the root of the word 'entitlement', and indeed the concept of entitlement links the status of individuals with the rights to property. Within the domain of society, a title indicates a rank; the Oxford English Dictionary (OED) provides this definition: 'an appellation attaching to an individual or family in virtue of rank, function, office or attainment, or the possession of or association with certain lands, etc'. Within the domain of law and politics, a title demarcates legitimate ownership of property; the OED definition states: 'legal right to the possession of property (esp. real property); the evidence of such right; title-deeds', and also defines real property as 'immovable property, such as land and anything erected on or attached to this'. These uses have a deep history within anthropology; for example, both occur frequently in 'Notes and Queries on Anthropology' (RAI 1951).

Sen's focus on famine and food scarcity might account for his attention to land and food, and his relative inattention to water. Aside from brief references in quotations and footnotes, he mentions water only once in his book *Poverty and Famines,* in a comment on the marginal position of people who earn their living as water carriers. But the relative absence of water from the literature on entitlements, even from environmentally oriented research (Leach, Mearns and Scoones 1999), may stem from more general sources. Recent scholarship on entitlements continues to discuss land, food and famine, and addresses several other domains as well (general frameworks of social welfare policy; specific government programmes that provide income supplements or social services; and psychological notions of personal empowerment). However, aside from a small set of papers on water markets in eastern Australia, this body of research does not address water issues. It is perhaps not a coincidence that both the definitions of title, mentioned above, are closely associated with land, and, moreover, that water can represent a particular challenge to systems of title and, more generally, to systems of property. Land is fixed in place, it can be easily bounded, and individuals can be excluded from a particular piece of land. By contrast, water moves and flows, and is less easily bounded; it can readily be shared by individuals. Although land can be eroded by water or wind, it is essentially permanent, remaining in place and retaining its physical state. In contrast, water can evaporate or be absorbed by the earth; it moves and it changes its state. It is therefore easier to associate a title (in the sense of rank) with lands than with water, much as it is easier to grant permanent, exclusive title (in the sense of property rights) to land than to water (Orlove and Caton 2010). We return to these issues in the conclusions, where we discuss them in the context of this case.

Water Regimes Worldwide and in Burkina Faso

The current forms of water governance and politics in south-western Burkina Faso can be located in the context of two recent phases of global water regimes, the dam-building period of the mid twentieth century, centred on technology and increase of supply, and the more recent period that replaced it, known by the ungainly name of Integrated Water Resources Management (IWRM), which is centred on administration and limitation of demand.

The period of large dam-building projects reflects the importance of irrigation and the generation of electricity. While small dams date back to prehistory, the construction of large ones expanded rapidly in the mid twentieth century, supported by the availability of new technologies for building massive structures of concrete. This period opened during the Depression and peaked in the postwar period, roughly from the 1950s through to the 1980s. One of the first of these new dams, Hoover Dam on the Colorado River, was completed in 1936. It reflects the economic goals of its builders, since it supplies water for both irrigation and hydropower; it addresses other purposes as well. Though initially planned in the 1920s, it garnered political support when it became an important public works project during the Depression. It also has important aesthetic and ideological dimensions. As Nye argued in his classic work *American Technological Sublime* (1996), Hoover Dam conveyed ever-expanding technological progress and control over nature, which provided Americans with a feeling of national distinctiveness and unity. His analysis opens up the possibility of locating nationalist impulses and the modernist aesthetics in other dam projects. Many of the major dams reflect a period of strong state involvement in national development, including several in Africa, such as the Akosombo Dam which formed Lake Volta, a triumph for newly independent Ghana in 1965, and Kossou Dam in Ivory Coast, that country's reply in 1973 to its neighbour. The Aswan High Dam in Egypt, completed in 1971 and forming Lake Nasser, is another major example in a different portion of the continent of a dam being used as a sign of state power. These dams are, in a sense, visible responses to a neocolonial dam at Kariba, sponsored by the settler state the Federation of Rhodesia and Nyasaland, nominally independent and run by small-minority white landowners. Kariba Dam supplied power to the copper mining district in what was then Northern Rhodesia and is now Zambia. But nations learned that dams were expensive and often disappointing. Dam building had fallen off by the 1980s, although a second phase of dam building is now beginning, in which China and Brazil are particularly active. These new dams are being contested much more extensively than earlier ones.

The growing challenges to dam construction are evident in the history of the International Commission on Large Dams. This international organization was founded in 1928. It focused on improving the planning, design, construction, operation and maintenance of large dams, and drew its membership largely from Europe and North America in its early decades. It added Latin American members in the 1950s and 1960s and then expanded to include Asia and Africa; its first congress outside Europe and the United States was held in India in 1961. By the late 1960s it had moved beyond mere technological optimism to address other issues, such as safety, the management of ageing dams and economic accountability. It also became more engaged in public information campaigns in response to the challenges that dams were facing, as their economic and social costs were becoming evident.

A more substantial critique came from the World Commission on Dams, founded in 1997 by twelve concerned individuals, including the anthropologist Thayer Scudder. Its final report, 'Dams and Development: A New Framework for Decision-Making' (World Commission on Dams 2000), articulates the concerns: though dams have brought many benefits, they have also brought social and environmental costs by displacing people whose lands were flooded, creating tax burdens to pay for the dams, and harming ecosystems. Moreover, they are often more costly than alternative water and energy systems. The report calls for a more open, participatory process that recognizes the multiple economic, environmental and social consequences of dams.

To summarize, the period of dam building corresponded to a model of economic development promoted by strong states, which made large-scale investments to provide highly visible signs of this development to the citizens of their nations. Its alternative, Integrated Water Resource Management, is somewhat more diffuse, and can be traced to the 1990s. The Rio conference on Environment and Development in 1992, being the 20th anniversary of the United Nations Conference on the Human Environment held in Stockholm in 1972, was a major appearance of environmental issues in a global arena.

A meeting that formed part of the lead-up to the Rio conference was the International Conference on Water and the Environment, held in Dublin in January 1992. It addressed the issues of water scarcity and water equity – both little recognized in the early optimistic decades of dam building. It issued four guiding principles, which would hold at local, national and international levels. They are as follows:

> Principle 1: Fresh water is a finite and vulnerable resource, essential to sustain life, development and the environment.
>
> Principle 2: Water development and management should be based on a participatory approach, involving users, planners and policy-makers at all levels.
>
> Principle 3: Women play a central part in the provision, management and safeguarding of water.
>
> Principle 4: Water has an economic value in all its competing uses and should be recognized as an economic good.

These principles were agreed upon, though there was particular debate over the fourth principle; some attendees wanted to have water defined as a human right, rather than as an economic good or resource. These principles were summarized into a fifth overarching principle at the Rio conference, proclaiming what has become the familiar trinity of IWRM: Integrated Water Resources Management is based on the equitable and efficient management and sustainable use of water. This has been restated as the three Es of water: efficiency, equity and environmental sustainability. These principles, known as the Dublin–Rio Principles, are only one version of IWRM; many other formulations have been provided by international organizations and NGOs.

To underscore some of the contrasts between dam building and IWRM, the dams emphasize technology, where IWRM stresses management and governance. Dam building focuses on increasing supply, IWRM on controlling demand. They offer contrasting sorts of entitlements. Dam building is on a national scale, and includes citizens as passive recipients of state benefits – 'transfers' in Sen's terminology, which provide free or heavily subsidized water through government programmes. IWRM operates on multiple scales, and emphasizes users as participants – in Sen's terminology, a combination of 'trade' (since water, as a good, has a price, and is sold) and 'transfer' (since water allocations involve planners and policy makers, who establish procedures to distinguish holders of water rights from others who do not hold such rights). Within IWRM, this issue of participation is important; it is mentioned in the second principle. In a way, IWRM has created social spaces of participation, which could be termed, to adopt a phrase from the great political scientist Benedict Anderson, 'imagined communities'. However, the participatory watershed committees – often created from above and managed by universal principles – are quite different from the more spontaneous, bottom–up national communities that Anderson (1983) presented as emerging from self-organizing networks.

The water regime in contemporary Burkina Faso, like many other issues in that country, can be linked to the key shifts during the presidency (1983–87) of a leftist military leader, Thomas Sankara, who promoted nationalism, inter-ethnic harmony, socialism, self-sufficiency and the prioritization of basic human needs such as food and health. He was killed in a coup led by his former associate, Blaise Compaoré, who remained in power until 2014. Though the new government of Michel Kafondo has introduced new policies in a number of areas, the key elements of water governance remain in place. The 1991 constitution, which strengthened the position of the presidency, affirmed a variety of principles of development, and stated that natural resources, including water, belong to the public and should be used to raise living standards – one of the elements of continuity with Sankara's vision for the country in that constitution. Integrated Water Resources Management is known in Burkina Faso by its French equivalent, Gestion Intégrée des Ressources en Eau (GIRE). A water management law of 2001 explicitly recognized IWRM as the appropriate framework for developing water.

An action plan to promote this system, called Plan d'Action pour la Gestion Intégrée des Ressources en Eau (PAGIRE), was adopted in 2003. PAGIRE created local water management committees (Comités Locaux de l'Eau, known as CLE, a name that is a play on words, almost certainly an unintentional one, since *clé* – a homonym of CLE – means key). A CLE is supposed to act as a local-level forum for consultation among all stakeholders with an interest in water management in a particular water system. It is made up of representatives from the state (both administrative and technical), water users, civil society and local authorities (communes or municipalities, including the traditional authorities). In this way, the CLEs are important sites for two key concepts in integrated water resources management and indeed in a great deal of contemporary policy in environmental and other realms: stakeholders, called *usagers* in French, and participation. The CLEs are designed to function 'as platforms for consultation, mobilization and promotion rather than [as] a decision-making body with enforcement prerogatives' (Roncoli et al. 2009: 701), since higher-level organizations have, in theory, greater power to enforce decisions; however, the authority of the CLEs to manage water can give them considerable influence in water issues. Some of them, including the CLE in this region, received a general mandate for the management of water, which has led them to issue annual release plans (*programmes de lâchure*). These plans, which ideally emerge in a consensual manner from extensive discussion, propose water allocations from reservoirs through canals and other infrastructure to meet the needs of users (Dowd-Uribe, Roncoli and Orlove 2012). Because these plans can vary from year to year, they have the potential to incorporate climatological and hydrological forecasts, which project fluctuations of water in this region of varying rainfall.

In addition to the CLE, PAGIRE established water management units at other scales, including water agencies, and a large unit in each of five river basins (two branches of the Volta River, two branches of the Niger River, and the upper reaches of the Comoé River). These water agencies are directed to establish basin management committees, which then prepare plans for water development and management. In theory the lower-level CLEs at the local level coordinate with the higher-level water organizations.

The first pilot phase of PAGIRE ran from 2003 to 2009, with support from Swedish and Danish bilateral assistance; and the country is now in the second phrase, 2010–2015, supported by the U.S. government agency Millennium Challenge Corporation as well as by the previous Scandinavian donors. Although PAGIRE is already ten years old, its implementation is still far from complete. The water agencies are at different points of their development; many CLEs have not yet been established, or have adopted only a subset of tasks (managing the water in one reservoir, for example).

This chapter focuses on one particular CLE, that of the Upper Comoé, which began operating in 2009 after two years of planning meetings. Its founding document lists the thirty-two members of the CLE, including the president of the Regional Council (a grouping of major officials), the mayors of the five communes in the area, regional directors of several ministries, agricultural and natural resource management projects, civil society organizations (women's groups, local NGOs), customary and religious authorities, economic enterprises, and user groups, including both the rice and vegetable farmers. This large group has only met a few times since the foundation of the CLE. The more active group, which meets several times a year, is the smaller fourteen-member Select Committee (Comité Restreint), including the two leaders, the president of the Regional Council (who also presides the CLE), mayors of three of the five communes involved, a few representatives from ministries, the user groups (though not the riparian farmers), and a few civil society organizations. Within the Select Committee, three or four individuals are particularly active and influential; others attend less consistently.

Water Users in the Upper Comoé

The Upper Comoé watershed is located in south-western Burkina Faso. As one of the moistest and hilliest regions in the dry and flat country, this availability of water and topography supports the construction of dams. The Upper Comoé water management system is centred on three reservoirs, which capture the waters of the Upper Comoé River and some of its tributaries, feeding them into a system of pipelines that operates by gravity, exploiting the natural slope of the land. They are Lobi, Toussiana and Moussoudougou, built in 1976, 1982 and 1991 respectively. Moussoudougou is the largest (with a total capacity of 38 million m^3), while Lobi and Toussiana hold about 6 million m^3 each. Lobi, however, is only partially filled, because of the deteriorating state of the dam. A number of user groups engage directly with this system of reservoirs and canals, using the water for domestic consumption or agricultural production. These users have different kinds of economic interests and levels of political influence, and include a sugar-cane plantation enterprise, an urban water supply utility, a union of farmer cooperatives, and a number of smallholders who grow vegetables along the river.

The first user group is a sugar processing company. It is a fascinating turn of history to see the role this crop is now playing in this part of West Africa, since the sugar cane plantations of Brazil and the Caribbean were central for the development of the slave trade from Africa, a connection well known to anthropologists through Sidney Mintz' magisterial *Sweetness and Power* (1985). About 10 per cent of the world's sugar cane is now grown on the continent of Africa, with most of it coming from North Africa, South Africa and Zimbabwe. However, a number of countries, including Burkina Faso, meet a portion of their demand through local production (Hassan 2008). This makes SOSUCO, a company known by its acronym (derived from the *Societé Sucrière de la Comoé*), an interesting variant of large-scale agriculture in the context of West Africa, where plantations are largely associated with the production of export crops in coastal regions under colonial rule.

SOSUCO was established in the early 1960s, shortly after independence, with French capital and on village land expropriated by the state – a transfer that still mars the relationship between the company and those communities. In the 1970s, the shareholding majority was transferred to the state and SOSUCO functioned as a parastatal until 1998, when the company was privatized. With a labour force composed of thousands of permanent and seasonal workers, SOSUCO is the second largest employer after the state in Burkina Faso, which gives it considerable economic and political clout. By a convention with the state, which financed the construction of the reservoirs, SOSUCO maintains and operates the reservoirs, controlling the sluice gates that allow water to flow downstream. Its ability to expand its operations is limited by the fact that most lands surrounding its plantation are either unsuited to irrigation due to topography, or occupied by local communities, which, in the current political climate characterized by a thrust towards democratization, are unlikely to tolerate further expropriations. SOSUCO currently operates about 4,000 ha of irrigated fields planted with sugar cane, plus a sugar processing plant, which also uses considerable amounts of water. The tall cane plants, an intense light green for most of their growth cycle, form a dramatic feature of the landscape. From a nearby escarpment, they are seen as a broad expanse; but from the dirt roads that run alongside and through the SOSUCO fields, they are a high wall. They are a popular backdrop for photographs, since visitors from other parts of Burkina Faso like to bring home pictures that show the spiky plants reaching far above the heads of even the tallest people.

The second major user group is the urban population of Banfora, a regional administrative and commercial centre with a population of about 63,000. Although there is a deep history of urban settlement in parts of West Africa, in pre-colonial times this region consisted largely of autonomous villages. Banfora was founded as a military post by the French in 1903, growing after the arrival of the railroad in the early 1930s, which connected the colonial hinterland to the Ivory Coast (Côte d'Ivoire) and the coastal region. Most travel and trade are now served by the road system rather than the railway, but urban growth has continued to be fed by the indirect economic effect of SOSUCO as well as by foreign tourists attracted by the picturesque landscape and its vicinity to popular destinations in Mali. The town is supplied with water by a public utility company, the Office National de l'Eau et de l'Assainissement (ONEA), created in 1977 and operated as a state enterprise until the early 1990s. At that time, in step with the neoliberal model embraced by the Burkinabé state, ONEA improved its management by raising rates, shedding personnel, and improving accountability; it also received substantial amounts of foreign aid (Marin, Fall and Ouibiga 2010). Still a state-owned utility, ONEA currently functions as a private enterprise under an agreement that grants it administrative autonomy on condition of financial solvency. Water use in Banfora and the other towns served by ONEA is metered, and fees are charged according to a graduated scale based on consumption levels, being relatively inexpensive for small users but quite costly for large consumers, such as hotels. ONEA intake is linked to a pipeline that channels water from the Moussoudougou and Lobi reservoirs to the SOSUCO fields. Legally, the urban population has priority in water allocation, but ONEA's water demands are relatively limited and easily met, compared to those of SOSUCO. A higher proportion of residents receive piped water in Banfora than in many cities of comparable size and wealth elsewhere in the interior of West Africa. Nonetheless, the continued expansion of Banfora means that peripheral neighbourhoods still obtain their water from carts and pedal-tricycles that carry jerry cans or barrels.

The third group – the Karfiguela irrigated farmer cooperatives – also represents an important aspect of African history, centred on rice cultivation. A species of rice was domesticated about 2,000–3,000 years ago in what is now Nigeria, about 700 km to the east of Banfora, and has been cultivated continuously ever since. This is a more recent domestication than the earlier, and closely related, Asian species. The accumulated knowledge of rice varieties, technologies and water management techniques is extensive, and was transported by slaves, along with seeds, to the British colonies in the Carolinas, as Judith Carney (2002) has documented. Rice remains a staple in urban areas of Burkina Faso. The Karfiguela irrigation cooperative reflects a sharp shift from the customary techniques of water management and from the African to Asian rice species. The initial 75 ha were developed in 1975 with assistance from the government of Taiwan, seeking opportunities to build international support at a time when it was isolated internationally. Importantly, it drew farmers who had been displaced from their lands by the formation of SOSUCO. This area expanded the following year to the current area of 350 ha, with the help of Chinese foreign aid. Currently the cooperative (technically a union of five cooperatives) involves about seven hundred farmers from seven villages.

The irrigated perimeter spans over the territory of the two dominant villages, Karfiguela and Tengrélà, the latter having the largest number of farmers and considerable political clout as the home village of a major national politician and a powerful chief. Most of the residents belong to the Karaboro and Gouin ethnic groups, having inhabited the area since the eighteenth century (Ouédraogo 1997). In this area women have traditionally been involved in rice production in the wetlands, while men cultivated upland fields. The development of irrigation schemes by government and development projects, such as the Karfiguela perimeter, deprived women of their land use rights, as men took control of irrigated land (van Koppen 2000). This follows a broader movement in regional agricultural development towards cash crop cultivation, which shifts formerly women-dominated crops to men. The shift towards irrigated agriculture turned rice into a cash crop dominated by men. In addition, women's work burden increased, because they were now obliged to work on men's irrigated plots, in addition to their own fields. Currently, less than 20 per cent of the Karfiguela cooperative members are women.

The perimeter lies downstream from the main sluice gate whereby SOSUCO controls the level of water in the river. The water that reaches Karfiguela is part of what gets released into the Comoé River after the SOSUCO main diversion. From the river, water is diverted by a gate to the primary canal, which releases water into four secondary canals that divide the territory of the five cooperatives that make up the Karfiguela union. The perimeter is divided into plots ranging in size between 0.25 ha and 0.75 ha, which are differentiated in terms of water access and land quality. Some plots have rich soils and are easily irrigated, supporting rice production for most of the year, while other plots barely receive any water because of distance, elevation or deteriorating infrastructure – but they can be planted with vegetables, maize or cassava, which require less water. Farmers complain that the construction of the SOSUCO reservoirs, particularly Moussoudougou, the largest one, has substantially reduced the availability of water in the Comoé River. The scarcity of water has forced the cooperatives to establish a rotation system whereby half of the perimeter receives water during one dry season, and the other half does so during the following dry season.

A fourth group, of growing importance, comprises the riparian farmers who cultivate along the riverbanks. This practice, too, reflects both the long history of African agriculture and its recent developments. Farmers in this region and further north have long cultivated the banks of rivers, lakes and wetlands, using manual or gravity irrigation, or simple technologies (Norman 1997). Until a decade or two ago, many farmers irrigated small plots next to permanent wetlands by carrying water in clay vessels – a process that was laborious and tiring, but which, even carried out on a small scale, allowed the production of vegetables in the dry season, providing a valued addition to the daily diet and a source of additional income as well. Most farmers currently irrigate their plots along the Comoé and its tributary, the Yannon, by means of diesel-powered water pumps. Streambank plots range between 0.12 ha and 5 ha, and are mostly cultivated with vegetables during the dry season and maize during the rainy season. They form a belt that hugs the river, a zone that is attractive not only for its productivity but also for the coolness that comes from the shade of the fruit trees and the evaporation of moisture from the gardens. It is a space of socialization as well as work, since neighbours pause to greet each other as they pass down the narrow paths on foot, donkey or bicycle, or riding the inexpensive Chinese motorbikes that have flooded the region in recent years.

Besides annual crops, cassava, papaya, banana and mangoes are also grown. Vegetables include a mix of indigenous African crops (okra and a local eggplant variety), crops introduced in pre-colonial times such as cabbage and onion, and other crops brought in by colonization (hot peppers and tomatoes). The crops are sold in urban markets and used for the sauces that complement the starchy staples that form the basic meals consumed by rural and urban households in Burkina Faso and elsewhere, as Jack Goody has discussed in his synthetic work *Cooking, Cuisine and Class* (1996). Most riparian farmers are residents of local communities, but they also include migrants who returned from the Ivory Coast, as well as Banfora residents with some income to invest. As is the case with the Karfiguela cooperative members, riparian farmers use part of the water that is released into the Comoé after the main SOSUCO diversion. But when river levels are low, most of the water that reaches the Karfiguela diversion is channelled into the irrigated perimeter. In such cases, conflicts may arise between Karfiguela and riparian farmers, particularly those who are located north of the confluence with the Yannon, which replenishes the river flow. On the other hand, riparian farmers are often blamed by the other user groups for provoking water shortages in the system. This has particularly been the case in the last decade, which has seen a significant expansion of their activities, driven by the subsidies for water pumps provided by the government as a way of promoting food security and economic growth through small-scale irrigation. There are currently over 600 ha being cultivated along the riverbanks downstream from the Karfiguela plain. Some of these riparian farmers are organized into committees, while others operate independently. There is also one large individual riparian farmer, a wealthy private individual who cultivates about 60 ha of banana trees; he is a wealthy trader from Banfora, who bought the land from an expatriate Frenchman settled in Ivory Coast, who in turn had received it as a concession from the government a number of years ago.

Other important groups that are not directly involved in water allocation decisions but do use local water resources include pastoralists and fishermen. Fulani agro-pastoralists tend local farmers' cattle and live in camps on the outskirts of villages. They maintain patron–client relationships with farmers, through whom they obtain fields to supplement their pastoral livelihood with crop production. During the dry season, transhumant pastoralists from the Sahelian zone also cross the province on their way to wetter areas further south. Access to water for animals is a serious problem for livestock husbandry in the area. The river and several lakes in the area cannot be easily accessed, being enclosed by cultivated fields, which have equally taken over the old cattle corridors used for seasonal transhumance. As a result pastoralists have no choice but to trespass into planted areas to get to water and pastures, which often leads to conflicts with farmers.

In addition to pastoralists, the river and the lakes are also a source of livelihood for fishers, who are drawn particularly from the villages that lost their land and who were forced to relocate when SOSUCO established its sugar cane plantations. At the same time, changes in quantity and quality of the water resources in the area are negatively affecting fishing revenues. The river no longer has enough water for fish to thrive, and so fishing is now limited to the wetlands and the lakes. But even there, fish populations are declining because there is less water for habitats and because lower rainfall means less run-off to replenish nutrients. Residents in the area also voice concerns about pollution from the agro-chemicals leaching from the SOSUCO cane fields and the rice fields into water sources (Painter and Sanou 1996). Other environmental changes are also making fishing more laborious: in the last several years, an invasive weed has proliferated in Lake Lemouroudougou, providing fish with hiding places and hindering the manoeuvring of watercraft and gear. Both pastoralists and fishermen are organized in associations and federations that represent their interests vis-à-vis the state and other relevant actors. These organizations participate in the CLE.

Water Conflicts in the Upper Comoé

The relations among these different groups of water users have led to overt conflicts on three occasions in the last decade. An examination of these three incidents shows that the groups compete for finite water resources, seeking to use connections with powerful individuals and organizations to obtain more water, especially in times of perceived scarcity. It also shows that the groups differ in terms of knowledge systems: they have distinct ways of observing and measuring water to assess its current and projected availability.

In the following discussion, each of the three incidents is assigned a name, based on an aspect of the incident that attracted a good deal of attention. However, the incidents themselves did not receive names by which they were discussed.

2007: THE FARMERS MARCH TO TOWN. Although the 2006 seasonal precipitation was well above average (1,300 mm), for the first time in local memory the Comoé downstream of Karfiguela ran dry in March and April. The riparian farmers were the ones who were most troubled, but the Karfiguela rice producers were also concerned because the water was not sufficient to grow rice. Both groups contacted government authorities and asked them to intervene with SOSUCO in the hope that water could be released from upstream dams. However, SOSUCO said that the lack of rainfall meant that the reservoirs were low, and so they had to save water for irrigation in the following dry season.

The riparian farmers from the village of Sitiena organized an expedition to visit the largest dam, Moussoudougou, to see for themselves how much water was in it. This trip entailed some expense to arrange for a vehicle to carry them to the reservoir. It was also a somewhat assertive act on their part, since the reservoir lay at some distance from their village, within areas generally under the authority of SOSUCO. The farmers assessed that there was enough water for releases to be made. They concluded that the problem was not as SOSUCO had claimed. After that, they organized a march on Banfora to the offices of the high commissioner and the prefect, who were respectively the government representatives at secondary (or provincial) and tertiary (or departmental) administrative levels. At the time, the governor, located at the primary (or regional) level, had just been installed. Since the regions were relatively new entities, local farmers were not as familiar with him as they were with the high commissioner.

Two villages, Sitiena and Siniena, were the main organizers of the march. The water problem was particularly severe in Sitiena because it is at a slight distance and higher elevation from the river, so water can only reach them when the river has sufficient flow. Moreover, the villagers recognized that they were wholly dependent on flows from further upstream. The villages lie below the confluence of the Comoé with the outflow stream from Lake Tengrélà, which ordinarily supplements the flows from the higher reaches of the Comoé, but the lake had receded that year so that its outflow stream was also dry.

The main target of attention was SOSUCO, but some of the tension was directed towards the Karfiguela cooperatives, whose union controlled the Karfiguela diversion of water from the Comoé. The commercial banana plantation (60 ha) downstream of Karfiguela was also extracting a large quantity of water from the river.

The regional and provincial directors of agriculture did not know about the march in advance, or at most had only a general sense of some discontent in the area. They only learned of the march when the villagers arrived in town. At that point they had no information about the level of water in the reservoir, since there was no established channel for them to receive this information. The story was picked up by the national newspapers, which in turn led the national government to become involved. About three weeks later, the minister of commerce was dispatched to 'calm the people's spirits'. He organized a meeting at the Karfiguela cooperative headquarters. The downstream villages also had representatives, and SOSUCO technicians attended as well. The farmers at the meeting accused SOSUCO of creating problems, but some of the downstream villages also blamed the Tengrélà banana plantation, which had been damming the river with sandbags to create a large pool of water, but which could be pumped out. The minister concluded that the problem was 'a lack of communication' between SOSUCO and the other producers (Ouattara 2007). This view helped to advance the negotiations for the establishment of the CLE. These efforts continued in the following months and advanced in September. It is unclear whether SOSUCO agreed to release more water following the visit by the minister. It seems that the crisis was resolved when rains began to fall, providing water for the rice cooperatives in Karfiguela and the riparian farmers downstream.

2009: THE GATE IS OPENED. A dry spell of two weeks' duration occurred in late July, well into the rainy season. The Karfiguela farmers were concerned because their rice crops were at the critical stage of head formation when the panicle – the organ which bears the rice grains in formation – emerges from within the leaves. This is a period when they visit their plots with particular concern, keeping a close eye on the plants. The Karfiguela farmers held a meeting among themselves. They wanted to ask SOSUCO to release water. As was usually the case during the rainy season, SOSUCO was not irrigating, but rather storing water for release in the dry season. After some pressure, SOSUCO agreed to meet the farmers, who asked SOSUCO to open the gate.

In the past, Karfiguela farmers would have gone to the provincial agricultural office, using their contacts with agricultural extension officers. The head of the Provincial Directorate of the Ministry of Agriculture would have called SOSUCO technicians. On this occasion, though, the president of the union of cooperatives in Karfiguela and the head of cooperative five went to see the president of the Regional Council to ask him to convoke the Select Committee of the CLE to discuss their problem with SOSUCO.

The Karfiguela cooperatives organized themselves to work for one week cleaning the canals to avoid potential loss of water. They also replaced the wooden gate at the Karfiguela diversion site that serves to redirect water from the Comoé to their fields. They hired a local artisan to make another gate, paying him with funds that they had received from the regional agricultural office and a World Bank project.

Additional meetings were also held. The provincial agricultural director personally intervened with SOSUCO on behalf of the Karfiguela farmers, because the Ministry of Agriculture stood to lose a great deal of money if the farmers could not repay them for the fertilizer that they had purchased on credit for rice production.

The SOSUCO technician opened the gate for a week. Interestingly, different individuals who were interviewed described the flow in different ways: one reported a release of 200 l/sec, another of the gate being opened 19 cm. With this supplement, the Karfiguela farmers had a substandard though adequate crop, and repaid much of their loans. A representative of the regional agricultural director on the CLE and leaders of the riparian farmers travelled along the canal to make sure that the water was being released. They did not measure volume directly.

A number of actors observed the situation closely. By August, the technician reviewed the level of water in the reservoir. At that time of year, with the rains well advanced, he could estimate the total inflow for the season and project SOSUCO's water situation in the dry season that would soon begin. Other groups in the region, such as the herders who water their animals from the canals, observed this flow and inferred that the CLE had influence. Some commented on the power of the provincial agricultural director as well.

2012: THE FARMERS' MARCH IS AVERTED. During the months of September, October and November of 2011, a small group from the CLE met. It included representatives from three organizations: SOSUCO, the regional agricultural director's office, and the local NGO and consulting firm AEDE (Association Eau Développement et Environnement, or the Association for Water, Development and Environment). Noting the low level of water in the reservoirs, they decided not to produce the annual water release programme. In particular, SOSUCO claimed that a water release programme could not be made since precipitation during the previous rainy season was insufficient, and there were problems with the dam in Moussoudougou, the largest reservoir, which prevented the storage of sufficient water. This decision was not made public or even discussed at a CLE or Select Committee meeting.

But before word of the lack of a water release schedule was somehow divulged and became an issue, the minister of agriculture demanded a water release programme to make sure that there would be sufficient water to grow maize. The dry season maize crop was in response to low rainfall and an inadequate harvest in the northern part of the country. It became a national priority to grow an off-season maize crop to deal with potential issues of food insecurity. The minister charged the newly installed water agency (Agence de l'Eau) to organize such a water release programme. However, since the water agency was not yet fully functional, it apparently fell to the Regional Directorate of the Ministry of Agriculture to ensure that water releases were planned.

This decision led to a series of smaller meetings between November and January. A group of individuals, who also happened to be members of the Select Committee, put together a water release programme. The key individuals at these meetings were from SOSUCO, ONEA, AEDE, and the regional office of the Ministry of Agriculture.

A water release programme emerged from these meetings. The programme saw that there was demand for 46M cubic metres of water, but there were only 27M stored in the reservoirs. It was decided at a Select Committee meeting that this 19M cubic metre deficit would be shared 'equally' between the three major user groups – SOSUCO, Karfiguela and the riparian farmers. In addition, the representatives at this meeting calculated reductions in planted areas that fell unevenly across the groups. They stated that this revised plan would require SOSUCO to reduce its planted area by about 20 per cent, from 4,000 to 3,250 hectares; Karfiguela by about 30 per cent from 350 to 250; and riparian farmers by 35 per cent from 2,000 to 1,300.

This water release programme was never officially approved and never went into effect. SOSUCO technicians reviewed the calculations, which had been done by AEDE, and informed AEDE and the regional agricultural director's office that they contained errors. Those three parties bickered over the programme, but never agreed to one. ONEA, whose water allocation was small, and legally guaranteed, did participate actively in these discussions.

In January 2012, the farmers on the Karfiguela plain had not yet planted their rice or maize crop, an activity which takes place around mid February. At this time, they were not taking water from Comoé, but the river was beginning to dry out near the village of Sitiena.

The regional agricultural director's office called a meeting to discuss water shortages and the water release programme. This meeting gathered representatives of the organizations who would ordinarily participate in CLE meetings, including SOSUCO, the regional and provincial agricultural director's offices, and the rice cooperatives of Karfiguela and riparian farmers committees from Sitiena. The upshot of the meeting was, given that there was no consensus on a water release programme, that SOSUCO would conduct water releases as it saw fit but it would provide an exceptional water release so that Sitiena would receive water.

The release did not reach Sitiena right away. In February, farmers from Sitiena visited the gates at Karfiguela and demanded that they be opened in order to let water down the river. They also gathered as a group and travelled down to the makeshift sandbag dam that the banana plantation had constructed in the river to facilitate pumping water; they worked together to dismantle the dam, walking directly into the river to remove it piece by piece. A leader from Sitiena would call people to ensure that the gates were indeed open. Eventually the gates were opened, but there was some significant tension between Sitiena on the one hand and the upstream villages of Tengrélà and Karfiguela on the other.

In March and April there was a second water shortage, felt most acutely in Sitiena and Siniena, the largest downstream villages of riparian farmers. The president of the irrigators committee of Sitiena went to Banfora, where he visited several parties in succession to complain about the lack of water: first to the president of the Regional Council (who is also the president of the CLE), then to the regional agricultural director, the first deputy mayor of Banfora, and finally to the prefect, who called the president of the Regional Council.

The leader from Sitiena then went to see the canton chief in Tengrélà, and informed him that if there was no water by the following Monday, a few days hence, the farmers would march to Banfora. He returned to Banfora to a previously scheduled Select Committee meeting of the CLE and discussed the march there as well. The march would be composed of producers from the downstream villages. They were going to meet just outside Banfora on the road to Karfiguela. In response, the Select Committee decided to release water exclusively for the Comoé River for four days and make sure that it arrived at Sitiena before closing the gates at the Karfiguela diversion so that the water would flow again to the Karfiguela cooperative farmers.

A delegation visited Sitiena and Siniena, along with other smaller downstream villages. It included the chief of the canton and representatives of the regional agricultural director's office and the regional agricultural chamber (an association, established in the mid-2000s, which includes a number of different agricultural interests in the area). This visit happened the day before the producers were going to march, as a way to quieten them down and to raise their awareness about the multiple factors that contribute to water shortages. (Officials describe this with the French term *sensibiliser,* which means mean to 'sensitize' or to raise awareness, with an implication of acceptance as well.) They were able to calm the people by explaining that the dams were in a bad state, and the dike needed repairing. Using an established proverb, they said *'tout le monde n'a qu'à mettre la main dans la pâte'*. A literal translation would be 'everyone has only to knead the dough', implying that this effort is required for everyone to eat; a freer translation would be 'everyone has to roll up their sleeves if we're going to get the work done'. The villagers responded positively to the visit, and cancelled the march. SOSUCO released enough water for the crops to be irrigated. And when water levels in the river began to decline again, the rain came, saving the growing season. A number of villagers stated that it was the minister of agriculture who ultimately intervened and told SOSUCO to release water.

Sitiena sent men to the Karfiguela gates to spend all day and night there. Officials also reported that people from the village did *'menacer de casser les vannes'* (threaten to break the sluice gates) if they found them closed. Four would go and spend the day, and then they would be relieved by four more who would spend the night until the next set of four arrived, and so on. They carried out this surveillance to ensure that the gates remained open to let water pass down the river to the downstream villages.

Discussion: Knowledge and Governance

At first glance, these cases might not seem to be particularly noteworthy. They could seem to reveal little more than the ability of wealthy and well-connected organizations to garner scarce resources, such as water. One could simply state that the most powerful actor in the system, the large sugar cane producer SOSCUO, sits highest up in the system of reservoirs – both topographically and politically – and controls the gates, keeping nearly all the water for itself while also regularly releasing small amounts for downstream users if they complain loudly enough. As for the IWRM process, it is so poorly organized and so lacking in technical capacity to monitor and regulate flows that it makes little difference. This would seem to be a simple story of gross power inequities and ineffectual governance, much like other such stories from around the world. At most one might say that the introduction of the IWRM process around 2008 opened the system up a small amount, allowing channels for requests and communication so that the disorder of the march in 2007 was not repeated.

On closer analysis, the cases show the complexity rather than the simplicity of water politics. Rather than merely being an issue of distribution of water, the cases point to the importance of knowledge and of governance. More generally, the cases show that entitlements are socially and culturally based. It might seem that they are simple, consisting of assertions that a particular person or group has the right to access what Sen calls a 'commodity bundle' – a particular quantity of a particular resource, under specified conditions. These cases show the complexity and variability of these terms. 'Access' can include various uses and actions beyond simple possession and consumption, such as display (the visual properties of water feature in these cases). The 'quantity' can be assessed or measured in different ways, and the 'conditions' can rest on different social ties, which in turn can be narrated and performed in different ways. Indeed, the contestations over entitlements can involve not only the access, quantities and conditions themselves, but the terms by which these three are defined.

For the question of knowledge, one may note that there are two modes for thinking about water in the Comoé watershed: vernacular or folk knowledge of the farmers, and scientific or technological knowledge of the officials and of IWRM (Orlove and Caton 2010). Indeed, the actors in the Comoé watershed think of water in different ways. Firstly, they use distinct systems to measure the quantity of water. The officials in the CLE and the SOSUCO technicians emphasize the quantity of water in terms of volume. They speak of the stock of water in the reservoir in terms of millions of cubic meters, and view flows as 'drawdowns' of these stocks. By contrast, the rice farmers from Karfiguela and the riparian farmers further downstream emphasize the quantity of water in terms of flow rather than volume. They speak of water flowing through the river and through canals for a certain amount of time. When they speak of the quantity of flow, they use simple vernacular measures. They might note that the height of the water is up to the level of a person's knee, for example, or that the width of the water in a specific locale extends out to cover the wooden supports of a bridge. This contrast shows the importance of metrology, the study of measures (Kula 1968). To be sure, these two descriptions, one in terms of volume and the other in terms of flow and time, are equivalent, much as a trip could be described in terms of the distance, or in terms of the speed and duration. But although the two may be formally or logically equivalent, they direct attention to different aspects of it.

Secondly, the actors emphasize different spaces within the water system. The officials in the CLE and the SOSUCO technicians speak more often of the reservoirs, while the farmers focus on the river and the canals. Certainly water flows from the former to the latter, but these spaces are managed differently. Access to the reservoirs is limited as the dams lie at a distance from Banfora and the agricultural areas, and so only the SOSUCO technicians and the leading government officials, with ready access to vehicles, can visit them easily. By contrast, the river below Banfora and the canals pass through public space between villages and fields. The gates, which figure so prominently in these cases, are important not merely as nodes in a water network, but as social boundaries as well, being the locations where these distinct domains meet.

Thirdly, the farmers emphasize the visibility of water. It may seem rather trivial to comment that water can be observed as it flows through rivers and canals, but this visibility plays a role for farmers. It is part of their everyday working lives to notice the amount of water in the river and in the permanent wetlands, much as they also notice the state of their crops as they mature and of their animals as they either grow fatter in times of abundance of pasture or leaner in times of scarcity. At times of crisis, they make particular efforts to observe water delivery continuously and in a collective fashion, in the 2012 case in particular organizing teams to watch the gates, river and canals. This visibility is an element in the importance of water in political systems as well as in economic livelihoods. Water is not only a resource, which permits farmers to provide their households with food and income; it is also a tangible element in the systems of political relations. Leaders among farmers garner support because their followers can see the water, and because other actors in the region can see it and comment on it as well.

For the question of governance, one may note that there are two systems for managing water in the Comoé watershed: a customary system, with elements of clientelism, that links farmers and officials, and the more recent system of IWRM. Much like the question of knowledge, the question of governance also contains several elements. Firstly, there is the matter of whether political power is located in individuals or in political offices and organizations, somewhat analogous to the question of how water is measured. On the one hand, important people have influence because they occupy specific roles – the high commissioner, or the regional director of agriculture, or head of the irrigators' committee in a village of riparian farmers. On the other hand, these important people are known by name, as individuals, with specific histories. The relations that actors have with these influential individuals are also personalized and long lasting. In the narratives in which actors described the events, they spoke of both aspects.

Secondly, the actors emphasize different spaces within the political system, directly analogous to the spaces within the water system. When the rice farmers from Karfiguela or the riparian farmers from the downstream villages make requests, they travel to the town of Banfora, to the offices where the powerful individuals sit and receive others, or sometimes call them (lower-level ones especially) on their cell phones. But when government officials make concessions to the farmers, they have meetings in the villages, typically gathered, as is the custom across rural Africa, in the shade of a prominent tree. To be sure, such patterns of visits occur in other settings, and may appear to be a natural way of showing respect in order to gain favour; but they also reflect a distinct understanding of politics, quite different from suggesting that the different actors are all stakeholders in a participatory framework.

Finally, the theme of violence is implicit in the discussions, most strongly in the 2007 case when political officials were concerned to 'calm the spirits' of the farmers who had come to Banfora to demonstrate, but present as well in the 2012 case. It seems possible that the farmers do not threaten to commit acts of violence, but rather that they present themselves, and are understood, as people whose feelings are so strong that they might suddenly give way to violent impulses – if faced with a gate that blocks water from reaching them, or with officials who refuse to grant them water. This undercurrent of violence may be understood as an echo of the displacement of villagers from their lands (and in some cases from their homesteads) half a century ago when the SOSUCO plantations were created. The new lands of Karfiguela and the newer possibilities of riparian cultivation do not fully compensate for this dislocation, and they require a supply of water. One might even speculate that the theme of violence in water governance would correspond to the theme of visibility for water knowledge, since it is the absence of water that provokes the possibility of violence. The French word *pagaille,* commonly used to describe violent political events here and in other parts of the country, is also used to describe less dramatic instances of disorder and disagreement, such as domestic quarrels, unruly classrooms, and even barnyard scenes of squawking chickens, barking dogs and panicked pigs. It links violence and vision by denoting both the disorderly actions of people (speech, movement, blows, smashing, etc.) and the disorderly arrangement – evident in the visual realm – of objects and buildings that results from their actions. Moreover, the political costs the authorities face when the demonstrations take place come from the challenge to their positions when angry demonstrators are seen in public places, as well as from any actual harm to people or damage to property that the demonstrators might cause.

Are there associations to be explored between these two disjunctures – the one between the two systems of knowledge and the other between the two systems of governance? There is at least some degree of correspondence between the technical knowledge of the officials and the formal governance institutions on the one hand, and between the vernacular knowledge of the farmers and the clientistic networks on the other. One can note the gap that separates the official discourse of the IWRM, with its efforts to produce an orderly system of governance (expressed in forms like annual release plans of specific volumes), from the concerns of the farmers, who mobilize at specific times in order to obtain flows – for example, when the Comoé ran dry late in the rainy season in 2007, during a long dry spell in the middle of the rainy season in 2009, and during a water shortage late in the dry season in 2012. One could add that these alternatives represent two ways of dealing with the challenges of climate at the edges of the Sahel, including both the variability of weather from year to year and decade to decade, and the long-term trends of climate change, which will only make water scarcity more acute. The IWRM can incorporate findings from climate science, which provides forecasts of expected rainfall in the coming year and on longer timescales, and which can be discussed at annual meetings; the farmers' view recognizes that the challenges are often on shorter timescales – for example, shortfalls that occur as dry spells within the rainy season, or early terminations of the rainy season – and cannot be easily forecast, but to which responses can be elicited by mobilizing clientistic ties.

Nonetheless, the gap is not so absolute. Most concretely, the leaders of the farmers' organizations (the Karfiguela union of cooperatives, and the associations of riparian irrigators) and the officials in key agencies are connected both through the IWRM organizations and through the clientistic networks. In addition, the CLE meetings seem to have promoted a greater awareness on both sides of the schedules within which the other operates, so that the SOSUCO technicians and the rice farmers have a better sense of the timing of the other's needs. They differ in terms of the ways they measure the quantity of water – in volume and in flow. They also differ in their reckoning of time, since the agencies operate exclusively with the global twelve-month calendar, and the farmers often use a local system that incorporates both the Islamic calendar, especially Ramadan, and periods tied to the seasons ('the moon of steady rains', usually August; 'the moon of great heat', typically April). Nonetheless, they share an understanding of the annual cycle of rainy and dry seasons, and they acknowledge the specific requirements of different crops within this cycle. Moreover, the CLE committees provide additional organizational ties to connect the different actors. In 2009 and 2012, the farmers who sought additional water releases used their CLE connections as ways to contact powerful individuals, most of whom they would have known earlier but with whom they now have additional ties.

One can note both exclusionary and inclusionary aspects of these annual release plans. For the former, they seem oriented outside the region. The annual release plans allow the local CLEs to articulate with the government water offices at regional levels, providing them with numerical information that can be moved from report to report. The plans serve well to incorporate technical information from other sources, such as climate forecasts. And they enact the sort of orderly logical thinking that is implied in the 'management' part of IWRM, especially in its French expression of *aménagement et gestion*, more than the kind of impromptu adaptive management that the farmers prefer. In addition they serve other functions; they work well as a focus of attention for the CLE, with its large number of members, and the participatory approach leads to a broad inclusion of many actors, creating committees that can address large issues on an annual basis but cannot respond quickly to short-term demands. In this sense, they resemble Scott's insights (1999) into the operations of centralized governments, which conceptualize resources in formal ways that are at odds with the empirical knowledge of local populations. They point as well to Ostrom's discussion of the management of commons (1990), in which she describes a number of cases of irrigation that are being managed well by small-scale groups of self-organizing users who needed little more than general recognition from a central state.

On the other hand, the IWRM may be more inclusionary than Scott or Ostrom envisaged. The meetings create an additional context for exchanges. The conversations at the meetings seem to have built a kind of awareness of each other's activities, frameworks and needs, and to have extended the network of social ties in the region; the Karfiguela rice cooperatives have been more fully incorporated than the riparian vegetable farmers, but both are involved to some extent. Moreover, two common critiques of IWRM do not seem to apply fully here. It does not privilege technical and scientific information as fully as it is said to do in other places, such as Brazil (Taddei 2011); the illiterate farmers (whether in riparian areas or on the Karfiguela plain) who may speak two or three African languages but who know little or no French, have limited access to the CLE, but their organizations at least have seats in the general assembly, and their position is acknowledged. Nor does this case suggest the neoliberalism of IWRM and its insistence on the treatment of water as a commodity used to produce marketable goods and services (Bakker 2005); rather, this case seems to accommodate a variety of users.

The reading one can make of IWRM depends on the reading of the relations between the more orderly functioning of the CLE meetings and the water release plans, on the one hand, and the marches and tensions of these cases, which occur every other year or so, on the other. One might see the cases as a sign of the incompleteness of the introduction of IWRM, as remnants of earlier political forms of brokerage, which should be replaced by the more progressive IWRM. One might read the cases as political movements of opposition to IWRM, which voice alternate concerns. Or one might read the two more recent cases as efforts of the poor and the weak to press the IWRM process to open up. At a minimum, they suggest that the system has begun to acknowledge the riparian farmers, some of whom were formerly referred to as 'pirates' – illegal and informal actors with no legitimate claim on water.

Conclusion: Citizenship and Entitlement

This discussion of the riparian farmers and informal economies brings to mind James Holston's use of the term 'insurgent citizenship' in his discussion (2009) of urban politics in São Paulo, Brazil. He shows that the contrast between legal neighbourhoods and squatter settlements in that city is a relative rather than an absolute one. Title to property is rarely entirely firm, since the state can exercise eminent domain; it is rarely entirely lacking, since state agencies give at least partial acknowledgement to even the most apparently marginal settlements. (Where anthropological maps of Brazilian cities used to make black and white distinctions between shanty towns and legal neighbourhoods, Holston sees many shades of grey.) Moreover, relations among the residents of poor neighbourhoods, which exist outside the sphere of state agencies, interact with the ties within organizations chartered by legal systems.

The efforts to make claims more solid is the insurgence he describes, which animates political activity in the area; he sees broad issues of citizenship within the workings of urban groups to address their concerns in the context of unequal access to state recognition.

In the Upper Comoé, the conflicts are over water rather than land, but the diverse and uneven nature of state recognition of claims is similar. The state might seem to be the ultimate arbiter of water, since the dams are, in theory, the property of the state, and the water allocations are decided each year by the CLE, an organization chartered and supervised by the state (with the lion's share going to SOSUCO, the local user with the greatest national importance). But the poor farmers can exercise their claims to water, much as squatters can exercise their claims to land in Brazil. The farmers emphasize the long-standing basis of their claims, evoking the times before the construction of the dams when the flows of the Comoé offered abundant water to Karfiguela, or recalling the times before the arrival of motor pumps, when farmers watered their vegetable plots by hand. They call on the clientistic ties with officials, dating back a number of years, to offer a counterweight to the discussions within the CLE that might cut allocations in any given year. The central elements of titling – a stable system of social ranks and a shared recognition of bounded property – are weakly present in the case of water. In these ways, access to water differs from the entitlements that Sen envisaged, because it is more the product of bargaining than of exercise of firm claims, more contingent, more changing – in a sense, more fluid, and visibly so.

In this way, the example of the Upper Comoé opens the question of 'fluid entitlements'. In this case, water entitlements might be an example of the 'transfers' that Sen envisaged in his writings in the early 1980s, since the government is, in theory at least, the owner of the dams and the reservoirs. (If the proposed system of water fees, discussed in some government circles in Burkina Faso, is ever established, that would add an element of 'trade', in Sen's terms.) But these entitlements are fluid, not just because water is fluid, but because of the way they change and unfold over time through ongoing negotiations in multiple channels – a sharp contrast with the relative fixity of land rights. Different groups may contest the rights to use a plot in the city of São Paulo, and their disputes may occupy the attention of political organizations, government agencies, courts and the media, but at any given time the boundaries and uses of the plot are evident and its area is fixed. The group that uses a plot will continue to use it unless it is dislodged by another; it may acknowledge the neighbouring groups that control other plots, but it exercises domain over its area. By contrast, the volume of water that flows downstream from the dams into the Comoé is always changing, always shared – even if unequally – among different users. The group that diverts water one day may continue to divert it, or may be pressed to relinquish it. In these ways, water does not match well with the elements – stable, exclusive claims over bounded entities – that are associated with the discussions of entitlements. Each diversion may serve to stake a claim for future diversions, but such claims are endlessly negotiated. The variability of rainfall and river flow in this region contribute to the importance of negotiations, since each year presents a novel situation, but negotiations would be present even in areas of less variable climate.

This question of citizenship is perhaps the most fundamental one. For Holston, urban land is only one of the many domains in which citizenship is contested in São Paulo, Brazil, though it is one of the most important ones. The same may be said of water in the Comoé watershed in Burkina Faso. The variety of forms of political action in this region is striking, including older institutions from a centralized state, newer decentralized organizations and local village organizations. The IWRM offers the promise of participatory decision making, a kind of neoliberal ideal in which politics is replaced by governance. Do the interactions of the IWRM deliberations and the pressures represented by the three cases move towards a fuller citizenship, in which the weaker farmers – both the rice farmers in Karfiguela and the riparian farmers downstream – exercise their voice, or does the power structure remain fundamentally unchanged? The answer to this question will only be answered in the future, as water politics in the region unfolds. These examples show the importance of water in the redefinition of citizenship in the contemporary world. And they show the importance of recognizing the inherent fluidity of entitlements. They demonstrate that disagreements over entitlements are not simply disputed claims of individuals and collectivities to 'commodity bundles' – objects, spaces and other valued entities. They are occasions when conflicts rise to the surface, conflicts between different social and cultural modes of defining collectivities and defining entities in the material world. The conflicts are as much about naming, seeing and knowing as they are about owning and using.

Acknowledgements

Major funding was provided under the cooperative agreement NSF SES-0951516 awarded to the Center for Research on Environmental Decisions. The study builds on previous research funded by the Sectoral Application Research Program of the United States National Oceanic and Atmospheric Administration (NOAA).

Notes

1. This chapter draws on the authors' field experience in the region and in Burkina Faso. Ben Orlove travelled to the field site in 2011 and 2013, for two weeks each time. Carla Roncoli spent a total of two months in Banfora between 2007 and 2012, in addition to regular research trips to different parts of Burkina Faso since 1995, averaging 8–10 weeks per year. Brian Dowd-Uribe visited Banfora in 2011, 2012 and 2013, totalling three months; he also spent fourteen months in Burkina Faso between 2008 and 2010. The chapter also draws less directly on other fieldwork carried out in Africa by the authors: in addition to some shorter stays in a number of countries, this included two years in Ghana for Roncoli, two years in Togo for Dowd-Uribe, and four months in Zimbabwe and Uganda for Orlove.

References

Anderson, B. 1983. *Imagined Communities: Reflections on the Origin and Spread of Nationalism*. London: Verso.

Bakker, K. 2005. 'Neoliberalizing Nature? Market Environmentalism in Water Supply in England and Wales', *Annals of the Association of American Geographers* 95(3): 542–65.

Carney, J.A. 2002. *Black Rice: The African Origins of Rice Cultivation in the Americas*. Cambridge, MA: Harvard University Press.

Dowd-Uribe, B., C. Roncoli and B. Orlove. 2012. 'Water Grows Food: Dry Season Farming, Food Sovereignty, and Integrated Water Resource Management in Burkina Faso', *Bulletin of the Association of Concerned Africa Scholars* 88: 11–19.

Goody, J. 1996. *Cooking, Cuisine and Class: A Study in Comparative Sociology*. Cambridge: Cambridge University Press.

Hassan, S.F. 2008. 'Development of Sugar Industry in Africa', *Sugar Technology* 10(3): 197–203.

Holston, J. 2009. *Insurgent Citizenship: Disjunctions of Democracy and Modernity in Brazil*. Princeton, NJ: Princeton University Press.

Kula, W. 1986. *Measures and Men* (Translated by R. Szreter). Princeton, NJ: Princeton University Press.

Leach, M., R. Mearns and I. Scoones. 1999. 'Environmental Entitlements: Dynamics and Institutions in Community-Based Natural Resource Management', *World Development* 27(2): 225–47.

Marin, P., M. Fall and H. Ouibiga. 2010. *Corporatizing a Water Utility: A Successful Case Using a Performance-Based Service Contract for ONEA in Burkina Faso*. Washington, DC: The World Bank.

Mintz, S.W. 1985. *Sweetness and Power: The Place of Sugar in Modern History*. New York: Viking.

Norman, W.R. 1997. 'Indigenous Community-managed Irrigation in Sahelian West Africa', *Agriculture Ecosystems & Environment* 61(2/3): 83–95.

Nye, D.E. 1996. *American Technological Sublime*. Cambridge, MA: MIT Press.

Orlove, B., and S.C. Caton. 2010. 'Water Sustainability: Anthropological Approaches and Prospects', *Annual Review of Anthropology* 39: 401–15.

Ostrom, E. 1990. *Governing the Commons: The Evolution of Institutions for Collective Action*. Cambridge: Cambridge University Press.

Ouattara, L. 2007. 'Une crise d'eau fait des dégâts', *L'Observateur Paalga* (Burkina Faso), 5 April 2007.

Ouédraogo, J.-B. 1997. *Violences et communautés en Afrique noire : la région Comoé entre règles de concurrence et logiques de destruction (Burkina Faso)*. Paris: L'Harmattan.

Painter, T. and S. Sanou. 1996. *La gestion décentralisée des ressources naturelles au Burkina Faso*. Ouagadougou, Burkina Faso : PADLOS/CILSS.

Roncoli, C., et al. 2009. 'From Management to Negotiation: Technical and Institutional Innovations for Integrated Water Resource Management in the Upper Comoé River Basin, Burkina Faso', *Environmental Management* 44(4): 695–711.

RAI [Royal Anthropological Institute of Great Britain and Ireland]. 1951. 'Notes and Queries on Anthropology', 6th edn, revised. London: Routledge and Kegan Paul.

Scott, J.C. 1999. *Seeing Like a State: How Certain Schemes to Improve the Human Condition Have Failed*. New Haven, CT: Yale University Press.

Sen, A. 1981. *Poverty and Famines: An Essay on Entitlements and Deprivation*. Oxford: Clarendon Press.

———. 1984. *Resources, Values and Development*. Oxford: Basil Blackwell.

Taddei, R. 2011. 'Watered-down Democratization: Modernization versus Social Participation in Water Management in Northeast Brazil', *Agriculture and Human Values* 28(1): 109–21.

Van Koppen, B. 2000. 'Gendered water and land rights in rice valley improvement, Burkina Faso', In Bruns, B. R. and Meinzen-Dick, R. S. (eds.), *Negotiating water rights*. London: Intermediate Technology Publications. pp. 83–111.

World Commission on Dams. 2000. 'Dams and Development: A New Framework for Decision-Making: The Report of the World Commission on Dams'. London and Sterling, VA: Earthscan Publications.

3

Raining in the Andes

Disrupted Seasonal and
Hydrological Cycles

Astrid B. Stensrud

> 'The rain rains when it feels like it'
> (Maria, 37)

People in Colca Valley in the Peruvian Andes are currently experiencing changes in weather and seasons. The rain seems to be even more unpredictable than before, and this creates uncertainty in the everyday lives of farmers and herders. There is a general experience of belated rains and dwindling water supplies, but on the other hand, when the rain finally arrives, it is more massive and intense than usual. Also, the glaciers, which are natural water reservoirs, are predicted to disappear all over the Andes due to their sensitivity to global warming (Bates et al. 2008; Vuille et al. 2008). In this chapter I explore how we can think about rain in terms of time and space, according to different scales. By focusing on knowledge practices and performativity, I ask how rain is known, related to, and anticipated. This entails an exploration of how rain is configured in daily practices, speech, memories, knowledge and narratives. What are the consequences of irregular rain, and how is it understood, explained and acted upon today? Profound changes in rain patterns and seasonality make rain a matter of concern, and affect how people predict future rain, how they remember past rain, and how they practise rain in the present. There are different ways of producing knowledge about rain and the changes that occur, based on bodily experience, narratives and science. Different forms of rainwater management in Colca Valley include technologies for measuring rain, infrastructure for harvesting rainwater and ritual performances for summoning rain clouds from the ocean. I suggest that engagements with local environments perform rain into being in different ways – ways that are not stable, but fluid and emergent. Barnes and Alatout (2012) argue that water is multiple, not only in its meanings, but in its very materiality, and that scholarship on water can benefit from a close attention to water's multiple ontologies (ibid.). I argue that in the Andes this multiplicity does not just entail the different versions of water that are enacted by different material practices, like in Mol's (2002) study of the body multiple in a Dutch hospital, but also sentient non-human beings and vital forces that partake in the relational ontologies in the Andes (cf. de la Cadena 2010; Stensrud 2014). As these beings are part of the world, they also are affected by global warming, and should therefore be accounted for in the studies of climate change effects.

I draw on ethnographic material generated during eight months of fieldwork in 2011 in Colca Valley, located in the Arequipa region of southern Peru. Here, I studied water-related practices in the Colca-Majes watershed, which comprises the water sources, streams, rivers and canals from 6,000 metres above sea level to the Pacific coast. I was based in the small town of Chivay, which is the provincial capital of Caylloma, located between the agricultural districts in the valley and the herder communities in the highlands; and I also visited sixteen other villages at different altitudes in the watershed. The fieldwork was not only multi-sited, but also involved looking at multiple scales of water practices as these were enacted by the actors (cf. Latour 2005). I thus aimed to follow the different actors in their scaling exercises emerging through narratives and activities. The methodology included mapping, surveys, interviews with local leaders, and – most importantly – participant observation among farmers, artisans, merchants, engineers and activists, as well as in different water-users' organizations.

Living with Rain: The Fluidity of Seasonality

Most of the inhabitants in Colca Valley are bilingual speakers of Quechua and Spanish, and the economy is mainly based on small-scale farming and alpaca pastoralism, as well as commerce, handicrafts and tourist-related activities. There are about ten thousand farmers in the valley who cultivate potatoes, barley, beans, peas, quinoa and maize on approximately 12,000 hectares of land – thus an average of 1.2 hectares of land per farming family. The agricultural activities are highly dependent on irrigation, and the vertical landscapes are inscribed with centuries-old agricultural terraces and crisscrossed with networks of irrigation canals made of earth or cement. The farmers are organized in irrigation associations where they elect leaders for four-year periods and distribute water among the members on a daily basis. For the last four decades, anthropologists and geographers have been analysing the social organization of irrigation in Colca, which is intrinsically related to rainfall patterns (see, among others, Guillet 1992; Guillet and Mitchell 1994; Paerregaard 1994; Treacy 1994; and Gelles 2000). These scholars have focused on local forms of water distribution, in terms of power and control, and they have discussed the changes and conflicts related to state intervention in community-based irrigation. With the changing climate, the melting glaciers and the increasing pressure on water resources, these issues are becoming even more critical as people are becoming more dependent on technologies to gather rainwater and save it for irrigation. Hydrological measurements in weather stations all over the southern Peru show an overall precipitation decrease between 1950 and 1994 (Vuille et al. 2008: 83–84). The so-called *veranillos* – defined as strong precipitation for two days, followed by a lack of rain for fifteen to twenty days – have also become more frequent. Moreover, according to the fourth assessment report of the Intergovernmental Panel on Climate Change from 2007, the annual precipitation is likely to decrease further in the southern Andes in future, although changes in atmospheric circulation may induce large local variability in precipitation response in mountainous areas (Christensen et al. 2007).

Rain is already scarce on the western escarpment of the southern Andes, where the Colca Valley is located between the wetter *altiplano* and the arid coastal zone. The ecosystem of Colca is defined as semi-arid, with a mean rainfall figure of 422.7 mm in the period 1951–1982, based on measurements from the weather station in Yanque village (Guillet 1992: 47; Winterhalder 1994: 39). Guillet describes the seasonal rainfall patterns in the Colca Valley from the 1950s to the 1980s, where the rainy season begins slowly in August, picking up during September and October, and increases dramatically during November. Although there are year to year variations in the monthly distributions of rain, most of the annual rainfall usually comes in the five months from November to March (Guillet 1992: 48), and this is what people in Chivay today would refer to as 'normal'.

During the last few years, however, the farmers in Colca have perceived abnormal rainfall, and they tell stories of the environmental consequences of changing rains. Between August and October 2011, a local field assistant and I conducted a survey among the inhabitants of Chivay. We asked eighty respondents, aged between twenty-three and eighty, whether and how they had experienced any changes in the environment. There was an overall agreement among the respondents that the weather had changed during the last twenty years and that there was less water. Over 90 per cent of the respondents stated that the seasonal variations in temperature (the heat and the frosts) are more extreme, as are the daily variations (warmer by day and colder at night). Rain, however, seemed not to be agreed upon: 30 per cent stated that the rain had increased, while 42.5 per cent claimed that it had decreased; and 30 per cent had experienced the rain as more irregular, while 2.5 per cent said that it remained the same as always. The discrepancies between the perceptions of more and less rain may possibly be explained by different ways of thinking of rain as 'more'; some respondents referred to the incidents of heavier rain, falling in large quantities in a short period of time, while others thought of the more frequent rain showers expanding into the dry months. The respondents stating that the precipitation had decreased may have been referring to either the late start of the rain season or to the total decrease in the quantity of rain, and only according to their memories. Some respondents would pick more than one alternative and stated that it had been raining more than usual the last season, but that in general the rain pattern had become more irregular. Like Luis said: 'The rain is not the same as before; sometimes it rains a little and sometimes it rains a lot'. The main concern is that there is no known pattern anymore that people can relate to. The regular rain cycle has been disturbed, and people in Chivay say things like: 'it rains at any random moment' and 'the rain comes when it feels like it'.

The responses in the survey concurred with my fieldwork material generated through informal daily-life conversations, public assemblies, and in interviews with leaders of water-user organizations in different villages in Colca. The leader of one of the irrigation associations in Yanque said: 'Each weather had its period, we used to know when it would rain, but now we don't know, at any random moment it rains and that harms us, there is a lot of variation'. Several farmers complained that the rain starts later (December/January) and ends earlier (late February/ early March) than it used to, which means that where they used to cultivate potatoes using only rainwater, now they need to irrigate. The leader of one of the irrigation associations in Chivay said:

> This rain used to accompany us in the sowing, but not any longer; now the rain practically comes only from December, January, February, nothing more. It used to come in September, October, when we were sowing potatoes; we used to sow in the rains. So this tells us that the situation of the year is changing.

An irrigation leader in Maca village stated:

> Where it has changed ugly is in the aspect of the rain. The rain is no longer as it was before. I remember when I was little it started from the month of September. Now it starts the fifteenth of January, and it rains January, February, March, nothing more; in the middle of March it is already retreating. The time of the rain has been shortened.

Others emphasize that, on the contrary, the rain has started to continue into the dry months of May and June, making the potatoes rot. Maria, a market vendor and farmer from Chivay, commented:

> The climate is changing a lot, it is warmer, stronger winds, and earlier the rain came in November, there were already clouds. Now it comes in December and it is stronger in February and March – they call it 'Crazy February'. Earlier it was no longer raining in April, and now it rains in April and May, and it destroys the harvest. The rain makes the potato rot, and we must dig them up in the rain.

Based on how people talked about the rain – and they talked about it a lot – we can see that there are some strong ideas that the rain should come at specific times, and many people said things like 'it rains when it shouldn't rain' and 'in the months that it should rain, it doesn't'. The expected points of commencement and termination of the rain season are strongly connected to the agricultural cycle, which should start with the sowing in September and end with the harvesting in May (Treacy 1994: 56). This cycle has developed over generations and has been adapted to the local environments and the weather seasons.

Drought is nothing new in Colca, but farmers remember how earlier generations had methods to predict whether the coming year would be a good year with sufficient rain or not, and they would prepare themselves accordingly. People knew how to read the signs of nature, a knowledge that today is seen as having been lost to a large degree. The mayor of Canocota village, who was also a farmer, told me:

> Earlier, if there would be a dry year, we the people took precautions, because we knew, we knew how the nature expressed itself, for example in the plants or in the earth ... or in how the fox cries. The animals and the plants manifest themselves, and the Andean man observes and he knows what is going to happen and he prepares.

The people who still pay attention to these signs, like this mayor, look at the earth beneath the stones, observe the flowering of the plants, and listen to the crying of the foxes. If they observe that the river comes with green algae, they know that it will be a good year; and if the seagulls fly up the river from the ocean, they know that the rain is approaching. Treacy (1994) has described how the farmers in the village of Coporaque in the 1980s would take into account the strengths of the rains in September and October, the amount of snow on the mountains, and the early flowering of the plants as climatic indicators (ibid.: 56). In today's Chivay, however, people complain that this knowledge has been lost. Moreover, the signs and the patterns are changing, which makes it harder every year to anticipate and prepare for anything.

The only thing that all of the respondents in the survey agreed on is that water will be scarcer in the future. Many predict that the water will disappear completely, and the time span of their predictions varies between 'a few years' and 'in about thirty years'. The predictions of a waterless future are explicitly linked to the lack of rain, as the leader of the irrigation association in the village of Lari stated in an interview: 'In the long run, the water will always be scarcer. The problem is that it will no longer rain, and the sources of water will not be filled'. When scarce precipitation fails to feed the springs and the glaciers, and the short and intense February rainfalls cause soil erosion, it makes the future unbearable. People fear that they will no longer be able to sustain life, as these statements from the survey bear witness to: 'The water will dry out and there will be nothing to irrigate our crops'; 'Fifteen years from today, the water will decrease, and we will no longer be able to supply ourselves; with so little water, we will lose harvests, animals, and more'; 'It will dry out. If the water runs out, we cannot live'; 'It will continue to decrease while there is global warming'.

Climate uncertainties such as these are multiplying around the globe, and everybody has to negotiate the boundary between manageable risks on the one hand, and fears that are unknown both in origin and scope on the other (Hastrup 2013). New kinds of uncertainties are created when the limits of time and space no longer correspond to what people recognize and can anticipate. In his book *Liquid Times,* Zygmunt Bauman states:

> [I]t is the insecurity of the present and uncertainty about the future that hatch and breed the most awesome and least bearable of our fears. That insecurity and that uncertainty, in their turn, are born of a sense of impotence: we seem to be no longer in control, whether singly, severally or collectively. (Bauman 2007: 26)

The changing rain in Chivay is seen as being caused by human activities on local and global scales, and global connections are never more acutely experienced as in the effects of global climate change. The 'time–space compression' of the postmodern global village (Harvey 1989) is felt not only through mobile phones, internet and cheap airlines, but as local effects of actions conducted in other parts of the globe – one of these effects being the changing rain patterns in the Andes.

Measuring Rain: The Destabilized Hydrological System

Today, narratively, the focus has moved from weather to climate all over the world (Hastrup 2013: 8). Among the farmers in Colca, too, observations of weather are compared to memories of past weather and lead to experiences that are expressed in terms of climate change. Farmers have become used to the climate concept and say things like 'the climate change is strong'.

Anthropological research on weather and climate has focused on how all people perceive climate change through cultural lenses, and scholars have pointed out that people comprehend what they see depending on what kind of knowledge they possess (cf. Roncoli, Crane and Orlove 2009: 88), as well as their livelihood and interests (Marin 2010:165). 'Memoryscapes' (Nuttall 1992) evolve as people accumulate experience and encounters in the physical environment. In the words of Mark Nuttall, memoryscape 'is constructed with people's mental images of the environment, with particular emphasis on places as remembered places' (ibid.: 39). I would like to add time as remembered time. However, if we understand knowledge, narratives and memories as practice, we see that memories of how it used to be are not static; they tend to change according to changing circumstances. The narrative of global warming, climate change and a future water crisis is gaining ground in the Andes, and it seems to have a lot of resonance among the farmers who recognize patterns from their own experiences and thus find approval and explanations for their own observations.

By shifting the focus from cultural representations of the environment to practices – body practice, earth practice, water practice – we can explore how people know that the climate is changing. In their daily practices, Colca farmers notice changes in water supply, the soil and the crops, and they are concerned by how changes in the weather affect their bodies. Moreover, people tend to see changes and illnesses in bodies, plants and the environment as being connected. In Chivay, people often say that the changing climate and the irregular rains bring new and unknown insects and diseases that people do not know how to prevent or cure. Farmer and market vendor Miriam said:

> Ay, the change affects us a lot; it affects us badly, because the babies and the elderly, we are sick with the bronchitis, the cough; the illnesses that come.

> Many illnesses that we have not known before, now we see these illnesses. I think it is because of the change of the climate.

Of the eighty respondents in my survey, sixty (75 per cent) mentioned that the changes in the climate are causing illness among people, because of the intensities and irregularities of cold, heat and rain. 'The rain brings illnesses, like the flu and the cough, and it brings mosquitoes', Luis said. Changing weather, extreme heat and cold, and irregular rain also produces sickness in the crops, as Maria talked about:

> Earlier they [the farmers] used to have good harvests. But there are no longer [many] beans and potatoes, because the heat burns it, and the frosts also burn and that affects us. When it rains, it produces worms [in the potatoes], and it makes the beans sick; they call it chocolate when the leaves of the plant blacken. Then they must fumigate.

I suggest that these attributes of rain, and the idea that irregular rain contains and produces illness, is related to the perception that the rain cycle is out of balance in terms of time and space. Late rains make the potatoes rot and cause other diseases in the crops. This is analogous to ideas of the body: a body should be in equilibrium to be healthy. If the fluids and substances of a body are out of balance – if the body is too hot or too cold due to environmental impacts or intake of food – it gets sick and has to be treated with hot or cool food, herbs and drinks (Lira 1995). The principle of equilibrium, of substances, energies and relations, is essential to live well in the world (Stensrud 2011), and I suggest that the same goes for the planet earth; when the rainwater is out of balance, it influences the entire web of relations and causes disequilibrium and illness in the world. In the relational ontological practices of the Colca farmers, everything is interconnected and interdependent, and rainwater is part of the seasonal cycle, which includes humans, plants, water, land, spirits, lakes, mountains, the living and the dead (Gose 1994; Harris [1982] 2000). The rain is supposed to feed the earth with water, which ideally is stored in the earth and later comes out of the springs. The mayor of Canocota village explained it like this:

> The globe is pure water. Underground there is water; there are veins ... In the rain season, the rainwater is stored there and then the water comes out. The rainwater gathers; it is filtered in the earth, which is like a sponge or a mattress. The globe has these veins of water.

The highland habitat of the llamas and alpacas consists of *bofedales*: cushion bogs that retain rainwater before it filters into streams and springs. Scarcer rain causes the *bofedales* to deteriorate, enhancing the need for irrigating pastures. However, due to irregular and hard rainfalls, floods and erosion, the ability of the earth to store water is also weakening. Moreover, as glaciers are disappearing due to the warmer climate, the Andean highland environment is becoming ever more vulnerable. As the leader of the water association in the highland community of Callalli expressed it:

> Today there are no snowfields (*nevados*), and thus there are no water mattresses that are deposited under the mountains, within the Apus [the mountain lords], like I consider them to be. Sometimes it rains a lot, it falls in January, February, but it rains like it were raining on a mirror or on a rock or on cement or something like that. It is raining, but it runs directly to the streams and rivers and watersheds, and those waters go directly to the Pacific Ocean.

Rainwater is what connects glaciers, mountains, land and *bofedales*, and irregular rain together with increased temperatures result in glacier shrinkage, soil erosion and dry springs and pastures. This is a matter of great concern, which is exacerbated by the difficulties of anticipation. In recent years, predictability – as a measure of the regularity of a periodic phenomenon (such as seasonal rainfall), or as the statistical certainty of the state of a phenomenon (such as quantity of rainfall) given information about time (for example, month of the year) (Winterhalder 1994: 34) – is becoming harder as climate change makes the weather more and more uncertain. Anticipations of climate change may be based on direct experiences of greater weather variability and intensified weather events, or it may be based on statistical models. All of the anticipated scenarios build upon a knowledge that is captured somewhere (Hastrup 2013: 2). There are some underlying similarities in different ways of observing variations in weather (Peterson and Broad 2009: 76), and studies have shown a remarkable overlap between local observations and instrumental climatological records (Marin 2010: 163). Anthropological research has also shown important points of congruence between traditional and scientific knowledge, as in the article by Orlove, Chiang and Cane (2000), where they examined how potato farmers in the Andes observe star constellations in June in order to forecast the rainfalls and plan the sowing of potatoes accordingly. All kinds of knowledge are complex, relational and affective processes, and acknowledging that scientific knowledge is not achieved through 'discoveries' of singular 'natural' facts, but rather as a craft, in which people do things and make things (rather than simply find things out), enables us to understand science as a kind of practice that is equivalent to other ways of doing and making things (Harvey 2012: 119).

In Chivay, there is a meteorological station that measures precipitation, wind, temperatures and solar radiation. Its conventional system from 1961 is operated manually by a local woman who is employed to observe and report the weather data several times a day by telephone to the central office. The station also has an automatic computerized system from 1997, but according to the regional director of SENAMHI (the national meteorological and hydrological service SENAMHI [*Servicio Nacional de Meteorología e Hidrología del Perú*]), the reports from the *señora observadora* are more reliable and quicker than the automatic data transmitted by satellite. The weather data for the last five years, registered in Chivay's conventional weather station which is located at 3,661 metres above sea level, are available at SENAMHI's webpage. From January 2008 to December 2011, an average annual precipitation of 459 mm was recorded. However, more than half of this rain – 263.8 mm on average – came during the two months of January and February. Earlier, the precipitation in Chivay seems to have had a more equal monthly distribution; according to SENAMHI's measurements referred to by Treacy, the average monthly precipitation in Chivay in the period 1973–1982 was 96.7 mm for January and 83 mm for February (Treacy 1994: 55).

However, the Colca farmers did not pay much attention to the measurements made by the SENAMHI stations; I never heard anyone talk about the weather stations or about the rain in terms of numbers. In their stories they referred to the rain in terms of timing and annual cycles; the onset and length of the rainy season, as well as their own experience of irregularities. Counting millimetres and telling stories about rain-related practices (like sowing and harvesting potatoes) are complementary ways of measuring changes in weather and climate. Information from

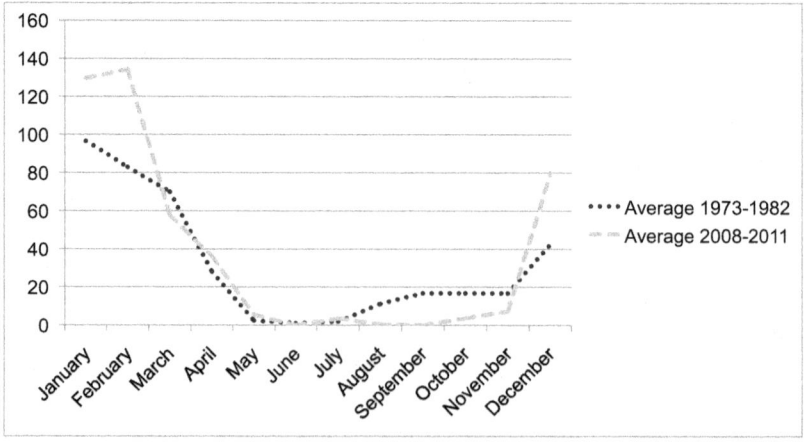

Figure 3.1 Average yearly precipitation in Chivay, 1973–1982 and 2008–2011.

technologies of measurement and observations made by farmers tend to confirm each other. However, weather stations do not measure the human experience of different kinds of rain, like 'hard' and 'soft' rain (cf. Marin 2010). The 'hardness' of the rain is experienced through the effects on bodies, soil, grass, animals and crops. Different forms of knowledge make different spatial and temporal scales, yet they are relative to each other. By understanding scaling as a practice, according to Bruno Latour (2005), scale cannot be seen as one of the many variables that social scientists need to set up *before* doing a study. Instead, scale could be seen as a product achieved by scaling, spacing and contextualizing each other; the actors' are the ones defining relative scale (ibid.: 184). Knowledge and scales of change that arise from the bodily experience of cultivating the land and memoryscapes are different from the meteorological data that are abstracted from the local environments and standardized according to universal scales. Both forms of knowledge relate to both local and global scales in different ways; ideas of the global are always locally made and understood.

Making Rain: Sowing and Harvesting Water

The hydrological cycle encompasses water that moves in time and space – clouds, rain and rivers – water in perpetual motion, as in a 'fluidscape' (Strang 2009). Water is part of the universe, or *pacha* – a Quechua concept that incorporates both temporal and spatial dimensions, and can be translated as 'era' or 'period' referring to either unique or repetitive events, or it can mean 'earth' or 'world'. It can be seen as an ordering principle, as a means of getting to grips with the world in which one lives and which is ever changing (Saenz in Dransart 2006: 25). The most precise meaning would be 'the world existing in time' (Allen 2002: 32). Some of the interviewees alluded to both space and time in their responses about climate and rain. For example, the leader of the irrigation association in Ichupampa said: 'The change can be noted quite a lot in respect to the volume of water. The rains have moved away a little'. While he, as most of the respondents, talked about the decrease in rain in terms of timing, he also referred to how the rain has moved in space.

Kay pacha ('this world') is the name of the space–time that we currently live in and which we experience in our daily lives. What happens when this world is changing? People repeatedly said that without water there can be no life. If the rain and the water disappear in the future, then the world as we know it will end. As time is seen as cyclic and spatial, this can however also mean the beginning of a new world, a *pachakuti*, which means a change of worlds. It can also imply the return of a past world in a new form, as *kutiy* means to return. *Pachakuti* would then be both a catastrophe and a restoration of equilibrium and a renovation. Popular sayings about how 'the world turns' (*el mundo da vueltas*), which can be said to mean 'what goes around comes around' and which is based on the principle of reciprocity and the ideal of universal equilibrium, convey certain moral concerns about actions and consequences: what you do to other beings, whether human or non-human, will eventually come back to you (Stensrud 2011). As part of *pacha*, water is perceived and related to as an animate substance, an other-than-human being and a female source of life. In Chivay she is called *Mama Choqueshisha* out of respect. Valderrama and Escalante, who studied water in Yanque in the 1970s, say that water is 'a vital force, a principle of life, a living being which, like ourselves, participates in the universe' (Valderrama and Escalante 1988: 206). According to Treacy who studied irrigation in Coporaque in the mid-1980s, the people there used to say *yaku karpay, yaku yachachiy*, which in Quechua means 'to irrigate is to teach the water', because when the farmer guides the water with a shovel so that it flows over the field, he or she teaches the water to flow over an uneven surface (Treacy 1994: 113–14). Sometimes, even rain is talked about as having animate properties, like when Maria said that 'the rain rains when it feels like it'. When I interviewed Miriam in October 2011, she talked about the rain as 'thinking':

> And also the rains, it seems like the atmosphere has changed quite a lot. In this time, it should get cloudy, because in November it should be raining. Because we are already beginning to sow, and therefore the rain should now be thinking and ripening, but now we see that no, the frost continues. There is no rain yet. Then there are seasons when you would not wait for the rain, and it rains. It has changed a lot.

In a world where elements in the environment can think, feel, act and react, rain can also respond when it is called upon. The calling for rain is a technique that performs the hydrological cycle in order to call the water from the ocean and make clouds and rain. It is performed by a ritual expert (*paqu*) as part of the offering rituals made to the springs in the mountains. The *paqu* puts seawater brought from the Pacific Ocean in a small plastic container, and he covers it with a piece of cotton. After libations and invocations, he places these items – together with a starfish from the sea – into the mountain spring. During one of these 'callings' in Chivay in August 2011, the *paqu* told me that he put the seawater in the spring 'so that it will call for more water', and then he explained that the cotton is 'clouds, so that there will be rain'. Then he described how he put the starfish there 'so that the water will continue to come out of the mountain'.

These miniature items are parts of the ocean, the clouds, and other water bodies. I here follow Catherine Allen who asserts that ritual practices in the Andes are 'premised on a principle of consubstantiality, the assumption that all beings are intrinsically interconnected through their sharing a matrix of animated substance' (Allen 1997: 75). Through the ritual, the hydrological cycle – in which the ocean is the origin of all water – is performed. Jeanette Sherbondy has described how the ocean plays an important role in the Andean cosmology: as *mamacocha* – mother lake – it is associated with the origins of the world. In the highlands, the lakes are perceived as minor parts of the ocean and as the origin of other water sources. Water bodies are furthermore connected by the underground canals, which communicate between the lakes and other sources of water (Sherbondy 1982). Ritual action in the Andes tends to 'include the envelopment of the whole as part of a larger whole' (Allen 1997: 75). Similarly, Sarah Lund Skar has shown that pebble amulets coming from a powerful mountain will always be part of the mountain and contain some of the force of its source, although separated (Lund Skar 1994: 67). I suggest that the small portion of seawater, although separated, is still connected to and a part of the Pacific Ocean, and therefore the ocean's properties can be performed, like the ability to make clouds. Hence, these miniature objects and the performed hydrological cycle are not only simulations, but ontologically real in the performance. Similar points have been made about rain-making rituals in other parts of the world. Veronica Strang argues about water in the aboriginal cosmos in Australia: 'the ancestral cycle of movements not only mimics but in effect *is* the hydrological cycle that, rising from the landscape, creates the rain that (on re-entering the land) generates all the living things upon which human societies depend' (Strang 2009: 89). This is also true for the ontology of ritual in Colca; the focus is on the action itself and the effects produced. As Todd Sanders argues about rainmaking in Tanzania: 'rainmaking does not make sense because it symbolizes, metaphorizes, or evokes other things: rainmaking makes sense because it brings rain' (Sanders 2008: 10–11).

Ontological statements about ritual reality could most fruitfully be understood as part of a certain way of perceiving relations among persons, things and landscape, and as a powerful strategy of comprehending and controlling the surroundings (Stoller 1995: 122; Willerslev

2007: 96). By focusing on how ritual practices perform particular relations and connections, I suggest that they also make relational worlds or ontologies. The practice of relating certain objects – like the cloud, the star fish and seawater – with specific properties, and giving them to the springs and mountains, produce new relations, attract rainy clouds and make new worlds. These relations have to be performed regularly in order to bring these worlds into being. Ritual offerings to mountains and springs are normally performed twice a year in Chivay and other villages in Colca Valley. In light of these practices, the statements on how 'the rain is thinking' and that 'it comes when it feels like it' appear as non-metaphorical observations of rain with a potentiality for having sentient properties, in a relational world where everything can be connected to everything else, through fluid substances, energies and relations, and where certain practices scale the world in distinct ways.

Rainmaking rituals can be seen as attempts to control the environment, but gaining a sense of control is becoming ever more difficult with the new kinds of climate uncertainties. In order to prevent a water crisis, people engage with different kinds of knowledge and technology in order to maximize the control over the flow of resources, like water, money and products. It is not enough to summon the rainwater – it should also be gathered when it comes pouring down. Projects of tree planting and the construction of micro-dams – called 'sowing and harvesting water' – have become increasingly popular during the last few years as a response to climate change. When the glaciers as natural reserves of water disappear, people take action to gather the rainwater in other ways. The micro-dams are seen as important, because they collect water when the heavy rains come in January and February, and can distribute the water in irrigation canals evenly throughout the year. Making such projects implicates the need to negotiate relations with powerful water bodies like lakes and mountains that demand offerings before they will permit the humans to proceed with the projects. The humans in Colca take these powerful other-than-human beings seriously, as they are dependent on their good will to get enough water. But they also need to negotiate with other humans in private companies and governmental bodies, as the projects need money to finance the constructions. The water that they harvest in the highlands is eventually channelled down to the lowland pampa where profits are made in large-scale export agriculture, and the political leaders in the highlands have demanded that the lowland farmers contribute financially to the micro-dam projects. In 2010, money was for the first time transferred from the lowlands to micro-dam projects in the highlands, thus establishing reciprocal relations of water and money within the watershed. In order to gain control over the hydrological cycle, it is not enough to call the rainwater; in the world of today money also needs to be called and collected.

Conclusions

> 'The seasons of frost, rain and heat were different ten years ago. You saw that it rained yesterday; it shouldn't do that. The climate change is strong'. (Miriam, 55)

Rain in Colca Valley is configured in particular scales of time and space, and disruptions of the time–space cycle caused by climate change affect a relational world of human and other-than-human bodies. When the rain changes, all the relations that rainwater is part of also change, unsettling the connections that make up the world. Rain is not a pure fact that can be found in 'nature'; rain is made through the conjunctions of agencies by the sun, the sea and the winds, as well as human engagements with the environment, non-humans and technologies. Rain is inherently fluid and in constant movement between the sky, the mountains, the land, the fields and the sea. Humans – especially in dry areas of the world – have always tried to control its fluidity in both time and space, by measuring, calling, directing and harvesting the rainwater. Hence, rain engages different knowledges and practices, which in turn produce different versions of rain: vital or sick rain; measured or remembered rain; rain that is sentient and responsive; rain that is harvested, distributed, and taught to irrigate fields; or rain that is late, untimely, scarce or destructive. Hence, 'what rain is' differs with the environmental and cultural practices in which people engage with rain.

These different practices and relations make different rain ontologies, which will always be changing, emergent and even fluid. When rain is related to as a responsive agent that connects with other elements of the world, the changes in the rain cycle will always affect the relations to the land, the plants, animals, the mountains and the other non-human beings inhabiting the world. When the seasonal weather cycles are disrupted, and the frost, heat and rainfalls can no longer be predicted as they used to be, the time and spatial scales collapse. Humans are no longer able to anticipate the availability of water in their surroundings, and local worlds destabilize. Rain irregularities produce disturbance and uncertainties about the present and the future. However, the new fluidity of the world may also induce flexibility and a dynamic ability to change; the future will show whether people in Colca Valley will find other ways of living with rain.

Acknowledgements

This research has been conducted as part of the project 'From Ice to Stone', funded by the Danish Research Council and led by Karsten Pærregaard, in close collaboration with the Waterworlds research project at the Department of Anthropology, University of Copenhagen. This text was written while I was part of the Overheating project funded by the ERC Grant Agreement n. 295843 and the NFR project n. 222783. I am grateful for the generous comments on the manuscript from the editors Kirsten Hastrup and Frida Hastrup.

References

Allen, C.J. 1997. 'When Pebbles Move Mountains: Iconicity and Symbolism in Quechua Ritual', in *Creating Context in Andean Cultures,* edited by R. Howard-Malverde. New York: Oxford University Press.
——. 2002. *The Hold Life Has: Coca and Cultural Identity in an Andean Community.* 2nd edn. Washington, DC: Smithsonian Institution Press.
Barnes, J., and S. Alatout. 2012. 'Water Worlds: Introduction to the Special Issue of Social Studies of Science', *Social Studies of Science* 42(4): 483–88
Bates, B.C., et al. (eds). 2008. 'Climate Change and Water'. Technical Paper of the Intergovernmental Panel on Climate Change, IPCC Secretariat, Geneva, p. 210.
Bauman, Z. 2007. *Liquid Times: Living in an Age of Uncertainty.* Cambridge: Polity Press.
Cadena, M. de la. 2010. 'Indigenous Cosmopolitics in the Andes: Conceptual Reflections beyond Politics', *Cultural Anthropology* 25(2): 334–70.
Christensen, J.H., et al. 2007. 'Regional Climate Projections', in *Climate Change 2007: The Physical Science Basis.* Contribution of Working Group I to the Fourth Assessment Report of the Intergovernmental Panel on Climate Change [S. Solomon et al. (eds)]. Cambridge: Cambridge University Press.
Dransart, P. 2006. *Kay Pacha: Cultivating Earth and Water in the Andes.* BAR International Series, 1478.
Gelles, P.H. 2000. *Water and Power in Highland Peru: The Cultural Politics of Irrigation and Development.* New Brunswick, NJ and London: Rutgers University Press.
Gose, P. 1994. *Deathly Waters and Hungry Mountains: Agrarian Ritual and Class Formation in an Andean Town.* Toronto: University of Toronto Press.
Guillet, D. 1992. *Covering Ground: Communal Water Management and the State in the Peruvian Andes.* Ann Arbor: University of Michigan Press.
Guillet, D., and W.P. Mitchell (eds). 1994. *Irrigation at High Altitudes: The Social Organization of Water Control Systems in the Andes.* Washington, DC: Society for Latin American Anthropology.
Harris, O. (1982) 2000. 'The Dead and the Devils', in O. Harris, *To make the Earth Bear Fruit: Ethnographic Essays on Fertility, Work, and Gender in Highland Bolivia.* London: Institute of Latin American Studies, University of London, pp. 27–50.
Harvey, D. 1989. *The Condition of Postmodernity: An Enquiry into the Origins of Cultural Change.* Oxford: Basil Blackwell.

Harvey, P. 2012. 'Knowledge and Experimental Practice: A Dialogue between Anthropology and Science and Technology Studies', in *The SAGE Handbook of Social Anthropology*, R. Fardon et al. (eds). Los Angeles: SAGE with the Association of Social Anthropologists of the United Kingdom and Commonwealth, pp. 115–29.

Hastrup, K. 2013. 'Anticipating Nature: The Productive Uncertainty of Climate Models', in K. Hastrup and M. Skrydstrup (eds), *The Social Life of Climate Change Models: Anticipating Nature*. London: Routledge, pp. 1–29.

Latour, B. 2005. *Reassembling the Social: An Introduction to Actor-Network-Theory*. Oxford: Oxford University Press.

Lira, J.A. 1995. *Medicina Andina. Farmacopea y Rituales*. 2nd edn. Cusco, Peru: Centro de Estudios Regionales Andinos 'Bartolomé de Las Casas'.

Lund Skar, S. 1994. *Lives Together – Worlds Apart: Quechua Colonization in Jungle and City*. Oslo: Scandinavian University Press.

Mol, A. 2002. *The Body Multiple: Ontology in Medical Practice*. Durham, NC: Duke University Press.

Marin, A. 2010. 'Riders under Storms: Contributions of Nomadic Herders' Observations to Analysing Climate Change in Mongolia', *Global Environmental Change* 20: 162–76.

Nuttall, M. 1992. *Arctic Homeland: Kinship, Community and Development in Northwest Greenland*. London: Belhaven Press.

Orlove, B., J.C.H. Chiang and M.A. Cane. 2000. 'Forecasting Andean Rainfall and Crop Yield from the Influence of El Niño on Pleiades Visibility', *Nature* 403(6765): 68–71.

Paerregaard, K. 1994. 'Why Fight over Water? Power, Conflict and Irrigation in an Andean Village', in D. Guillet and W. Mitchell (eds), *Irrigation at High Altitudes: The Social Organization of Water Control Systems in the Andes*. Washington, DC: Society for Latin American Anthropology.

Peterson, N., and K. Broad. 2009. 'Climate and Weather Discourses in Anthropology: From Determinism to Uncertain Futures', in S.A. Crate and M. Nuttall (eds), *Anthropology and Climate Change: From Encounters to Actions*. Walnut Creek, CA: Left Coast Press.

Roncoli, C., T. Crane and B. Orlove. 2009. 'Fielding Climate Change in Cultural Anthropology', in S.A. Crate and M. Nuttall (eds), *Anthropology and Climate Change: From Encounters to Actions*. Walnut Creek, CA: Left Coast Press.

Sanders, Todd. 2008. *Beyond Bodies: Rainmaking and Sense Making in Tanzania*. Toronto: University of Toronto Press.

Sherbondy, J. 1982. 'El regadío, los lagos y los mitos de origen', *Allpanchis* XVII(20).

Stensrud, A.B. 2011. '"Todo en la vida se paga": Negotiating life in Cusco, Peru'. Ph.D. dissertation, Faculty of Social Sciences, University of Oslo.

———. 2014. 'Climate Change, Water Practices and Relational Worlds in the Andes', *Ethnos: Journal of Anthropology*, DOI: 10.1080/00141844.2014.929597.

Stoller, P. 1995. *Embodying Colonial Memories: Spirit Possession, Power and the Hauka in West Africa*. New York: Routledge.

Strang, V. 2009. *Gardening the World: Agency, Identity and the Ownership of Water*. Oxford: Berghahn Books.

Treacy, J.M. 1994. *Las chacras de Coporaque. Andenería y riego en el Valle del Colca.* Lima: Instituto de Estudios Peruanos.

Valderrama, R., and C. Escalante. 1988. *Del Tata Mallku a la Mama Pacha: Riego, sociedad y ritos en los andes peruanos.* Lima: DESCO.

Vuille, M., et al. 2008. 'Climate Change and Tropical Andean Glaciers: Past, Present and Future', *Earth-Science Reviews* 89: 79–96.

Willerslev, R. 2007. *Soul Hunters: Hunting, Animism, and Personhood among the Siberian Yukaghirs.* Berkeley: University of California Press.

Winterhalder, B. 1994. 'The Ecological Basis of Water Management in the Central Andes: Rainfall and Temperature in Southern Peru', in D. Guillet and W.P. Mitchell (eds), *Irrigation at High Altitudes: The Social Organization of Water Control Systems in the Andes.* Washington, DC: Society for Latin American Anthropology.

4

Respect and Passion in a Lagoon in the South Pacific

Cecilie Rubow

Muri lagoon is an extraordinary place on the rim of Rarotonga. On a bright day, the lagoon has white beaches, turquoise water, green palms and a blue sky. It looks like a perfect tourist destination, a tropical blue lagoon, and so it is. Muri is also home to three women – Mii, Anne and Sahron – my protagonists in this chapter. Differences apart, Mii, Anne and Sahron share a marked concern for the lagoon they live by. Beach erosion, pollution, algae bloom, sedimentation, coral bleach and many more troubling changes are common topics in their daily conversations, mixed with frequent expressions of praise and admiration of the beauty of the beach and the lagoon. I met them in the lagoon, and talked about leaking sewers, new schools of baby parrotfish, spiky urchins, bygone Maori fishing practices and the local management of the environment.[1] This chapter is a story about their concern for the lagoon: how they worry about the changes they observe, how they admire the island and the ocean, how they seek political influence, and how they call upon the wider community for environmental care.

This chapter is also dedicated to certain analytical problems, since I want to dwell not only on what Mii, Anne and Sharon are concerned about, but also the ways in which they are concerned: *how* they relate to the lagoon, and *how* changes in their concern involve the landscape; in other words, how concerns and landscape are mutually implicated. This aim is closely tied a critique in the anthropology of the environment of a modernist stance to nature (Descola 2006; Latour 2009; Ingold 2012).

This volume too speaks of 'fluid environments', thereby stressing that landscapes are socialized and incorporated into a human world of resources and imagination, a relationship that has not only become more evident with global warming, but also far less bounded and definite.

My intention with the stories and the conceptual work is to link the acknowledgement of the entwinement of society and nature in anthropology with a critical approach within philosophical, theologian, anthropological and sociological studies, where modernist conceptions of the secular and the religious as separate domains are challenged (Cannell 2006; Taylor 2007; Maintenay 2011; Jørgensen 2014). With the concept of immanent transcendences I will search out the blurred zones between nature and culture, and between the secular and the religious. Thus, my purpose in this chapter is twofold: first, ethnographically I will present different narratives about a particular lagoon that I have encountered during fieldwork; secondly, I will seek out links between the anthropology of the environment, bridging gaps between nature and culture, and broader social scientific efforts to bridge notions of the secular and religion. Although notions of transcendence are often tied to meanings associated with the supernatural or divine, the point here is to show how a philosophically and anthropologically grounded environmental ethics may include notions of immanent transcendence based on everyday experiences of a vibrant living world as an 'otherness' that entails respect and passion.

Beach Erosion: From Nature to Environment

Reports from the Intergovernmental Panel on Climate Change (IPCC) (Minura et al. 2007; Church and Clark 2013) have established that small low-lying islands will suffer from devastating floods and a breakdown of vital infrastructure if measures are not taken to decrease the developed nations' contribution to global warming, and if local adaptations are not set in train. While climate sciences are trying to overcome the uncertainties in climate projections, in their ways people living along the coasts are also engaged in understanding and dealing with the astonishing changes they are witnessing in their surroundings.

I shall begin the story with Mii, a businesswoman in her forties, and also the chairperson of Muri Environmental Care Group (MECG), which consists of a core group of around ten people. On a stormy day, I meet up with her at Sails, a café and club house, formerly called The Yacht Club, right on the beach and with a magnificent view of the lagoon. On that particular day rumbling waves were beginning to build up. We had a view of tourists surfing, small islets with dense vegetation, and further out, breaking waves at the reef crest. Pop music, gusts of wind and the drumming of the slit gong from a glass-bottomed tourist boat were transforming into scratchy sounds on my voice recorder. Nevertheless, Mii's voice is clear. She tells me how MECG was formed.

> It started, I would say, about four years ago when the National Environment [Service] was holding awareness programmes in our village. These workshops highlighted to me that I was very ignorant about the environment. I got to know the reasons why there is a lot of damage on land – and how what we do on land affects the lagoon big time. The other reason why I got involved is that I live in the village Ngatangiia, in Muri, and I own one of the prime pieces of land on Muri Beach, and at the back of my mind I know that if my lagoon is going to be destroyed I have nothing to look forward to in life. Also I have got a daughter, and I look into the future of my grandchildren too.

Ngatangiia is the main village in Muri, with 204 households and 38 businesses, farms and community houses (Herrmann 2011: 7). The piece of land that Mii is referring to is next door to the café, a plot of a quarter of an acre. Mii's plot is the only one on the beach not being developed. The rest of the beachfront is dotted with tourist accommodation ranging from large complexes to small cottages, and some private houses. Large ironwood trees planted to provide shelter from the south-easterly winds balance on the slope between the upper shore and the sandy beach. One of them has finally died and with its man-like form of the branches and the exposed roots it seems to be on a determined walk into the water. As Mii, and Anne, a stakeholder in the café and also a member of MECG, relate, this tree and the rest of the row of ironwood trees are of major concern to the villagers. Everybody who knows this stretch of the beach can see that something problematic is going on. The beach is obviously eroding, and why this is happening, and what should be done about it, is the concern of Mii and Anne and the wider community. I ask Mii what she meant by saying that she was once 'ignorant' about the environment:

> Being ignorant is being without knowledge about the impact of what I'm doing to the environment. Before, my rubbish all went into one bag. After finding out it goes to the landfill that will be full in five years time, I take all my bottles and glasses to a guy who crushes it and makes slabs out of it. So already my little input is not going to be buried in the soil. My cans, I'm washing them before I separate. So I'm doing that.
>
> I'm very concerned about the septic too, so if I ever build again I'm aware of what kind of septic I'm using; I'm knowledgeable about the types of soil, where you are building. Of course, if I build on the beachside, it is only a few

> metres to the water, so what happens there? I'm very aware of streams being the vessel from the land to the lagoon. I'm horrified when I see pigs tied by the stream. The pigs' waste is going into the stream and now I'm aware that the pigs waste is three times more condensed than the human waste. It is just the knowledge I have acquired over the years. Before, I did not care. I saw the water as a place to swim – and I had no respect for the lagoon.

When I ask her about her newly found respect, she answers by referring to her new way of orientation in the landscape that she knows so well. Where Mii once saw a magnificent lagoon offering beautiful scenery, she has now become preoccupied with the lagoon as a precarious environment, and her new worries give her a new passion.

> Basically, I'm not really a beach person, but before I would come down to my beach – and I would probably have a barbecue and I would look out and just think how amazing it looks, but now when I see a build-up of algae bloom, I know in my mind that something terrible is going on – a build-up of nutrients – and I know what the reasons are: the septics flow off, the waste, soap powders and the chemicals used. Now, I see dogs running around with no collar doing their business – is it like, please, who does this dog belong to? And people leaving their rubbish on the beach, mums bringing their children and just like not even caring about the nappies and just leaving them on the side of the beach. It's, yeah, I don't know whether I'm getting – what's the word – too passionate.

For Mii the lagoon has turned into a fragile ecological system, actually and potentially suffering from extensive overuse. Dark chapters of the past and present management of the lagoon often turn up in conversations with Mii and other residents. The burning of stacks of coral (dead and alive) in large kilns, a technique introduced by the missionaries in the early nineteenth century for the construction of limestone houses and churches, was only recently prohibited. Enterprising land reclamation projects are found everywhere, and many other practices now deemed inappropriate are within memory: extensive mining of sand and gravel for the construction of roads and houses, filling of wetlands, and blocking and redirecting of streams. Fishing with explosives and the use of large amounts of local plant-based poisons have been banned for a long time.

The workshops held by the National Environment Service changed Mii's understanding of the lagoon. Not only did she learn about the waterways and how the practices on land affected them. As I understand Mii, the story she tells is more comprehensive. Firstly, it is a story about how she changed her household habits, her engagement in community work, and her relation to many people upholding practices that she now found unsustainable. The changing relation to the lagoon clearly had social implications. Secondly, it is a story about a personal transformation, going from a relationship with the lagoon as nature – as beautiful scenery detached from her – to an understanding of the lagoon as an environment in which she and the rest of community are enmeshed. Her re-orientation from ignorance to respect embodied a new relationship with the lagoon – one of *passion*, in her own words. Before I suggest how this change may be seen as an opening for a certain mode of transcendence, I shall introduce my second protagonist.

Soap Talk: Environmental Concerns

Anne, a keen sailor from New Zealand, currently commodore of the yacht club and a long-time resident of the island, was equally intrigued by the erosion of the beach, not least because she also had observed that the lagoon seemed more and more shallow. Now she found it much easier to wade through the waters to the small islets, and more difficult to manoeuvre boats with kilns into shallow areas. Processes of sedimentation, the influence of old fish traps and other possible sources of the changes were intensely discussed in the local community and among sailors in the yacht club. Cursory references were made to climate change as a driver, but most often, the shallowness was linked to an increasing frequency of algae blooms, sometimes converting the sparkling waters to a stinking, green and brown substance. The underlying mechanism theorized and debated was that the lagoon was no longer flushed effectively by fresh ocean water. With the lagoon floor being too high, not enough water from the ocean was able to pass inside, and instead the lagoon was filled with water from the streams contaminated with soil, waste water, chemicals, and – as they came to understand – high levels of nutrients from laundry detergents and other soaps.

As a fellow member of Muri Environmental Care Group, Anne, also with a newly acquired environmental perspective on the lagoon, searched for ways in which she and the wider community could contribute to an improved water quality. In this process, Mii and Anne's shared passion became the local use of soap, especially laundry detergents. Soap had become bit of an obsession to her, Anne told me: 'The soap lady' was one of her nicknames. This interest was spurred, she said, by being warned by the National Environmental Service about the negative effects of overuse of fertilizers in the gardens in the hills. Flushed into the lagoon, sometimes together with large amounts of soil sediment due to logging, it causes high levels of nutrients in the water, to the detriment of the marine life. Later, she said, they became aware that extensive use of non-biodegradable soap has the same negative effect, resulting in more algae blooms, especially in the hot season. This prompted Mii and Anne to make a survey, entitled 'The Soap Saga', of the different washing soaps available on the islands. They did this together with schoolchildren on a so-called Lagoon Day, when they and other stakeholders encouraged children to take care of the environment. 'BOOM Fresh and Bright', the cheapest laundry detergent on the island, turned out to contain by far the largest amount of nutrients. 'BOOM for bloom', as one of the students had it. At a later stage, MECG members wrote petitions to the importers of this particular soap and to the government in order to put a stop to the import, and they addressed everybody on the island who cared to listen about the negative effects on the waterways. Eventually, they also applied for funds to upgrade the community sewage system in order to secure better waste water treatment.

Anne browsed the internet to learn more about nutrients, fillers (apparently paper is a regular ingredient in cheap laundry soaps), import bans, importers, water quality and so forth. Becoming more and more engaged, she also registered that not everyone in the community shared her concern, let alone changed their washing habits. The damaging detergents were still available in the shops, often in very large quantities. Anne was curious about it. To her the change in washing (and cleaning) habits and techniques seemed perfectly logical, and she quickly developed a personal and embodied distaste for certain types of soap. Therefore, she laughingly confided, she felt utterly embarrassed, when she one day discovered that her own house cleaner was using the nutrient-rich soaps and cleaning agents.

Getting more and more involved and developing a deeper concern for the lagoon, Anne nevertheless recognized that the cheap soap was a good buy for many people in the community, with its strained economy. The higher cost of biodegradable soap, and the fact that nobody really understood the exact biological mechanisms going on in the waterways, was to her the explanation for why some residents held on to their nutrient-rich soap. Scrutinizing her own former use of soap that she now considered inadmissible, she became fascinated by the wider implications of soap use. Anne recalled her mother's use of soap and how the introduction of very foamy soaps was promoted as being more effective – the more foam the better. But why? Does it help at all? Is it just a story told by the advertising industry? What do the bubbles indicate? And why do young women today, as she was told, wash their often very long hair two, three or four times in order to reach the right feeling of cleanness? In interviews she and other residents also linked the soap habits to the one-time colonial preference for the colour white in clothes, buildings and pathways. Another striking example with strong historical and colonial roots was pointed out in soap conversations I had with other members of the community: the churchgoers dressed all in white on Sundays for celebrating Holy Communion: suits, shoes, hats and dresses, spotless and shining clean.

The soap saga did not end there. In fact, it proliferated along many waterways and seeped into many cultural domains. It became a passion, and while they occasionally joked about it, they continued their efforts by writing irate letters and attending meetings that in their view led to far too little action. A sense of urgency and impatience were driving the activities. As the print on their T-shirt on Lagoon Day said: 'We are the problem. We are the solution'.

One particular offshoot of the soap saga that I discussed briefly with Anne, came from the backlist of scientific studies on beach erosion in tropical lagoons, which I had compiled before and during the fieldwork. Sharing the pile of reports with Anne, who turned out to know quite a few beforehand, one day we came upon an account by Patrick Nunn, a renowned specialist of the geography and geology of the South Pacific. To our surprise he mentions a case from Fiji where a small island had lost its beach; the sand had simply vanished, revealing a hard layer of beach rock underneath. The explanation given was this: too many nutrients from soap may strip off the sand of a beach, because the nutrients damage the coral reef and the marine life that actually make the sand (Nunn and Mimura 2007). Further to this explanation, the sand in these lagoons is coral sand consisting of carbonates that are entirely skeletal – billions of marine animal skeletons squashed, shattered and smashed into sand by parrotfish, sea cucumbers and other sea animals that eat the coral and excrete it as sand (cf. Ong and Holland 2010). Thus, we speculated, in the end the soap story *could* be the same story as the beach erosion story.

Spectacular Nature

So far, I suggest that Mii and Anne's stories show how they understand and live by the lagoon as 'nature' and 'environment'. I have highlighted a remarkable change that they pointed out themselves in our conversations. Years back they saw the lagoon as healthy, beautiful, robust nature, whereas now they are preoccupied with the precariousness of the lagoon as an environment. Mii expressed the change explicitly in the interview at the café, and my impression from other meetings confirmed a sense of pressing concern, expressed in an ongoing dialogue with other people in the community and an ongoing effort of trying to make sense of the changes in the lagoon. Based on the conversations I had on the beach with both visitors and residents, my impression is that Muri lagoon readily stands out as an instantiation of 'nature' in a most spectacular version. Remarkably often it was portrayed as untouched – 'pristine in a way', as Mii once noted. As least, as many tourists emphasized, it is not considered to be as spoiled as many other beaches at tourist destinations around the world. In an interview, Anne pointed out that one particular view of the lagoon, with an uninhabited islet, Koromiri, in the background, is reproduced by tourist agencies over and over again. Photographs in brochures and travel books endlessly cultivate the lagoon as a landscape without any traces of human activity. 'And what is special here', Anne remarked, 'compared to many other tourist front pieces around the world: here it is actually readily accessible. You can take the direct flight from Auckland, Sydney or Los Angeles, and when you get out of the airport, it is just 20 minutes away. You can see the joy of recognition in their faces when they come down here'. Clearly, many visitors and residents are amazed by the beauty of the lagoon.

A second point, by telling the soap saga, was to show that Mii and Anne's engagement with the lagoon was mediated by a host of agents. The soaps, the importers, the laundries, nutrients, hotels, shell fish, hair-washing girls, politicians were all involved in an intense engagement with the landscape. This is not to conclude that Mii, Anne and the rest of the members of MECG always considered the lagoon as a precarious environment, and even less to suggest that they were always in one mind about it. Most people I met in Muri, including my protagonists, were often shifting from one kind of concern to another. Having a barbecue at the beach on a bright day does not necessarily prompt worries about the water quality.

Now, in the next section, I will turn to show how people's concerns about the lagoon can be understood as involving immanent transcendences without necessarily implying any conventional references to religion, but by referring to particular ways of socialization of and involvement with one's surroundings, human and non-human. During conversations, my interlocutors would sometimes refer to the beauty of the lagoon as being something other than just a spectacle or an environment with extraordinary qualities. There was something more to it, I thought, challenging established distinctions between 'nature' and 'environment', when they talked about respect, anger and passion – and when they engaged in innumerable actions in their own households and in the wider community.

Immanent Transcendences

According to Tim Ingold, Western conceptions of the natural world connote distance; we tend to think of the natural world as external, whereas 'environment' is the world that exists around somebody, 'forged through the activities of living beings' and 'continually under construction' (Ingold 2000: 20). Whereas 'nature' is something outside the human world, 'an environment' is socialized in many ways. What I would suggest here is that this distinction, although it is important and helpful in many contexts, misses out that a lagoon (and many other places) may also act as a *source* of imagination, rather than simply an *object* of imagination.

The modern conception of nature as an externality has been criticized in many quarters. Environmentalists of all descriptions have pointed out the wide gap that the-world-seen-as-nature is creating between human beings and the world to the detriment of the ecology of the world (e.g. White 1967; Pálsson 1996; McFague 2008; Morton 2009). This is an important critique in many contexts and places associated with dilapidation of natural resources, extinction of endangered species and so forth. But, according to other important strands of Western thinking about nature, this critique also tends to carry a limited understanding of what nature as external or even distant may offer. Here we enter the domains of the imagination – and the immanent transcendences.

One view of this is Vincent Crapanzano's notion of 'horizon' as a frontier 'that extends from the insistent reality of the here and now into that optative space or time – or time-space – of the imaginary. This is the realm that gives us an edge ... on the here and now ... and allows us to transcend (*dépasser*) the immediacy of the present' (Crapanzano 2004: 19). Here, quoting among others Jean Starobinski, Crapanzano speaks of modes of imagination that are notoriously difficult to describe, but nevertheless permits 'fiction, the game, a dream, more or less voluntary error, pure fascination. It lightens our existence by transporting us into the regions of phantasm' (ibid.). Poems and paintings and other aesthetic genres originate from and spur experiences of 'edges' or 'frontiers', but, Crapanzano states, the imaginative horizon is by no means restricted to the arts. 'It figures in accordance with prevailing genres of communication in everyday discourse and in oral and written language'. He mentions sunsets, old oaks, and mountains, all of them both very real *and* imaginative. What would art do without landscapes? And we can add, what would societies do?

Another tradition of philosophy building on Baumgarten, Heidegger and Benjamin has worked out alternative notions of transcendence, bridging aesthetics and post-modernist theological traditions. According to the philosopher Dorthe Jørgensen, these conceptualizations of immanent or aesthetic transcendences build on experiences of an emergent surplus of meaning that '*occurs* – that happens to somebody who, in the situation is not the subject of something, but is rather the object of the event which this experience constitutes' (Jørgensen 2014: 955). A step closer to the environmental issues discussed in this chapter is the suggestion made by Andre Maintenay, also drawing on phenomenology (Husserl, Heidegger and Merleau-Ponty), that we by immanent transcendences should understand an acknowledgement of 'otherness in nature, that is a natural process *larger* than (and thus in some sense transcendent of) humanity, in which we participate', which 'entails respect and responsibility' (Maintenay 2011: 270). Close to a recent paper by Ingold, who argues that natural materials are not bits of nature, but rather 'sources of vitality' (Ingold 2012: 428), Maintenay argues with David Cooper that immanent transcendences are made of the stuff of 'primordial "selfblossoming emergence" and "upsurging presencing" for us of the natural world'. In this conception, immanent transcendences are felt, experienced, with a certain depth or fullness that transcends the here and now and invites a sense of respect and responsibility. Thus, what is conceived as ***distant*** nature and often criticized as the outcome of a Cartesian dualism that misrepresents social-natural networks (Pálsson 1996) may in other influential traditions, often on phenomenological grounds, be celebrated as an *otherness* that sets a new horizon, a potentiality of surplus of meaning, and thus constitutes a source of transcendence.

The pressing question now is whether we can talk meaningfully about experiences of immanent transcendence of time and place in the stories from the Muri lagoon, extraordinarily beautiful, but apparently also strained. Importantly, as noted, the term transcendence should not necessarily ring any religious bells, as implied also by Crapanzano and the phenomenologically inspired philosophies, who in this sense are on a par with postmodern metaphysics (Latour 2009: 463; Maintenay 2011; Jørgensen 2014: 553–83). Phenomenologically, and obviously in an increasingly secular world, religion cannot monopolize the experiences of transcendence (Luckmann 1967, 1990). However, the point is also that immanent transcendences *could* be understood as religious as far as the term remains central to religious adherents seeing the transcendent as something ontologically beyond the realm of the supernatural or the 'wholly other' (Maintenay 2011: 269). Mii, Anne and Sahron, my third protagonist – none of them, from what I gathered, declared any particular interest in religious matters. However, as I will show, religious notions and contexts do make their presence in the lagoon.

Ancestors, Mother Nature, and God

Sahron is one of the few villagers still using the lagoon as a 'cupboard of food' for her own consumption and as a major contributor to all kinds of functions and celebrations in the community. On two occasions, as I was following her into the lagoon through the shallow waters at low tide, she pointed out various sand spits, rocks, wrecks, buildings and dozens of types of fish, seaweed and shellfish. With a large knife she poked to purple urchins and squeezed the fascinating spaghetti slugs that secrete a substance you can use as an emergency 'Band-Aid' if you get a cut on the sharp coral reef. She showed me how she looks out for air bubbles in certain stretches of sand that might be hiding a tasty shellfish (*ka'i*), and she told how, as a child, she and her friends used blue starfish as Frisbees and how they surfed on the high waves on car tyres during storms and cyclones (if they could sneak out). Walking all the way out to the reef crest with her on one occasion, hardly able to keep upright owing to the strong current, and scarcely able to hear each other's voices over the tremendous noise of the breaking waves, she pointed out certain landmarks and recounted how her ancestors used them for wayfinding; and we had a conversation about the skills of her Maori ancestors that she truly admired. At one point Sahron expressed her affection for the ancestors' way of life so explicitly that I asked whether, if she could choose, she would prefer to live as they did, say two hundred years ago, before the English missionaries arrived. She did not hesitate a second and said that she had actually discussed with her sons what they would choose if it was possible for them to give up their houses, cars, electric kettles and so forth, and live an entirely different life. Two of the sons, she said, told her that she was crazy, but one of them was quite positive about the idea of moving into one of the valleys with the intention of trying to live as the ancestors did, off the land and the sea.

When Sahron and I waded through the knee-high waters, the lagoon was clearly not only made up of urchins, ancestors, and a myriad of other beings in an insistent here and now. The lagoon was also, in my understanding, acting as an 'edge' and as 'a pristine source' that opened up for another life in the past and in the future, a world of old and new possibilities. In this sense, with her veneration and passion, she transcended the here and now in multiple ways through urchins and currents, and through the recollections and dreams about other times. Sahron's imaginations of the lagoon often took different directions to those of Mii and Anne. Among other things, Sahron said she thought that 'the environmentalists' are exaggerating the level of degradation, and that this is because environmentalists in general do not know as much about the lagoon as they think they do. They worry a lot, but 'they are never here', she says, and 'they don't know where to find or recognize the species they talk so much about'. Clearly, people in the community do not share all their concerns for the lagoon. They socialize it differently. Whereas Sahron happily uses BOOM, the nutrient rich soap, because from her observations she cannot confirm any damaging effects, for Mii and Anne the soap at times tends to transfigure the whole lagoon and its inhabitants as an entity.

However, back at Sails, the café, Mii also in more explicit ways invoked the changing landscape as a source of imagination. Troubled by the algae that had once again been building up, she sighed, but then she suddenly said with great relief: 'Luckily, Mother Nature did a wonderful clean up yesterday', referring to the exceptionally high waves spilling over the reef into the lagoon and thereby providing it with clean, oxygen-rich ocean water. This flushing of the lagoon was frequently on the minds of Mii, Sahron and Anne when they discussed their doubts and envisioned the different future possibilities for the lagoon. This time Mother Nature did the work. On other occasions Mother Nature also popped up into conversations in the village, usually denoting nature's nurturing and self-dependent power. Crossing many cultural contexts, Mother Nature as a symbol has proven to align well with both Christianity and Polynesian cosmology, in which Papa, the earth mother, and Tumu, the father, give birth to light, feeling, waters and many gods (cf. Turua 2003: 70). Thus today, in a secular environment, non-metaphysical notions of Mother Nature are also working well. On Rarotonga, for instance, inhabitants may refer to Mother Nature as a source of unknown processes in the management of the environment.

Indeed, neither villagers nor visiting experts claimed to know everything worth knowing about the relations and causalities involved in the changes observed in corals, water quality, the sedimentation budget, and so forth. The variability and complexity of the lagoon clearly exceeded the knowledge and reach of any individual or any single body of knowledge. As a (decaying) environment, it was conceived of as consisting of extremely complicated, interrelated processes in which the villagers, visitors, animals and plants, geomorphological features and the sea were all taking part. In this sense, it was an environment offering many 'edges', and a sense of otherness. An endangered red-footed crab, or an exposed bedrock, or certain soaps, or birds, or motor boats: all were possible edges in an environment with an excess of uncertainty, complexity and fragility, prompting the imagination of a restored and healthy lagoon.

But what about religion in its institutionalized form; does it also enter the lagoon, perhaps with more classical modes of metaphysics? Rarotonga has harboured a strong Christian tradition ever since the missionaries arrived almost two hundred years ago, and the old beliefs were abruptly overturned (Gilson 1980). On several occasions I have asked members of MECG and other church members in the lagoon whether the Christian churches have a voice in MECG's work or in any other way engage themselves in environmental issues. Parallel to other parts of the Pacific (Rudiak-Gould 2013), they unanimously told a story of the church's limited engagement in environmental issues, such as land degradation, pollution, overfishing and, lately, climate change. Certainly, there have been efforts by Oceanian theologians to develop new forms of eco-theologies addressing many issues of environmental change and, specifically, climate change (cf. Tofaeono 2000; Halapua 2008) within the frames of a liberal academic contextual theology. As such, the emerging eco-theology in Oceania draws on pre-Christian worldviews and practices, which include notions of interconnectedness, belonging, sharing and reciprocity, respect, reconciliation rituals and the sacredness of the land, sea and air (Rubow and Bird, in press). In the context of ecological crisis and climate change, liberal theological versions thus express a need for theologies that are more earth-oriented and not overtly other-worldly focused (ibid.). This is, obviously, an understanding that speaks up against salvation as an other-worldly, spiritualistic, individualistic and futuristic eternal existence, which according to Ernst (1994, 2006) is a characteristic feature of new religious groups in Oceania but which is also present in mainline churches.

In the Cook Islands there is so far no specific, formal eco-theological engagement. The official forms of theology are indeed coming in other-worldly forms nesting more or less informal theological reflection about the environment and the potential threat of climatic change to the islands and islanders. Prayers are obligatory at the opening and closing of most meetings in the communities, so ministers often attend official workshops and meetings. At meetings with environmental questions on the agenda this means that a minister may deliver a short exegesis about man's place in the world and the importance of fulfilling man's role as steward – a role given by God. As I learned during conversations with ministers in the Cook Islands Christian Church, the somewhat reluctant and ritualized environmental concern does not mean that they do not engage vividly in the environment they live in, such as their gardens. Without exception, the ministers related extraordinary experiences: one minister had experienced that mango trees died from not being talked to, and according to him, caterpillars were disappearing from his crops when he told them to by weeding and singing. Another minister often experienced that plants started to flower when they were scorned, and a third minister related how a whirlwind, as a response to his prayers, had once carried him over a large lagoon. Clearly, this group of ministers had an engaged relationship with their environment, involving respect and passion for nature's grandiosity, diversity and strength. However, they were not as worried as the environmentalists about the health of the land and the waters, and they certainly did not conflate nature (as God-given) and God. According to their theology, the pristine sources to be respected with passion are rather one's soul or God's spirit (or both), the sources from which the rightful actions – including those concerning the environment – will spring.

Ecological Crises – and an Abundance of Transcendences

The members of MECG were acutely aware that their view of the lagoon was not shared by all villagers. Many did not attend the workshops and/or could not afford the more expensive, environment-friendly, phosphate-free soap powders; also they did not see the point in separating their rubbish or in stopping burning most of it on their own land. MECG members knew that they did not reach out to the whole community and they had a growing awareness that they would never be able to do so. Therefore, they said, they prioritized awareness programmes targeting children, extensive lobbying and applications for grants locally, regionally and overseas in order to provide financial support to various projects. An updating of the sewage system had already been set in train.

Now, to return to the initial question concerning climate change, one might ask whether the rising sea levels due to global warming were a potential or real driving force in MECG's understanding of the changes in the lagoon. They are after all living on an island in the Pacific with severe beach erosion. The local and regional news and many workshops on the island often reported that sea level rise was one of the present and future effects in the South Pacific. Furthermore, some geo-scientific reports state that the sea in this area is presently rising by 4.4 mm a year, which is double compared to thirty years ago (SEAFRAME 2011).

When asked directly, MECG members all acknowledged that global warming 'is for real', but they did not consider a rising sea to be a threat to this particular island, at least not at present. 'We have not seen too much on our island, but we have seen enough evidence to say that it is something we need to take seriously', as Mii said. In a speech at the opening of an exhibition on Muri lagoon, when considering what islanders can do in order to alleviate future risks such as more severe cyclones and higher sea levels, a climate change officer from the National Environment Service noted: 'Keeping the lagoon healthy may turn out to be the best way to prepare for climatic changes'. A resilient lagoon due to an updated sewage system – and as Anne noted, the use of biodegradable soap – would prepare for the unknown. As such, climate change was not conceived of as a separate danger, but as an emergent change to the environment they live in. Targeting climate change by constructing coastal protection devices might turn out to be the right solution for future generations, they speculated, but here and now the landscape was open to many more concerns – and options. A healthy lagoon with clean waters and a living marine life was an option with many promises.

Not infrequently, climate scientists scorn the wider community for not taking the climate sciences and their scientific revolutions seriously (cf. Lucht 2012), and perhaps rightly so. However, scientific facts and projections cast in numbers and curves (with many uncertainties about the specific local consequences of global warming), cannot shape the social capacity for reorientation unaided. Science is not the only supplier of edges between the known and the unknown – nor is religion. Forecasts of an immediate apocalypse installing a supernatural, otherworldly register do occur in the Pacific and elsewhere, but you need not go to the churches to find the kind of passion that might fuel new environmental action and ethics.

As in Muri, people are moved by amazingly different properties in the landscapes they inhabit. All sorts of edges, otherness and self-blossoming spur the imagination: soaps, urchins or sediments, sometimes it is the work of the moment, sometimes it sparks off an enduring respect and passion. What is lacking, therefore, when impatient scientists call for action is not necessarily seriousness, knowledge, respect or passion for a changing environment. The engagement with the socialized landscapes as a pristine source creates an abundance of transcendences – open for both secular and religious types of engagement. What is lacking is rather the coordination of actions and a management fuelled by political, scientific and everyday concerns in socialized environments. It presupposes a language and an understanding of the different ways that passion and respect are created through experience of the material sources of vitality that can be prompted both in laboratories (Latour 2009) and lagoons; an understanding that anthropology, among others, can help to promote.

Notes

1. The fieldwork on Rarotonga was undertaken in June–July 2010 and June–July 2011. Thanks to Mii, Anne, Sahron, Mene, Jean, Makiuto and Tekao for sharing their insights; and to Waterworlds Research Centre at the Department of Anthropology, University of Copenhagen, Denmark, for financial support.

References

Cannell, F. 2006. 'Introduction. The Anthropology of Christianity', in F. Cannell (ed.), *The Anthropology of Christianity*. Durham, NC: Duke University Press.

Church, J.A., and P.U. Clark. 2013. 'Climate Change 2013: The Physical Science Basis'. Contribution of Working Group I to the IPCC Fifth Assessment Report. Final Draft Underlying Scientific-Technical Assessment. Available online: www.climatechange2013.org.

Crapanzano, V. 2004. *Imaginative Horizons: An Essay in Literary-Philosophical Anthropology*. Chicago: University of Chicago Press.

Descola, P. 2006. 'Beyond Nature and Culture'. Radcliffe-Brown Lecture in Social Anthropology, 2005. *Proceedings of the British Academy* 139: 137–55.

Ernst, M. 1994. *Winds of Change: Rapidly Growing Religious Groups in the Pacific Islands*. Suva: Pacific Conference of Churches.

———. 2006. *Globalization and the Re-Shaping of Christianity in the Pacific Island*. Suva: Pacific Theological College.

Gilson, R. 1980. *The Cook Islands 1820–1950* (ed. Ron Crocombe). Wellington, NZ: Victoria University Press.

Halapua W. 2008. *Waves of God's Embrace: Sacred Perspectives from the Ocean*. Norwich: Canterbury Press.

Herrmann, T., et al. 2011. 'European Union Muri Water & Sanitations Project. Final Completion Report'. Avarua Cook Islands.

Ingold, T. 2000. *The Perception of the Environment: Essays on Livelihood, Dwelling and Skill*. London: Routledge.

———. 2012. 'Toward an Ecology of Materials', *Annual Review of Anthropology* 41: 427–42.

Jørgensen, D. 2014. *Den skønne tænkning*. Aarhus: Aarhus Universitetsforlag.

Latour, B. 2009. 'Will Non-humans be Saved? An Argument in Ecotheology', *Journal of the Royal Anthropological Institute* 15(3): 459–75.

Lucht, W. 2012. 'Global Change and the Need for New Cosmologies', in D. Gerten and S. Bergmann (eds), *Religion in Environmental and Climate Change, Suffering, Values, Lifestyles*. New York: Continuum.

Luckmann, T. 1967. *The Invisible Religion: The Problem of Religion in Modern Society*. London: Collier Macmillan.

———. 1990. 'Shrinking Transcendence, Expanding Religion?', *Sociological Analysis* 30(2): 127–58.

Maintenay, A. 2011. 'A Notion of "Immanent Transcendence" and its Feasibility in Environmental Ethics', *Worldviews* 15: 268–90.

McFague, S. 2008. *A New Climate for Theology: God, the World, and Global Warming*. Minneapolis, MN: Fortress Press.

Minura, N., et al. 2007. 'Small Islands', in M.L. Parry et al. (eds), *Climate Change 2007: Impacts, Adaptation and Vulnerability*. Contribution to Working Group II of the Fourth Assessment Report of the Intergovernmental Panel on Climate Change. Cambridge: University of Cambridge.

Morton, T. 2009. *Ecology without Nature: Rethinking Environmental Aesthetics*. Cambridge, MA: Harvard University Press.

Nunn, P., and N. Mimura. 2007. 'Promoting Sustainability on Vulnerable Island Coasts: A Case Study of the Smaller Pacific Islands', in L. McFadden, R.J. Nicholls and E. Penning-Rowsell (eds), *Managing Coastal Vulnerability*. Amsterdam: Elsevier.

Ong, L., and K.N. Holland. 2010. 'Bioerosion of Coral Reefs by Two Hawaiian Parrotfish: Species, Size Differences and Fishery Implications', *Marine Biology* 157: 1313–23.

Pálsson, G. 1996. 'Human–Environmental Relations: Orientalism, Paternalism and Communalism', in P. Descola and G. Pálsson (eds), *Nature and Society: Anthropological Perspectives*. London: Routledge.

Rubow, C., and C. Bird. In press. 'Eco-theological Responses to Climate Change in Oceania', *Worldviews: Global Religions, Culture and Ecology*. Worldviews.

Rudiak-Gould, P. 2013. *Climate Change and Tradition in a Small Island State*. London: Routledge.

SEAFRAME. 2011. 'The South Pacific Sea Level and Climate Monitoring Project. Sea Level Data Summary Report. July 2010 – June 2011'.

Taylor, C. 2007. *A Secular Age*. Cambridge, MA: Harvard University Press.

Tofaeono, A. 2000. *Eco-theology AIGA – The Household of Life: A Perspective from Living Myths and Traditions of Samoa*. Erlangen: Erlangen Verlag.

Turua, B. 2003. 'Kia Pu'era: An Oral Tradition of Rarotonga Origins', in R. Crocombe and M. Crocombe (eds), *Cook Islands Culture: Akono'anga*. Suva, Fiji: Institute of Pacific Studies, in association with the Cook Islands Extension Centre, Rarotonga, University of the South Pacific, the Cook Islands Cultural and Historic Places Trust, and the Ministry of Cultural Development.

White, L. Jr. 1967. 'The Historical Roots of our Ecological Crisis', *Science* 155(3767): 1203–7.

5

West African Waterworlds

Narratives of Absence versus Narratives of Excess

Mette Fog Olwig and Laura Vang Rasmussen

In the 2000s, West Africa experienced unusually heavy and persistent rains that caused extensive flooding. During our fieldwork in northern Ghana and northern Burkina Faso in 2009 and 2010, the evidence of destruction from flooding was dramatically present, yet narratives of flooding remained remarkably absent. We found instead a preoccupation with insufficient rains, which is likely related to the power of an overarching desertification narrative that has dominated the perception of the area. The desertification narrative, which essentially blames local resource mismanagement for causing droughts and desertification, gained considerable ground during the great Sahelian droughts of the 1970s and 1980s. This explanation of drought has received repeated and severe critique, yet still seems to be a dominant environmental narrative for the West African Sahel (e.g. Leach and Mearns 1996; Marcussen 1999; Rasmussen, Fog and Madsen 2001; Olsson, Eklundh and Ardöm 2005). Thus, as we will show, even though too much rain leading to flooding has caused substantial damage, alongside the adversities from drought, when asking about pressing environmental problems and how they can be solved, the local population and development staff repeatedly reverted to the desertification narrative by emphasizing the absence of water and the need to rectify local resource mismanagement. As a result, while there was a call for humanitarian assistance due to the destruction caused by the flooding, there was a notable lack of knowledge or narratives relating to excessive rainfall and flooding.

Leach and Mearns (1996: 3) have illuminated how 'received wisdom' about environmental change obscures a plurality of other possible views, and often leads to misguided or even fundamentally flawed development policy in Africa'. In the following we will exemplify the way in which the 'received wisdom' of resource mismanagement leading to desertification still dominates in northern Ghana and northern Burkina Faso, despite criticism, and despite the fact that floods have become an increasingly tangible problem in addition to droughts. We thereby show how powerful environmental narratives can highlight certain phenomena, such as 'desertification', and shadow others, such as 'flooding' – regardless of their empirical relevance. Such narratives, we propose, retain their power by creating a bridging effect between the social, natural and applied sciences. We will suggest, however, that narratives pertaining to global climate change may turn out to be powerful enough to sway the desertification narrative's dominance by proving equally useful to the development sector as a means of providing a straightforward storyline that fits the prevailing crisis discourse.

Conceptual Framework: Environmental Narratives

In this chapter we examine the nature of key West African Sahelian environmental narratives, and the role they play in influencing everyday life and policy decisions. We are thus exploring recognized narratives, not performing a discourse analysis per se. Adger et al. (2001: 685) explain that '[w]ithin discourse analysis, expressive means have been analysed in terms of narratives, storylines and metaphors, and other rhetorical devices'. Describing the make-up of a typical narrative, they summarize that, 'First, a narrative is a story with a chronological order (beginning, middle and end) ... Second, a narrative constitutes a particular structure with respect to an involved "cast" of actors [such as] *heroes*, *villains* and *victims*' (ibid.). In the desertification narrative, the local population – the development recipients – are both the 'villains' and the 'victims', being portrayed as having degraded their own environment, while the development practitioners and donors are the 'heroes' who will save the environment, as well as the livelihoods of the victims/aid recipients, by teaching them new and better ways (Marcussen 1999: 101).

Environmental narratives focus 'not directly on a specific phenomenon itself, but rather on claims concerning this phenomenon, claims-makers and the claims-making process' (Adger et al. 2001: 683). In this study of environmental narratives, we are therefore not making an argument concerning the validity of the scientific claims supporting the narratives.

In fact, the scientific validity of a narrative has often proved irrelevant to its success (Roe 1991). According to Roe, 'Rural development is a genuinely uncertain activity, and one of the principal ways practitioners, bureaucrats and policy makers articulate and make sense of this uncertainty is to tell stories or scenarios that simplify the ambiguity' (ibid.: 288). Roe later elaborates that these narratives are not necessarily scientifically valid, and 'there is no pretense otherwise for many of them' (ibid.: 269). Ferguson (1994: 69) takes a more critical stance by arguing that 'an academic analysis is of no use to a "development" agency unless it provides a place for the agency to plug itself in, unless it provides a charter for the sort of intervention that the agency is set up to do'. He further explains that through a 'natural selection' those analyses and narratives will be embraced that require 'precisely those things [that] "development" agencies are set up to provide', which is to say, an apolitical and technical intervention (ibid.: 69–70). As pointed out by Adger et al. (2001: 283), the oversimplification of the local situation by narratives supporting development agency interests often leads to a narrative disconnect: '[S]ince global discourses are often based on shared myths and blueprints of the world, the political prescriptions flowing from them are often inappropriate for local realities', resulting in 'striking discrepancies between discursive simplifications and the diversity of situations within local contexts' (ibid.: 709).

The influential 1996 publication *The Lie of the Land: Challenging Received Wisdom on the African Environment*, edited by Leach and Mearns, was a culmination of repeated critique of 'orthodoxies concerning African environmental change' (Leach and Mearns 1996: 3). The publication stressed the need to question the narratives, blaming local land-use practices, worsened by overpopulation, for land degradation, desertification and deforestation. Despite the growing evidence questioning the scientific foundation of such neo-Malthusian narratives, and the general recognition Leach and Mearns' analysis received, the desertification narrative, as we will show, remains strong in a West African Sahelian context.

Scientists have been concerned, from as early as the 1920s, with the apparent advance and spread of the desert in West Africa, the cause of which was thought to be mismanagement of land resources (Batterbury and Warren 2001). The focus on human mismanagement of resources persisted in the following decades when Stebbing (1937), among others, identified the causes of land degradation in British West Africa to be the shortening of agricultural fallow periods and overgrazing. In other words, degradation was regarded as place-specific and caused by humans – and therefore treatable. Following this interest in human-induced degradation, the term 'desertification' emerged. It was first coined in 1949 by the French botanist Aubréville, who used it to describe the change of productive land into desert as a result of human activity in the tropical forest zone of Africa (Aubréville 1949).

While the focus on land degradation and desertification received less attention during the decades of exceptionally high rainfall in the 1950s and 1960s, the severe drought and famine in the 1970s again revived the desertification concept, resulting in the United Nations Conference on Desertification, held in Nairobi in 1977. The focus on desertification further intensified when droughts hit the region again in the 1980s (Timberlake 1985). During these decades, droughts were explained by endogenous causes – what became known as the Charney hypothesis. Charney, Stone and Quirk (1975) used a global circulation model to show a positive feedback mechanism between decreasing plant cover and a corresponding decrease in precipitation via increasing albedo. With this hypothesis they argued that desertification actually contributed to drought, and not vice versa. These explanations of drought, however, are now largely rejected by climate researchers (Tschakert et al. 2010).

Since the term desertification was first used, more than a hundred definitions have been formulated (Rhodes 1991). The 'Agenda 21' document of the 1992 United Nations Conference on Environment and Development (UNCED) defined it as 'land degradation in arid, semi-arid, and dry, sub-humid areas resulting from various factors, including climatic variations and human activities'. In contrast to the early definitions of desertification, the UNCED definition ascribed desertification interchangeably to anthropogenic and natural processes. The desertification narrative was first institutionalized through the United Nations Convention to Combat Desertification (UNCDD), ratified in 1996.

There is significant ambiguity about the nature of land degradation and desertification, and a lack of measurable criteria to document such environmental changes (e.g. Roe 1991; Leach and Mearns 1996; Marcussen 1999; Herrmann and Hutchinson 2005). Some recent studies even suggest a possible recovery of rainfalls and a greening of the Sahel (Rasmussen, Fog and Madsen 2001; Herrmann, Anyamba and Tucker 2005; Fensholt et al. 2012). Nevertheless, land degradation and desertification narratives are still prevalent in research and policy agendas. While drought is a problem, these narratives oversimplify the problem and present it in a way that calls for the type of intervention favoured by NGOs – apolitical and technical interventions (Ferguson 1994) such as educating locals and planting trees (Olwig and Sejersen 2014). The general mental image of West Africa is thus still dominated by the drought/land degradation/desertification narratives, with famine, hunger and food insecurity constituting the quintessential core (Tschakert et al. 2010). In effect, for many it can be extremely difficult to imagine the Sahel in any other way – for example, as a flood-prone area (ibid.). Nevertheless, here not only drought, but also too much rain are major problems, as will be seen below.

Setting the Scene: Too Much and Too Little Water?

During 2009 and 2010 we carried out fieldwork in two different locations in the Sahel: in the Upper East Region in Ghana, the north-easternmost region of the country located in the southern part of the Sahel; and in the northernmost region of Burkina Faso located in the northern part of the Sahel. In Ghana, fieldwork took place in Bolgatanga, the capital of the Upper East Region, as well as in villages in Bolgatanga Municipal District, located on the outskirts of Bolgatanga, and in villages in Bawku West District located around Sapeliga, near the border with Burkina Faso. In Burkina Faso fieldwork was carried out in Dori and Gorom-Gorom, the capitals of the Seno and Oudalan provinces in the Sahel region, and in two small villages in the provinces of Seno and Oudalan respectively. While these locations represent very different areas of the Sahel, with the northern part of the Sahel in Burkina Faso being significantly drier than the southern part in Ghana, they have in common the dual problem of having too much and too little water.

In recent history droughts have hit the general Sahel region during the 1970s and 1980s, while floods have battered different parts of the region with some regularity since the 1990s, with especially severe consequences in 2002, 2003, 2005, 2006, 2007 and 2010 (EM-DAT 2008; Tschakert et al. 2010; Direction de la Météorologie, Burkina Faso 2010). In the 1980s, there were large-scale droughts that affected most of the Sahel, and since then there have been equally severe droughts and flooding events that have affected specific areas of the Sahel (Direction de la Météorologie, Burkina Faso 2010). The southern part of the Sahel witnessed, for example, the most substantial flooding in 2007, while the northern part of the Sahel experienced severe flooding in 2010. In sum, 'the region has a long history of climatic stress and extreme events', and these include both floods and droughts (Tschakert et al. 2010: 472). When drought and flooding affect the same region during the same year, damages are intensified. Rainfall leads to floods, and not only from overflowing lakes and rivers. When the soil is very dry, excessive amounts of rainfall can cause flooding in areas far away from bodies of water because the soil cannot absorb the rainwater fast enough. This causes wide-ranging flooding, leading, for example, to the collapse of homes that are commonly made of mud and therefore cannot withstand being immersed in water for extensive periods.

The recent history of drought and flooding in the Sahel in general, as well as in the more localized study sites, indicates that more climatic extremes are likely to characterize the region over the next century (Tschakert et al. 2010). Climate projections for the Sahel are, however, particularly challenging for two reasons. Firstly, the great climate variability observed throughout the twentieth century makes it difficult to extract a clear sign of climate change above the background noise of an ever-varying climate; and secondly, some of the most credible models predict opposite outcomes for this region (Tschakert et al. 2010; Buontempo 2010). According to the 2007 IPCC report, 'half of the 21 models in the MMD-A1B simulations project an increase in precipitation over the next century, and the other half does not' (Tschakert et al. 2010: 495). Regarding the annual rainfall, model predictions for the Western Sahel include significantly drier conditions as well as wetter monsoons with 20–50 per cent more precipitation (Mitchell et al. 2000; Haarsma et al. 2005; Zhang and Delworth 2006; Kerr 2005; Knight et al. 2005; Lu and Delworth 2005; Hoerling et al. 2006; Tschakert et al. 2010). Turning to extreme events, very little modelling or observation evidence on trends exists for the Sahel (Christiansen et al. 2007). There is no consensus among models whether extremely dry or extremely wet seasons are likely to become most common, but the ENSEMBLES data that combine four regional circulation models nested in four global circulation models corroborate the IPCC projections of an increase in the frequency of dry spells and intensive rainfall events (Mertz et al. 2011). Despite the prevalence of both wet and dry periods and extreme events, there has nevertheless long been an overwhelming emphasis on drought, and specifically on the desertification narrative in policy and practice concerning the Sahel. In fact, the desertification narrative still dominates to the degree that we experienced, during our fieldwork, difficulty engaging in discussions concerning solutions and preventive measures regarding flooding, even though flooding was a tangible problem.

Methods: Talking about Water?

In 2010, Laura Vang Rasmussen undertook fieldwork in northern Burkina Faso in order to study land use changes and the drivers of these changes, such as population growth, shifting market conditions and climate variability. She was not particularly concerned with flooding. Nevertheless, she became aware of the contradictions between some of the statements that informants made and the obvious problem of too much water, as will be outlined below. Furthermore, she was surprised at the almost exclusive focus on developing agricultural extension services, even though agriculture was only one of many other sources of livelihood in the region, such as seasonal migration. Thus for Rasmussen, there was a need to come to terms with the way in which questions of too much water slowly seeped into her data – thus making her aware of issues she had not entirely expected, yet which never quite came to the fore.

Mette Fog Olwig did fieldwork in northern Ghana in 2009–2010 as part of her research on how the notion of climate change affects the development sector. Northern Ghana was particularly interesting because of the unusually severe 2007 flooding attributed to climate change, and because of the prevalence of development organizations. During fieldwork she asked many questions related to the flooding. Informants showed her strong evidence of the flooding's destruction in the form of destroyed buildings as well as items ruined by the water, yet it seemed that even though she was asking about flooding, they were somehow talking about drought. This became apparent, for example, when informants kept emphasizing the importance of planting trees because they would bring more rain, even though the conversation had been about the problem of too much rain. The conversation had inconspicuously changed from being about floods to being about the problem of drought. Thus for Olwig an important research question became the disjuncture between wishing to discuss flooding issues and receiving responses concerned with drought. This paper is thus partly based on findings that were not intentionally sought, and partly on data that was intentionally sought but not found. Based on semi-structured interviews with local development practitioners and local development recipients in both areas,[1] we will analyse our encounters with the desertification narrative in expected and not-so-expected circumstances.

The Absence of Flooding: Not Seeing the Rain for the Trees

During fieldwork in northern Ghana, the local emphasis on tree planting as an optimal solution to disaster and climate-related problems immediately became apparent. A farmer told Olwig during an interview in 2010:

> Climate change affects the weather, for instance when cutting down the trees. The trees help the rainfall; when there is rainfall the weather is wet and cool. I have heard a lot about [this] from all the [nongovernmental and governmental] organizations that I mentioned that work here; they tell us the importance of growing trees. We have therefore formed a committee to protect trees; it will go and find out why you are cutting a tree and arrest you.

The importance of trees was largely linked to the desertification narrative, and the local population repeatedly explained that the planting of trees would lead to rainfall while the cutting of trees would lead to drought, in accordance with the Charney hypothesis. Furthermore, there was little mention of the connection between trees and flooding – even though tree planting could equally be presented as an adaptation strategy to flooding, due to trees' ability to absorb rainwater. This bias towards droughts became clear when, in 2010, Olwig attended a seminar in Denmark entitled 'Climate changes – now what?',[2] organized by an NGO called 'The Ghana Friendship Groups in Denmark', which included several participants from Ghana. Even though the images illustrating the seminar programme showed drought and flooding, many of the speakers only talked about issues related to drought. The head of the Environmental Protection Agency (EPA), Northern Region (Ghana) asserted, for example: 'Bush fires and the cutting of trees are the main problems'. The seminar also contained a skit by four Ghanaian teachers who were on teacher exchange in Denmark. The programme stated that they would 'demonstrate, through a dramatic skit, the consequences of climate change for a family in northern Ghana'.[3] The skit turned out to be about tree cutting and bush fires. When a professor from the Faculty of Agricultural Sciences, University of Aarhus, and a member of IPCC, gave a presentation that only discussed adaptation to drought, Olwig asked why he did not talk about adaptation to flooding. He answered: 'Adaptation strategies to flooding? That's correct, I haven't mentioned any. That's because they are more complicated'. The professor was perhaps referring to the more resource-demanding and largely infrastructural dimensions of flood control, which a smaller NGO like The Ghana Friendship Groups in Denmark would have difficulties administering. Flood control is in general, however, a notoriously contested and complicated issue at many levels – social, economic and political (see e.g. Colten 2009). Adaptation strategies to drought, on the other hand, are largely linked to changing local practices – a more straightforward NGO agenda – as we will further discuss below.

In northern Burkina Faso, Rasmussen similarly found a considerable focus on droughts and little focus on flooding. During conversations with a local NGO leader in Gorom-Gorom, it became obvious, for example, that many of their strategies were based on an underlying assumption that drought is the only climate-related problem: 'The main problem in the area is that there is not enough food due to the low rainfall. Our main effort is concentrated on helping the local population by delivering millet at subsidized prices'. He further explained that their choice of strategies was influenced by Burkina Faso's NAPA (National Action Plan for Adaptation) from 2007, which notes that '[t]he permanent drought has accelerated deforestation and desertification' (NAPA, Burkina Faso 2007: 3). This view that droughts are by far the most important climate-related factor affecting the natural resource base, food production and local people's livelihoods is very persistent in the region. While drought has been a major problem in this area, the overwhelming focus on drought as opposed to flooding is problematic for several reasons.

A 'Dangerous' Discourse

> On the ground, the vast majority of subsistence land users, agricultural extension agents, and regional policy makers are also still entrenched in the lingering drought and desertification discourse. Most participants in our project see a direct link between land degradation, deforestation, agricultural overexploitation, and drought. Repeatedly, farmers insisted that cutting down trees brought droughts, whereas shady canopies attracted rains. This discourse is dangerous as it underestimates the real threat of externally driven wet extremes and flooding, suggesting that they are a temporary albeit troublesome anomaly. (Tschakert et al. 2010: 496)

In addition to being a problem for the researcher trying to learn about local understandings and practices related to flooding and environmental management, the overemphasis on the desertification narrative is dangerous because it may result in other environmental issues, such as floods, being overlooked. This not only has consequences for research and development policy and practice but, as we will illustrate here, it shapes local fears, hopes and strategies.

The fear that comes with not knowing or understanding a phenomenon such as flooding is reflected in the following conversation between Mette (Olwig), Raymond, a young man still in school, and the interpreter Lawrence, another young man who had recently graduated from high school.

> Mette: Why do you think the flood happened?
> Raymond: I don't know. I don't know what brought about that, so that is why I am afraid. Because if you know what brought about something, you may tackle it.

Mette: Did your teachers talk about the flooding when you returned to school?
Raymond: I never heard anything about it from them ... It was something strange; I expected them to say something about it.
Mette: Do you have an idea why they didn't? [long pause] Why do you think they didn't [now addressing Lawrence]?
Lawrence: Well, one of the things is that our teachers, some of them, didn't experience destruction from the flood; sometimes they didn't think of what happened. It may tend to be a laughing matter to them.
Mette: A laughing matter?
Lawrence: Yeah. Because, you see, they may group and say: 'Ah, water picked people away' [Raymond laughs] – they are laughing like that. You see, you see that? Because, some of them, they are able to build houses out of cement [as opposed to mud, which the poorest use to build their homes] and the cement structures remain standing during flooding. Even some laugh, some people, because of that. They say, 'Ay, you are just poor, living in a mud compound'. You see? You know, the teachers think that a poor person has a poor mind.

Because the teachers did not discuss the flooding in school, Raymond and Lawrence feared the flooding and believed that the teachers were not concerned with the flooding as they felt it only affected poor people who deserve such disasters because of their ignorance.

In northern Burkina Faso, it became apparent to Rasmussen that the overemphasis on droughts within policy and practice had an impact on local strategies. Lack of food due to low rain was indeed reported as a major concern among the local population, but Rasmussen noticed during her fieldwork in the local villages that the flooding of 2010 had also damaged many fields. Most of them were located close to a kind of temporary lake, called 'mare' locally, that had exceeded its bounds due to the heavy rains. People had earlier learned from agricultural extension officers that they should relocate some of their fields from a large sand dune to the areas close to the mare as a way of adapting to the annual rainfall variability. When rainfall was low, the soil close to the mare would remain relatively moist. They were also taught to build a granary close to these new fields in order to save time, as they would avoid transporting the harvest back to the dune. However, the risk of flooding from the mare was clearly not incorporated into these new strategies, and the flooding thus left the villagers with ruined fields and granaries. Rather than including the risk of flooding in agricultural strategies, people continued to focus only on droughts, based on what they had learned from the agricultural extension officers. This is illustrated by a local villager talking about the flooding in 2010: 'I also lost a granary, the one close to the mare. I had two before, one by each field. But I will build a new one ... Yes, I'll build it at the same location close to the mare. It saves a lot of time when you have your granary close to the field'.

Part of the reason for the narrow focus on too little water, despite an obvious problem with too much water, can be linked to the strategies of aid and development agencies.

Narratives of the Unnatural versus the Supernatural

As discussed earlier, the physical characteristics of the desert are believed to be linked to local resource mismanagement and therefore to be 'unnatural' (i.e. caused by humans): 'This [desertification] is an indication that the natural balance between the populations of the Sahel and the natural environment has been upset, and that there are no steps in the direction of an acceptable new balance' (CILSS and Club du Sahel 1980; cited in Rossi 2006: 31). Regardless of the somewhat questionable scientific validity of this statement, it has become prominent and has led to policies aiming to change the local population's agricultural practices. This policy has been internalized, at least discursively, by the local population, as exemplified by the following comment made by a female Ghanaian farmer when asked about climate change:

> I have heard about climate change. I have heard it on the radio [FM Bolga station]; the radio tells us we should stop causing deforestation and stop burning the bush. If we stop, it will help us get better rains. If we don't and we continue, then we will get worse rains. If we deplete the forest and continue burning, it will rain where the forest is and leave the place that is bare with no or just light rain.

Flooding, because it is sudden and dramatic, is often treated as an 'act of God', not only in religious terms (as recounted, for example, in the Biblical book of *Genesis*, where God is punishing people for their sins), but also in secular contexts where the phrase is applied, for example, by insurance companies to flooding disasters (Tuan 1968; Colten 2009). This perception of flooding is also prevalent in the local areas concerned. When asked why the flooding happened, another female Ghanaian farmer responded that it was God's decision. When this response was followed up by questions concerning whether she knew of anything the government could do to minimize damages from the flood, she responded:

> I didn't even know that the government can help us; if there is something the government can do to prevent those things, it is good. Any government

that is prepared to do that, we will be happy about, and whatever they can do will be welcomed. But I attribute all to God.

Scholars have suggested that the dominant African environmental narratives that emphasize local practices as the cause of, for example, desertification, have prevailed largely as a result of the need to legitimize international intervention. As argued by Leach and Mearns, 'received wisdom about African environmental change has had the instrumental effect of promoting external intervention in the control and use of natural resources' (Leach and Mearns 1996: 19–20). By emphasizing the problematic actions of 'the victims', policies concerning desertification and drought stress the need to teach the local population not to burn the bush but to plant more trees, and thereby underscore the importance of external intervention. When framed as supernatural, it is not as easy to attribute flooding to 'the victims', which could explain why there has been such a strong emphasis on desertification as opposed to flooding. Furthermore, adaptation strategies in relation to flooding, as mentioned earlier, are likely to be structural and on a larger scale, and therefore costly and difficult to implement by NGOs and GOs (e.g. Colten 2009).

Bridging Effects and Powerful Narratives: The Emergence of Climate Change Narratives

The common assertion by members of the local population that local resource mismanagement is causing drought demonstrates the pervasiveness of the desertification narrative; these assertions also, however, reflect local people's ability to say what they think potential donors want to hear, as well as their skill at speaking the development language. In contrast, they did not know 'what to say' concerning flooding. While the prevalence of the desertification narrative may derive partly from its connection to potential funding, an article by Moseley and Laris (2008) provides a good example of the power of the desertification narrative, regardless of such motivations. Moseley and Laris describe and reflect on their experiences as Peace Corps Volunteers with 'no apparent incentive – financial or professional – for supporting the dominant narrative' of desertification (ibid.: 61). Although they suggest different reasons for why they supported the narrative, one of the authors notes that he 'is disturbed that he was not able to turn his critical eye on his own left-leaning, neo-Malthusian environmentalism of the time, which underlay much of his then tacit support for many aspects of the desertification narrative' (ibid. 73). Only in the years that followed in graduate school did he realize that the desertification narrative was highly problematic. Narratives, in other words, can be both disarmingly simple and disarmingly effective at bridging the worlds of scientists, development practitioners and local populations. It is perhaps this bridging effect that gives such narratives their power. Narratives of climate change, as we will discuss in the following paragraphs, may prove powerful enough to affect the way in which NGOs and GOs approach flooding. There are two probable reasons for this. Firstly, the crisis narratives of climate change feed well into the overall crisis discourse that predominates for the area. Secondly, by attributing the 'blame' of flooding linked to climate change to the global community this narrative can provide the NGOs with renewed justification for intervention. The climate change narrative may thereby be able to create the same bridging effect as the desertification narrative.

The resource base of countries in the Global South is thought to be particularly vulnerable today because of the perceived threat of climate change, and associated natural disasters, as this threat will amplify the already considerable internal social, political and economic inequalities within the Global South and between the Global North and the Global South (Gado 1993). Areas in the Global South, such as West Africa, are highly influenced by international donor, development and humanitarian agencies. This is partly because of the global crisis discourse that these organizations produce and sustain concerning these areas. Reflecting this, West Africa, and in particular the Sahel, has been presented as a 'basket case', to use the ideologically loaded argument of the biologist Garrett Hardin, quoting Wade (1974): 'A whole vast area which might with appropriate management have become a breadbasket providing beef for half of Africa instead became a basket case needing more than $100 million worth of imported food just to survive' (Hardin 1977).

Hardin promotes two powerful narratives[4] concerning the Sahel: one maintaining that the local populations are completely dependent on the natural resource base for their survival, and one holding that the local populations have destroyed this resource base because of poor environmental practices, the 'Paradise Lost' narrative (Marcussen 1999: 96). Such narratives, in turn, lead to two widespread perceptions about the area, one emphasizing that the natural resource base in the Sahel is poor, and one contending that the local populations are dependent on external interventions in order to manage their environmental resource base, and thus survive. These story lines have led to the desertification narrative, as well as other, often critiqued, crisis narratives (ibid.: 96–97). West Africa, for example, has been presented as an area with rapid deforestation. Small-scale subsistence farming and logging companies are seen as the most important causes of deforestation with the expansion of subsistence farming being fuelled by rapid population growth, land degradation and poverty (Adger et al. 2001). The broad range of crisis narratives (degradation, desertification, deforestation, drought, hunger, etc.) has thus established an overall crisis discourse. By retaining West Africa in an overall crisis discourse, the continuous need for international development interventions has been validated (Leach and Mearns 1996) and, as Marcussen points out, 'actors in the environmental political arena remain in business' (1999: 99).

One alternative argument has had some success in countering the crisis narratives and the victim-blaming storyline by emphasizing the validity and value of local knowledge of the environment and environmental management. It is increasingly being argued, however, that, as a result of climate change, the natural environment is changing, making local knowledge and understandings of this environment obsolete (e.g. Anderson, Gundel and Vanni 2010). Since it is predicted that the Sahel, as a result of climate change, may have more floods and be more prone to drought, this, in effect, means that agricultural areas near the rivers and lakes are increasingly perceived to be threatened because of flooding. At the same time, areas far away from the rivers and lakes are believed to be equally threatened as they can be difficult to irrigate – and thus would not survive spells of drought. Narratives of climate change thereby fit well into the overall crisis narratives about the area and may therefore be effective through manipulating instead of attempting to displace the overall narrative: 'being consistent with the development narrative that has hitherto resisted all manner of assaults on it ... the narrative's blueprint becomes one way of altering rather than displacing the narrative itself' (Roe 1991: 292).

It is deplored that local communities in the Global South do not have the technology or science to predict and adapt to climate change (Tschakert et al. 2010). Furthermore, many global climate change mitigation and adaptation funds are likely to be so bureaucratic and technical in their requirements for funding that local populations and organizations are unable to access them without external assistance. External development interventions thereby arguably retain their raison d'être by playing a crucial role in enabling local populations to develop their knowledge so that it can be relevant in a world changed through global warming. In this case the 'villains' in the narrative are the countries that have emitted too much carbon, the 'victims' are the people living in the Global South whose life conditions are changing as a result of these climate changes, and finally the 'heroes', once more, are the NGOs that will come to the rescue. The flooding of agricultural fields fits well into this new crisis narrative and therefore it is possible that the problem of flooding will eventually find articulation through climate change narratives. Furthermore, the type of intervention called for through this narrative is of the apolitical and technical kind favoured by NGOs, as pointed out by Ferguson (1994). Thus, it calls for the need to provide technology (e.g. improved seeds) and science (e.g. weather predictions). Roe argues that the displacement of a development narrative 'requires an equally straightforward narrative that tells a better story' (1991: 290). Globally induced climate change narratives may prove to be the 'better story' that can overcome the power of the desertification narrative while being consistent within the overall crisis discourse that prevails for the area, thereby allowing a place for stories of water's excess in addition to stories of its absence.[5]

Will Narratives of Water's Absence Remain More Powerful than Narratives of its Excess?

Northern Ghana and northern Burkina Faso are both areas where the natural resource base is often presented as being so poor that dependency on development aid and agricultural extension services has become a primary means of survival for the local population (Porter and Lyon 2006; Whitehead 2006). This situation is seen to be exacerbated by climate change leading to new climate change crisis narratives. The new narratives on climate change may prove as simple and straightforward as the desertification narrative, capable of bridging the social, natural and applied sciences and thereby becoming as powerful as the desertification narrative.

The climate change narratives provide a useful narrative for the legitimization of development intervention, and may well prove so powerful that they can bring to the fore the subject of flooding, which until now has been largely hidden by the desertification narrative. Climate change narratives are, furthermore, consistent with the overall crisis discourse that dominates the area. Climate change narratives, however, are also problematic because they, like the desertification narrative, have the tendency to overemphasize some phenomena and to overshadow others. With the climate change crisis narratives, for example, the primary premise that local populations are mostly dependent on natural resources for their survival – particularly agricultural production – is given support, while other important livelihood strategies, including seasonal migration, are marginalized. Furthermore, climate change crisis narratives downplay the value of alternative positive scenarios, thereby disregarding the strength of politically and spatially peripheral regions.

Our experience during fieldwork in the Sahel suggests a number of key points with regard to the intersection of environmental narratives and development policies. Firstly, it is vital that academic discourse of the social sciences does not take place in isolation from that of the natural sciences or from that of development practitioners and the local population. The distinction between basic social science, natural science and applied science is not useful here because it distracts from the ways the discourses in these spheres are entangled with each other. It thus becomes more complicated to deal with the amelioration of flooding, not simply because of technical reasons, but because society's understanding of the Sahel is locked into a desertification narrative that makes it difficult to change the interpretive framework on the terrain of facts alone. Environmental narratives can thus only be countered by approaching them not simply from a social, applied or natural science perspective, but through approaches that show how these narratives interlink differing approaches. There is thus a need for studies that deal with all perspectives, and which are not conceived to be simply basic, applied science, or professional in character.

Notes

*All names of informants are pseudonyms.
1. For more on the methods used in our studies, see Rasmussen and Reenberg 2012 and Olwig 2012.
2. Translation by authors from Danish ('Klimaændringer – og hva' så?').
3. Translation by authors from Danish.
4. Roe points out that '[t]he most obvious feature of the "tragedy of the commons" ... strongly exposited by Hardin, is its status as narrative' (Roe 1991: 288).
5. This analysis finds further support in a comment made by a speaker at the 2013 conference in Copenhagen on 'Climate Change and Development Politics' to the effect that the development sector is using climate change as a 'lifeboat'.

References

Adger, W.N., et al. 2001. 'Advancing a Political Ecology of Global Environmental Discourses', *Development and Change* 32: 681–715.
Anderson, S., S. Gundel and M. Vanni. 2010. *The Impacts of Climate Change on Food Security in Africa: A Synthesis of Policy Issues for Europe*. London: International Institute for Environment and Development.

Aubréville, A. 1949. *Climats, forêts et désertification de l'Afrique tropicale*. Paris: Société des Editions Geographiques, Maritimes et Coloniales.

Batterbury, S., and A. Warren. 2001. 'Desertification', in J.S. Neil and B.B. Paul (eds), *International Encyclopedia of the Social & Behavioral Sciences*. Oxford: Pergamon, pp. 3526–29.

Buontempo, C. 2010. *Sahelian Climate: Past, Current, Projections*. London: Met Office Hadley Centre.

Charney, J., P.H. Stone and W.J. Quirk. 1975. 'Drought in the Sahara: A Biogeophysical Feedback Mechanism', *Science* 187: 434–35.

Christiansen, J.H., et al. 2007. 'Regional Climate Projections: Climate Change 2007: The Physical Science Basis', in S. Solomon et al. (eds), *Contribution of Working Group I to the Fourth Assessment Report of the Intergovernmental Panel on Climate Change*. Cambridge: Cambridge University Press, pp. 847–940.

Colten, C.E. 2009. *Perilous Place and Powerful Storms: Hurricane Protection in Coastal Louisiana*. Jackson: University Press of Mississippi.

Direction de la Météorologie, Ouagadougou, Burkina Faso. Data derived October 2010.

EM-DAT. 2008. 'Emergency Events Database'. Available via http://www.emdat.be/Database/ (accessed December 2012).

Fensholt, R., et al. 2012. 'Greenness in Semi-arid Areas across the Globe 1981–2007: An Earth Observing Satellite-based Analysis of Trends and Drivers', *Remote Sensing of Environment* 121: 144–58.

Ferguson, J. 1994. *The Anti-Politics Machine: 'Development', Depoliticization, and Bureaucratic Power in Lesotho*. Cambridge: Cambridge University Press.

Gado, B.A. 1993. *Une historie des damines au Sahel: études des grandes crises alimentaires, XIXe-XXe siècles*. Paris: L'Harmattan.

Haarsma, R.J., et al. 2005. 'Sahel Rainfall Variability and Response to Greenhouse Warming', *Geophysical Research Letters* 32: L17702.

Hardin, G. 1977. 'Ethical Implications of Carrying Capacity', in G. Hardin and J. Baden (eds), *Managing the Commons*. San Francisco: W.H. Freeman.

Herrmann, S.M., A. Anyamba and C.J. Tucker. 2005. 'Recent Trends in Vegetation Dynamics in the African Sahel and their Relationship to Climate', *Global Environmental Change – Human and Policy Dimensions* 15: 394–404.

Herrmann, S.M., and C.F. Hutchinson. 2005. 'The Changing Contexts of the Desertification Debate', *Journal of Arid Environments* 63: 538–55.

Hoerling, M., et al. 2006. 'Detection and Attribution of 20th Century Northern and Southern African Rainfall Change', *Journal of Climate* 19(16): 3989–4008.

Kerr, R. 2005. 'Atlantic Climate Pacemaker for Millennia Past, Decades Hence?' *Science* 309: 41–42.

Knight, J.R., et al. 2005. 'A Signature of Persistent Natural Thermohaline Circulation Cycles in Observed Climate', *Geophysical Research Letters* 32: L20708.

Leach, M., and R. Mearns. 1996. 'Environmental Change and Policy: Challenging Received Wisdom in Africa', in M. Leach and R. Mearns (eds), *The Lie of the Land: Challenging Received Wisdom on the African Environment*. London: The International African Institute, pp. 1–33.

Lu, J., and T. Delworth. 2005. 'Oceanic Forcing of the Late 20th Century Sahel Drought', *Geophysical Research Letters* 32: L22706.

Marcussen, H.S. 1999. 'Environmental Paradigms, Knowledge Systems and Policy: The Case of Burkina Faso', *Danish Journal of Geography* 2: 93–103.

Mertz, O., et al. 2011. 'Adaptation Strategies and Climate Vulnerability in the Sudano-Sahelian Region of West Africa', *Athmospheric Science Letters* 12: 104–8.

Mitchell J.F.B., et al. 2000. 'The Effect of Stabilizing the Atmospheric Carbon Dioxide Concentrations on Global and Regional Climate Change', *Geophysical Research Letters* 27 (18): 2977–80.

Moseley, G.M., and P. Laris. 2008. 'West African Environmental Narratives and Development-Volunteer Praxis', *The Geographical Review* 98(1): 59–81.

NAPA, Burkina Faso. 2007. http://unfccc.int/cooperation_support/least_developed_countries_portal/ldc_work_programme_and_napa

Olsson, L., L. Eklundh and J. Ardöm. 2005. 'A Recent Greening of the Sahel – Trends, Patterns and Potential Causes', *Journal of Arid Environments* 63: 556–66.

Olwig, M.F. 2012. 'Multi-sited Resilience: The Mutual Construction of "Local" and "Global" Understandings and Practices of Adaptation and Innovation', *Applied Geography* 33: 112–18.

Olwig, M.F., and F. Sejersen. 2014. 'Water Technologies: Mirroring Great Expectations in Greenland and Ghana', in K. Hastrup and C. Rubow (eds), *Living with Environmental Change: Waterworlds*. London: Routledge, pp. 146–51.

Porter, G., and F. Lyon. 2006. 'Groups as a Means or an End? Social Capital and the Promotion of Cooperation in Ghana', *Environment and Planning D: Society and Space* 24: 249–62.

Rasmussen, K., B. Fog and J.E. Madsen. 2001. 'Desertification in Reverse? Observations from Northern Burkina Faso', *Global Environmental Change – Human and Policy Dimensions* 11: 271–82.

Rasmussen, L.V., and A. Reenberg. 2012. 'Land Use Rationales in Desert Fringe Agriculture', *Applied Geography* 34: 595–605.

Rhodes, S.L. 1991. 'Rethinking Desertification: What Do We Know and What Have We Learned?' *World Development* 19: 1137–43.

Roe, E.M. 1991. 'Development Narratives, or Making the Best of Blueprint Development', *World Development* 19(4): 287–300.

Rossi, B. 2006. 'Aid Policies and Recipient Strategies in Niger: Why Donors and Recipients Should Not Be Compartmentalized into Separate "Worlds of Knowledge"', in D. Lewis and D. Mosse (eds), *Development Brokers and Translators: The Ethnography of Aid and Agencies*. Bloomfield, CT: Kumarian Press, pp. 27–49.

Stebbing, E.P. 1937. 'The Threat of the Sahara', *Journal of the Royal African Society* 36: 3–35.

Timberlake, L. 1985. 'The Sahel: Drought, Desertification and Famine', *Draper Fund Report* 14: 17–19.

Tschakert, P., R. Sagoe, G. Ofori-Darko and S. Codjoe. 2010. 'Floods in the Sahel: An Analysis of Anomalies, Memory, and Anticipatory Learning', *Climatic Change* 103: 471–502.

Tuan, Y.-F. 1968. *The Hydrologic Cycle and the Wisdom of God: A Theme in Geoteleology.* Toronto: University of Toronto Press.

UNCED (United Nations Conference on Environment and Development). 1992. 'Managing Fragile Ecosystems: Combating Desertification and Drought, Chapter 12 of Agenda 21'. Rio de Janerio, Brazil, 3–14 June 1992.

Wade, N. 1974. 'No Victory for Western Aid', *Science* 185(4147): 234–37.

Whitehead, A. 2006. 'Persistent Poverty in North East Ghana', *Journal of Development Studies* 42(2): 278–300.

Zhang, R., and T.L. Delworth. 2006. 'Impact of Atlantic Multidecadal Oscillations on India/Sahel Rainfall and Atlantic Hurricanes', *Geophysical Research Letters* 33: L17712.

6

To the Lighthouse

Making a Liveable World by the Bay of Bengal

Frida Hastrup

Introduction: Collaborations on the Shore

In early 2010, the foundations for a new lighthouse on the beach of the coastal village of Tharangambadi in South East India were laid. A flat cement base covered with water for it to harden and measuring about 9 square meters had been moulded at a spot near the waterfront, right next to the main landing site of the local fishing boats and the village's fish auction building. Metal bars protruded from the four corners of the base, showing where the tall iron construction holding the guiding light would later be attached. Since the Asian tsunami swept across numerous villages along the coast of the Indian state of Tamil Nadu in December 2004, a whole range of projects have been implemented in the region, introducing all kinds of new objects, structures and buildings to the coastal village landscape (cf. F. Hastrup 2011). Used to discussing, receiving and being informed of the many such projects aimed in one way or another at managing nature's unruliness, the villagers knew perfectly well what was going on at this particular construction site, and they readily explained. When, during my fieldwork in Tharangambadi, we talked about the construction work on the beach, the locals would usually say something like 'They're making a lighthouse', or 'It's the government and some NGO', or 'The government is in charge'.

When I came back to Tharangambadi to do more fieldwork in 2011, the construction of the lighthouse had been completed. Towering over even the tallest palm trees in the village, the lighthouse was now a prominent feature of Tharangambadi's modest skyline. Like the year before, people would tell me that the Tamil Nadu state government had constructed the lighthouse, perhaps with the aid of 'some NGO'. In response to my questions of what they thought about the new addition to the coastal vista, I was repeatedly told by the villagers that they appreciated the lighthouse. 'It's good', or 'the government put it up, because we live here', or 'we appreciate it' would be frequent statements offered by people in the course of our conversations.

Nightfall is sudden and swift in Tharangambadi, and on many days it would be dark before I made my way to my lodgings. Walking through patches with irregular or unreliable street lightning, often I could not see a thing. Stumbling along, I would look around – for the lighthouse, among other things – only to find its lights dim, and on many nights next to invisible. To find and see it, I needed to know in advance where to look for it and its guiding light.

I do not mean to judge the usefulness or success of the lighthouse by the degree to which it lights the way home for a visiting fieldworker. Yet it puzzled me to learn that the fishing people in Tharangambadi spoke quite highly of the lighthouse when, apparently, it did not really provide much in the way of a guiding light to be seen from afar. What did the lighthouse accomplish to merit the local appreciation? How did it function? What did it light up?

In this chapter, I want to explore what I see as a series of intriguing collaborations that have gone into making the lighthouse work, however modestly – for the government in charge of its construction, for the fishing people living by it, and for other analysts engaged in life along the water's edge on the Tamil Nadu coast. What I want to show is that the lighthouse is both a light technology spurring playful comments and a weighty intervention in life by the sea, and as such it is a vital participant in making up a particular local world, which is at once liveable and imperfect – and shared by everyone in it. By being available as a common means of qualifying coastal life in such a complex manner, one function of the lighthouse becomes to highlight the fact that people may sometimes live well together even with inadequate interventions. In fact it may be the very shortcomings that make them useful as shared points of reference.

My suggestion is, then, that the lighthouse occasions realistic local analyses of coastal life, and to unfold this I will discuss three enigmatic articulations of the construction generated in the course of my fieldwork. First, I will look at the official policy and reasoning that have put the lighthouse in place; second, I will focus on its role as a measure of precaution and expression of care provided by the state; and third, I will explore how the specific construction of the lighthouse seems to make it impossible for it to fulfil its own stated purpose. In conclusion, I suggest that these articulations, with the incompleteness and ironies they point out, make the lighthouse a valuable and common analytical resource that calibrates expectations for a shared coastal life – the one field of concern that all actors present in this chapter address. In consequence, I want to argue that the lighthouse does *not* work in multiple ways or as different lighthouses, but as a joint, collaborative and singular attempt at making a less than perfect life on the shore viable. Now let me turn to the policy of guiding lights.

Reliable Sources of Power

Near the top of the lighthouse, a noticeboard states that it is a 'Wind–solar hybrid lighthouse', a fact that explains the construction's propellers whirling around in the breeze. The use of renewable energy sources is directly linked to the formal purpose of the lighthouse, the stated intention of which is to guide the fishermen safely home from their fishing trips, without there being the risk of a power cut. In a policy note from the Tamil Nadu Government Fisheries Department in charge of the project I read about the 'Provision of Guide Lights in Coastal Areas'. I need to quote the note at some length here. It says:

> Fishermen living in coastal areas mainly depend on beaming lights that can be seen when they venture [out] to sea for fishing, and for safe returning to land. Due to absence of such lights, there are occasions of drifting of fishermen and losing their way to land. However, due to fluctuation in the power supply, the illumination power of the light gets affected. In order to overcome these practical difficulties, installation of a hybrid light system which utilises both wind and solar energy to produce electricity is found to be more useful. The solar module will be a standby arrangement [that] assures continuous power supply. Moreover, the provision of Light Emitting Diode (LED) ensures uninterrupted power supply for brighter light source to the guide lights. Hybrid guide lights will be installed in 5 selected locations at an estimated cost of Rs.30.00 lakhs [100.000] during 2009–10. (Policy Note 2009–2010)

From my fieldwork I know that fluctuation in the power supply to the village is indeed a fact of life in Tharangambadi, just as daytime sunlight and wind are constant features. The idea of a self-sufficient lighthouse based on durable energy sources as explained in the policy note was apt, it would seem. If we take a closer look at the quote above, though, even for all its matter-of-fact style, we can see that the policy note is ripe with interesting considerations that point to issues beyond the obvious helpfulness of green energy. As Andrew Mathews has observed, no rule or regulation contains enough information for it to fully explain itself and how it gets implemented (Mathews 2011: 238). There is thus reason to look at some of the assumptions that feature in the policy document. The note starts off by making a straightforward claim about fishing life, more specifically about what the fishermen need in order to practise their trade safely, namely beaming lights on the shore to prevent drifting. However, for reasons unexplained, there are 'practical difficulties' that make such lights absent or, at least, fluctuating. In consequence, the policy note then states that the provision of more reliable guiding lights is the responsibility of the government, which has allotted thousands of rupees to be spent on an uninterrupted power supply.

What we can read from the note, I suggest, is a first instance of how the lighthouse serves as an analytical resource enabling the Tamil Nadu state government to attune its efforts to the Tharangambadi coastal reality. The lighthouse, as described in the policy note, materializes a measure of realism in the sense that it articulates an acknowledgement of the fact that the state apparently cannot provide the whole village and area with a regular wired supply of electricity. There are just too many practical difficulties for this to be feasible. Instead, and as a response, the government somehow scales down its sphere of responsibility to cover only the provision of a guiding light on the beach for the fishing people, run by energy sources allegedly unaffected by political priorities, technical problems or heavy bureaucracy, or whatever the practical difficulties in question might be. The implicit irony in the state policy note's description of the lighthouse is that it seems to acknowledge that, when it comes to the provision of electricity, sun and wind are more reliable powers than the Tamil state apparatus, which in a sense is too big and difficult for its own good. Through the lighthouse and the way it is described, the state government may thus be seen as attempting to resolve the fact that the very same government cannot provide a steady supply of electricity to Tharangambadi. In this way, the lighthouse is articulated as an intervention that creates a new governed terrain of a manageable scale on which to exert authority and indeed care for a population living off a particular practice. An uninterrupted power supply from the government is provisioned by trustworthy sun and wind, and thus by a kind of distributed responsibility.

The lighthouse as it appeared in the policy note, then, shows a government taking the opportunity to act as a reliable actor in coastal life, caring for its population in a way that would perhaps be unnecessary had the same government been able to get its act together. What is on offer here, I suggest, is a downsized state, emitting its power from sources other than itself. True to the difficult practical realities of shoreline governance, what we see in this case is a kind of hesitant bureaucracy that samples, among other things, wind, sun, technical know-how, views on fishing life, and fluctuating power to make a humble intervention. This approach perhaps also accommodates the expectations of those governed (cf. Mathews 2011: 235). Let me now turn to conversations with some of the people who populate the officially downscaled terrain by the sea, made manageable by the implementation of a particular and modest policy of uninterrupted power supply.

Faint State Interference

During my fieldworks, the fishermen of Tharangambadi articulated an ambiguous view of the lighthouse. Repeated statements from local villagers asserting that it was a welcome new arrival in the village made me want to talk more about its function and capacity. It does not really light up the sea or even the shore or the fishing village very much. 'I can hardly see it at night-time', I would say to the appreciative fishermen, who would respond that no, certainly it does not provide much light. They would often elaborate on this by explaining that the light it radiates is not nearly strong enough for them to navigate by during nights in the boats, but they would also state that this is exactly the purpose of the lighthouse, almost as if quoting the policy note discussed above. I was intrigued – and probably more so than the people I was with. The dimness of the light, it seemed, was not a problem to them at all. Most often the fishermen would simply laugh at my question about whether they would actually need a construction such as a well-functioning lighthouse to find their way back from the sea if they went fishing during the dark hours of night. How then, the fishermen humorously replied, would they ever have managed to come back from fishing trips before the very recent construction of the lighthouse? Occasionally, the fishermen would joke even more explicitly and tell me that the only way the lighthouse guided them was if they singled out the dimmest light along the shore and steered towards that to get back to Tharangambadi.

Jokes aside, it did not seem to occur to the fishermen I worked with to think that their government could or should actually do anything more to guide them safely across a darkened sea. If the state government, as I suggested above, limited its sphere of responsibility by turning to sun and wind to light up a small portion of coastal land, rather than aiming to supply the whole village or even state with reliable electricity, then the fishermen, too, had only limited expectations of state protection. Surely, even the most efficient government could not be held accountable for the vagaries of the sea at night-time and in rough weather. I learned from the fishermen that this was not what was expected of a government intervention. The very fact that a lighthouse had been constructed at all and placed in the heart of the fishing village was apparently enough – a sufficient and expectable formal recognition of the life ways of a particular group of citizens; in the words of the fishermen, the lighthouse was built 'because we live here'. What warranted the local appreciation of the lighthouse, I think, was in a sense exactly the very location of the lighthouse combined with the dimness of its light that, so to speak, kept it in place. In a way, it seemed as if the beams of the lighthouse had just the right range in the eyes of the fishermen. The lighthouse had enough energy to make the local coastal world emerge as visible to and thus not forgotten by its formal government, while its power was still light enough to permit the fishermen to do what they do, more or less uninterrupted. In other words, the fishing people seemed to live well by the guidance of a state that is not the exclusive source of power.

One important lesson here is that the degree of local appreciation of a construction like the lighthouse did not depend on the extent to which local villagers were granted or assumed ownership of it. Ownership of the lighthouse never appeared to be a concern for the fishermen. The construction remained the government's project. I do not think, however, that this can be ascribed to lack of mobilization, lack of communication, or any such identifiable deficit. The South Indian fishing villagers are known to be good at organizing themselves in quite strong and independent societies – trade organizations and village councils play a big role in structuring life, often implicitly as a balance to the state authorities (Subramanian 2009; F. Hastrup 2011). One example of this surfaced in the aftermath of the Asian tsunami in 2004. After the disaster, all fishing families were relocated in new settlements on land provided by the Tamil Nadu government further from the shore, and the households were initially required to hand over their former settlement areas. Due to mobilized and state-wide protests from fishing organizations, however, the Tamil Nadu government decided to let the fishing people retain the use right (which was what they also had before the relocation) over the areas close to the sea, the argument being that their livelihood practice necessitated free access and proximity to coastal land.

Part of the fishermen's notion of citizenship, then, seemed to be a shared understanding that the state should only interfere in a limited way in their life practices; it seemed a citizenry right of the fishermen to, as it were, cut the state authority down to size – and sometimes laugh about it. Indeed, on many other issues discussed during fieldwork I came across lots of vocal and serious disappointment with regard to the services provided by the authorities, such as the provision of drinking water, the issuing of legal documents, and the allocation of support for children's education among other things. Hardships in these matters are not hard to come by. I do not mean to paint a picture only of harmonious relations between the Tamil Nadu state and citizens, nor do I criticize (or excuse, for that matter) the state government for not providing a sufficient level of service. I am not involved in project evaluation here, as if an external consultant of sorts. What I do mean to point to is the workings of the lighthouse as a common analytical resource – with critical potential, of course – adjusting and commenting on expectations of proper and realistic relations between state and citizens; a kind of understood collaboration that implied no homogeneity, satisfaction or even equality (cf. Tsing 2005: 245). The fishermen were not asked whether they wanted a lighthouse in the first place, and they did not speak of it as their project; I am not inferring participant democracy or shared decision making. But as long as state interference was imperfect enough to leave the fishermen be, they welcomed it as a token of at least some measure of care from the authorities, apt for making independent citizens exactly because of its faintness. Let me now move on to the technicalities – and further potential – of the faint light on the beach, to explore how the lighthouse, too, curiously scaled itself down.

Partial Solutions

Drinking coffee with my friend Arivu during my 2011 fieldwork, we discussed the lighthouse more. Arivu, who is originally from a Tharangambadi fishing family and who, at the time of my fieldwork, was finishing a Ph.D. in physics on nanotechnology and solar cells in the city of Coimbatore, seemed interested in talking about it. We spoke about the dim lights. 'There's too much salt in the air for it to work properly on solar power', he explained. Laughingly, Arivu added that it would take as much man power as solar power for the guiding lights to function; careful and steady upkeep of the solar cells would be needed. So much, we agreed, for the stated self-sufficiency of the lighthouse. Apparently, the salty winds constantly blowing onshore from the Bay of Bengal will interfere with the delicate technology of the solar cells, impeding the energy transfer, if the construction is not carefully maintained.

Another irony of the lighthouse is dawning here: it was located too close to the sea for its own good. If, as I suggested above, the Tamil Nadu government compensated for its own lack of control by downscaling its ambitions, and the fishermen accepted the authorities' intervention because of its faintness, the lighthouse was in a sense a literal expression of this incomplete power transfer in that it had impossibility built into it. The location of the lighthouse so near to the seafront, which was of course a given because it was meant to serve as a landmark for people fishing, spurred another problem: the lighthouse could not properly perform as itself. For all the clear identification of problem and solution expressed in the policy note, the lighthouse worked as a downscaled version of itself; minding its own business, as it were, by running on natural energy and not having the power to impose itself too much on the local setting.

Considering Arivu's description, then, the lighthouse comes to life as a complex analytical resource, employed by people living with it as a commentary on what it means for power to be self-sufficient. Self-sufficiency here is the capacity to be humble enough to work imperfectly and shed light inwards, so to speak, on the problems that are built in by the construction. What interests me in Arivu's analysis is that the lighthouse light's lack of range due to impeded energy transfer caused by its particular location and perhaps construction is not readily critiqued. He did not write the lighthouse off as a failed project. The manpower that Arivu talked about as necessary seems to also imply an acknowledgement that some projects work by not really working. If, again, we think about the lighthouse as a realistic object that calibrates different people's expectations, one might say that what we see here is another articulation of the incomplete nature – and indeed success – of the lighthouse. Its very construction makes it impossible to be anything other than a limited and partial intervention – and as such it becomes a materialization of a set of relations between a downscaled state and its citizens that I discussed above.

What is important here is that there seemed to be no drive on the part of anyone to improve the efficiency of the lighthouse; it was never a matter of some blaming others for not taking or giving ownership over the lighthouse, or for not maintaining it, or even for delivering it in the first place. If ownership or lack thereof were at all the issue here, people might either talk about the lighthouse an as improper state intrusion, or take it upon themselves to carefully maintain the solar cells, or just complain about the lighthouse as a flawed project. Here, though, I see the fact that such evaluative statements were never voiced as a measure of the lighthouse's success. There seemed to be no other motor in the life of the lighthouse than for different people to use it as one available means to make the shared coastal world liveable for those who care about it. At issue was not the matter of making project plans and practices co-extensive and have them respond to a defined problem – there was no quest for total solutions to fix life on the shore. Those living it, whether from state offices or sandy beaches, seemed to be the first to know that such immodest criteria of success and agreement would not be of much use.

Discussion: Calibrating a Common Field

The question of how to live in the space between the promise and disappointment of development processes and welfare interventions often features in postcolonial rural India, according to Anand Pandian (2009: 227). In the three sections above, we have seen a state government that provides a faint, short-range guiding light, seemingly recognizing that it is beyond its means to ensure regular state-wide electricity, and a fishing population who appear content to become visible as citizens in the dim lights and attendant shades provisioned by the state; and we have talked to life a lighthouse constructed so that it cannot perform in a way that is true to itself, so to speak. These articulations could be heard as localized answers to Pandian's question: how do we make an imperfect world liveable?

What I have explored here has been a particular kind of realism materialized by the lighthouse; it expressed mutually approved downscaled sets of expectations as to what can and should be done by whom – in terms of concerns about electricity, safety, the sea, citizenship, state projects, dark nights, delicate technology and salty winds. The capacity to subsume these concerns and somehow address them in a realistic key makes the lighthouse appear as a lifelike object, at once a success and a failure, supporting and generating collective analytical processing of life by the sea.

In her book *Friction*, Anna Tsing has discussed collaboration as difference within a common cause, stating that in the forest conservation campaign she explored, 'undifferentiated unity was not a prerequisite for success' (Tsing 2005: 246). The idea of a common cause is important here. I do not mean to suggest that the articulations of the lighthouse imply unanimity – as I have suggested, they may be responses to a less than perfect management of the coastal zone. But, importantly, nor do I mean to present a compilation of three different versions of the lighthouse. What we have seen are not discrete perceptions of the lighthouse, conceived from given positions within, say, a hierarchy of power; and my purpose here has not been to collate separate accounts of the lighthouse from respective and shifting points of view. This is not a matter of pluralism, as if the lighthouse were merely a passive object coincidentally placed in the middle of different people's unconnected lives (cf. Mol 2002: 4). On the contrary, the point here is that anyone even thinking about the lighthouse, however differently, already addressed it as located in a particular common coastal sociality, shared by people who work and live there. The lighthouse would not be what it is, were it not produced for and by an already joint and composite world where different analyses intersect to form a specific – and needless to say complex – coastal world. Think only of the fishermen's assertions that the government put up the lighthouse because they live on the beach.

In much current anthropological work influenced by science and technology studies we learn of different enactments of knowledge claims and of how various technologies can be seen as fluid and working in multiple ways. I am influenced by such work myself, such as the elegant and subtle writings of Annemarie Mol (e.g. Mol 2002; de Laet and Mol 2000) and others, who make a strong case for particular practices being sites of knowledge making and constitutive of subjects and objects. However, it seems to me that some of the subtlety of these studies is lost if the notions of fluidity or fluid technology are taken to imply that objects such as the lighthouse simply work differently for different groups of people, as if the object itself could either remain stable or be atomized into different fragments, and the analyst jumps around from one point of view to the next, adding them together as if from an external position. Rather, what I have stressed here is all the connections that the lighthouse materializes and the way they work to analyse relations between, for instance, state and citizens, or between solar cells and their upkeep. One might say that I have addressed and engaged in a kind of interdisciplinary collaboration that proposes the lighthouse as a shared research object or perhaps even method, which connects and discusses different actors' respective knowledge practices or 'disciplines', including those of an anthropologist interested in a new addition to the Tharangambadi skyline. This is what I mean by calling the lighthouse a shared analytical resource.

My aim here has been to show that, rather than encountering either different people's private (unrelated) lighthouses or one stable public construction perceived in different (unrelated) ways, in fact the three articulations of the lighthouse I have presented above seem to club together to perform a singular task, namely that of qualifying how life along the coast is liveable, even for all the imperfections that loom. Rather than trying to ascertain whether the beach of Tharangambadi is home to one or many lighthouses, I suggest that fluidity (of technologies such as the lighthouse) is perhaps the analytical capacity, which gets mobilized to make a practice collaborative, partial and realistic – indeed, lifelike enough for it to contradict itself; that is, to materialize inadequacies and ironies without falling apart. As I see it, this is at the heart of responsible anthropology: to situate knowledge and world-making practices in the one field that engages both anthropologist and interlocutors and to view partiality as a stance of productive openness to common grounds (cf. Haraway 1988). The kind of anthropology that I pursue is not a consultancy business, which seeks to combine and take into account different stakeholders' respective views on the usefulness or uselessness of something or other. As Marilyn Strathern has observed 'The idea of there being numerous perspectives and viewpoints "on" phenomena implies that one could ideally formulate some kind of summation of all possible views' (Strathern 2004: 108). Such a position would assume that analytical work offers a kind of overview and endpoint, which does not sit well with the kind of incompleteness of coastal life that I have taken the lighthouse to articulate when explored from within the range of its functioning. Partial solutions make up the singular shared fields that anthropologists, too, find interesting. This goes to show, I think, that neither governance nor indeed living together is a fault-finding mission, which is either successful or fails. Interesting anthropological analysis, in my opinion, is not troubleshooting. Rather, it is a generative mode of thinking and conversing, in which the gaps that come from knowing that imperfection is here to stay give us somewhere 'to extend' (ibid.: 115). Incompleteness, it seems, can work as an analytical motor.

Around the lighthouse, at least, people chipped in responsibly and realistically, calibrating features of their world including state intervention, sun, wind, darkness, waves and salt against one another. For all actors involved, partial collaborations seemed to be the central analytical unit. Together, these people and things contributed to building a jointly owned lighthouse, which was powerful because it was anything but self-sufficient and accordingly shed just the right amount of light.

References

Haraway, D. 1988. 'Situated Knowledges: The Science Question in Feminism and the Privilege of Partial Perspective', *Feminist Studies* 14(3): 575–99.
Hastrup, F. 2011. *Weathering the World: Recovery in the Wake of the Tsunami in a Tamil Fishing Village*. New York and Oxford: Berghahn Books.
Laet, M. de, and A. Mol. 2000. 'The Zimbabwe Bush Pump: Mechanics of a Fluid Technology', *Social Studies of Science* 30(2): 225–63.
Mathews, A. 2011. *Instituting Nature: Authority, Expertise, and Power in Mexican Forests*. Cambridge, MA: The MIT Press.

Mol, A. 2002. *The Body Multiple: Ontology in Medical Practice.* Durham, NC and London: Duke University Press.
Pandian, A. 2009. *Crooked Stalks: Cultivating Virtue in South India.* Durham, NC and London: Duke University Press.
Strathern, M. (1994) 2004. *Partial Connections.* Walnut Creek, CA: Altamira Press.
Subramanian, A. 2009. *Shorelines: Space and Rights in South India.* Stanford, CA: Stanford University Press.
Tsing, A. 2005. *Friction: An Ethnography of Global Connection.* Princeton, NJ: Princeton University Press.

7

Enacting Groundwaters in Tarawa, Kiribati

Searching for Facts and Articulating Concerns

Maria Louise Bønnelykke Robertson

Introduction: Closer to Water

Water has not always been an obvious concern in anthropology, not even in the Pacific. Thus, Stefan Helmreich (2011: 134) has pointed out that for Malinowski, in his classic *Argonauts of the Western Pacific,* the ocean was perceived as detached from the ethnographic pursuit. That is, water appeared as mere description. However, water has received increased attention as an object in its own right from anthropologists and locals in the field, instead of simply being something they drink, swim in, seek shelter from, gaze upon, and so on. The current ethnographic interests range from rivers (Strang 2005; Toussaint 2008) to lakes (Orlove 2002), oceans (Helmreich 2009, Schneider 2012, Maxwell 2012) and irrigation systems (Lansing 2007). This chapter will add to the rising ethnographic interest in water, even if the water I am concerned with here could only partially be engaged with and could not be seen. This water is the groundwater found in Kiribati, an atoll nation in the mid Pacific Ocean.

Various social actors were involved in trying to understand the groundwater. How much water was there? Whose water was it? And how should it be used? I shall explore how villagers and development practitioners practised the groundwater and made it tangible, and their ideas about what was happening to it. For this purpose I will draw on empirical material of how development practitioners and villagers understood the effects of pumping up groundwater for reticulated use on Kiribati's main island, Tarawa. I hope to demonstrate that even if not visible to the eye, the groundwater was not an abstract object. Rather, it was made concrete through different practices such as measurements and assessments.

As we shall see, there was no absolute agreement between the actors. Groups of experts (who were commissioned, based on their knowledge and skills, to implement water technologies) and counter-experts (the receivers, users and people otherwise affected by the water infrastructure) practised water differently, and through their practices different waters emerged that were in a relationship of convergence or divergence. In my analysis I present experts and counter-experts separately, while also examining cases of overflow (Callon, Lascoumes and Barthe 2009: 28) where science flows into everyday life, and conversely, where expert knowledge is challenged. This implies that the same 'thing', the groundwater, was enacted in different ways by the villager and the development practitioner, and these differences sometimes gave rise to controversy. Meanwhile, this analytical sensitivity towards multiplicity also enriches our understanding of the stakes involved in water management. Other scholars have worked with the multiple nature of water. Veronica Strang's analysis of the Brisbane River in Australia highlights the multiple nature of this particular water flow:

> The Brisbane River starts high in the Jimna Ranges in a network of small streams that are often no more than a thread of green in the dusty hills. By the time it reaches the Port of Brisbane, it has been captured, used and turned into many things: beef and vegetables, fruit and wine – things that can be bundled into containers and shipped to the trading partners on [whom] Australia relies. (Strang 2006: 9)

Once the river serves multiple purposes it is never 'the same'. That 'the river is never the same' might be an idea easier to agree with than 'the groundwater is never the same'. We may even hear the faint echo of Heraclitus' renowned quote, 'no man ever steps in the same river twice'. However, on the strength of my ethnographic material, I argue that the groundwater on the atoll was never the same either. The groundwater served many purposes, established alliances and created tensions.

This chapter contributes to a tradition within anthropology that studies the relationship between science, technology and indigenous knowledge in the implementation of development projects (Silitoe 1998: 226), and that explores how natural resources are managed through traditional ecological knowledge (Olson 2013: 141). To build the theoretical foundation for this analysis of multiplicity I will draw on literature concerned with multiplicity and controversy within the field of science and technology studies (STS). This approach allows me to unravel the different ways in which the groundwater is practised while giving each version the same weight – privileging neither one nor the other. Sheila Jasanoff, in a comparison of biotechnological innovation and governance in Britain, Germany and the United States, reminds us that not taking objects for granted but exploring how and by whom they are co-constructed gives insights into how such objects function in the world:

> the products of the sciences, both cognitive and material, embody beliefs not only about how the world is, but also how it ought to be ... Accordingly, to understand how social entities such as the 'state' or natural entities such as the 'gene' function in the world, one has to ask how diverse actors use and understand the concept, how it is articulated through formal and informal practices, where and by whom it is contested, and how it reasserts itself in the face of challenges to its integrity or meaning. (Jasanoff 2005: 19)

Following Jasanoff, the social entities in this chapter are the tools for understanding and the technologies for extracting the water from the ground, and the actors are the development practitioners and the villagers who use different tools and technologies and thereby enact different groundwaters. This is not a matter of applying different perspectives on the groundwater; I echo Annemarie Mol, who advocates that different practices enact different objects altogether. In other words, objects are manipulated through practice (Mol 2002: 4–5). Like the veins and the blood circulating through them in Mol's examination of how atherosclerosis is performed in practice, I look at the pipes and the water moving through them to examine how water is performed in practice, and how objects are performed into being, not in singular but in multiple ways (Mol 2002: vii). As I will show, simply investigating the biochemical structure of water, H_2O, and the contaminants it may contain – or in Mol's case the biochemical imbalances in blood – ignores the practices by which water is enacted and where water multiplies, in this case through technologies, scientific methods, or ancient stories of spirits. If water is multiple then the next question should be: 'How do we understand the relationship between waters?' This chapter will give no clear-cut answer to this question. The waters enacted and the relations between them are a matter for empirical investigation. That is, the relationships between waters are uncertain. Phrasing John Law when describing how nature itself is enacted: 'Perhaps, sometimes, they fit together neatly. Perhaps they contradict one another. Perhaps they pass each other by without touching, like ships in the night. Perhaps they are included in one another ... Perhaps they are deliberately kept apart because any encounter would be a collision' (Law 2004: 6).

Tracing Networks of Water

Where is the groundwater found on the main island Tarawa in Kiribati, and how is it managed? Hydrological and geographical studies answer some of these questions – answers that I outline below. Kiribati is an atoll nation covering a vast area in the Pacific Ocean. The country has a modest land area of 726 square kilometres spread across thirty-two islands, but is located in an Exclusive Economic Zone of 3.5 million square kilometres of ocean (ADB 2008: 12). The country comprises low-lying coral atolls with no surface water, making the population entirely dependent on the groundwater (Kuruppu 2009: 799). Kiribati, then, has more ocean than land, and it has scarce freshwater resources, suggesting the crucial role of providing clean potable water to the population. Throughout history water has caused controversies if not conflicts. More recently, the water reserves in the villages Buota and Bonriki, from where water is pumped to service the entire urban South Tarawa, have experienced longstanding vandalism from villagers assumed to live in the area; a conflict that, despite numerous efforts from the government, has not been resolved. The vandalism takes place because the villagers living on the land from where water is pumped have experienced a decrease in the yield of their crop trees growing near the pumps. The villagers believe that this decrease is a direct result of a lower water table due to pumping.

The groundwater, which is referred to in hydrological terms as a freshwater lens or a Ghyben-Herzberg Lens, is the result of numerous ecological and social interactions. Firstly, it is dependent on precipitation for recharge, and therefore climatic variability, like drought and flooding, and saltwater inundation shape the groundwater (White and Falkland 2010: 227). Secondly, the rural–urban dilemma, a term coined by policy makers and development practitioners to describe the uneven demographic distribution on the islands, is reflected in the groundwater resources. Tarawa is heavily populated, leading to overuse and contamination of the groundwater (White et al. 2008: 282, 284). Within the island of Tarawa itself there is another rural–urban divide. Almost half of the entire population of around 100,000 people live in one urban centre, South Tarawa. This demographic intensity has led to the abandonment of groundwater resources in the area due to contamination from overpopulation (ibid.: 284; White and Falkland 2008: 8). Meanwhile, South

Tarawa is the only place with a reticulated water supply in an attempt to meet the growing demand for water here. As a result, groundwater is pumped from the outlying rural areas and piped to South Tarawa. In the rural North Tarawa and on the outer islands people rely solely on well water and scattered rainwater harvesting. However, despite these differences in access to water it is a general condition across the islands, even on South Tarawa, that people must engage daily in the laborious activities of acquiring and storing water: pumping it, collecting it, keeping it in various containers, and treating it for contaminants. Hence, the groundwater cannot simply be considered as the product of precipitation; it is an emergent property entangled in many different interactions between humans and non-humans. One could say that the groundwater is an emergent property of a network of water, as I explain in greater detail below.

Across Kiribati people practised a close relationship with the groundwater resources. This was not only because villagers had to consider their need and consumption of water daily, but also because there was no national water legislation. Traditionally, and even still today, the water resources under the ground were considered to belong to the individual landowner. In political debates and national policies this tenure system made ownership of groundwater a contentious subject. Furthermore, people lived in very close physical proximity to the groundwater. On the atoll the groundwater floated on top of the surrounding salty ocean, transitioning from fresh to increasingly salty, and was usually found only one to two metres below the surface of the ground. This made access to the groundwater simple in the sense that you could just dig a shallow well, but this configuration of water also made it susceptible to pollution from different land-use activities, such as using pit toilets, keeping pigs and discarding car batteries. Hence, different versions of water, which usually demanded practices of keeping separate the salty from the fresh and the dirty from the clean, were often in contact and appear in transition zones.

On the island of Tarawa the water infrastructure was highly visible. Private wells were dug on each plot of land. Rainwater harvesting tanks were connected to public buildings, churches and a growing number of private houses – the ones that could afford them. Public water towers appeared in every village, and the pipes were now and then exposed along the shoreline where erosion had carried away the sediments that once concealed and protected them. Through these technologies, diverse actors made their relationships with and claims on water tangible. However, as with any groundwater resource, the water in the ground did not render itself visible to the eye. The groundwater had to be measured, or materialize through stories, depending on the actors enacting it. It could be through expert knowledge: models, measuring tools, or ancient local stories; through technologies: pumps, pipes and wells; or through the vegetation receiving nourishment from the groundwater: the babai (Cyrtosperma chamissonis), an important staple cultivated around the centre of the island where the groundwater lens was thickest. The groundwater may have been invisible, but it was enacted through knowledge, technologies and agriculture.

Enacting Water: Convergence and Divergence

The principle agent supporting life on atolls is the small freshwater lens on each of the islets (Spenneman 2006: 45). Among the development practitioners, the groundwater on atolls was talked about as this lens-shaped curved body of water extending under the ground, mirroring the silhouette of the island. Technically, it was explained as a system, which could be confined and modelled; a system ruled by cause and effect and linear development. In other words, the lens was subject to the laws of physics, and its processes were measurable. Development practitioners were preoccupied with understanding the capacity of the lens by calculating the rate of recharge, and the losses due to evaporation and transpiration. Through such calculations sustainable yields were estimated, and such estimations shed light on the interaction between supply and demand. In other words, calculating the sustainable yield could provide guidelines as to how much water could be extracted without doing permanent damage to the lens.

The groundwater in low coral atolls was hydrologically described as a thin lens of fresh water, which floated over seawater in unconsolidated coral sediments and consolidated limestone formations (White and Falkland 2004: 6). It was a thick brackish transition zone, which separated the fresh water from the seawater. The freshwater lens on the atoll was depicted as a much simpler system than other watersheds the development practitioners encountered through their work. The lens consisted of known inputs and outputs, and together they defined the capacity and the sustainable yield of the lens. Jake, an engineer who was contracted to refurbish the reticulation system for urban South Tarawa, explained:

> Your average annual rainfall dictates your inputs into the system, and your outputs are water consumption and losses, transpiration from plants, fresh water mixing with saline water, and losses to the ocean ... You have this

confined water budget, so you can conceptualize the water system and the water cycle easily ... Then you can work out the sustainable yield. Once the lens is developed the inputs will dissipate over time because it is in equilibrium; it is in balance. So the average annual input will equal the average annual output. But some of this output that dissipates into the ocean, we can suck up from the lens. We cannot alter the evaporation or the transpiration, but we can work out what the other losses are and take that, without disturbing this equilibrium – and that is the sustainable yield of the lens.

Jake painted a compelling picture of a scientific enactment of the lens. Through numerical models you could calculate the capacity of the lens, the extent to which it was recharged, and the losses occurring. He revealed a complex balance when he suggested that the lens existed in equilibrium, and that extracting too much water from it would disturb this equilibrium. Jake's main objective was to understand how much water could be taken from the lens without disturbing the way it worked; or in other words, to calculate the sustainable yield. Crucial in this quantification of water was the premise of the groundwater as a stable entity. The enactment of the groundwater as a stable entity in equilibrium – predictable, certain and representing an unquestionable 1:1 relationship with reality – was not a neutral enactment. It played an important role in legitimizing certain other practices, like the pumping of groundwater for reticulated use. Jake's models and calculations carefully took uncertainties into account and reached tangible results. In other words, the lens was a stable entity where input equalled output. If the groundwater fluctuated, oscillated, or in other ways appeared ambiguous, Jake risked overexploiting the water resources that nurtured so many people on the island.

When villagers spoke of the groundwater, it was not enacted as an easily demarcated system, but rather as a phenomenon emerging through numerous relations between people, spirits and ancient migration stories. One afternoon my field assistant Taati and I had lunch with Thomas and Jane, two water engineers working on Tarawa. As I explained that I was looking into the local knowledge and stories about water and change, Jane's face lit up, and she said:

> I think there are many stories like that. I remember when we took the village elders to the bush to show them where we are building the new water pump, we said to them, 'This is where it will be, and that is because this is where the water lens is thickest'. The old men nodded and said, 'Yes, we know', and then they told us a story about an ancient spirit that swam all the way from Samoa, and she arrived in the village. She was very thirsty and dehydrated, so she dug the first well with the best water, and that was where we were constructing the pump.

Taati added: 'When you go Makin Island you have to go to the beach and dig a hole. When you reach the water you drink it. If the water is fresh the spirit likes you, and you will not be harmed'. Jane remarked to Thomas with a look of mutual understanding: 'That would be where the fresh water lens discharges into the ocean. That is why you can find fresh water there'.

In the dialogue, different enactments of the groundwater appeared. It was an entity of water that had to be carefully and scientifically measured and calculated to ensure the right location for extraction. Meanwhile, water also materialized through connections to ancient spirits where the location of the extraction had always been in place, and in the right place. Between development practitioners and villagers, the groundwater was enacted in highly divergent ways. In consequence, the practices that held the groundwater in place in one enactment could not replace the other. Ancient spirits could not be included in the hydrological account, and vice versa. Yet, there were striking confluences between Jake's and Jane's confined water system, and the water enacted through Taati's and the village elders' connections to ancestors. All were concerned with the capacity of the groundwater resources, where the groundwater was thickest, and how it dissipated into the ocean. There was no single neutral version of water; rather there were different practices and styles of knowing (cf. Mol 2002: 1) and enacting multiple waters. Even if the enactments differed and almost accomplished the transformation of one physical lens into two different objects, they also hung together (cf. Mol and Law 1994: 658).

Instead of insisting on identifying some sort of common ground on what the groundwater is, we can gain insight from an analytical openness towards the convergence and divergence that characterize these different ways of enacting water. Convergence reminds us that we live in and share a common world. However, when enacting water, different actors rely on different practices in arranging the same material. The field of controversy within science and technology studies (STS) examines scientific and public controversies over scientific and technical issues (see Martin and Richards 1995; Callon, Lascoumes and Barthe 2009). Controversies can enrich our understanding of a technoscientific project. When exploring the extent of controversies as opposed to agreement, a particular space is carved out for uncertainties, and varying demands, expectations and concerns can be articulated. However, instead of controversy, as developed within STS, I instead want to stress the divergence of perceptions. My study is not only concerned with groups who disagree over technical issues, but also with materialities, and the way they were meaningfully connected in different ways – for example, how fresh water dissipated into the ocean through physical or spiritual connections. That is, I am concerned with the plasticity of the freshwater lens, which was stretched and bent every time it was enacted, yet never torn apart.

In the encounters between the villagers and the water engineers there were moments of convergence, when both engineers and villagers agreed where the groundwater was thickest, or that it was possible to find pure fresh water along the salty beach. In fact, the water enacted by the water engineers and Taati shared many qualities: it flowed and dissipated in a similar manner. In these moments of convergence the different enactments of water momentarily overlapped. However, the styles of knowing, which gave the waters their credibility and legitimacy, still differed greatly, and there was no intention of reconciliation or surrendering the particular ways of enacting water.

Articulating Concerns and Searching for Facts about Water

In *Acting in an Uncertain World,* Michel Callon, Pierre Lascoumes and Yannick Barthe (2009) examine how scientific and public controversies about nuclear waste and the potential health risks associated with living close to high voltage lines create uncertainty, but may also be productive in exploring the possible states of the world (ibid.: 32). Their overall contribution should be understood as a pursuit of a technological democracy where decision-making processes, usually left to politicians and experts, are opened up to a wider public. They suggest a radical form of democracy, not based on representational democracy, where one person represents a wider public opinion, but rather one where the public represents itself qua its interest in a certain project. In short, a public does not seek to transcend its 'situatedness', but is engaged in particular projects precisely because it has a stake in them. Callon, Lascoumes and Barthe propose hybrid forums where experts and counter-experts can debate the implications of political decisions as an experimental and almost playful approach to democracy (ibid.: 118–19). In similar vein, Bruno Latour (2005b: 23) wants to let the actors deploy the full range of controversies instead of imposing some analytical order beforehand. Latour's notion of an 'object-oriented democracy' reminds us that we are deeply connected to each other through shared matters of concern, and that each object or issue gathers around it different assemblies of relevant parties, which in turn trigger new differences and disputes (Latour 2005a: 14–15).

Even if there were no hybrid forums where experts and counter-experts could debate water management on Tarawa, we can use these notions of democracy to explore what was at stake in water management by listening to the many voices involved. If we do so, facts about water reveal themselves to be far from indisputable truths, which in turn create specific scientific and public concerns. Rather, facts appear to be produced because of specific concerns. Once listening to these many voices on water management we detect that there is not one overarching concern but several, sometimes conflicting concerns. The concern of the development practitioners was how to implement an infrastructure that could provide clean drinking water. The concern of the villagers was how to sustain their agricultural production if water was also to be extracted for potable use in the southern urban area.

In the previous section we saw how the hydrological enactment of water among development practitioners depended on demarcation and calculations. However, demarcation processes also played a role in the villagers' enactment of the groundwater – if of a different kind. To the villagers who lived on and from the groundwater it was considered a privately owned substance. The property boundaries running across the land cut through the groundwater, making it the unequivocal possession of the landowner. Through this notion of water tenure, the landowner had access to water for domestic purposes and to sustain the crop production on his land.

Veronica Strang, focusing on the River Stour in Dorset, points out that the people in her study are unaware of where their water comes from, and few actually see the environmental degradation that results from water overuse (Strang 2004: 197). As Tarawa is a small island of roughly thirty square kilometres, this was not the case here. There were only two water reserves from where water was drawn for reticulated use, so people shaped their use of water around scarcity. Furthermore, there were widespread concerns about the impact of pumping water from the ground on the agricultural productivity.

The report 'Effects of Pumping from Infiltration Galleries on Crop Health and Production in Low Coral Atolls: Groundwater Impacts' (2004) by Ian White, a hydrologist, and Tony Falkland, a water engineer from the Australian National University, framed much of the debate about the pumping of water and agricultural productivity. This piece of 'grey literature', where scientists were commissioned to carry out scientific studies so as to inform policy decision-making, examined what effect the pumping of groundwater had on crop production. The report reached an unambiguous conclusion: compared to other variations in the groundwater, pumping had little or no effect on crop production.

This report turned out to play a prominent role throughout my fieldwork. I was encouraged by various development practitioners to read it and become familiar with the results. Furthermore, some community consultants memorized the findings in the report and used them when consulting communities in an attempt to rule out the villagers' concerns about the decline in crop yield as an effect of pumping, and to legitimize their own concerns about access to clean drinking water. Latour argues that scientific facts should always be understood as an expression of a particular concern (Latour 2004: 231–32), but through this specific scientific report the development practitioners attempted to make the villagers' concerns appear as unfounded rumours, while their own concerns appeared to be supported by undisputable facts. White and Falkland described the villagers' concern in this way:

> Traditional landowners in areas used for ... freshwater reticulation systems in low atolls are concerned over the impacts of groundwater pumping on the health and productivity of traditional crops. The concerns centred on the effects of pumping, which was imagined to lower the water tables so that Babwai were unproductive or coconut yields were reduced. (White and Falkland 2004: 6)

The villagers living in the vicinity of the reserves were much more dependent on agricultural production in their daily lives than the villagers living in the urban areas. Therefore, when they discussed their concerns about how the pumping affected the agricultural production, the land and its productivity appeared more important to them than clean drinking water. Maria, a water engineer working for the government, said about her early career in Kiribati:

> There are some [villagers] who are angry about the water reserve. When I was new in the country, in this job, I went to the water reserve, and this man came out and said, 'Are you an Australian?' I said yes. And he replied: 'All you Australians care about is the water, that is all you care about. You don't care about the land, you just care about the water'.

Similarly, while travelling to rural North Tarawa on an outrigger canoe, I spoke to one of the passengers next to me who recognized me from earlier trips to there with the government's water team. We talked about the construction of new pumps in the rural north. Initially, he spoke in positive terms about the project, but as the conversation progressed, he unveiled a more critical perspective: 'What about our forests? We earn our money from cutting copra,[1] but if we take the water from the bush then where will the plants get their water from? Yes, it is good that we can drink, but what will happen to how we earn a living?'

It seemed that every time a water infrastructure project was proposed it immediately led to concerns about the agricultural productivity. Therefore, providing clean drinking water using scientifically robust and sustainable methods was not a project everyone supported. More important to the villagers was *how* and *what* the groundwater could sustain if it remained under the ground, not to *whom* and *where* it could be transported as a service if extracted.

Copra, mentioned in the quote above, was not the only crop that was brought up by the villagers. Throughout history on these islands the giant swamp taro or te babai (cyrtosperma chamissonis) has been an important staple. It was both ritual food, and, in times of drought, it was carefully dried and prepared to serve as a famine food (Campbell 2006: 19). Today, with increased urbanization and reliance on imported foods, the babai has become a luxury in many areas and is reserved almost exclusively for ceremonial purposes (Thaman 1990: 12). The babai is planted straight into the surface of the groundwater. Little baskets of Pandanus (Pandanus tectorius) leaves are woven and placed around each babai to keep added organic material in place close to the root (Neemia and Thaman 1993: 292). This agricultural practice and the pits themselves are ancient. Many people have no recollection, or only mythical stories, about their origin (Catala 1957: 68). In the pit, each row of babai is planted for a specific purpose: 'first row for weddings, second row for Maneaba gatherings, third row for newborn baby ceremonies' (Baiteke 1994: 7). It was not only the villagers but also the development practitioners who were concerned about the babai, but for very different reasons, as Jake, a water engineer, explained:

> If you have babai and you can bring it to the Maneaba [public meeting house], it is seen as an important part of the village system. It goes beyond just eating it. So there have been a lot of negotiations. How can we still have this infrastructure, and a better water supply, without impacting too much on the agriculture? We have tried to use locations with less [sic] babai pits, but it is difficult because you dig a babai pit where the freshwater lens is thickest, which is generally at the centre of the island, and that is also the best place to put the pump.

Jake pointed out a dilemma. At the centre of the island pumping was most sustainable because here the groundwater lens was thickest. This was also where one found the ancient babai pits, because the thick freshwater lens ensured enough water to nourish the babai. The agricultural practices depended on excavating the topsoil, thereby exposing the surface of the groundwater to sunlight. Furthermore, the organic materials added to fertilize the babai could contaminate the water and could eventually damage the whole lens. To the villagers cultivating, sharing and consuming the babai constituted the community. I recall during a visit to an outer island, Marakei, an old man named Peter explained that it was impossible for him to return to Tarawa without bringing the babai root from his extended family's land. Before leaving Marakei he carefully wrapped a big root, weighing between seven and ten kilos, in an old rice bag, brought it to the small domestic airport, and checked it in. Even if the cultivation of babai exposed the groundwater to contamination, this crop was known as the one staple that had nourished families on these islands since time immemorial. The development practitioners, on the other hand, were driven by concerns over the impact of this agricultural practice on the quality of the drinking water. Kiribati has one of the highest infant mortality rates in the Pacific region. The cause, the development practitioners pointed out, was the poor access to clean water, making diarrhoea the second highest cause of death among children under five (UNESCO 2009: 7, 10). The development practitioners were mindful of the obvious social entanglements of the babai cultivation, as Jake showed in the quote above, but they were also constantly questioning whether this practice should be abandoned for the sake of the quality of the groundwater. Clean water could lower the number of lives lost every year due to contaminated water.

Overflows of Water: Experts and Counter-Experts

Both development practitioners and villagers were concerned with and cared for the water, but each in their own way. White and Falkland's scientific study in 'Effects of Pumping' (2004) produced facts to support specific concerns and rule out others. They concluded that the effect of extraction of water was minimal and should not be harmful to agricultural production. Their findings suggested that the natural fluctuations occurring in the lens were much more dramatic than the fluctuations caused by pumping:

> Simple water balance estimates before and after pumping ... suggest that pumping may have lowered the water table by up to 140 mm. Measurements reveal that intense rainfalls cause rapid rise in groundwater by up to 650 mm. The maximum amplitude of diurnal change in the watertable due to tidal forcing was 300 mm, and groundwater could fall by up to 440 mm in prolonged droughts ... These measurements and calculations demonstrate that drawdown due to pumping from infiltration galleries is at least in an order of magnitude smaller than that caused by natural factors such as the tidal fluctuations, intense rainfall or prolonged droughts. (White and Falkland 2004: 4)

In the report the uncertainties of the effects of pumping were put to rest through what resembled a SWOT (strengths, weaknesses, opportunities and threats) analysis, which is often used for decision making in development work. White and Falkland could not rule out any effect whatsoever, but they suggested that, even with no human interference, natural variation was more significant than the variation caused by pumping. In other words, the weaknesses and threats were not considered to outweigh the strengths and opportunities of pumping water. This legitimized the need to continue the work of providing clean drinking water, and was thought to calm the villagers' concerns.

The earlier hydrological enactment of the groundwater where sustainable yields were identified by conceptualizing the groundwater as a confined system in equilibrium with known inputs and outputs was replaced in White and Falkland's study by a highly dynamic process existing in interaction with tides, droughts and precipitation. White and Falkland described the groundwater as highly fluctuating, and in states far from equilibrium. The groundwater existed, in their account, with some degree of uncertainty. It was dynamic and alive. The development practitioners' enactment of the groundwater as a stable entity *and* in fluctuation seemed to aim less at establishing singular coherent facts than at facts that could support the continued pumping of groundwater. Sometimes a strong, durable enactment required loose networks that could be reconfigured when needed. There was no stable conclusion about what the groundwater was, yet controversies were still absent. Hence, the incontestable truth of the scientific facts faded away, and instead the political nature of the numbers, the models and the calculations was revealed. The facts legitimized the need to act on one specific concern through technological practice: the pumping of drinking water.

Callon, Lascoumes and Barthe introduce the notion of overflow, which is, needless to say, fitting when dealing with issues of water. But more specifically overflow captures the way science flows over into everyday life, which in turn challenges specialist knowledge. In these moments of overflow, controversies may appear that 'help to reveal events that were initially isolated and difficult to see, because they bring forward groups that consider themselves involved by the overflows that they help to identify' (Callon, Lascoumes and Barthe 2009: 28). However, overflows and controversies can be productive as they expose 'different dimensions of what is at stake in a project' (ibid.: 29–30). Until now, the villagers' and the development practitioners' enactment of the groundwater have been explored separately. Below I present a case of overflow in which new and unexpected dimensions of a water infrastructure project were revealed once White and Falkland's scientific findings had been used strategically among the villagers. This discussion ties into questions about deliberation and participation in the public sphere, influenced by John Dewey's classic work *The Public and its Problems* (1927), in which Dewey develops his ideas of democracy.

According to Dewey, and also later pointed out by Callon, Lascoumes and Barthe, democracy should not be based primarily in parliament where a select few represent the larger public, but rather should be what might be called 'participatory democracy', where distinct publics emerge around a specific concern. It is pivotal to Dewey's theory that a public emerges only once people perceive indirect consequences as consequences of some activity, *and* when they take collective action to stop the cause of these consequences. Only then has a public found itself. That is, 'inclusion is by way of effects, not by inherent nature or right' (Dewey 1927: 72). Along similar lines Callon and Rabeharisoa (2008: 232), exploring how relations are shaped between technoscience, politics and economic markets, similarly point out that group identity is an achievement rather than a starting point. Villagers and development practitioners should likewise be considered as groups of publics brought together as a response to particular harmful indirect consequences – in this case, the simultaneous lack and provision of clean drinking water to the islanders on Tarawa.

I was invited along to listen in to an interview by a community consultant, Alice, who worked on a rural water project funded by the World Bank. The interview took place in one of the two hospitals on Tarawa because the interviewee was a doctor, and it related to a technology called a water infiltration gallery. Most wells fitted with electric pumps extracted water deeply from one point, thereby increasing the risk of penetrating the freshwater lens and mixing it with the surrounding saline water. The infiltration gallery was designed for atoll islands and, according to the development practitioners, it sustainably pumps water from the ground by skimming water horizontally from the top of the lens as opposed to pumping vertically and deeply. This technology was to be constructed in the northern rural village of Taborio in the grounds of a Catholic school, where the pumps would supply the schoolchildren with clean drinking water. Before the interview took place, rumours about how the pumps affect the productivity of crops were widely debated. Villagers who lived close to existing infiltration galleries blamed them for the loss of agricultural productivity. Development practitioners argued that the loss of productivity was simply a result of a restriction on how close to the pumps new crops and trees could be planted. The reduction in agricultural productivity, from their point of view, was just caused by aging crops with decreasing yields.

This interview was part of a larger baseline data collection in which the government documented the condition of the land around the proposed pumps in order to identify the long-term effects of pumping on crop production and, in turn, the villagers' livelihoods. Alice collected data from the landowners of the Catholic school and from landowners with land bordering the Catholic school. Socioeconomic data was collected about the households, their livelihoods and the crops they cultivated. Furthermore, the salinity of the groundwater was measured. Pictures were taken from the construction site, from the land bordering the Catholic school, and from the next islet to the north. This data was given to the landowners involved and to the government.

Alice and I were waiting in a small clinic, brightly lit by fluorescent light; a noisy air-conditioning system on the wall made the room feel chilly. The doctor, Tioti, entered and took a seat behind his desk. Alice and I sat beside each other on an examination bed across from the desk, our feet dangling above the floor. Alice explained the purpose of the interview, and about the rumours surrounding the pumps. She referred to White and Falkland's study, underlining that the natural fluctuations of the groundwater were more dramatic than the fluctuations caused by pumping. She explained:

> There was a case study in 2003 that suggests that the effects of the water infiltration gallery should be minimal. In the study the water lens was lowered by around 14 cm because of the pumping. The same study showed that the tidal changes could affect the level of the water lens by up to 30 cm, and that during droughts the water lens can fall by up to 44 cm. So when you have that information you can see that the infiltration gallery should have minimal effect on the water on your land. But this interview is to give safety to you, to the school and to the government…

Tioti interrupted her: 'So are you trying to convince me to use my land as a water reserve?' The government had declared land near the water pumps for reticulation water reserves, thereby restricting landowners' land use activities, especially agricultural production. To this question Alice replied: 'No, not at all! All we want to do is to collect data about your land, and give it to you, to the school and the government, so that in the future you all have the same data. You can use the data to look at how the land has been affected'.

Despite Alice's starting point that the groundwater was dynamic, uncertain and oscillating, she attempted to fix the groundwater through the collection of baseline data, which captured a specific variation of the groundwater. Styles of knowing were flowing and moving, and it seems that the findings of the report 'Effects of Pumping' and the baseline data that Alice had collected served two different purposes. The report established the groundwater as a highly fluctuating and dynamic entity. The baseline data attempted to pin down the groundwater, and give it a particular consistency and certainty, despite its dynamic nature. The baseline data was to be handed over to all the actors who had a stake in the project in an effort to create convergence and limit future controversies.

As the interview continued, Alice once more explained that some people were concerned that drawing water from the infiltration galleries affected the productivity of their crops, and that was the reason for collecting this data. Tioti commented: 'Everybody knows that if the vegetation dies on the land it is because of climate change. But if you take the water out of the ground of course it will have an effect'. Alice tried to be more specific: 'According to our calculations the freshwater lens on your land will only be lowered by two centimetres'. Tioti promptly replied with a mocking smile on his face: 'Two centimetres, you say that, but how can you know this? It is under the ground no one can know what is going on there'.

The project had been opened up to allow in different actors, such as Tioti, who it was thought could contribute to making the project successful by aligning the different parties who had a stake in the project. However, far from giving the project his support, Tioti was challenging it by asserting that if water was pumped from the ground then of course there would be less water available. Along with the openness of including Tioti in the first place, new matters of concern were raised, and expert knowledge, that the lens will only be lowered by two centimetres, was questioned. It was not only Alice who suggested, backed up by White and Falkland's scientific study, that the groundwater was slippery and ambiguous, so did Tioti. His knowledge also flowed and moved when he insisted that a simple manoeuvre, such as pumping water, could produce complex responses, and that climate change, and other unforeseen events, simultaneously affected the groundwater. In contrast, the two centimetres, which was a number extracted from the scientific study, seemed a perfectly unambiguous finding. Tioti put an end to the interview by demanding an equally unambiguous figure in compensation for the water extracted from his land:

> It will take years for [the groundwater to be damaged by the pumps]; I will be long gone. It will be my children who will suffer the consequences, and people will talk about me. Tell me, how will you compensate me? You are taking the water from my land, and I want compensation! You will give me peanuts! I want a contract that says that if my land is affected I want one million dollars! But if you tell me it is climate change, then what will I get? Nothing.

In an impressive way, Tioti articulated his concerns about the implications of a political decision to provide schoolchildren in rural North Tarawa with clean drinking water – the same children at risk of dying from waterborne disease. He tried in creative ways to challenge the knowledge produced in the water project, and suggested the many ways in which the development practitioners did not own a singular enactment of the groundwater. With his final comment he demonstrated that there was no space for convergence. He rejected the project, and his exaggerated proposal of requiring one million dollars in return for his water suggested that he did not expect to come to any agreement about compensation. Even if White and Falkland's scientific study was so intended, it did not inform Tioti's decision. He was aware that in the future the groundwater could be re-enacted as damaged by climate change, which is out of the government's hands and cannot be linked to pumping, and therefore is not a legitimate foundation for compensation.

In the end, the water infiltration gallery was constructed, and whether Tioti received any compensation for his water is beyond my knowledge. Even if the consultation process was an attempt to allow the public to voice their concerns and include them in political decisions it does not necessarily alter power relations. Their overall contribution should be understood as a pursuit of a technological democracy, where decision-making processes, usually left to politicians and experts, are opened up to a wider public. The encounter between Alice and Tioti shows that even if different concerns are successfully articulated it may not always affect the outcome. As Mike Michael reminds us in a discussion of public engagement with science, just as the encounter between Alice and Tioti gave voice to a public, the encounter was also part of a production of a particular political subject (Michael 2012: 531). It shows that, even in cases of overflow, the articulation of concerns does not necessarily alter outcomes. Even if publics articulate and deliberate their concerns, inequality and power differences are not simply wiped out.

Concluding Remarks: Stretching the Lens through Flowing Styles of Knowing

This chapter has made it clear that the question 'what is the groundwater on Tarawa?' allows no straightforward answer. Rather, when scrutinizing the way water is enacted, the answer continues to emerge through the empirical examination, and it depends on whom you ask and what concerns that person has about the groundwater. Not only have multiple waters been described throughout this chapter, but they have also turned out to be fractional; they both contradict and complement each other, and they are sometimes mutually inclusive (cf. Law 2004: 6). Styles of knowing about water are flowing and moving. In the encounter between Tioti and Alice, there was no agreement on what water was, what was happening to it, or what purpose it should serve. And the water became obviously partial once the development practitioners enacted it as both a stable and a fluctuating entity in order to legitimize the pumping. The partiality did not make the enactment any less durable; it still supported the pumping of groundwater.

Groups of actors were formed around specific concerns with water. When examining the groundwater through the perspective of convergence and divergence, I have shown that there was no enduring agreement about how much groundwater there was, who it belonged to or how it should be used. Or rather, there were multiple agreements. The otherwise invisible groundwater appeared in different ways, depending on the concern that gave it shape. When the development practitioners identified the sustainable yield of the groundwater it was a predictable and demarcated entity with known inputs and outputs. When examining whether pumping affected the agricultural production, the groundwater was an unpredictable phenomenon emerging in interaction with other ecological interactions. An analytical sensitivity towards both convergence and divergence has enriched the understanding of what is at stake in water resource management on Tarawa. Enactments of water in Kiribati have centred on groundwater as a system in equilibrium, as a process unfolding in interaction with numerous ecological interactions, as a substance sustaining agricultural and social practices, and as a resource sustaining human bodies. Exploring the many ways the groundwater is practised has opened up new avenues for thinking about what the groundwater *can* be, and it has shown that enacted practices multiply and cannot be fully known.

Notes

1. Copra is the dried meat of the coconut, the leading export of Kiribati.

References

ADB. 2008. 'Kiribati Social and Economic Report: Managing Development Risk'. Philippines: Asian Development Bank.
Baiteke, A. 1994. 'Traditional Agriculture in Kiribati', in J. Morrison, P. Geraghty and L. Crowl (eds), *Science of Pacific Island People: Land Use and Agriculture*. Suva: Institute of Pacific Studies.

Callon, M., P. Lascoumes and Y. Barthe. 2009. *Hybrid Forums in Acting in an Uncertain World: An Essay on Technical Democracy.* Cambridge, MA and London: The MIT Press.

Callon, M., and V. Rabeharisoa. 2008. 'The Growing Engagement of Emergent Concerned Groups in Political and Economic Life: Lessons from the French Association of Neuromuscular Disease Patients', *Science, Technology, and Human Values* 33(2): 230–61.

Campbell, J.R. 2006. 'Traditional Disaster Reduction in Pacific Island Communities'. GNS Science Report 2006/38.

Catala, R.L.A. 1957. 'Report on the Gilbert Islands: Some Aspects of Human Ecology', *Atoll Research Bulletin* 59.

Dewey, J. 1927. *The Public and its Problems.* 1st edition. New York: Henry Holt and Company.

Helmreich, S. 2009. *Alien Ocean: Anthropological Voyages in Microbial Seas.* Berkeley and Los Angeles: University of California Press.

———. 2011. 'Nature/Culture/Seawater', *American Anthropologist* 113(1): 132–44.

Jasanoff, S. 2005. *Design on Nature: Science and Democracy in Europe and the United States.* Princeton, NJ: Princeton University Press.

Kuruppu, N. 2009. 'Adapting Water Resources to Climate Change in Kiribati: The Importance of Cultural Values and Meanings', *Environmental Science and Policy* 12: 799–809.

Lansing, S.J. 2007. *On Priests and Programmers: Technologies of Power in the Engineered Landscape of Bali.* Princeton, NJ: Princeton University Press.

Latour, B. 2004. 'Why Has Critique Run Out of Steam? From Matters of Fact to Matters of Concern', *Critical Inquiry* 30: 225–48.

———. 2005a. 'From Realpolitik to Dingpolitik – or How to Make Things Public', in B. Latour and P. Weibel (eds), *Making Things Public: Atmospheres of Democracy.* Cambridge, MA and London: The MIT Press.

———. 2005b. *Reassembling the Social: An Introduction to Actor-Network-Theory.* Oxford: Oxford University Press.

Law, J. 2004. *Enacting Naturecultures: A Note From STS.* Lancaster, UK: Centre for Science Studies, Lancaster University (http://www.comp.lancs.ac.uk/sociology/papers/law-enacting-naturecultures.pdf).

Martin, B., and E. Richards. 1995. 'Scientific Knowledge, Controversy, and Public Decision-Making', in S. Jasanoff et al. (eds), *Handbook of Science and Technology Studies.* Newbury Park, CA: Sage.

Maxwell, I. 2012. 'Seas as Places: Towards a Maritime Choreography', *Shima: The International Journal of Research into Island Cultures* 6(1): 22–24.

Michael, M. 2012. '"What Are We Busy Doing?": Engaging the Idiot', *Science, Technology and Human Value* 37(5): 528–54.

Mol, A. 2002. *The Body Multiple: Ontology in Medical Practice.* Durham: Duke University Press.

Mol, A., and J. Law. 1994. 'Regions, Networks and Fluids: Anemia and Social Topology', *Social Studies of Science* 24(4): 641–71.

Neemia, U., and R. Thaman. 1993. 'The Environment and Sustainable Development', in H. van Trease (ed.), *Atoll Politics: The Republic of Kiribati*. Suva: Institute of Pacific Studies.

Olson, E.A. 2013. 'Anthropology and Traditional Ecological Knowledge: A Summary of Quantitative Approaches to Traditional Knowledge, Market Participation, and Conservation', *Culture, Agriculture, Food and Environment* 35(2): 140–51.

Orlove, B. 2002. *Lines in the Water: Nature and Culture at Lake Titicaca*. Los Angeles and London: University of California Press.

Schneider, K. 2012. *Saltwater Sociality: A Melanesian Island Ethnography*. New York and Oxford: Berghahn Books.

Silitoe, P. 1998. 'The Development of Indigenous Knowledge: A New Applied Anthropology', *Current Anthropology* 39(2): 223–52.

Spenneman, D. 2006. 'Freshwater Lens, Settlement Patterns, Resource Use and Connectivity in the Marshall Islands', *Transforming Cultures eJournal* 1(2): 44–63.

Strang, V. 2004. *The Meaning of Water*. Oxford: Berg.

———. 2005. 'Common Senses: Water, Sensory Experience and the Generation of Meaning', *Journal of Material Culture* 10(1): 92–120.

———. 2006. 'Turning Water into Wine, Beef and Vegetables: Material Transformations along the Brisbane River', *Transforming Cultures eJournal* 1(2): 9–19.

Thaman, R.R. 1990. 'Kiribati Agroforestry: Trees, People and the Atoll Environment', *Atoll Research Bulletin* 333: 1–29.

Toussaint, S. 2008. 'Kimberly Friction: Complex Attachments to Water-Places in Northern Australia', *Oceania* 78(1): 46–61.

UNESCO. 2009. 'Country Programming Document. Kiribati 2008–2012'. Published by the UNESCO Apia Office.

White, I., and T. Falkland. 2004. 'Effects of Pumping from Infiltration Galleries on Crop Health and Production in Low Coral Islands: Groundwater Impacts'. Australia National University and Ecowise Environmental.

———. 2008. 'Report on the Protection and Management of Water Reserves, South Tarawa. Preparation of Water Master Plan for Tarawa'. Kiribati Adaptation Project Implementation Phase II.

———. 2010. Management of Freshwater Lenses on Small Pacific Islands', *Hydrogeological Journal* 18: 227–46.

White, I., et al. 2008. 'Safe Water for People in Low, Small Island Pacific Nations: The Rural–Urban Dilemma', *Development* 51: 282–87.

8

Mapping Urban Waters

Grounds and Figures on an Ethnographic Water Path

Astrid Oberborbeck Andersen

In early March 2011, one month after I arrived in Arequipa to explore how water scarcity is produced and acted on by different actors in an urban context, and how water management and governance take new forms (discursively and materially) in the light of climate change, a particular event took place in the city: the carnival.

In Arequipa, as throughout Peru, the days before the Catholic Lent are marked with a public and popular celebration where water plays a central role. The festivities around *carnavales* are characterized by a playful practice with water that is not experienced at other times of the year; water suddenly stands out as a festive element.

In the days before and during the carnival, children and youths were throwing water balloons at each other on the streets and in public squares; when walking in the street I was told to continuously watch out for buckets being emptied from above or from around the corner. The carnival itself was celebrated with a '*Corso de las flores*', a colourful parade where public institutions, private companies, schools, cultural associations, and other groupings dressed up in traditional costumes or as crazy devils, and passed through the streets, playing music, singing and dancing. The parading crowd was cheerful and festive – the crazy devils were armed with long whips, foam or coloured powder, and would periodically invite spectators to dance along, and finally smear them with stuff, or whip their feet. The spectators, standing on the pavement or on the roofs of buildings, were armed with buckets and water balloons, and when the parading crowd was passing, the spectators would greet them by launching water at them. At times, the crowd would yell '*Agua, Agua!*' – water, water – and they would, from either a bucket, a balloon or a water pistol receive a soaking from the precious fluid. Some of the participating groups were dancing a folkloric 'water dance' from the Andean region of Huancayo. The dancers, men and women, were carrying artisanal water pipes made of bamboo, clay jars and buckets, and simulating an irrigation infrastructure while moving along choreographed rhythms and formations to the melody of a cheerful *huayno*. In the parade, water was enacted as a festive element to celebrate and play with, and in the dances water was enacted as a life-giving element linked to a particular Andean cosmology incorporating water as a sacred and central matter. At the same time, during the carnival days, the municipal company for drinking water and sanitation, SEDAPAR, would send out communications to the public of Arequipa, through newspapers, television and radio, recommending 'the rational use of water, in order to avoid affecting the distribution of drinking water to parts of town that suffer from restricted service'. Also, by distributing the slogan '*gota a gota el agua se agota*' [drop by drop, the water is used up], the water company was aiming, through the festive play, to sensitize the general public to be more conscious of the value of water. During the carnival, multiple actors engaged in defining and valuing water in differing ways – through discourse, practices or material engagement. In other words, water was known and done differently by different actors.

I attended the carnival parades and dance competitions and wondered how to understand the relations, interconnections and disconnections between the stated scarcity and enacted abundance of water that were played out by different actors during the carnival. How did buckets, taps, water balloons, costumes, whips and play work together to transform water from being scarce to being abundant? How did institutions, expertise, slogans and discourses work to make it scarce again? How could I understand the different ways of knowing and doing water at play during carnival? And how could I possibly localize sites and modes of production of these different characteristics related to water? During my year of fieldwork, a methodological starting point for exploring these questions was to experiment with an ethnographic form of mapping water in Arequipa.

The aim of this chapter is to answer the questions that sprang out of the carnival in Arequipa. By exploring how water becomes both scarce and abundant in the city of Arequipa I ask how we as ethnographers can respond to such a paradox, and I suggest that one way of proceeding is by experimenting with mapping as an ethnographic practice and as a strategy for studying social aspects of urban waters.

In the first part of the chapter, after a brief discussion of maps in anthropology, I describe how I used mapping as a methodological starting point for studying urban waters in the city of Arequipa. An ethnography of fluid environments requires analytical concepts as well as methodological approaches that capture not only cultural and social life around water, but place water and its materiality centrally in the analysis. I thus looked to mapping as a practice that systematically follows connections, links activities and events, and hence unpacks the material, discursive and practical relations and configurations in which water is produced in a particular social situation. What emerges when mapping urban waters, I suggest, is a water ethnography that shows a complex interplay of social, material and political life around water in urban ecologies.

In the second part of the chapter, I narrate the experience of assembling a map, on the basis of other maps, that brought together the multiple layers of water and its infrastructure in Arequipa in one graphic representation. Each layer of the map makes visible a particular configuration of relations in the urban waterscape, and as such each can be said to carve out and project a particular perspective onto a territory, as well as onto the actor who produced the map: showing some elements and leaving others invisible. Comparing different cartographic maps relating to the same territory can be an important contribution to the analysis of human–environmental relations.

In the final part of the chapter, I use these findings to discuss the potentials and implications of mapping as an ethnographic practice that highlights the intertwinement of method and analytical perspective by seeing these as mutually constitutive elements in an iterative process of knowledge making. I ask what mapping can do in the generation of ethnography in an urban 'waterworld', and how the experiment of mapping can add to a discussion of the relation between method and analysis in the process of generating knowledge about human–environmental relations. Before engaging with the urban waters in Arequipa in this manner, let me review some literature on the use of maps and mapping in anthropology and other disciplines engaging with ethnography as method.

Maps and Anthropology

> A map represents the world, or portions of it, as a set of features divided into a small number of recurring types (rivers, towns, national borders, etc., each indicated by a conventional symbol) that are related to one another by contiguity and distance. (Orlove 1993: 29)

The use of maps as part of scientific methods to explore social and environmental worlds is not new. In anthropology, maps of territories and cartographic practices are elements that recurrently appear in accounts of environmental issues and in studies of spatiality. In such literature, maps have been included into ethnographical analysis in various ways.

One focus of study is the use and effect of maps in situations where several kinds of knowledge coexist. Frequently, the ethnographic and analytical objects of such studies are power relations, conflicts and colliding knowledge and value systems related to a territory and its natural resources, where indigenous and nation-state ways of representing and managing a territory are analysed as highly diverging. This divergence, then, is often articulated in the production and use of maps, which are included as parts of the ethnographic analysis (Anderson [1983] 1991; Orlove 1993; Møhl 2012). Also focusing on the epistemological aspect of maps, David Turnbull examines maps and cartographic practice, through a historical and ethnographic perspective. In his book *Maps are Territories, Science is an Atlas*, the making of and work of maps is accounted for as a kind of scientific or managerial practice embedded in a specific Western ontology and epistemology (Turnbull [1989] 1993). As Turnbull states, the spatiality expressed in maps, with square grids, is a particular European spatiality; a way of perceiving, ordering and practising space, which contrasts to other ways of space making and representation. Another aspect discussed through maps is the relation between territory and representation, as well as between perception, experience, movement and knowing a landscape (de Certeau 1984; Ingold 2007).

Approaches within science and technology studies (STS) elaborate critical methods for using maps or mapping to examine knowledge controversies (Chen 2003; Whatmore 2009). Likewise, the early Chicago school and newer approaches of situational analysis have worked with strategies of mapping for the analysis of social situations and worlds (Clarke 2005: 37–41). Both STS and the new situational analysis emphasize the inclusion of non-humans in the spatial and relational analysis of the worlds being studied. There are thus various ways in which maps have been included in the analytical and theoretical work of social sciences and anthropology. The approaches mentioned here are mainly of critical character, emphasizing the unequal power relations between the ones making and using the map and the ones being mapped. As Perle Møhl states when writing about the history and consequences of cartographic practices in French Guiana, 'Maps are powerful both as representations of the world and as agents in the world' (Møhl 2012: 74).

When it comes to methodological tools for examining social worlds, mapping has been proposed to be productive to ethnography in a variety of ways (Clarke 2005; Strang 2010). Veronica Strang broadens the idea of mapping to entail other practices than strictly two-dimensional cartographic practice; she outlines 'cultural mapping' as an ethnographic method that 'explores people's historical and contemporary relationships with local environments' (Strang 2010: 132). Under the term 'cultural mapping' Strang includes a variety of methodological tools: phenomenological walkabouts, video, formal and informal interviews, sketches, as well as digital methods such as GIS tracking (ibid.: 139, 141). By using these tools in combination, including a broad range of data in the ethnographic analysis, such as topographic information, local histories, ecological knowledge, economic practices, and aspects of rights and ownership (ibid.: 133), what is obtained is 'an in-depth, holistic view of people's engagements with the places that they inhabit, and to illuminate particular cultural and ethno-historical landscapes' (ibid.).

In this chapter, I borrow the critical gaze and the focus on non-human objects as a part of the practice of mapping from STS and new approaches within situational analysis; additionally, I draw on Strang's broadened notion of mapping, which includes histories from an experience near perspective. Obviously, mapping as an *ethnographic* tool must be distinct from a cartographic or geographical form of mapping. Although I show how maps can be used as ethnographic material, when working with maps ethnographically, it is crucial to go beyond the idea of maps as objective representations of certain features within a limited territory, and examine maps as objects embedded in history and politics (Orlove 1993: 29). Maps both represent and project onto the world (Anderson 1991; Møhl 2012). This resonates with arguments raised in human geography about cartography being transitory and processual rather than representational, which implies that maps are contingent and actively *mapping* (Kitchin and Dodge 2007). This means that neither maps nor mapping can ever be neutral. Maps do something to the world they are made to represent or relate to, and mapping can be seen as a particular practice that can generate ethnography about a particular problem, in this case the simultaneous production of water as scarce and abundant in Arequipa.

To use mapping and maps as part of an analytical process rather than giving them the status of a finished product, I suggest, makes them interesting in more than one sense. Since mapping is a practice through which certain things in the world are carved out and made visible in a specific way, while other are left invisible, it follows that, inherently, mapping entails interconnected elements of method and analysis. In that sense maps enact a certain figure that is carved out and holds a specific perspective (Brichet and Hastrup 2011: 120). Reading a map, then, or mapping elements in a given context, entails analytical work – making the map unfold something in the world on the one hand, and telling something about the map maker on the other. This relates to the process in which objects of ethnographic analysis become visible as entities of interest – what Nathalia Brichet and Frida Hastrup call 'figuring' of the world (ibid.). In order to elaborate my argument about maps and mapping as having both methodological and analytical potential, I use the concepts of figure and ground (Strathern 2002; Brichet and Hastrup 2011) to argue that the methodological steps of mapping make up a process of carving out analytical figures for further study. The methodological outset of mapping is thus inherently analytical, and vice versa. It seems obvious, then, that the relation between map and territory is a complicated one, and never just one-to-one (de Certeau 1984; Turnbull 1989; Møhl 2012).

The above discussion paves the way for asking what maps and mapping can do for us when understanding how water is produced as both scarce and abundant in Arequipa in particular, and when studying waterworlds in an urban context generally.

Mapping Urban Waters

Arequipa is the second largest city in Peru, located at 2,400 metres above sea level, on the northern limit of the Atacama desert, between the Pacific coast and the Andean highlands. The urban topography in Arequipa is characterized by verticality, with three volcanoes embracing the city, pointing towards the high Andean ridge, and generating a particular hydrology for life in the city. Without these volcanoes, Arequipa would be desert, like its surroundings. The vertical topography gives direction to natural water flows, and verticality shapes access to water as well as water technology. Also, social life influences the flow and quality of water. Agriculture, industry, generation of hydropower, tourism, mining and a growing urban population use the same water; in different ways these users alter the quality and characteristics of water before returning it to the river.

The rainy season spans from December to March or April, and the rest of the year is sunny, warm and dry, which makes it pivotal to have the capacity to store vast volumes of water. When arriving to Arequipa, you soon notice that the urban landscape of industry, roads, houses and commerce is regularly mixed with cultivated fields, which stand as green contrasts to the dry and brown slopes of the mountains and volcanoes with no vegetation. There are as many canals as roads; reservoirs and ponds frequently meet the eye, and mobile water tanks circulate all day to provide the neighbourhoods that are not connected to the potable water system with water. All these features appear as material evidence of the work and resources it takes to manage water; it does not take long to notice what difference irrigation and water make in this landscape. If water is not stored, given direction and controlled, little life can be sustained. Furthermore, people in Arequipa are among the 90 per cent of the Peruvian population living on the arid Pacific slopes of the Andean ridge. This population has traditionally been dependent on run-off from melting Andean glaciers. During recent decades, due to global warming, these glaciers have been melting rapidly, generating an extra level of concern about future water availability in Peru (Oré et al. 2009: 56; Mark et al. 2010).

Water reaches the city via the Chili River and originates from the same sources, hundreds of kilometres away, at over 4,000 metres altitude. Rainwater is captured in glaciers or swampy areas in the highlands, and is stored in one grand hydraulic system: five dams, rivers and canal connections in the highlands, from where it is regulated and released to reach its functional destinations in the city. This infrastructure makes the Quilca-Chili watershed one of Peru's most 'intervened'; without the dams there would not be enough water to feed current and growing levels of human activities in Arequipa. In this context of changing water demands and shifting conditions of availability, there is frequent debate among engineers, politicians and in media about whether or not water is scarce.

In order to explore the relations of and around water in Arequipa, and try to untangle the mystery of how water becomes both scarce and abundant, I developed a method of 'water mapping'. One intention of this mapping was to get to know the city with water as a starting point. In other words, to follow the water and discover flows, connections, disconnections and obstructions, materiality of and around water, as well as problematic places and issues; take a step back from presuppositions and let the water lead to the matters of concern (Latour 2004) and of relevance for the people inhabiting Arequipa.

Starting to Walk: Modes and Dimensions of Mapping

With the aim of becoming familiar with the locations and directions of flows of water, I started doing a physical mapping, consisting of identifying bodies of water, flows and infrastructure. Where does water come from? How is water given direction and by whom or what? These questions guided my initial weeks of fieldwork in the city. I walked along the river, the canals for irrigation, and the empty *torrenteras* – ravines for rainwater – identifying different uses of water as well as types of infrastructure, focusing on the materiality and physical characteristics of and around water: what kind of materials were used to build canals, pipes and valves? How many treatment plants for potable water and wastewater were functioning in the city, and where were these located? Along the way I talked to people, asking questions about how water reaches the city, and what it is used for. I watched and listened to water and the people around it.

This physical mapping of water brought to the fore several figures. Firstly, it generated a kind of overview or understanding of the city through the lens of water. Secondly, it showed how multiple collective actors, natural and constructed, make up the urban waterscape.[1] This mapping provoked a focus on non-human and hybrid actors. Thirdly, tracking the different waters physically showed that water from one origin becomes 'many' when arriving in the city. Although Arequipa is placed in a semi-arid region, there is water flowing everywhere. Water comes from a few, relatively limited sources, but when water reaches the city, it can become irrigation water, regulated, raw, measured, drinking water or wastewater; different kinds of chemicals, technical devises, pipes and expertise transform water into many – what some political ecologists conceptualize as a metabolism that urbanizes nature (Swyngedouw 2004, 2006; Gandy 2005).

Initially, I thought physical mapping to be one of three kinds of water mapping to be done in Arequipa. Besides physical mapping I had the idea of doing institutional mapping: identifying the organizations and institutions that manage and govern water in the city, as well as examining institutional practices related to water, and epistemological mapping: examining different ways of knowing water, exploring values and beliefs linked to water, thoughts about where water comes from and what position it takes up in the world and the universe. However, while walking along the urban waterscape, it soon became obvious that the physical aspect of water cannot possibly be separated from institutional and epistemological aspects. Each infrastructure, use and enactment of water takes physical place, and while taking place – or being thrown in a balloon – water is known in a particular way, which relates to a specific ordering of practices, organizations and institutions that partake in managing water. Hence, instead of seeing the physical, institutional and epistemological dimensions of mapping as separate domains, waiting out there to be plugged into a map, these dimensions should be understood as being produced in particular configurations, and becoming figured in the practice of mapping itself. A flow of water through a canal is thus never a mere material or physical matter, because it is always embedded in particular institutional and epistemological relations. Likewise, each water organization or institution is situated in a network of physical relations (pipelines, technologies and water flows) that are embedded in and enacting particular ways of knowing and valuing water. It follows, then, that mapping institutions that work to manage and govern water in Arequipa entails understanding how a particular water epistemology is produced and enacted around each institution, through a material ordering and physical enactment of water.

Mapping Institutions: Multiple Scarcities

In Arequipa, the celebration of carnival is linked to the rainy season, and the playful engagement with water is explained by some people to be related to the joy of having water in abundance. In 2011 it did indeed rain a lot; at the end of February the reservoirs were reported full, and the institutions governing and managing the Quilca-Chili watershed announced that they had stored enough water for two consecutive years. Rainfall generated abundance in the system; for a while Arequipans could forget that they inhabit an arid region. Yet, while water was abundant in the major system of dams and in terms of amount of cubic metres flowing down the Chili River per second, no more potable water could be produced than usual. Let us have a look at the institutional landscape of water in Arequipa, and then dig into the different layers of scarcity.

Many institutions and actors (individual as well as collective) engage in water management in Arequipa. Roughly, these can be grouped in state or public institutions, civil organizations and private and semi-private companies. Among public institutions we find the earlier mentioned municipal drinking water company SEDAPAR, the local and regional offices of the national water authority, the regional authority of agriculture, and AUTODEMA, the regional institution that operates the major hydraulic system of dams. Among civil organizations we find boards and committees for irrigation water users, dwellers in new urban neighbourhoods that organize to claim and obtain running water to their homes, and NGOs working with water and sanitation in different ways. Water governance is organized and ordered around state institutions; some semi-public and private companies also have a major influence in the field of water governance in Arequipa: the copper mining company Cerro Verde and the hydropower company EGASA. Less influential, although pushing towards inclusion in decision making, are the NGOs and the organizations of urban dwellers. Organizations of irrigation users are traditionally influential, but with a new national water legislation being implemented, these organizations are losing participation in influential organs.

Some of these institutions and actors come together in the Comité Multisectorial, the multisectoral committee, an organ where representatives of the most influential water users meet every second week to collectively decide how many cubic metres of water are to be released from the dams through the different water systems, and to deal with different issues related to water availability and management. In this committee six organizations of irrigation water users were members, as well as a mining company, the Arequipa electricity company, the national water authority, the regional institution AUTODEMA (mentioned above) that operates the grand hydraulic infrastructure of dams and canals, the national authority for agriculture, the national meteorology and hydrology service, and SEDAPAR, the municipal drinking water company.

Water is given direction and flow through material infrastructure as well as through technical devices and institutional connections (and disconnects). Hence, each institution engaged in managing water, works within a particular water epistemology, and performs and produces scarcity or abundance in specific ways. Thus, when mapping the institutions and the relations between them, and when interviewing officials about general aspects of water availability, management and governance in Arequipa, different kinds of scarcities and the different kinds of abundances became notable. Let me exemplify by looking at two institutions and two maps; each depicts different objects, according to the institutional functions, objectives and interests.

The two maps show different parts and functions within the same urban watershed, bringing to the fore different scopes, different main actors and particular relations. In the scheme of AUTODEMA (Figure 8.1), the dam 'Embalse Aguada Blanca' and the Chili River serve as main actors, making the system work through storage, regulation and distribution. The major water users of the watershed are depicted either by the amounts of water they get (SEDAPAR receives 1,500 litres per second and the mining company receives 960 litres per second), or in terms of the production (the hydropower plant EGASA produces 196.9 megawatts, and the six irrigation organizations together irrigate 25,325 hectares of land). In terms of territory, Figure 8.1 extends beyond the city; only three of the depicted users are located within the urban frontiers: SEDAPAR and two of the irrigation organizations. The users depicted in Figure 8.1 are also the institutions that participate in the Comité Multisectorial, and are thus influential in making decisions about distribution, management of dams and construction of new ones.

Figure 8.1 The hydraulic scheme and system of distribution of water by AUTODEMA, the operator of the major hydraulic system. Central to this system are the dam 'Embalse Aguada Blanca' and the Chili River, which together store, regulate and distribute the water. The squares and photos depict the different major water users: the electricity company EGASA, six irrigation organizations, potable water company SEDAPAR, and the copper mine Cerro Verde. Produced by AUTODEMA (Arequipa, Peru) and printed with permission.

Figure 8.2, the plan of SEDAPAR, depicts the system of production and distribution of water for population use; it zooms in on and specifies the system that circulates the 1,500 litres per second, which in Figure 8.1 are depicted as 'SEDAPAR 1500 lps'. The plan emphasizes reservoirs, pumps and supply pipelines as the central actors that make the system work. In this map of SEDAPAR, water scarcity is not revealed, but will arise if users consume more water than has been calculated, and more than the treatment plant can produce. Within this system, scarcity occurs when users consume more than the treatment plant can produce. This is why responsibility for scarcity during carnival was placed on the urban water consumers: 'drop by drop, the water is used up'. The amount of water put into this system is constant, and agreed about in the Comité Multisectorial in relation to overall demand and availability of water in the watershed. These 1,500 litres per second correspond to the capacity of the water treatment plant, how much it

Mapping Urban Waters 173

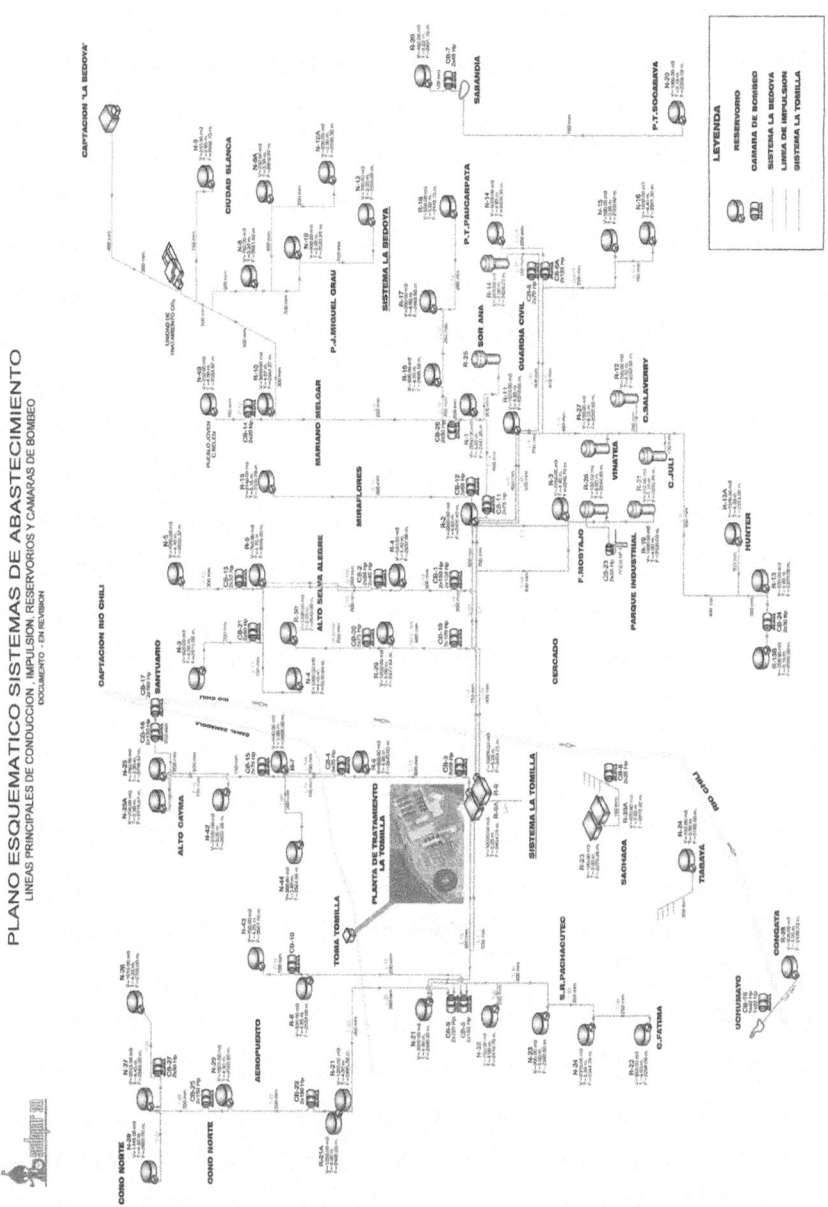

Figure 8.2 Plan of the SEDAPAR system of distribution of drinking water. This system supplies close to 80 per cent of the population of Arequipa. Central to this system is the drinking water treatment plant, which is emphasized with a small photo. Produced by Sedapar S.A. (Servicios de Agua Potable y Alcantarillado de Arequipa, Peru) and printed with permission.

can transform per second from crude water into potable drinking water. The map does not reveal that the actual demand for drinking water among the urban population is much higher than that; more than 20 per cent of the urban dwellers have no running water in their homes, which means that the system of SEDAPAR functions within a larger system of scarcity. Both figures leave out dysfunctions, leaks and human beings, while also producing different potential scarcities and overflows; hence they reveal that water scarcity and abundance in Arequipa can be produced in different scales and sites.

The hydraulic scheme of AUTODEMA, which is the overall scheme of water availability and distribution in the regulated system of Arequipa, requires several elements and efforts in order to avoid scarcity: precipitation, storage capacity and efficient management. This system produces abundances and scarcities on a different scope than that of SEDAPAR. In the system in Figure 8.1, scarcity can be a product of missing rainfall, bad management of the dams or reduced storage capacity. The year 2011, when I did fieldwork in Arequipa, was a year with heavy rainfall. The system of dams and reservoirs was full after only one month of rain. It kept raining, and soon a risk of collapse of dams made AUTODEMA release huge amounts of water into the Chili River, resulting in a few days of flooding of cultivated fields as well as closing down production of potable water and electricity.

While the two maps presented here do not describe human activity and are completely free of humans, they do tell us about social life. They are produced in social contexts, and as such they are indicators of social relations and particular visions of social reality. To map water is a part of its management. In this sense, the institutional maps in figures 8.1 and 8.2 reveal how maps are embedded in a specific way of knowing, doing and giving value to water. Maps and visual representations produced by institutions, then, perform particular ways of knowing, and project particular possible practices and relations. In the maps presented here, the institutional way of knowing is constituted by infrastructure, measurement and technology; together they highlight engineering practices with water dominant. Through the institutional mapping, water management and governance become visible as engineered fields. Engineer ways of knowing become instituted and enacted in the maps, and other ways of knowing water do not easily find their way onto two-dimensional graphics and maps.

The figures presented are just two of many maps, schemes, plans or other visual representations that are produced and used by institutions to order, control and manage the water they are assigned. What emerges by looking at these maps, and when examining institutions, is a multiplicity of ways in which water is instituted, meaning that each institution is capturing, knowing, defining and practising water in a particular way – or even in several ways. Every institution responds to particular demands and necessities, and works within different ranges of availability and criteria of scarcity and abundance. Further, when looking at the institutions, water emerges as an element embedded in political intention and relations of power. Water flows through a network of institutional relations, with alliances and conflicts along some of the relations: the logics and frames of management of one institution do not correspond to those of another.

When it comes to understanding how different maps perform particular ways of knowing, Tim Ingold's (2007) distinction between the 'sketch map' and the 'modern cartographic map' is helpful. Ingold uses the notion of lines to explore human experience and life in a given environment. He states that 'the knowledge we have of our surroundings is forged in the very course of our moving through them' (ibid.: 87–88). This movement creates a line, which can be engaged through a journey or through storytelling, generative of a path that others can follow (ibid.: 84). The 'sketch map' – ephemeral lines of movement or gestures through a terrain – contrasts to the 'modern cartographic map', which contains permanent lines on a surface, and creates borders of occupation and appropriation of space. Where the sketch map shows how people inhabit the world, the cartographic map shows how the world is occupied (ibid.: 85). According to Ingold, these two modes of relating to a territory are configured by different ways of knowing: inhabitant knowledge and occupant knowledge. Inhabitant knowledge is characterized by 'knowing while going along the line of a travel', as a path of movement through the world, and occupant knowledge is 'founded upon a categorical distinction between the mechanics of movement and the formation of knowledge' (ibid.: 89). Following Ingold, it would be easy to state that during carnival in Arequipa, the people who engaged in festive play with water were manifesting inhabitant knowledge of water, while SEDAPAR, encouraging people to use water rationally, was manifesting occupant knowledge. However, in this chapter the point is not to categorize maps and knowledge according to ways of experiencing and practising a territory; rather, the point is that in order to grasp how people in Arequipa know water in different ways, and how water is scarce and abundant simultaneously, a mapping of maps, or a gathering of diverging maps, can be useful as a way of gathering diverging perspectives on and enactments of urban waters.

Scales of Scarcity and Abundance

The description of the varying enactments of water during the carnival of Arequipa and in the managerial practices of institutions has shown that water in Arequipa is not one but many, and that the generation and performance of different ways of knowing water are productive of particular relations that have political and social implications. During the carnival, when Arequipans celebrate traditions and engage playfully with each other and authorities in public space, SEDAPAR participated to produce institutional legitimacy by campaigning water as scarce, and appealing to people to be responsible and rational in their use of water. The head of public relations in several conversations told me that if SEDAPAR were seeking to earn more money then they would be encouraging people to consume more water. Yet, SEDAPAR was an institution interested in the well-being of all citizens, and was therefore seeking to sensitize Arequipans to consume less water. Enacting water as scarce hence reaffirmed SEDAPAR as a capable and responsible institution in terms of managing potable water in Arequipa. The contrary was the case when heavy rainfalls obliged AUTODEMA to discharge huge amounts of water into the Chili River. SEDAPAR then had to stop production of potable water for some days due to *turbidez* – too much pressure on the flow of water; the solids such as stones and sediment the water was carrying along could ruin the infrastructure of the water treatment plant. Further, due to the heavy rains, the sewerage system, also administered by SEDAPAR, was collapsing, causing flows of excrements in several streets in Arequipa. On this occasion, an extreme abundance of water at one scale of the urban waterscape was producing extreme scarcity at another scale. For SEDAPAR, flooding of excrements and cuts in the production of potable water led to them being blamed and heavily criticized, and this compromised the institution's legitimacy in the eyes of the population, media and political authorities.

Through ethnographic mapping it becomes clear that the practice of mapping is productive of particular perspectives or figurations of relations. It should be clear by now that the mapping proposed here is about exploring the flows, directions, intentionalities and infrastructures of water itself, as well as the fluidity and shapes of social life that water is part of. By mapping we make a path through the urban landscape (Ingold 2007), and thus create a particular narration and perspective (de Certeau 1984). Through the practice of mapping – understood as methodology, description and analysis – objects are carved out; mapping is hence about figuring the world with the aim of understanding specific aspects and relations in it.

Assembling a Multilayered Map

What happens when, instead of looking at the maps from the different institutions next to each other, we put them on top of each other, superposing instead of juxtaposing? In November 2011, about three months before my fieldwork in Arequipa was due to end, I got the idea that I wanted a map of the different networks that distribute water through the city of Arequipa. I imagined a map of several layers, each depicting a system of distribution of water, plotted on transparent paper. I wanted to put each of these layers on top of each other in order to be able to see the layers simultaneously. My wish was that such a visual document would graphically perform the complexity of the water systems of the city, and show that although Arequipa is located in an arid region, there is water flowing everywhere.

When first sharing my idea with a young architect in the cadastre office of SEDAPAR, I thought making such a map would be a simple task – just a question of plotting the different maps on several transparent papers, and then putting them on top of each other. It turned out to be more complicated than that. The architect, with the approval of his boss, a female engineer in charge of the cadastre office, agreed to help me to make the maps; and the boss allowed us to use the institutional plotters for making the maps. While the first obstacle, human and material resources, was thus soon overcome, the rest of the map-making process turned out to be more difficult.

Digital versions of the different maps had to be collected from different institutions. Back in SEDAPAR, the maps turned out to be in differing formats. It took the work of several people at the cadastre office and the acquisition of special software to open all files in one document. The maps from the different institutions were divergent in scale and content. For instance, the curves of the Chili River, which runs through the city as a central vein of water, were not the same on one map as on another. Surely, it was not surprising that water management is distributed between various administrative entities. However, it was significant that the maps of one institution did not correspond to those of another, either in terms of scale or in terms of the objects depicted, relational distances, or accuracy. Mapping, then, can be used to enlighten more than the objects and relations they depict two-dimensionally on a flat piece of paper. Superposing maps from several institutions can point us towards an understanding of how urban water is instituted fragmentally.

I spent several days in the cadastre office. Whenever I was there I sensed an atmosphere of a place working hard with limited human resources. The director of cadastre, a friendly but firm engineer in her late forties, was running the office and its eight employees with an efficient attitude. The office was full of archives, desks and stands with old maps of the city and its potable water infrastructure, containing a long history of urban development. The team was always plotting new plans, making inventories, and reorganizing – the urban water infrastructure as well as the institution itself, it seemed.

After a few days the digital work was done. We had one file showing almost all the layers of surface water running through Arequipa, and its infrastructure.[2] We gave the systems and elements different colours, and made a legend for the different layers: a hydrographical map showing natural water flows, a map of potable drinking water connections, a map of the sewerage system and wastewater flows, a map of irrigation canals, a map of the cultivated fields, and a ground map of the streets and districts of the city. We plotted a ground sheet in white, showing the city and the division of districts in black. Then we plotted four sheets: natural water flows in dark blue, irrigation canals in light green, drinking water connections in light blue, and drains and the sewerage system in orange and brown. There were symbols for water treatment plans, directions of water flows, and fire taps. A few days before leaving Arequipa I went out of the cadastre office with my printed maps and a copy of the digital version in my baggage.

The narration of the challenging assembling of the maps of the systems of water in Arequipa shows, on one hand, that it takes effort to make a map to explain something about the world. On the other hand, the narration is a window into a research process, making my path through a physical setting as well as a theoretical endeavour (Sanjek 1990: 396–99).[3] In the process of making the layers fit to my wishes, institutional and epistemological differences were erased in order to make something else visible.

In Ingold's terms, we could categorize these maps as manifestations of occupant knowledge. However, the point here is not to categorize knowledge as either occupant or habitant. Rather, the idea is to use the maps productively to make the Arequipan waterscape visible as complex, consisting of multiple layers. Each layer of water system and infrastructure is linked to different lived realities, knowledge, practices, materiality, technologies, politics, interests and economies that sometimes work together, sometimes against each other, to make water flow. Knowing that each infrastructure (marked by different colours) is linked to differing materialities, institutions and practices indicates that water becomes multiple when entering the city (Barnes and Alatout 2012). The different layers and colours in the map point towards moments

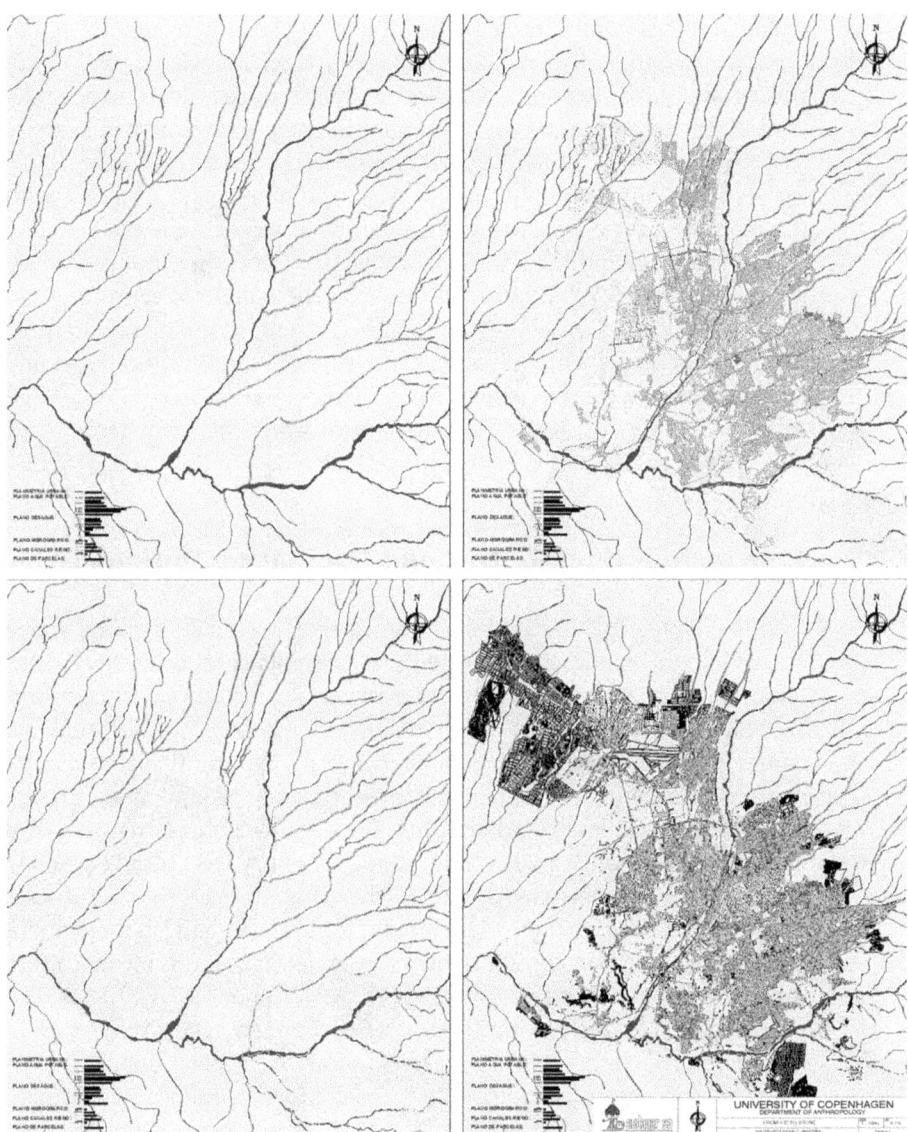

Figures 8.3–8.6 The multilayered map of Arequipa, made with the architect in SEDAPAR, January 2012. Scale 1/1000. Upper left, 8.3: Natural flows of water. 8.4: Natural flows and irrigation canals. 8.5: Potable water, wastewater, irrigation canals and natural flows. 8.6: Potable water, wastewater, irrigation canals and natural flows, and a ground plan of buildings (black). Produced by author, in collaboration with SEDAPAR S.A., and printed with permission.

where water becomes 'many' when entering the city, which are at the same time moments of political and social intensity. Hence, the juxtaposing and superposing of different maps produces different perspectives of the urban waterscape; ethnographic mapping is then an exercise that can gather and figure various things and relations in the perspective that emerges through mapping. Further, looking at and thinking with the maps brings us to new questions: In what ways do the maps depict different objects and relations? Whose way of knowing is not present in any of the layers? What kinds of water do the maps not capture? Who uses maps? Who does not? What kind of relations of inequality do these maps talk to or silence? Each map alone shows a simplification of reality and establishes an order, while several maps – superposed or juxtaposed – point towards a complex multiplicity of water. By comparing maps and perspectives new questions can be generated.

Conclusion: Carving Out and Oscillating Perspectives

In this chapter I have explored how water is produced as both scarce and abundant in the city of Arequipa, in events such as carnivals and flooding, and in the discursive and material practices of institutions. When assembled in layers, maps point to depth and multidimensional complexity, and I suggest that the multiplicity and multilayered quality of the waterscape is what characterizes water in Arequipa as 'urban'. Many actors – human and non-human – partake in configuring and enacting water, sometimes as scarce and sometimes as abundant, along connected or disconnected flows. To the ethnographer, the map shows as much about the institution that is making and using the map, as about the territory it claims to represent. What mapping does is to offer room for oscillating perspectives (Strathern 2002; Wagner [1987] 2012).

Then what is the position of the ethnographer when mapping? In this chapter, diverse graphic representations have been considered as maps, and various methodological steps grouped as mapping. Mapping is composed by selection and production of a variety of perspectives through which figures, actors, silences, flows, relations and disconnects emerge. Our interests, questions, gazes carve out an object for analysis and orient our further questions. I have presented mapping as an explorative practice; each map is carved out by a particular perspective *and* carves out an analytical figure. When using mapping as a method, the path of mapping draws a line in a social-material world; as such it marks an analytical process, since when mapping we start to see some things and leave out others; we carve out an analytical object (Brichet and Hastrup 2011).

There is analytical work to be done when we try to make maps speak to us about their objects, functions and context. The map becomes visible as we walk, but also makes things visible or invisible. What becomes visible as figure and ground as we follow the water ethnographically in an urban context? What configures 'the social' when we see it through water as well as social and physical infrastructure around water? It is not the aim here to provide a full answer to these questions, but to anticipate that the practice of mapping can bring about a grip on urban waters, where physical, institutional and epistemological aspects configure the urban waterworld. What becomes visible along this ethnographic water path is a complex web of relations and positions; water becomes many as it circulates and is transformed through infrastructures, practices, technologies and knowledge regimes.

The world does not present itself in separable layers, and water is present in every day practices as well as intense moments like carnival festivities, flooding and sensitizing campaigns. In these events, water enters social worlds and becomes productive of different relations, which take on social, political and material dimensions. Although the world does not present itself in layers, the practice of mapping explored in this chapter has shown that an understanding of the waterscape of Arequipa, as that of any waterworld, can have many layers. Such a methodological practice can help us to unravel how water becomes a contested element in particular contexts, valued in incommensurable ways by different actors (Andersen 2014). Depending on what we as researchers are interested in elucidating, mapping can help us to carve out objects and perspectives.

Seeing 'urban water' in Arequipa as a multiplicity, consisting of several layers, is the result of a particular carving out that takes place through a practice of mapping. Producing an ethnographic water path is not a question of describing all layers and including these in the same analysis. Nor is it a question of placing oneself in between the layers or on top of them. Rather, ethnographic mapping is about seeing all objects of study, including 'urban water', as results of a particular perspective, which emerges as a result of a particular carving out – a process that is equally methodological, descriptive and analytical.

The use of cartographic maps in ethnographic fieldwork, and the practice of ethnographic mapping proposed here, can be of benefit to interdisciplinary work, since maps and mapping are modes of inquiry that gather various academic and non-academic disciplines.

Notes

1. The concept 'waterscape' is a variation of the word landscape, bringing to the fore the importance of water in human–ecologic relations, or in society. Geographer Erik Swyngedouw (1999) defines 'waterscape' as water landscape, and uses waterscape to refer to natural flows as well as human intervention or use of water. Characterizing 'waterscape' as a hybrid character, he argues that nature is produced through changing societal and ecological conditions (ibid.: 444–45). Anthropologists Ben Orlove and Steven Caton define 'waterscape' as 'the culturally meaningful, sensorially active places in which humans interact with water and with each other' (Orlove and Caton 2010: 408), hence bringing to the fore the specific relation of humans and water.
2. Not all, of course, since new taps and reservoirs are constantly being constructed in new urban areas; also, the vehicles that take around drinking water to those urban areas without running water are not depicted on the maps.
3. In his chapter 'On Ethnographic Validity', Roger Sanjek (1990) examines the role of theory, method and fieldnotes when it comes to establishing the validity of ethnographic research. Sanjek argues that ethnography should be assessed and validated in its own right, through 'theoretical candor, the ethnographer's path, and fieldwork evidence' (ibid.: 395). It is Sanjek's idea of a path through field research that I evoke in the title of this chapter, and my aim is to lay out narrations here as evidence from the process of my research.

References

Andersen, A.O. 2014. 'Water is Life: An Ethnography of Urban Ecology and Water Politics in Arequipa, Peru'. Ph.D. thesis. Faculty of Social Sciences, University of Copenhagen.

Anderson, B. (1983) 1991. *Imagined Communities: Reflections on the Origin and Spread of Nationalism*. London: Verso.

Barnes, J., and S. Alatout. 2012. 'Water Worlds: Introduction to the Special Issue of Social Studies of Science', *Social Studies of Science* 42(4): 483–88.

Brichet, N., and F. Hastrup. 2011. 'Figurer uden grund', in *Tidsskriftet Antropologi* 64: 119–35.

Certeau, M. de. 1984. *The Practice of Everyday Life*. Berkeley: University of California Press.

Chen, C. 2003. *Mapping Scientific Frontiers: The Quest for Knowledge Visualization*. London: Springer.

Clarke, A.E. 2005. *Situational Analysis: Grounded Theory after the Postmodern Turn*. Thousands Oaks, CA: Sage Publications.

Gandy, M. 2005. 'Cyborg Urbanization: Complexity and Monstrosity in the Contemporary City', *International Journal of Urban and Regional Research* 29(1): 26–49.

Ingold, T. 2007. *Lines. A Brief History*. London: Routledge.

Kitchin, R.M., and M. Dodge. 2007. 'Rethinking Maps', *Progress in Human Geography* 31(3): 331–44.

Latour, B. 2004. 'Why Has Critique Run Out of Steam? From Matters of Fact to Matters of Concern', *Critical Inquiry* 30: 225–48.

Mark B., et al. 2010. 'Climate Change and Tropical Andean Glacier Recession: Evaluating Hydrologic Changes and Livelihood Vulnerability in the Cordillera Blanca, Peru', *Annals of the Association of American Geographers* 100(4): 794–805.

Møhl, P. 2012. *Omens and Effect: Divergent Perspectives on Emerillon Time, Space and Existence*. Meaulne, France: Semeion.

Oré, M., et al. 2009. *El Agua, ante nuevos desafíos: Actores e iniciativas en Ecuador, Perú y Bolivia, Agua y Sociedad*. Lima: Instituto de Estudios Peruanos.

Orlove, B. 1993. 'The Ethnography of Maps: The Cultural and Social Contexts of Cartographic Representation in Peru', *Cartographica: The International Journal for Geographic Information and Geovisualization* 30(1): 29–46.

Orlove, B., and S.C. Caton. 2010. 'Water Sustainability: Anthropological Approaches and Prospects', *Annual Review of Anthropology* 39: 412–15.

Sanjek, R. 1990. *Fieldnotes: The Makings of Anthropology*. Ithaca, NY: Cornell University Press.

Strang, V. 2010. 'Mapping Histories: Cultural Landscapes and Walkabout Methods', in I. Vaccaro, E.A. Smith and S. Aswani (eds), *Environmental Social Sciences: Methods and Research Design*. Cambridge: Cambridge University Press, pp. 132–56.

Strathern, M. 2002. 'On Space and Depth', in J. Law and A. Mol (eds), *Complexities*. London: Duke University Press.

Swyngedouw, E. 1999. 'Modernity and Hybridity: Nature, Regeneracionismo, and the Production of the Spanish Waterscape, 1890–1930', *Annals of the Association of American Geographers* 89(3): 443–65.

———. 2004. *Social Power and the Urbanization of Water*. Oxford: Oxford University Press.

———. 2006. 'Circulations and Metabolisms: (Hybrid) Natures and (Cyborg) Cities', *Science as Culture* 15(2): 105–21.

Turnbull, D. (1989) 1993. *Maps are Territories, Science is an Atlas: A Portfolio of Exhibits*. Chicago: University of Chicago Press.

Wagner, R. (1987) 2012. 'Figure-ground Reversal among the Barok', *HAU: Journal of Ethnographic Theory* 2(1): 535–42.

Whatmore, S.J. 2009. 'Mapping Knowledge Controversies: Science, Democracy and the Redistribution of Expertise', *Progress in Human Geography* 33(5): 587–98.

9

Water Literacy in the Sahel

Understanding Rain and Groundwater

Anette Reenberg

Background: The Global Importance of Water

Adequate and reliable water supplies are important challenges at the global scale, but perhaps an even more crucial issue to consider in the poorest parts of the world, particularly in sub-Saharan Africa (Falkenmark and Rockström 2006). It is well documented that hydro-climatic variability has a significant influence on economic growth (Brown et al. 2010); most importantly, persistent droughts have a consistent negative effect. The threat of water scarcity is global, yet most impacts of water shortage are felt at the local level. Freshwater remains essential to produce food and sustain life; today, however, it is estimated that more than one-third of the global population already lives in water-scarce regions. Rapid population growth, combined with changing lifestyles, has led to a dramatic increase in water needs in many regions, a situation that may be aggravated in some of them by adverse trends in climatic change. In regions like the Sahel – where water is already scarce, the population increase has accelerated, the economy is weak, and the state of food security is alarming – sustainable development scenarios for water use and management deserve specific attention in order to avoid putting livelihoods, the food supply, economic growth, and the environment at severe risk in the future (VEOLIA Water/IFPRI 2011).

The scale of calamities caused by lack of water is generally larger in poor countries, where they hit the fundamental basis of livelihoods. Water is a determining factor for human life and progress, and it has no substitute. Globally, it is not land that is a limiting factor for food and biomass production; variations in water quality and supply, together with soil characteristics, dictate the conditions for farming and pastoral productivity (Lundqvist and Falkenmark 2010). Water and land use are intimately connected. Land use decisions are also water decisions because they influence the allocation of water flows. A major challenge for future food production is meeting water requirements. This is not least true for the poor and water-scarce land use systems in the Sahel. It must be recognized that too heavy reliance on water from lakes, aquifers, and dammed reservoirs for agricultural production is not sustainable. The accumulated freshwater resources from the past seem to be inadequate for dealing with future challenges of ensuring water for livelihoods and sustainability.

Insights into the ways in which people appraise their water resources as well as insights into rationales behind people's efforts to improve the conditions of life in the face of the erratic and scarce water are important. They may serve as points of departure for finding suitable pathways for future change. The present chapter aims to provide a starting point for this broader reflection on important water literacy and sustainability concerns in the Sahel.

Water Literacy and Sustainability

The notion of water literacy offers a compelling lens to look more closely at the ways in which humans manage water – for example, for food production. In the Global North (www.allianceforwatereducation.org), the notion of water literacy has been developed and defined to mean 'knowing where your water comes from and how you use it'. This includes, but is not limited to, a basic understanding of water footprints, virtual water, groundwater recharge and consequences of over-drafting, how to move and control surface water, competing demands for water, and water conservation. Most Sahelian farmers never attended school, and these levels of abstraction and technical detail may be difficult for them to grasp. However, if we broaden the literacy notion to encompass the human ability to understand other water-related issues of importance, we can employ it as a simple heuristic to frame our exploration of the possible rationales that underpin Sahelian land and water use strategies. This broader notion of literacy is thus perceived as the capacity to assess (a) the impact of spatial and temporal rainfall patterns on the comparative advantage of different agricultural micro-strategies, (b) alternative ways of maneuvering to adapt to site-specific production potentials defined by water, and (c) long-term consequences of contemporary water use strategies.

The concept of 'water sustainability' has been suggested in different contexts and with different meanings. People's appraisal of resources has significant impact on use strategies and implications for the valuation of these. In Australia, for example, sustainability has been used as a label for wise use of water, specifically the need to avoid exorbitant water consumption by heavy industry and water-intensive agro business (www.benefits-of-recycling.com). This usage is on a par with the notion of wise management of water resources to avoid irreversible damage to ecosystems and chronic water shortages. Orlove and Caton (2010) link the term 'water sustainability' to different ways of valuing water, and thereby broaden the concept to include the themes of value, equity, governance, politics and knowledge. By doing so, they implicitly adopt a notion of multiple types of sustainability previously suggested by other scholars (e.g. Goodland 2002). In the present context, the term 'water sustainability' provides a loosely defined lens to explore strategies for wisely using the limited, erratic, and spatially and temporally fluctuating water resources of the Sahel. Land- and water-use strategies are considered to be sustainable if they: (a) give equal access to water for the local populations, (b) ensure a minimum loss of water to non-productive or destructive purposes, (c) support an ecologically sound agro-pastoral land use system, (d) correspond to local, cultural values, (e) follow established rules for governance and politically determined strategies, (f) do not exhaust finite resources that are crucial for the long-term functioning of the production systems, and (g) do not exacerbate vulnerability.

Fluctuating Water Conditions in the Sahel

The importance of securing water in the Sahelian region increases every day in light of the current population growth, economic development, and climate change projections. The variability and unpredictability of rainfall is the most hazardous dimension of climate and water resources, and a tangible development predicament (Lundqvist and Falkenmark 2010).

Historically, droughts and floods have severely challenged human efforts for survival and development. Variability of weather has always been one of the most important constraints to farming, in semi-arid tropics in particular. For millions of farmers in the Global South, the notion of average rainfall does not mean anything, and together with unstable market prices this makes the burden on their livelihood excessive

(Faurès, Bernardi and Gommes 2010). Devastating socioeconomic consequences of rainfall variations are found in many parts of the world (Brown and Lall 2006), and the already vulnerable Sahel is highly exposed. The very high variability in climate, specifically the spatial and temporal variability in precipitation both within and between years, is well documented and known to be a major challenge for local livelihood conditions (Dietz, Ruben and Verhagen 2004). Poor people are immediately forced, for example, to reduce herds or sell off any assets they may have at low prices since demand is low in times of crises. When the rain returns, the capacity to make optimal use of the available opportunities is hampered by the actions taken during periods of water shortage.

Seen in a long-term historical perspective, significant climate variability is a key issue (Brooks 2004). If we look back to 10,000 BP, the climatic situation in the Sahel was characterized by an intensified monsoon situation and the landscape was dominated by lakes and open woodland. By 5,000 BP, a final collapse of the monsoon was experienced after periods of abrupt arid crises, and cattle herders then migrated to the Sahel. More recently, in the 1950s and 1960s, the Sahel experienced unusually high rainfall, coincidentally with the independence of the nation states in the region. This co-development of the societal and environmental events created a great incentive to expand cultivation into marginal land, which has, in turn, led to profound implications for the vulnerability of this land use system on the edge of the desert.

Since the 1960s, the Sahel has been affected by a series of dramatic droughts. Long-term data sets from Niger (1940–2007) indicate that the Sahelian drought may to some extent have 'ended' in the early 1990s (Ozer, Hountondji and Laminou Manzo 2009; Niel, Leduc and Dielin 2009), but different rainfall indices still point to a significant downward trend. Importantly, it is also observed that the length of the rainy season has not changed, but the amplitude has become more pronounced, with negative implications for vulnerability (Eakin and Luers 2006).

It is a widely debated question whether a recent increase in rainfall may be interpreted as a return to previous levels or just as natural variability. Bolwig et al. (2011) summarize that, starting around 1986, rainfall generally increased compared to the dry 1970–85 period. There are regional differences within the Sahelian region, and recently rainfall seems to have recovered mostly in the southern parts of the Sahel (12–16°N), whereas drought intensified in the northern part (16–20°N). In the southernmost Sahel (12–14°N), conditions in the 1998–2003 period even seem to have been comparable to the very wet period in the 1950s and 1960s (Nicholson 2005). As regards future climate predictions, IPCC's Fourth Assessment Report is inconclusive (Christensen et al. 2007). The West African region is one of the regions of the world about which global climate models differ most in their predictions; yet, variability is likely to increase, and both prolonged droughts and extreme rainfall may become more common.

For agricultural and pastoral productivity, intra-annual and spatial variations in rainfall are as important as inter-annual variations. Vegetation dynamics are more or less determined by daily rainfall (de Ridder et al. 1982). Plant growth is determined by the distribution, number, amount and intensity of individual rains. Three months are of prime importance for plant growth: July, August and September. July determines the beginning of the growth; if July is dry, the number of growing days is limited. August is the month that may deliver some limited excess water for storage in the soil. September rainfall can influence the maturation periods of the plants. Apart from the important rainy season months, early rain may have adverse effects because it triggers early germination, and late rains may be disastrous, causing dry vegetation to rot. Hence, it is well documented that there is no simple correlation between the total amount of annual rain and yields, although the 'big patterns' of rain are, of course, reflected in the overall yield trends. The local plant production conditions are furthermore influenced by a significant spatial variability in the occurrence of showers. Rain may fall in one village, while the neighbouring village may not receive any.

Due to the high temperatures, potential evaporation is generally very high, up to six to seven millimetres per day (Kowal and Kassam 1978), and adequate water availability for plant production is highly dependent on a regular distribution of rainfall events throughout the growing season, not least because the surface run-off is normally high (due to crusts on the soil surface), and the soil water capacity is generally low (Claude et al. 1991). The hazard of dry spells (defined as a maximum of 5 mm of rainfall within a fourteen-day period) is therefore a major constraint to plant development (Barron et al. 2010), and there seems to be evidence that, for parts of sub-Saharan Africa, dry spells are becoming more frequent (Lundqvist and Falkenmark 2010).

Most of the aquifers in the Sahel do not contain abundant water resources (Kowal and Kassam 1978), and large quantities of water can only be secured by constructing artificial lakes. But these have a very low efficiency of conservation due to the high evaporation in the main period of storage. There are, however, water resources stored in deep water tables of sedimentary basins. There are considerable reserves, but at variable depths, sometimes at one to two thousand metres, and they are often non-renewable resources (fossil water) (OECD 2009).

In the following, four Sahelian cases provide an empirical platform for reflections on water literacy and sustainability in the Sahel. All of them are located in what could be considered the desert fringe of the Sahelian zone, areas that receive in the order of magnitude of 200–400 rainfalls per year (northern Senegal, northern Burkina Faso and south-eastern Niger. The examples serve to illustrate two different dimensions of water resources underpinning Sahelian livelihoods: water from the rain, and water from the ground.

Rainwater: Wise Adaptive Strategies

Yomboli is a village in the Oudalan province of Burkina Faso, approximately thirty kilometres north of Gorom-Gorom. Agricultural production and pastoral production are the main sources of sustenance for the population, and the land use system is basically a combination of cultivated fields and pastures. Rain is the primary source of water, supplemented only by traditional wells used for watering livestock. The rainy season lasts about five months, from May to September, and is characterized by a high inter-annual variability with an inter-annual coefficient of variation calculated to be 30 per cent (Rasmussen and Reenberg 2012).

The village is situated on a longitudinal east–west oriented dune that is superimposed on a pediplain cut by temporary river valleys. The dunes form barriers across natural drainage structures and create more or less temporary lakes (in French: *mare*) (Reenberg, Nielsen and Rasmussen 1998). The main crops are pearl millet and sorghum, while cowpeas are grown to a lesser extent. The villagers distinguish between two main locations of their fields: the dune and other locations (including the pediplain, the piedmont, and the border of the mare). Today, the majority of the fields are located on the sandy soils of the dune, where millet is cultivated as the sole crop. The soils on the pediplain, the piedmont, and the border of the mare are loamier, and can be used for mixed cropping of sorghum and millet.

Over the last six decades, however, a substantial, dynamic reallocation of fields has taken place. This pattern of change serves as a characteristic example of a noticeable systematic in the villagers' way of handling rain shortage or abundance. Starting in the late 1960s, with the onset of the dry years, and continuing until 1988, the field area was expanded primarily on the dune north of the mare. During the same period, villagers abandoned the southern fields on the pediplain. Since 1991, the location of fields has shifted southwards on the pediplain again. Villagers explained the recultivation of the pediplain as being due to different yield potentials in different locations with varying rainfall amounts. The pediplain fields were most productive in years with adequate rainfall but they also had the highest risk of production failure in very dry years, whereas millet cultivated on the dune was more resistant to low rainfall (Reenberg, Nielsen and Rasmussen 1998; Rasmussen and Reenberg 2012).

During the 1990s and early 2000s, the villagers noticed an increasing unpredictability in the rainy season. This observation was supported by rainfall data from the meteorological station in Gorom-Gorom, which showed greater inter-annual rainfall variability in this period, as was also seen elsewhere in the Sahel (Proud and Rasmussen 2010). The villagers seemed to address this by embracing different land use strategies from year to year (Rasmussen and Reenberg 2012). In dry years, 49 per cent of the respondents preferred to keep the field area constant, 44 per cent abandoned their fields, and the remaining 7 per cent enlarged their fields. In rainy years there was a clear tendency (72 per cent) to enlarge fields.

The villagers sometimes prayed for more rain. By explicitly wishing to stay in Yomboli and cultivate the fields, they deliberately signalled a sense of hope to the other villagers. Hence, the villagers' response to the changing rainfall conditions was determined by cultural norms rather than by agricultural goals. Rasmussen and Reenberg (2012) also observed that conditions in the recent past can be crucial for the current strategic choice. For example, because 2010 was a rainy year, agricultural expansion was expected to take place, but due to very dry conditions in 2009, many young men were forced to go on transhumance to Mali and Niger in order to find pasture and water for the animals, and no one was present in the village to do the work needed in the field when the rain came.

The correspondence between cultivation patterns and rainfall patterns in Yomboli illustrates some important traits that have also been observed elsewhere (e.g. Reenberg and Paarup-Laursen 1997; Nielsen and Reenberg 2010). One of these traits demonstrates the well-established traditional knowledge of the soil-water-crop productivity nexus – a type of water literacy. Local farmers are well aware of the comparative advantage of sandy and loamy soils under different rainfall regimes, and they manage their agricultural strategies accordingly to use the most productive parts of the landscape under given circumstances. These distinct patterns seem, however, to have become less prominent with time. This is most likely because agriculture, with increasing population pressure and the need for alternative income generation to support local livelihoods, has lost its prime importance as a means to supply food.

In a macro environment similar to that of Yomboli, approximately seven kilometres to the north of Gorom-Gorom lies the village of Touro, in the middle of the extended pediplain. This specific part of the pediplain is intersected by broad, shallow valleys (Fr.: *bas-fonds*), where huge amounts of surface run-off come together to form temporary river courses during the rainy season. In general, the soils of the pediplain are hard and covered with crust; hence, vegetation is often patchy and scarce. The bottom of the *bas-fond* hosts vegetation in the form of trees and scrubs. Cultivation is limited to parts of the pediplain that have a sandy cover, while most of the landscape is bare or used for grazing.

In the 1980s and 1990s, Oudalan attracted a great deal of attention in connection with large, integrated development projects under the umbrella of PSB (Programme Sahel Burkinabé). Major efforts were devoted to improving natural resource management strategies in the region and, in turn, to improving the livelihoods of people in this extremely poor part of Burkina Faso. Food security is a major issue; the fluctuating rainfall, together with the substantial increase in the population, has led to an almost chronic insufficiency of locally produced cereals since the late 1960s.

Hence, the vision of storing and utilizing the large amounts of surface run-off that runs through the valley systems in the peak of the rainy season seems obvious. As part of a large, integrated development project, a huge dam was built across one of the valleys to create a temporary lake, sufficiently large to remain a source of fresh water well into the dry season. A channel system was established behind the dam, which became the backbone of an extended area of rice fields in what had until then been an unused part of the valley bottom. There was great interest among local farmers. Towards the end of the twentieth century, rice had gradually become a 'prestigious' food item, which could be bought at the market at relatively high prices. The prospect of being able to cultivate their own rice attracted farmers from as far away as Gorom-Gorom, despite the time they would have to invest in walking to and from their fields.

The period within which the potential benefits of the large investment could be harvested proved, however, to be very short. On 9 August 2006 a severe rainstorm hit Gorom-Gorom. In four hours the region received 136 mm of rain, or around one-third of the 'normal' annual rainfall. This led to a major disaster, as was described on Burkina Faso's website (www.lefaso.net): 'What is most striking is the destruction. One of the city quarters is completely wiped out except for a few houses. Two others have half of the buildings left, and the marketplace was severely damaged, with huge losses for the shopkeepers. In all, 965 houses were completely damaged, and more than 5,000 people have lost everything' (author's translation from French).

While the rainstorm triggered the disaster, the root cause of the extreme event was found north of Gorom-Gorom. Figure 9.1 shows the dam after the disaster. All installations surrounding the rice fields have been wiped out – a result of the storm as well as gradual erosion in the years after the event. The location has reverted to pastoral use only. There seem to be no obvious prospects for trying to reconstruct the dam. Although major rainstorms may not be a frequent occurrence, the experience has shown the extreme vulnerability of the construction to events that could occur again at any time. Despite some requests from local authorities for assistance to reconstruct the dam, development agencies have so far been reluctant to provide the necessary financial support.

Rainwater resources are crucial for livelihoods in the Sahel; yet they need to be well understood to cope with their obvious limitations. On the one hand, the case studies illustrate that farmers have developed skills to adapt their land use, anticipating rainfall pattern, to obtain the best possible outcome. On the other hand, they illustrate that seemingly rational strategies can be vulnerable to extreme, but not unlikely, natural events.

Figure 9.1 The dam at Touro, northern Burkina Faso, following the storm in 2006, shortly after the construction. Photo by Anette Reenberg.

Groundwater: Spatial Distribution and Local Irrigation

The Ferlo region is located in the Sahelian zone of Senegal. The climate is characterized by a short, relatively well-defined rainy season. The greatest amount of precipitation falls in July, August and September, and the mean annual rainfall for the period 1986–1996 was approximately 200 mm in the north and 400 mm in the south. The coefficient of variation in annual precipitation is above 33 per cent. Sandy soils prevail, and ancient longitudinal dunes dominate the topography.

Historically, the rangelands of Ferlo served as a grazing area for pastoralists, who had to pursue large-scale migration due to the lack of permanent water supplies. The efficient use of natural resources requires pastoral mobility adjusted to the spatial and temporal variability of resources. In highly variable and unpredictable ecosystems, large-scale pastoral mobility is a common phenomenon. Pastoral mobility between different agro-ecological zones means that more livestock can be kept compared to a situation where livestock are permanently kept in one zone. By using drier places during the wet season and more humid places during the dry season, livestock can be ensured sufficient and high quality grazing.

Grazing resources were generally abundant, but as temporary waterholes dried out during the dry season, pastoralists moved north to the Senegalese river valley, or south and west to the peanut basin. In the 1950s, the French colonial administration made the first boreholes equipped with motor pumps in Ferlo. This meant that the pastures could be used on a permanent basis, and some pastoralists also engaged in rain-fed agriculture, especially in the southern part with the highest rainfall (Adriansen and Nielsen 2005; Adriansen 2008).

Since the great drought in the 1970s many pastoralists have abandoned cultivation, and only a small percentage of the area is cultivated today. Even though many pastoralists have become semi-sedentary, mobility is still an important part of livestock rearing in various ways.

Water is crucial for pastoralists in terms of providing for the animals' daily needs as well as ensuring productive pastures. In her compelling description of the pastoral areas in the northern part of Senegal, Juul (1996) summarizes how the imagination and innovative spirit of the herders have played a significant role in enabling a specific group of herders to overcome immediate water constraints and to engage in another form of mobile behaviour. In short, the historical situation is as follows. Over the last fifty years, pastoral areas have shifted considerably. There has been continuous pressure on the pastoral land from agricultural encroachment, but at the same time, the digging of wells has provided new opportunities by enlarging the areas that can be pastured in the dry season. After the boreholes were drilled in the 1950s, many Fulani herders gave up the previous annual transhumance and settled around the boreholes. During the serious droughts in the 1970s and 1980s, the pasture production was insufficient to feed the animals and the herders were severely hit, not least because they waited to move until very late, when the animals were already weakened. When a drought hit again in 1983/84, a large proportion of the herders decided to stay in the Ferlo region, where a new system of water transport had created a novel platform for prosperity. In the same period the emphasis in pastoralism shifted from cattle rearing to greater dependence on sheep.[1] Sheep have higher drought resistance and a shorter reproduction cycle; hence sheep herding allows herders to recover their losses more quickly. The growing importance of sheep was also due to a substantial rise in their market value. Small stock are easier to sell in general, and during the conflict between Mauritania and Senegal in 1989, imports from Mauritania were cut, which led to a considerable rise in the demand (and price) for sheep for the Tabaski (Juul 1996).

The most important factor in this transformation of the pastoral systems was the invention of a new system for carrying water over long distances: the use of huge tractor-tyre inner tubes and donkey carts. A major challenge during the dry season is to ensure optimal fodder conditions while limiting energy losses related to watering. Instead of moving the dry season camps close to the deep wells or watering points, the technological leapfrogging offered by the tubes enabled the herders to stay in the most productive pastures and bring the water to the animals. Small stock are more dependent than cattle on regular watering (Reenberg 1982), so the adaptation of tubes to carry water over long distances constituted a technological revolution. The 'triumph of the tube' was possible because the donkey carts were already widespread in the region, introduced as part of the general attempt to mechanize the agricultural sector, and they were gradually adopted by the herders during the 1980s.

The success of the pastoral production and the higher survival and reproduction rates of the herds are closely related to this new dimension of mobility; the new means of water transport hugely expanded the accessible pasture areas. In other words: while the situation in northern Senegal has become more difficult due to agricultural encroachment and severe drought periods, a simple but smart technological innovation for transporting water has enabled more animals to survive by making better use of grazing. As a result, many herders have become richer than they were before the drought forced them to migrate south.

The last case study site, Karagou village in Diffa province, is located in south-western Niger, on the border of what has been proved to be the maximum extent of Lake Chad (Grove 1985). The region is remote with respect to the administrative and commercial centres of Niger (almost 1,000 km from Niamey), but is adjacent to the Nigerian border. It has a relatively low population density, but the population has increased significantly in recent history and accelerated the need for food production to cover local needs. Rainfall is scarce and highly variable in time and space, with an average of around 300 mm per year. The landscape is dominated by large dunes originating from periods that were drier than at present. In previous, more humid periods, the dunes were partially inundated by Mega-Chad, and the depressions (*bas-fonds*) in the contemporary landscape originate from a hydrological network that functioned some 20,000–40,000 years ago. In subsequent drier periods, aeolian erosion deepened parts of the valley system and created approximately two hundred low-lying oasis basins, or cuvettes.

The potential for rain-fed agriculture is confined to a very limited range of crops (predominantly millet, sorghum and cowpeas). The traditional land use systems in the region are 'typically Sahelian', with two more or less interconnected components: (a) subsistence peasants, permanently settled in villages, who mainly cultivate millet in the *bas-fonds* or in the dune landscape, and supplement this activity with livestock rearing; and (b) pastoralists passing through the region with their herds.

The cuvettes are an important and productive niche in the region with their inherent potential for exploitation. They are used in three main ways: for agriculture, for grazing, or for a mix of the two. The use is linked to the groundwater levels of the respective cuvettes. In addition, the cuvettes are important for agroforestry products (doom palms and dates in particular), and they are important for salt and natron excavation (Reenberg, Mamman and Oksen 2013). Often, the land use is organized in concentric zones, especially in the water-rich cuvettes, where the outer part of the 'halo' is occupied by palms, the next concentric zone by cereals or fruit trees, and the third part by halophilic plants; and finally, in the centre, there is a bare surface covered with natron.

The land use in the cuvettes has shifted over the course of time and varies somewhat from one cuvette to another. When Karagou was founded, for example, the adjacent cuvette was the main source of food crops such as wheat, sugar cane, maize and melon, and later millet, sorghum and groundnuts. When the water table dwindled around 1920, the cuvette fields lost some of their importance for the production of the main staples. A survey conducted in 1992 (Oksen 1993) showed that a large number of crops were grown in the cuvettes. The most dominant were cassava and to some extent maize (used for both personal consumption and sale); other crops (in order of magnitude) were: wheat, sweet potatoes, sorghum and sugar cane; and in smaller quantities: pumpkin, tomato, lettuce, cabbage, pimento, aubergine, onion, melon, carrot and okra. The crops were often inter-planted with tree crops such as dates, mango, banana, citrus, orange, guava and papaya. The portfolio of crops/products remains basically the same today (Reenberg, Mamman and Oksen 2013). More significant changes are noted as regards the excavation of salt and natron in the cuvettes. Only powder natron was important in 2011; salt has lost importance. The main reason suggested for these changes is the lowering water table. No quantitative measurements are available, but the peasants agree that there has been a continuous decrease, which has not been ameliorated even in years of good rain. In the long run, this will have serious implications for the agricultural potential of the cuvettes. Dates, for example, are a very important resource and have long been a valuable export commodity, especially until approximately 1970, when the lowering of the water in the cuvettes had a negative effect on yields. Prior to that, dates were instrumental in providing cash that enabled local people to build up their livestock herds.

In the contemporary visions for improving the local livelihoods, cuvettes are considered to have significant potential for irrigated agriculture; the African Development Fund (2003) suggests in their appraisal of the Diffa region that there is scope for supporting the development of 300 hectares of irrigated agriculture in oasis basins. In practical terms, this is reflected in a number of small-scale irrigation initiatives adopted by the local farmers (Figure 9.2). They employ small motor pumps to harvest water for the irrigation of their vegetable crops in the fields in the cuvettes. This agricultural activity is presented with great enthusiasm and pride, and the irrigation obviously now provides the basis for an intensive and productive use of the cuvettes.

But there are reasons to ask whether the strategy will be sustainable in a longer perspective, not least because farmers seem to agree (and worry) that the water table at the wells is continuously lowering, even in years of abundant rainfall. The cuvettes are generally not well researched as regards the potential and development of the water resources. PAGRN (Projet d'Appui à la Gestion des Ressources Naturelles) (2005) provides some details for a small selection of the cuvettes in the Diffa region, primarily addressing the soil quality and the current level of the groundwater table. They distinguish between three main types of cuvette: those with high (< 1.5 metres), medium (1.5 – 4 metres) and low (>4 metres) water levels, noting that there is a general north–south gradient, with

Figure 9.2 Small-scale irrigation in Niger. Motor pumps provide water for agriculture in the cuvettes. Photo by Anette Reenberg.

the highest water levels being predominant in the south of the region. However, no in-depth information on the change in water tables seems to be available. This is a serious challenge, because water resource management in arid areas requires not only exploration and assessment of the available reserves but also a determination of groundwater recharge in order to evaluate the sustainable long-term yields of the resource. The mechanism of the recharge of wells around Lake Chad is neither uniform nor well documented (Ngounou Nagatcha, Mudry and Sarrot-Reynauld 2007).

Concluding Discussion

The Sahel has a legacy of 'difficult hydrology', characterized by a short rainy season as well as high inter-annual and intra-annual variability of rainfall. Extremes of occasional flooding and persistent droughts pose unpredictable risks to communities, and necessitate water storage. Regions with very low biological productivity, such as sub-Saharan Africa, certainly stand to gain most from a wiser use of water resources (Molden et al. 2009).

Water security is a special challenge in the Sahel. By water security is meant 'the availability of an acceptable quantity and quality of water for health, livelihoods, ecosystems and production, coupled with an acceptable level of water-related risks to people, environments and economies' (Grey and Sadoff 2007). In the current situation of potential adverse climate changes and accelerating population pressures, there is no immediate alternative to the adaptation of peasant and pastoral land use systems to the best possible management practices of scarce water resources.

The large body of literature about Sahelian issues that emerged specifically after the serious droughts in the 1970s (Bolwig et al. 2011) has been helpful to draw attention to the large number of scientific writings that, among many other issues, document how traditional knowledge embodies rich insight into wise human–environmental interaction. Many classic agricultural and pastoral practices are actually wise ways of coping with ephemeral and unpredictable water resources. However, it has also been noted (Desanker, Megadza et al. 2001; Dietz, Ruben and Verhagen 2004; Brooks 2006) that knowledge of climate variability and adaptation in the Sahel can be improved, and that better insight into some of the mechanisms that Sahelian communities have used to cope with current climate variability may be a useful complement to technological innovations.

The four examples from the Sahel provide glimpses of how local people deal with water constraints. They may help in understanding the complexity and entanglement of actions that are taken to deal with the difficult and erratic water situation in the Sahel. Such insight may, in turn, broaden and build on the concept of water literacy, and inform reflections on long-term water sustainability in poor arid environments.

The example from Yomboli presents a convincing case of wise usage of traditional knowledge about water availability in soils under different rainfall regimes. The ability of farmers to understand the soil–water related issues of millet cultivation (an example of water literacy in our broader conceptualization) has played a significant role in ensuring the best possible harvest in a given year. The strategic manoeuvring between different landscape elements determined by soil water has, however, gradually lost its prominent role as a means to ensure food security in the best possible way; as the population and food demands have increased, so other livelihood sources have necessarily become more important. The traditional field allocation strategies are still in use, but have taken on a more psychological meaning, being more a signal of trust in the future for the local community.

With the development project agenda, the possible potential of technological innovations has influenced the local water–agriculture nexus.

The Touro dam in the very poor region of northern Burkina Faso is a large-scale water intervention far beyond local peoples' economic capacity. The dream was to create a water reservoir that would be able to wipe out the Sahelian intra-seasonal water constraint, and, in turn, to enhance the water-limited agricultural production potential and enable the farmers to grow the new prestige crop, rice. The water literacy capacity of local people did not reach to encompass the functionality of novel, large-scale, technological inventions. Despite some possible theoretical reservations, such as longer travel distances for the farmers and huge water losses to evaporation, the dam was extremely well received by the local population. Obviously, the immense cost of the dam, which was covered by donor money, was not an evident part of the farmers' assessment of benefits versus costs. Hence, the success was only transformed to failure when the dam broke and created a flooding catastrophe in the nearby town. In a very narrow perspective, the dam could be seen as a means to create a certain type of water sustainability in a drought-prone region, which may have succeeded if it had not fallen apart due to the extreme rain event. On the other hand, it is not sustainable in a broader sense (e.g. economically, culturally, or with respect to vulnerability).

The Ferlo pastoralists demonstrate a high level of insight, that is a high degree of water literacy, in the importance of the prevailing water constraints for the optimal use of their scarce and scattered grazing resources. By shifting from moving the animals to moving the water they secured access to previously inaccessible productive pastures. Because the deep aquifers in northern Senegal seem to be a rich water resource, the strategy may be sustainable from a pure water perspective. On the other hand, the long-term sustainability of the greatly increased pressure on previously less used pastures could be worthwhile considering in more detail.

Lastly, the cuvettes in south-eastern Niger illustrate how people under pressure from climate changes, increasing population pressures, and poverty have managed to cope by gradually modifying their agricultural strategies. The current emphasis on irrigation agriculture in the cuvettes seems promising in a short-term perspective, but does not take the possible long-term implications of the water use strategies into account. If the farmers' explicit worries about (over-)usage of the groundwater correspond to the hydrological realities, the use of motor pumps will only provide a short window of opportunity, and will in fact accelerate the exhaustion of the water resources.

Four more or less randomly chosen cases cannot, of course, provide any wide-ranging lessons to be learned about people and water in the Sahel. Technology can have favourable as well as unfavourable impacts on society; for example, technology may remove the reasons for water to be the limiting factor. Yet, the implications of changed uses of technology for water access may affect other domains of importance – social, economic, political or ecological. Glantz (1997) emphasized this obvious fact early on, and urged the examination of unexpected side effects of technological development. While he mostly stressed the simultaneous effects, it seems relevant to consider the creation of possible lock-in effects – situations where new directions of change are hampered by continuous, smaller adjustments. A 'business as usual' way of 'living with water', based on step-by-step adjustments and adaptations as illustrated by these cases – both traditional 'wise' strategies and technology-aided strategies – can in fact sometimes lock people into an unsustainable pathway and effectively hamper a transition to a more permanent and desirable situation for local people. If this is the case, strategies based on traditional water literacy may in fact be viewed as a constraint, as opposed to a progression.

Acknowledgements

The research underpinning the chapter is funded by two major projects: a grant from Danida-FFU (09-001-KU) (a region-wide assessment of land systems' resilience and climate robustness in the agricultural frontline of the Sahel) and the ERC project 'Waterworlds'. The author also thanks the reviewers for their constructive comments.

Notes

1. Inspired by the pastoral people based on the southern fringe of Ferlo, sometimes referred to as Egge-egge.

References

Adriansen, H.K. 2008. 'Understanding Pastoral Mobility: The Case of Senegalese Fulani', *Geographical Journal* 174: 207–22.
Adriansen, H.K., and T.T. Nielsen. 2005. 'The Geography of Pastoral Mobility: A Spatio-temporal Analysis of GPS Data from Sahelian Senegal', *GeoJournal* 64: 177–88.
African Development Fund. 2003. 'Diffa Region Local Development Support Project (PADL-DIFFA)'. Appraisal Report. Department of Agriculture and Rural Development, Central West Region. Republic of Niger.
Barron, J., et al. 2010. 'Coping with Rainfall Variability in Semi-arid Agro-ecosystems: Implications on Catchment Scale Water Balances by Dry-Spell Mitigation Strategies among Small-Scale Farmers in Niger', *International Journal of Water Resources Development* 26(4): 543–59.

Bolwig, S., et al. 2011. 'New Perspectives on Natural Resource Management in the Sahel'. SEREIN Occasional Paper No. 21. Department of Geography and Geology, University of Copenhagen.

Brooks, N. 2004. 'Drought in the African Sahel: Long-term Perspectives and Future Prospects'. Tyndall Centre Working Paper 61. Norwich: Tyndall Centre.

———. 2006. 'Cultural Responses to Aridity in the Middle Holocene and Increased Social Complexity', *Quaternary International* 151: 29–49.

Brown, C., and U. Lall. 2006. 'Water and Economic Development: The Role of Variability and a Framework for Resilience', *Natural Resources Forum* 30: 306–17.

Brown, C., et al. 2010. 'Hydroclimatic Risk to Economic Growth in sub-Saharan Africa', *Climate Change* 106: 621–47.

Christensen, J.H., et al. (eds), 'Climate Change 2007: The Physical Science Basis'. Contribution of Working Group I to the Fourth Assessment Report of the Intergovernmental Panel on Climate Change. Cambridge and New York: Cambridge University Press.

Claude, J., et al. 1991. Un espace sahelien: la mare d'Oursi, Burkina Faso, 1 ed. Paris: ORSTOM.

Desanker, P.V., and C. Magadza (Coordinating lead authors; plus 11 lead authors and 13 contributing authors). 2001. 'Africa'. Chapter 10 of the IPCC Working Group II, Third Assessment Report. Cambridge University Press.

Dietz, A.J., R. Ruben and A. Verhagen (eds). 2004. 'The Impact of Climate Change on Drylands with a Focus on West Africa', *Environment & Policy Series* 39. Kluwer Academic Publishers.

Eakin, H., and A. Luers. 2006. 'Assessing the Vulnerability of Social–Environmental Systems', *Annual Review of Environment and Resources* 31: 365–94.

Falkenmark, M., and J. Rockström. 2006. 'The New Blue and Green Water Paradigm: Breaking New Ground for Water Resources Planning and Management', *Journal of Water Resources Planning and Management* (May/June): 129–32.

Faurès, J.M., M. Bernardi and R. Gommes. 2010. 'There Is No Such Thing as an Average: How Farmers Manage Uncertainty Related to Climate and Other Factors', *International Journal of Water Resources Development* 26(4): 523–42.

Glantz, M.H. 1977. 'Nine Fallacies of Natural Disaster: The Case of the Sahel', *Climate Change* 1: 69–84.

Goodland, R. 2002. 'Sustainability: Human, Social, Economic and Environmental', *Encyclopedia of Global Environmental Change*. Hoboken, NJ: John Wiley and Sons.

Grey, D., and C. Sadoff. 2007. 'Sink or Swim? Water Security for Growth and Development', *Water Policy* 9: 545–61.

Grove, A.T. 1985. 'Water Characteristics of the Chari System and Lake Chad', in A.T. Grove (ed.), *The Republic of Niger and its Neighbours*. Rotterdam: Balkema, pp. 61–76.

Juul, K. 1996. 'Post-drought Migration and Technological Innovation among Fulani Herders in Senegal: The Triumph of the Tube!'. IIED Drylands Programme Issue Paper 64. London.

Kowal, J.M., and A.H. Kassam. 1978. *Agricultural Ecology of Savanna: A Study of West Africa*. Oxford: Clarendon Press.

Lundqvist, J., and M. Falkenmark. 2010. 'Adaptation to Rainfall Variability and Un-

predictability: New Dimensions of Old Challenges and Opportunities', *International Journal of Water Resources Development* 26(4): 595–612.
Molden, D., et al. 2009. 'Improving Agricultural Water Productivity: Between Optimism and Caution', *Agricultural Water Management* 97: 528–35.
Ngounou Ngatcha, B., J. Mudry and J. Sarrot-Reynauld. 2007. 'Groundwater Recharge from Rainfall in the Southern Border of Lake Chad in Cameroon', *World Applied Science Journal* 2(2): 125–31.
Nicholson, S. 2005. On the question of the "recovery' of the rains in the West African Sahel. *Journal of Arid Environments* 63: 615-41.
Niel, H., C. Leduc and C. Dielin. 2009. 'Caractérisation de la variabilité spatiale et temporalle des précipitations annuelles sur le bassin de Tchad au cour du 20ème siècle', *Hydrological Science Journal* 50(2): 223–43.
Nielsen, J.Ø., and A. Reenberg. 2010. 'Temporality and the Problem with Singling Out Climate as a Current Driver of Change in a Small West African Village', *Journal of Arid Environments* 74: 464–74.
OECD. 2009. 'Regional Atlas of West Africa'. Paris.
Oksen, P. 1993. 'Naturresourcer og strategivalg i en landsby i det syd-østlige Niger'. Unpublished master's thesis, Department of Geography, University of Copenhagen.
Orlove, B., and S.C. Caton. 2010. 'Water Sustainability: Anthropological Approaches and Prospects', *Annual Review of Anthropology* 39: 401–15.
Ozer, P., Y.-C. Hountondji and O. Laminou Manzo. 2009. 'Evolution des characteristiques pluviométriques dans l'est du Niger de 1940 a 2007', *Geo-Eco-Trop* 33: 11–30.
PAGRN. 2005. Projet d'Appui à la Gestion des Ressources Naturelles, Typologies de Cuvettes et Bas-Fond et Possibilité d'Expoltation Agricole et de Valorisation. Karimou et al., http://www.reca-niger.org/IMG/pdf/Diffa_Typologie_cuvettes_Karkara-AFVP_2005.pdf (accessed July 26 2015).
Proud, S.R., and L.V. Rasmussen. 2010. 'The Influence of Seasonal Rainfall upon Sahel Vegetation', *Remote Sensing Letters* 2: 241–49.
Rasmussen, L.V., and A. Reenberg. 2012. 'Land Use Rationales in Desert Fringe Agriculture', *Applied Geography* 34: 596–606.
Reenberg, A. 1982. *Det Katastroferamte Sahel* – Tørke, imperialisme eller andre forklaringer. Brenderup: Geografforlaget.
Reenberg, A., I. Mamman and P. Oksen. 2013. 'Twenty Years of Land Use and Livelihood Changes in SE Niger: Obsolete and Short-sighted Adaptation to Climatic and Demographic Pressures?', *Journal of Arid Environments* 94: 47–58.
Reenberg, A., T.L. Nielsen and K. Rasmussen. 1998. 'Field Expansion and Reallocation in the Sahel: Land Use Pattern Dynamics in a Fluctuating Biophysical and Socio-economic Environment', *Global Environmental Change* 8: 309–27.
Reenberg, A., and B. Paarup-Laursen. 1997. 'Determinants for Land Use Strategies in a Sahelian Agro-ecosystem: Anthropological and Ecological Geographical Aspects of Natural Resource Management', *Agricultural Systems* 53: 209–29.
Ridder, N. de, et al. 1982. *Productivity of Sahelian Range Lands I*. Wageningen: Wageningen University.
VEOLIA Water/IFPRI. 2011. 'Finding the Blue Path for a Sustainable Economy'. Chicago: VEOLIA White Paper.

10

Deep Time and Shallow Waters

Configurations of an Irrigation Channel in the Andes

Mattias Borg Rasmussen

The Andean landscape is marked by lines of water that defy the rugged terrain. By way of low- and high-tech engineering, the propensity of water to take the fastest route downhill is manipulated. Low gradient waterways are carved into the terrain, concrete or wooden bridges bring the water across ravines and creeks, reservoirs contain the water, at times creating pressure for the final distribution. While a flow of water is by its very definition temporal, measured by litres per second, in this chapter I wish to open up a discussion of how the flows across the Andean landscapes are both embedded in and configure particular times.

Complex irrigation systems are epitomes of historical civilizations in the Andes. Both the Incas and those who came before were notable engineers of their landscapes, and today, both practices of engineering as well as many of the actual irrigation channels have long histories. This chapter centres around one such channel: the Querocoja 3 Bases (Q3B), located in Recuay in the upper part of Peru's Santa River basin. This channel, with its out-take just below the white peaks of the Cordillera Blanca, takes its water from the Querococha Lake from where it is distributed through dugout waterways to the three different communities that make up it bases of users. In this chapter I discuss how the channel has different times and how its users and builders may at times trace it back to the Incas, at times to the feudal structures of the hacienda era, and at times to the rural highlanders 'liberation endeavours' after the agrarian reforms of 1969. Furthermore, just as the channel has many histories, it may also have different imagined futures, and hence, many presents. Most notably I shall highlight the present that emerges with the prospects of the melting glaciers.

As a means of dealing with the inherent capriciousness of wind and weather, irrigation channels are constructed, maintained and put into use. A leading figure in both the past construction and the present management of the Q3B, Don Arturo, told me the long and complicated story that led to the construction of the much-wanted channel that brings water from the Querococha watershed across difficult terrain to his and two other villages. The construction of the channel had begun in the early 1980s as an extension of a previous, much smaller channel. In one of our conversations I asked why they chose this particular moment for constructing the channel, expecting that we would talk about the new institutions and reconfigurations of the territory that emerged after the agrarian reforms during the 1970s. He gave this rather surprising answer:

> Look, I had been anticipating myself with this work, because I already knew of the consequences that we are now living through due to the global warming, the melting glaciers, all of that. So I had prognosticated the situation; I already knew of these events that we would feel, that we would have. That is why I proposed that we should build that irrigation channel. There was no other reason than my own initiative because of this situation with the global warming.

The comment made by Don Arturo is remarkable because of the way in which it resituates the channel in terms of landscape, human agency, and temporal orientation compared to earlier lines of reasoning that he had given me. The Q3B is the centre of gravity in this chapter, as I explore the flow of water that traverses the high altitude grasslands known as the *puna*, from the Querococha watershed to the fields and houses of its users. By focusing on how the water is situated in time while simultaneously creating time I argue that water and time are linked through personal action, technologies of irrigation, expansion, construction and maintenance, and modes of local governance. In the first part of the chapter I explore how water is located within the landscape, how it is worked with by rural people, and how individual strategies converge with collective temporal repertoires of water management. The second part moves further into the temporality of water politics, scrutinizing how collective practices of maintenance, expansion and defence are extended into different pasts and futures, thereby reconfiguring the present. Water here is always a site of cultural and political struggle, and is thus deeply implicated with social lives.

This chapter is based on twelve months of ethnographic fieldwork between 2010 and 2011. Exploring the flows of water across the rugged terrain, I was able to identify the different connections that are created through water, and scrutinize how these entail contentious politics, collective aspirations and individual ambitions, as people were struggling to make ethical and moral imperatives meet the needs of the household and the cycles of the year. And I saw how the flows of water were not only inscriptions into the surface of the mountains, but that the very movement of water was an integral part of the flow of life in the Andes.

Waters of the Altitudes

The province of Recuay is located in the upper part of the valley known as the Callejón de Huaylas. The area is famous for being home to some of the most dramatic features of the Andes, as the Cordillera Blanca hosts a selection of the highest peaks of the continent. Across the valley, the landscape is different. Whereas the Cordillera Blanca in its white drama of glaciers reaches towards the skies, the Cordillera Negra is lower and softer. And the colours of white (Blanca) and black (Negra) that are used as adjectives to describe the two separate parts of these ranges give a clue to a vital difference between those who live east of Recuay and those who dwell on the western slopes: the availability of water.

On either side of the Santa River, which cuts through the bottom of the Callejón de Huaylas, water in its different forms is crucial to the lives of farmers, herders and occasional labourers. Indeed, I would often be told during the many meetings and discussions that I attended during my year of fieldwork in the area, 'water is life'. This is a truth of life that has been recorded on many other occasions, as in the work of Perreault (2006) analysing the gas and water wars in Bolivia. It would be stated at some point during virtually every meeting of the irrigation users' committees, and its ramifications move the liquid substance beyond biophysics and into vitality. As Jakobsen and McNeish (2006: 7) argue in their anthology on water politics and local knowledge in Bolivia and Ecuador, water is 'the provider of life and animation for the universe'. Thus, water in the Andes is imbued with power and cultural significance, which again raises questions as to how water works as a formative power, shaping and shaped by human lives (cf. Dransart 2006).

Rural people of Recuay would often tell me that they wait for the rain to come in order to sow. The temporality of weather, in terms of seasonal variability, permeates the productive and social activities, as farmers go about adjusting the yearly calendar of activities in accordance with the expected patterns of precipitation and temperature curves. Ingold has argued for an understanding of the temporality of the landscape in which no place is ever just the incidental locus of human action, but is always produced by it. Thus, 'the landscape is the world as it is known to those who dwell therein, who inhabit is places and journey along the paths connecting them' (Ingold 2000: 193). Because people undertake an array of activities, or tasks, that are 'constitutive acts of dwelling' (ibid.: 195), different temporalities intersect in the production of the landscape. The landscape is temporal because it is produced through dwelling and thus incorporates many different tasks. Ingold likens the workings of time in the 'taskscape' to that of music: each instrument follows its own rhythm, yet none can be said to mark the time alone. Instead, it is in their congruence that social time emerges.

Even though agriculture is predominantly rain fed, the rural dwellers of Recuay have a network of irrigation channels at their disposal. As highlighted in more classic Andeanist work on irrigation, it is a way of extending the agricultural cycle beyond the annual seasons (e.g. Golte 1980; Gelles 2000; Trawick 2003). It works differently at different altitudes, however. Recuay is located at 3,400 metres above sea level, which is close to the upper limit of meaningful irrigation. As the altitude increases, the crops are vulnerable to low temperatures, which threaten to 'burn off' (*quemar*) the crops and destroy the harvest. The irrigation channels that I had under exploration during fieldwork were all of limited use. Being the largest and oldest of the channels, the Q3B has had cycles of more intensive use in the past. But during my fieldwork, this channel brought little water to the fields. Instead, people relied on their auxiliary channels bringing water from nearby springs, or simply recurred to rain-fed agriculture only. Even so, vast amounts of time would be spent in the irrigation committees.

Following Ingold, I suggest that the temporality of water provides an apt starting point for understanding how the different social, political and economic activities of the Andean people relate to each other. The rhythms not only stem from human activities, but also from a wide array of movements, such as the shifting days, winds and tides. Consequently, temporalities emerge in the interplay between human and non-human forms of movement. Citing E.P. Thompson on eighteenth-century Sunderland, Ingold notes that 'the patterning of social time in the seaport follows *upon* the rhythms of the sea' (Ingold 2000: 200). To Ingold, resonance captures the intersections of these different temporalities that emerge between the movements of people, animals, wind and weather, as well as celestial spheres. Agriculture and the flow of water are thus embedded in a particular temporal logic.

Dwelling in the landscape, as herders and agriculturalists, labourers and migrants, rural people of Recuay are in a continuous process of creating and recreating the world that they inhabit. The everyday tasks they engage in must in different ways resonate with the movement of the water in the skies, on the mountaintops, in the riverbeds, and underground, as well as in tubes, pipes and channels. Intricate to landscapes, water marks the engagements of people and place. The waters of the altitudes are never just water. They become, as it were, the very materiality of social relationships, as human actions are done *with* water rather than to it (cf. Bender 2002: S104), embedded in particular times and places. Thinking about the temporality of the landscape, Tim Ingold writes that 'the stream does not flow between pre-cut banks, but cuts its bank even as it flows. Likewise, people shape the landscape even as they dwell. And human activities, as well as the action of rivers and the sea, contribute significantly to the process of erosion. As you watch the stream flows, folk are at work, a landscape is being formed, and time passes' (Ingold 2000: 203). Landscape, space and time infiltrate each other (cf. Massey 2006).

Here I am therefore interested in how certain 'temporalizing practices' (Munn 1992) are related to the flow of water. Like Ingold, Nancy Munn has a phenomenological take on time, highlighting how both conscious and tacit embodied knowledge bring out the inherent temporal character of social life. Water, here, is a particularly privileged site for considering not only how a sense of time is created through practice, but also how this practice relates to other kinds of movement. Building on philosophical traditions, and largely theoretical in scope, Gell ([1992] 2001) develops further a distinction between human (A-series) and objective (B-series) time. While events exist with definite relationships between them, it is through the temporality of the A-series that people subjectively perceive the passing of time as involving past, present and future. As ethnographers we are inclined to focus on the A-series, but should consider how these relate to each other. Gell proposes that 'time-maps' work as representations of time mediating between 'real time' and the personal experience of it. Bear moves on to suggest that time-maps 'knot together pragmatic concerns about navigating in time to the long-term fate of ethical and political relations ... As we navigate time, we co-ordinate various time-maps at once in relation to diverse social and non-human rhythms' (Bear 2014: 16). What I want to suggest, based on this all too brief review, is that the irrigation channel and the flow of water mediates human and non-human time.

In what follows, I shall make no sharp distinction between the water and the channels through which it carves its way through the landscape.

At high altitudes, water and channels implicate one another as people try to manage their landscapes and their lives by engaging with water in different ways. Calculations made by topographers with banded sticks and optical pointers – or, as was the case with Q3B, with wooden sticks crossing each other along the imagined course of the channel – predispose the flow of the water. But once water starts to flow, it begins to cut its own way, eroding the banks and defying the engineering efforts, at times led astray by alternatives cut open by villagers with other interests in mind. To understand how, we shall look closely into the social and political processes that made and make up the Q3B channel – that is, how people deal with the presence, absence, duration and intensity of water in the channel. For several reasons, the channel that is supposed to bring water from Querococha is actually of little use, but even so, people spend vast amounts of time and effort to secure, maintain, expand and defend the water. This paradox, I argue, can be understood by considering the temporality of the irrigation channel, and hence the waters that run through it, as will be shown below.

Water Works

The flow of water in the Q3B is only partially a matter of water quantity. Thus, while there must, obviously, be an available pool of water at the intake, questions of the management of the commons emerge along its course. These are questions of membership and access, distribution and equity, and legitimacy and authority. In other words, akin to Strang (2005) who in her analysis of the different actors along the Mitchell River in Australia finds that cultural visions of water are encoded with meaning regarding production and reproduction of human society, the following seeks to illuminate how individual and collective practices intersect with ecological issues, social issues, and conflicts over leadership and water legitimacy. The emphasis here is on the temporal practices of water management, and consequently, on how the movement of the all too often shallow waters connect deep times and everyday concerns.

The irrigation channels in Peru are organized in a nested hierarchy in which the users of the channels are the basic unit of the users' committee. The users' committee is headed by an elected president, whose legitimacy is therefore both stipulated by law and granted at grass-roots level. In matters of disagreement, if the president of the channels cannot solve the conflict it moves upwards in the organizational hierarchy, first to the users' commission, which is a gathering of individual channels, then to the regional junta, and finally to the national junta. This is not the place to go into any depth on the historicity of this structure (for a detailed analysis, see Oré and Rap 2009). What I wish to highlight is that to be a legitimate user of the water of the channel, one must be a member of the users' committee – in this case, of the Q3B.

In 2009 the national government promulgated a new law on water that reframed the terms of engagement amongst water users, drawing new lines between what can be considered legitimate and illegitimate users, as well as introducing new standards for the interactions between water users and the state. While the law stipulates certain courses of action in times of conflict, it also confirms the right to customary use. Therefore, while the presidency of the Q3B cannot guarantee the availability of water in general – both failing rains and melting glaciers are beyond their realm of influence – they can, and must, continually deal with nightly trout-fishers shutting of the sluice gates at the intake, illegitimate users creating little out-takes to water their fields in the upper part of the channel, eroding banks, filtrations and seepages, and distribution of water among the three bases and among the users of these bases, all while dealing with a local government of varying and often unpredictable levels of engagement in community affairs and needs. In other words, expanding, maintaining and defending the waters of Q3B places the presidency in a contentious field of intra- and inter-community politics.

Efforts to expand the irrigation channel take different forms. Back in the mid-1980s, community leaders of the three bases that were to make up the users of Q3B agreed upon the work that would expand by threefold the reach of the old irrigation ditch (*acequia*) of the former hacienda owners, who had been displaced by the agrarian reforms some fifteen years earlier. They were thus proposing an addition to the existing water infrastructure that would enhance the possibilities for the household to obtain a successful harvest, and one that would mimic the pre-Incaic waterway that was still evident in parts of the terrain. In order to obtain permission from the landowners, Don Arturo and Don Diosdado wrote in a letter to them that 'the small plots that we possess lack water, which causes the seeds that we put down to be unproductive and our economic situation to be much reduced'. The process that followed was tedious, involving a negotiation not only with authorities at different levels, but also with other communities. The expansion and basic alteration of the channel required that the local authorities had to deal with the relevant governmental institutions. Concerns about the present merged with concerns about the future, and they had to propose a solution that would cover both.

The Q3B was dug out over the course of approximately three months. Equipped with pickaxes and basic tents, the labour force spent the cold nights in the high altitudes while the work proceeded slowly. Organized as *faena,* the prospective users of the channel were obliged to participate in its construction. This type of labour can be seen as a citizenry obligation: if you wish to receive the benefits of membership you must contribute. A way of organizing labour during the hacienda era, it was institutionalized by the government of Leguía during the 1920s. The *faena* then emerged as a trade-off between a national government desperate to mobilize labour in order to expand the road network across the country, and the highland populations yearning for their own land and the acknowledgement that they were equal citizens (Gose 1994: 58). As a workforce related to citizenship, the *faena* has since then been integrated into peasant community organization as the clearest expression of the 'costs' of localized citizenship. It is the *faena* of construction along with the present day statutes of the association that define the legitimacy of the water users. Those who dug out the Q3B earned the right to membership for themselves and their heirs. One can, however, be a member without having participated, albeit at a considerable cost.

Implicitly, the politics of infrastructural enhancement deal with particular configurations of water scarcity. In late 1985, when Don Arturo and others took charge, the major concern was how to create stability in a landscape that was shaken by the political movements in the aftermath of the agrarian reforms and the subsequent (re-)emergence of the peasant communities (*comunidades campesinas*) as a new form of territorial ordering. Future prospects of water availability were therefore tightly connected to the perception of territories. In a landscape of emancipation and historical injustice, the construction of Q3B connected a past of Incaic grandeur and a prolonged, interim era of violent domination by landlord rule with the promise of future water equity and the long-awaited social justice.

New Engagements, Old Concerns

The utility of the channel is in itself bound to the seasonal variability: it is exactly in times of predicted water scarcity – that is, outside the rainy season – that the activities related to the maintenance, expansion and defence of the waters are most intense. These I understand as 'temporalizing practices'. Meetings of the committee are frequent and, at least during my time there, tense. During the rainy season, water is plentiful across the landscape. But once the clouds begin to disappear behind the peaks of the two Cordilleras that encircle the people of Recuay, the earth quickly dries up. These are times when water is needed, and times when conflicts and coordinated action is most likely to happen. First of all, after months of heavy rain the channel is in dire need of repair. The coordinated actions secure the continuity of the flow of water. Secondly, as water is once more becoming scarce, illegitimate users begin to appear and the users' committee must police their domains of interest. In the following I highlight how the work of the committee is embedded in temporal practices.

In the Andes, waiting for the rain is a finely attuned productive practice that relates to the cyclical time predicated by the seasonality of precipitation. It is waiting as timing. Looking at economic life beyond the fields, we see that many economic as well as domestic and social activities are related to this mode of waiting. Rather than being a passive activity, it would therefore be more adequate to describe waiting for the rain as being a suspension of certain agricultural activities 'until the time is right' (cf. Minnegal 2009). As Hage writes in his introduction to a recent volume on waiting, 'waiting happens in time, in the sense that time and time frames pre-exist the subjects that are waiting within them. On the other hand, waiting creates time. That is, various modalities of waiting produce their own temporality that may or may not be in tune with other social and natural temporalities' (Hage 2009: 7). Rain is thus an integral part of social time in the Andes, central to the emergent resonance between labour in the fields and homes, social events and religious celebrations. Harvesting in the field is tightly connected to practices of timing and anticipation, reading the signs in the environment and listening to the weather forecasts on the radio.

As observed elsewhere as well (Robbins, in Hage 2009: 9), the changes in the cyclical predictability of the rain that has come with climate change require that farmers and herders rethink their engagement with the environment. 'We are prone to change now', Don Aristes explained. 'Before, at this time I would be done, potatoes would almost be ready to eat and some were ready for harvest. Now there are none'. While climate change is not always the master narrative through which they express their being in the landscape, it provides a powerful language for understanding how the temporality of water configures the social life of agricultural production in the Andes. As a farmer or herder, the evacuation of the near future (Guyer 2007) is hardly a possibility. The cycles of the season combine with the passing of time extending itself until the end of time to create a situation of both immediacy of the near future (will the harvest be good?) and long-term worries of the far future (will there be a world for my children to inhabit?). Future and temporality, writes Guyer, can be reconfigured and rearticulated (ibid.: 416). Even though the near future remains present in the everyday temporalizing practices that are carried out in relation to the management of the water, the far future changes shape with the attention to climate change.

Whereas concerns about stability may in a sense be part of a narrative of loss connected also to the ways in which people talk about climate change and the shifting patterns of precipitation, there is also a different way of situating Q3B in the temporal landscape through a particular set of practices. Improvements to the channel aim at heightening the efficiency. In two of the villages, the inhabitants have found different solutions for improving their practices of irrigation. One has constructed a reservoir aided by the Recuay municipality; the other has installed a system of dispersers with the support of the Ticapampa municipality. Both these constitute new possibilities for enhancing the efficiency and range of the irrigation systems. Water here becomes connected to the future through the promise that, by technological intervention, things might be different. The basic components are present, and development becomes a question of ingenuity and initiative on the part of individuals, the will to act on the part of the local leadership, and responsiveness and capital on the part of the local government and the relevant NGOs.

Tasks of maintenance abound, because the steady movement of water and wind, and of animals and people, gradually erodes and tears down the walls of the channel. Whereas expansions and alterations reach into the future, ordinary maintenance is aimed at restoring equilibrium, optimizing the potentiality of the current configuration of the flow. Channels are cleansed, bridges built, walls restored. The work, however, is embedded in a temporal landscape, as the flow of water is both related to a concrete past just after the completion of the channel, when water flowed in abundance, and an imagined past when the original, pre-Incaic Q3B brought water to the archaic inhabitants of the ruins at Jekosh above Poccrac. As mentioned above, in the Andes communal work is what connects one to society, granting rights to water – among other things. Participating in the *faena* of construction and the present-day *faenas* of maintenance affirms the user's connectedness not only to the present community of water users, but also a historical community of Andean irrigators going back to the forefathers of the Incas.

The work of an irrigation committee such as that of Q3B oscillates between securing stability and opening the way for development. Often the capacity of the users' committee is limited to ensuring stability and continuity, but from time to time windows of opportunity emerge, as happened with both the reservoir and the dispersers funded by the participatory budgets of the local municipalities. These not only mark a chance for improving agricultural production, but also stand as proof that affairs need not stagnate or deteriorate as would happen to an irrigation channel that is only subject to maintenance. Cleaning up channels secures, at best, the status quo of the flow of water, but maintenance is an impossible and continuous battle against the forces of erosion, tectonics, animal movement and human imprudence. But importantly, ensuring that water can continue to flow retains the possibility that the capacity may be enhanced, and the water distribution network expanded.

Like maintenance, the defence of waters is a political and social practice that is embedded in certain versions of the present rooted in a known past. The landscapes that the water traverses are not the same as when the current version of Q3B was constructed. In territorial terms, new configurations of ownership have emerged since the post-reform efforts to establish large-scale associative enterprises (e.g. SAIS Atusparia) were replaced by the more localized and bottom–up initiatives to create the peasant communities. I shall not go into the details of the socio-political particularities of the different types of territorial ordering, but merely say that the reconfiguration of the territory created new alliances, which in the case of Q3B pose a challenge to the flow of the water which is therefore resituated within the landscape. The actions producing stability of the flow of water thus connect the channel to a past of social struggles. The history of the channel is a victorious story in which the founders managed to organize and carry out the work in a complicated socio-political field. In an area of heavy out-migration and a sense of social and moral decay, the task of maintaining the flow of water still signals a sense of social continuity. As production becomes increasingly individualized and directed towards the market rather than the community, water is the last realm that is inherently social.

Temporality and the Construction of Context

In this section I shall return to the quote that opened it, relating the words of Don Arturo. He grew up in Poccrac at the very same place where he now has his house and lands. In the meetings at the Q3B commission it would most often be people such as him who would set the tone. His relation to the political sphere has made him a trained speaker, and his proficiency in reading and interpreting allows him to deliver persuasive arguments to his peers during the meetings of the Q3B users' committee. These would often be made with reference to the twin challenges to life in Poccrac: a self-perceived backwardness and marginalization, and global climate change most evident from the bare rocks of the Cordillera Blanca.

On an earlier occasion, Don Arturo had told me how his grandmother had warned him against the coming disaster of glacial meltdown: 'When this peak ends', she said pointing towards a particular top in the Cordillera Blanca visible from Poccrac, 'it is going to be Judgement Day'. As highlighted by Robbins (2001) in his study on Papua New Guinean millenarism, this perspective on time indicates that, in Christianity, time not only has a fixed starting point but also a definite ending, perhaps followed by a new beginning. It is a working paradox of a time model that it is both continuous and susceptible to ruptures, telling people to engage themselves in this world while expecting it to end at any time (ibid.: 526). Whether put into a framework of Christian eschatology or the more mundane dynamics of water scarcity, the important point is that the canal was constructed by way of 'anticipation' (see Hastrup 2013a); that is, a projection of a flow of water into the future. Thus, people continuously engage in the maintenance, expansion and defence of the waters of the Q3B. But the grounds differ, and so do the landscapes.

The projection of water availability into the future is thus a matter of constructing certain scenarios. In that way, the future is brought into the present by adjusting one's actions to a scenario that is, in a sense, part of a social imaginary (see Hastrup 2013b). It is, however, also worth noting the very different future that is imagined in the quote that opened the chapter compared to the letter that Don Arturo and Don Diosdado sent to the leadership of the SAIS Atusparia in the initial phase of the construction. We have no way of knowing whether Don Arturo had actually prognosticated the situation back in 1985. What is important, however, is to consider how the flow of water becomes situated very differently within the landscape according to the chosen scenario; that is, the way in which the future is brought into the present. In short, a landscape of territorial and productive injustice differs from a landscape of climate change.

The channel had many authors, and many would disagree with Don Arturo's way of putting himself at the epicentre of the construction work. To Don Arturo, the reason for initiating the ambitious construction of Q3B over the course of twenty-three kilometres across difficult terrain was the imminent climate change; hence, a way of proactively countering the effects would be to lead water from the abundant Querococha watershed to the rather dry slopes in the vicinity of the three bases of the channel. While Don Arturo may, in a sense, reflect a retrospective afterthought of the reasons for extending the range of the old irrigation channel, his rationalization of the construction gives vital clues to understanding how present and future availability of water is imagined and acted upon.

The remark made by Don Arturo points towards the temporality of the irrigation channel and how it works as a time-map. By resituating the channel in terms of a future scenario, the channel changes its social and political significance. No longer being a matter of lack of water within the plots, the channel shifted horizons: the flow of water had to be established in order to pre-empt a predicted water scarcity. Strictly speaking, climate change as a process and a series of discrete events belongs to the B-series of time. But these events are brought into the A-series as the social imaginations of what this implies filter into the experience of time, the worries about the upcoming season and the imaginaries of the far future. The time-map that connects the B-series to particular events is being reconfigured by imagining a different modality of connecting past and future events. Don Arturo's tale of construction thus raises questions as to what contextualization does, not only when we as analysts employ it, but also how everybody, including the people we work with, create new contexts.

Here, we reach a point of contextualization akin to the challenge that anthropologists and other social scientists face. Originating in the Latin word for weaving, context is a matter of creating connections. As Dilley (1999) writes, 'connections made with one domain imply a series of disconnections with another: contexts not only include certain phenomena as relevant, they exclude others as marginal or put them out of the picture all together' (ibid.: 14). Through establishing certain connections through practice, discourse and – in this instance – talking to an anthropologist, Don Arturo draws forward the channel as a particular configuration. By invoking climate change as the master narrative of the channel, he establishes a set of connections to wider societal concerns, scientific discourses on climate change, and Christian concerns for the end of the world. Thus, the channel becomes situated within particular social and historical times and, accordingly, attains a specific purpose. By articulating these connections, Don Arturo simultaneously creates disconnections that would otherwise locate the channel differently in the shared temporal landscape of its users.

The activities connected to the establishment, maintenance and defence of the flow of water in the Q3B are contextualizing moves, locating the channel within particular temporal landscapes. As the different engagements with the landscapes from agrarian reforms via the efforts of contemporary engineers to climate change highlight, the meaning of the canal and the efforts that people undertake change accordingly. The materiality of the water and the channel through which it flows thereby become ways of imagining the passing of time. It is a time-map reaching both into the past and the future, connecting these in different ways through the present. But the activities of the everyday – those of maintenance that seek to secure the stability of the flow, the status quo of water availability – are directed towards the upcoming harvest only. Thus, people simultaneously work in and image themselves within different spatial horizons. And the flow of water therefore not only traverses the terrain, but also time.

Conclusion

Life in the high mountains is tightly connected to the seasonality of water availability. Even as the activities of the households have long since moved beyond work in the field, the coming and going of the seasons provides a scheme of probability and predictability. While being susceptible to short- and long-term fluctuations of water, the work connected to the channel and its shallow waters employ different temporal repertoires and strategies. By looking at the temporalizing practices of maintaining, expanding and defending the Q3B, I have wished to explore the temporality of water governance. The work that water and people in Recuay do is related to different temporal scales, relating both the seasonal changes and to the ways in which past, present and future intersect. Thus, the work of water moves beyond productive practices into imaginaries of the place and time of those who engage in manipulating its movements.

As a Gellian time-map, the irrigation channel and the flow of water that it carries mediates between human time and 'real' time. As climate change changes both the actual and the imagined flow of water, a new time-map emerges as the irrigation channel is being reconfigured. Therefore, I have argued that the waters and the channels are embedded in particular times, and that they also, by way of the practical engagement of individuals and collective imaginaries, create time. By focusing on how the water is situated in time while simultaneously creating time I found that water and temporality are linked through personal action, technologies of irrigation, construction and maintenance, and local governance. The temporality of the irrigation channel thus places the flow of water differently within the social and cultural landscapes. The intensity of water, its absence, presence and duration, infiltrate social lives along the course of the channel, evoking different horizons for action, and bringing new futures into the present.

References

Bear, L. 2014. 'Doubt, Conflict, Mediation: The Anthropology of Modern Time', *Journal of the Royal Anthropological Institute* 20(S1): 3–30.
Bender, B. 2002. 'Time and Landscape', *Current Anthropology* 43, Supplement: Repertoires of Timekeeping in Anthropology (Aug.–Oct. 2002): S103–12.
Dilley, R. 1999. *The Problem of Context*. New York and Oxford: Berghahn Books.
Dransart, P. 2006. *Kay Pacha: Cultivating Earth and Water in the Andes*. Oxford: Archaeopress.
Gell, A. (1992) 2001. *The Anthropology of Time: Cultural Constructions of Temporal Maps and Images*. Oxford and Washington, DC: Berg.
Gelles, P. 2000. *Water and Power in Highland Peru: The Cultural Politics of Irrigation and Development*. New Brunswick, NJ: Rutgers University Press.
Golte, J. 1980. *La Racionalidad de la Organización Andina*. Lima: Instituto de Estudios Peruanos. Colección Mínima No. 9.
Gose, P. 1994. *Deathly Waters and Hungry Mountains: Agrarian Ritual and Class Formation in an Andean Town*. Toronto, Buffalo and London: University of Toronto Press.
Guyer, J.I. 2007. 'Prophecy and the Near Future: Thoughts on Macroeconomic, Evangelical, and Punctuated Time', *American Ethnologist* 34(3): 409–21.
Hage, G. 2009. 'Introduction', in G. Hage (ed.), *Waiting*. Melbourne: Melbourne University Press, pp. 1–12.
Hastrup, K. 2013a. 'Anticipating Nature: The Productive Uncertainty of Climate Models', in K. Hastrup and M. Skrydstrup (eds), *The Social Life of Climate Change Models: Anticipating Nature*. New York: Routledge, pp. 1–29.
———. 2013b. 'Anthropological Contributions to the Study of Climate: Past, Present, Future', *WIREs Climate Change* 2013. doi: 10.1002/wcc.219.
Ingold, T. 2000. *The Perception of the Environment: Essays in Livelihood, Dwelling and Skill*. London and New York: Routledge.
Jakobsen, F., and J. McNeish. 2006. *From Where Life Flows: The Local Knowledge and Politics of Water in the Andes*. Trondheim: Tapir Academic Press.
Massey, D. 2006. 'Landscape as Provocation: Reflections on Moving Mountains', *Journal of Material Culture* 11(1/2): 33–48.
Minnegal, M. 2009. 'The Time is Right: Waiting, Reciprocity and Sociality', in G. Hage (ed.), *Waiting*. Melbourne: Melbourne University Press, pp. 89–96.
Munn, N.D. 1992. 'The Cultural Anthropology of Time: A Critical Essay', *Annual Review of Anthropology* 21: 93–123.
Oré, M.T., and E. Rap. 2009. 'Políticas Neoliberales de Agua en el Perú. Antecedentes y Entretelones de la Ley de Recursos Hídricos', *Debates en Sociología* 34: 32–66.
Perreault, T. 2006. 'From the Guerra del Agua to the Guerra del Gas: Resource Governance, Neoliberalism and Popular Protest in Bolivia', *Antipode* 38(1): 150–72.
Robbins, J. 2001. 'Secrecy and the Sense of an Ending: Narrative, Time, and Everyday Millenarianism in Papua New Guinea and in Christian Fundamentalism', *Comparative Studies in Society and History* 43(3): 525–51.

Strang, V. 2005. 'Water Works: Agency and Creativity in the Mitchell River Catchment', *The Australian Journal of Anthropology* 16(3): 366–81.

Trawick, P. 2003. *The Struggle for Water in Peru: Comedy and Tragedy in the Andean Commons.* Stanford, CA: Stanford University Press.

11

Moral Valves and Fluid Properties

Water Regulation Mechanisms in the *Bâdia* of South-Eastern Mauritania

Christian Vium

Introduction

Oualata, a town of some three thousand inhabitants, is situated on the south-eastern fringe of a geological basin area covering and giving name to the two provinces of Hodh Ech Chargui and Hodh el-Gharbi. The soil in the dried-out riverbed (*oued*) at the foot of the dark plateau upon which Oualata is founded is characterized by a particular capacity for harnessing precipitation, which percolates through the sand, filling a significant natural water reservoir which can be accessed all year round via the 17-metre-deep rain-fed well Ain al-Argoub ('the well at the foot of the escarpment') as well as two less important wells in the immediate vicinity. In large part due to this strategic location, Oualata developed into a prosperous caravan city in the early middle ages, and thrived for centuries as a crucial node on the trans-Saharan trade routes. Oualata was frequented by caravans operated by Touaregs, Moors and Berbers, transporting salt, gold, slaves, textiles and other commodities through the hostile desert expanses between a vast grid of enigmatic cities such as Tombouctou and Gao in Mali, Agadez in Niger, Tichit and Chinguetti in Mauritania and Marrakech and Fès in Morocco (cf. Bovill 1968; Austen 2010). Through time, the well Ain al-Argoub has thus nourished uncountable numbers of people and animals by affording water, an essential resource unparalleled in its capacity to assemble a vast array of actors in the arid landscape. Intense dramas and conflicts over access to this hole in the ground have abounded, and it has defined and determined life in Oualata (cf. Khaldún 1925; al-Mahjúbí et al. 1927; Marty 1927; Barth 1965; ibn Battuta 1981; Cleaveland 2002). Ain al-Argoub is, indeed, a very particular place invested with spectacular social density and political intensity, which continues to constitute a central node in the political economy of the area known as Dhar Oualata and its amalgam of nomadic collectives dispersed across the vast and immensely arid territory in the extreme south-eastern parts of Mauritania, which literally bridges the Saharan and Sahelian climatic zones. This well was the centre of part of my fieldwork, and it is at the core of the chapter.

From the plateau above Oualata, I had been observing one herd of animals after another arriving at the well Ain al-Argoub since the first rays of morning sun had begun illuminating the enigmatic landscape. Hundreds of animals and their herders, from a multiplicity of diverse tribal factions,[1] conglomerated in the dry riverbed (*oued*). The place was bustling with activities. A desaturated gauze of light enveloped the landscape in a delicate translucent veil. The sand faded to white, and the distant horizon dissolved entirely. In the foreground, the distinct

Figure 11.1 Morning view of the eastern fringes of the city Oualata, with the well *Ain al-Argoub* surrounded by animals in the dry riverbed (*oued*). Photo by Christian Vium.

geometrical architecture of the city blended in with the rocky plateau on which it was established, descending down to the *oued,* flanked on its eastern fringe by a scarred escarpment in shifting nuances of ochre. Beyond the escarpment, the *trâb el-beyda* (the white land), vast desert plains, moving sand dunes and rocky plateaus, which comprise the Sahara, extend for thousands of kilometres through Mali, Niger and Chad, before plunging into the Red Sea east of Sudan. In spite of the almost timeless vista, what was in fact unfolding in front of my eyes on this particular morning in January 2012 was an existential drama: increasingly desperate herders were conglomerating in still larger numbers, hoping to procure water for their weak and thirsty animals as a drought which, at the time, looked as if it could turn out to be the worst drought(s) in the region since the last of the so-called 'great Sahelian droughts' in the first half of the 1980s, was gaining momentum.[2]

The relentless heat was rising and the archetypical desert landscape imposed itself as a quivering wall of silence. I went down to the well. I was left confused as to what informed people's choices in the face of increasing water scarcity in the south-eastern frontier lands of Mauritania. What were the constraints and incentives motivating their actions, and how did they manage access to the water and pastures on which they based their livelihoods?

Arguably, the main challenge to life in the arid parts of the Sahara and the Sahel is the scarcity of water, or perhaps more correctly, the inadequate access to it (Toupet 1983; de Bruijn and van Dijk 1995; Thébaud 2002). The distribution and frequency of precipitation in south-eastern Mauritania is inherently ephemeral and unpredictable (Nouaceur 1995; Toupet 1995; Koechlin 1997; Raynaut 1997; Vermeer 1981), which makes permanent water points such as wells privileged nodal points in the dynamic desert topography. Elsewhere (Vium 2009a, 2009b, 2013), I have described the landscape in south-eastern Mauritania as fundamentally nomadic, arguing that it is defined by a particular form of shifting environmental topography and mobile social topology, in which wells such as Ain al-Argoub constitute 'singularities' (de Landa 2002: 14–19; Deleuze and Guattari 2004: 408), which attract and agitate sociopolitical intensities.

In arid environments, wells and pastures co-constitute each other. During the dry season in particular, when pastures are precarious, it becomes evident how wells enact the potentiality of the landscape that surrounds it. They 'open up' areas to pastoral exploitation. For this reason, the regulation of access to a given well is a means of controlling the number and movements of animals frequenting the surrounding area, thus balancing the rhythm of consumption of the fluctuating and often limited pastures. While appropriate management permits an optimal exploitation of the vegetal resources, mismanagement can lead to sustained degradation of the pastures in the vicinity of a given well (Thébaud 2002: 87). But how is control orchestrated practically in times of increasing scarcity? Which laws, codes, rules and principles do people refer to in their negotiations for access to water? In short, what are the concrete elements that constitute the water regime (Orlove and Caton 2010) in south-eastern Mauritania, and how do these manifest themselves at the well of Ain al-Argoub?

Proceeding from a description of the people frequenting the well and their practical activities around the well, and a discussion of its central position within the nomadic landscape of the Hodh Ech Chargui province during a critical period of increasing water stress, I shall argue that wells such as Ain al-Argoub can be understood as socio-political technologies which may be likened to valves, regulating access to water and facilitating its flow through a dynamic conflation of political and moral economies. More specifically, access to water, and thus by default to pastures, is regulated through a socio-political system based on ideas of collective property (*miri*) and communal management, which is largely configured by notions of solidarity (*assabiyya*), honour (*darje*)

Figure 11.2 Nomadic herders pulling water at the well *Ain al-Argoub* on the eastern fringes of the city Oualata. Photo by Christian Vium.

and personal integrity (*hárim*), and which make up an integral part of the politico-juridical cum moral bundle of rights assembled in, and thus constituting, the well. Wells, then, are socio-political cum moral epicentres in which the whirling landscape of ephemeral resources and dispersed nomadic collectives conjugate during droughts, and the activities constituting the wells are essentially collective mechanisms that serve the purpose of minimizing constipation and optimizing flows.

By scrutinizing the moral mechanisms of access to water, this chapter points to a particular form of auto-regulation enacted in the face of increased scarcity. The empirical material and the reflections of my interlocutors illustrate how the nomadic pastoralists, to a wide extent, restrain from engaging in open conflicts and abstain from procuring water from water points that are associated with specific groups. This, I argue, represents a concretization of a distinct form of solidarity embedded in notions of honour and moral integrity, which is a crucial ordering principle in a tremendously flexible collective property regime in which access to pastures and water is formally open to all and at the same time intricately managed on an ad hoc basis.

Ain al Argoub: A Nomadic Nodal Point

Like many nomadic pastoralists originating in the area, Médé had been frequenting Ain al-Argoub throughout his life. In a life predicated upon incessant movement, the well constituted an important site, as it afforded him the privilege to procure water, buy provisions and acquire information on issues crucial to his livelihood from other herders in the area (cf. Toupet 1983; Frérot 1993: 275). As he pragmatically said: 'For us, all that matters is water. If there is water it is good. If it is rare (*nath'ubet,* lit. scarce), we are in trouble. Ain al-Argoub unites us. It is a meeting place.'

At that time, Médé was camped with his own and four other families, one day's journey by foot from the well, and with his small herd of goats and sheep, he moved to and from the well in a coordinated schedule. Every third day, he would spend at the well; the days in between he would spend on pastures. The increased waiting time resulting from the growing number of herds at the well was bothering him because it left him with less time to let the animals pasture. On this particular day, Médé was waiting for his turn at the well together with relatives from other Edmaghratt encampments (*aïal*) dispersed in the vicinity of Oualata. They all confirmed that the situation was becoming increasingly precarious and difficult to navigate. They told me that since *Am*

Enaam ('the year of good seasons'), a period of three fertile years from 1994 to 1996, which was followed by a severe regional drought in the Dhar Oualata in 1997, there had not been any distinctively good years. Interested in understanding what governed access to water in times of scarcity, I tried posing what I thought was a straightforward question:

> Christian: Who owns the well (*el aïn*) here? Who decides who gets to take water and who doesn't, and when? It looks very confusing.
>
> Médé: Nobody owns Ain al-Argoub. It is for everybody.
>
> Christian: But how is that possible? I don't understand.
>
> Médé: As long as you respect the order and wait for your turn, it is fine. The problem is not the access ... It is the lack of water (*ma nath'ubet*) that concerns us.
>
> Christian: But I thought there were a lot of conflicts in the dry season. I mean, you are so many, and there is so little water...

Before I had chance to pose more questions, Islim, who was obviously a more short-tempered man than his friend Médé, exclaimed: 'What do you expect us to do? Fight? We have enough problems as it is. Look around. As if waiting didn't bother us!' I looked around. The order they were referring to was anything but evident. People were not exactly queuing up in a neat line. But neither did they fight or argue, at least not in any obvious way. The scenario at the well could, I thought, be seen as a form of ordered chaos. Somehow, the animals did eventually drink, and the herders filled their metal water barrels and proceeded to their encampments with their animals. People were 'behaving', but I was struggling to comprehend the logic of access, despite literally standing in the middle of this 'ordered disorder'.

A welter of activities was taking place around the well. Men[3] were hauling up water with the aid of a camel used as a draught animal under the direction of another man. In the vicinity, groups of men were attending to the hundreds of goats, sheep and camels, which were divided into smaller units according to some sort of logic. A couple of women arrived with donkeys equipped with barrels, which they filled with water before returning to where ever they came from beyond the plateau. Groups of men were discussing where the pastures were still adequate, drawing 'maps' in the sand to indicate the location of encampments, and the number of animals believed to be dispersed in the pastoral zone known as the Mantega Rehwa, which surrounded this particular water point. New herders arrived with their animals, while others left in all directions. Compared to the 'emptiness' of the surrounding desert landscape, the *oued* was like a nomadic intersection, and in spite of the apparent chaos, everybody, without exception, confirmed that here everybody were entitled to water – all that mattered was 'respecting the order', which they all seemed to take for granted. According to Cher, a member of the esteemed Kounta tribe, who had been frequenting the well regularly for the last seven years, this year, however, did not look promising.

> Normally, there are no severe conflicts here, but this year may turn out different. The herders all say that pastures are bad and they fear what will happen at the end of the year [i.e. at the peak of the dry season, which was still some months into the future]. ... We still have water, but this is only the beginning. Imagine how this place will be with twice as many animals and even less water in the well than now.

Because the well was rain-fed,[4] the volume of water it contained fluctuated depending on the amount of rain, and during periods of heightened demand and decreased volume, the situation could turn critical. Members of another group of herders, some having waited more than a day for their turn to draw water for their thirsty animals, had said the same thing when I asked them previously: 'For ten years now it has been difficult. This year, there is hardly any water in Mantega Rahouwiya [a 30–40 km pastoral zone surrounding Oualata] and we have to take the animals far to find pastures (*rahhâle*) during the dry season (*seyf*)'. I asked, 'But why are you here at Ain al-Argoub then? Shouldn't you be elsewhere?' They explained how, under the given conditions, Ain al-Argoub was the best option at this time. They would move further only later, when the pressure became too high here. This was one of the reasons why herders were constantly acquiring updated information on wells. Knowing the fluctuations – the flow of people, animals and water – enabled them to plan their itineraries, and this was vital, as even a slight miscalculation could mean that animals would perish. Timing was essential, particularly during times of scarcity. Hoping to make Cher elaborate further on what I had just discussed with Médé and the others, I decided to ask him about how access to the well was regulated practically.

> Christian: Who is in charge of the well?
> Cher: What do you mean? Nobody is in charge. It is a well.
> Christian: But there must be some kind of regulations, some kind of system.
> Cher: Of course there is. It is all written in the law (*sunna*).
> Christian: But what does it say, the law?
> Cher: That everybody here has equal rights (*miri*, lit. collective property) to the water in the well. That is what it says. Read it.

And so I did.

The Formal Water Regime

The two main law documents defining the juridical regime concerning water and the concepts and principles of 'rational management' of pastoral space are the Water Code (Loi no. 2005-030 portant Code de l'eau) and the Pastoral Code (Loi no. 2000-044 portant Code Pastoral en Mauritanie), which entered into vigour in 2005 and 2004 respectively. In addition, Decree no. 2000-089 of 17 July 2000, which abrogated and replaced ordinance 83.127 of 5 June 1983, and pertains to the reorganization of property and domains, is of importance.

In the Water Code (Loi no. 2005-030), water is defined as a common good and a resource appertaining to national patrimony (articles 2 & 6), stipulating that it is in the collective interest to 'respect natural equilibrium' (article 2). Any water infrastructure construed to domesticate water is subject to state regulation (articles 19–21). Water infrastructures for public distribution of water is the object of a service delegation, overseeing the distribution (article 49) and, in areas where such delegations are not present (i.e. in the Dhar Oualata), the conditions and modalities of distribution are defined by conjoint statutory order between the minister in charge of water and the minister in charge of local collectives (article 49). Any mismanagement of public water infrastructures are subject to government sanctions, and individuals or collectives failing to comply with the water law can be both economically penalized as well as incarcerated (articles 59–78).

The above applies to the entire national territory, but special legal conditions apply to what is labelled pastoral space. The Pastoral Code (Loi no. 2000-044) defines the concepts and principles of rational management of pastoral space, determining the rules concerning the ensemble of aspects of pastoral activity, to ensure the preservation and promotion of pastoralism within a framework of 'harmonious evolution of rural development' (article 1). Pastoral space is constituted by the ensemble of zones, in which pastoral resources exist, including the passage corridors that permit animals to access these resources (article 5). The right of access to and use of resources is defined as the freedom accorded to the herder[5] to use all resources in the pastoral space in respect of the norms fixed by the rules in vigour (articles 7 & 9). Of immense importance is the juridical recognition of the principle of communality of pastoral resources (article 8), which stipulates that pastoral mobility[6] is preserved under all circumstances (article 10), and that communal management of pastoral resources implies free access and use, and this communal management is accorded to the 'habitual users' (article 11). Pastoral space, then, is recognized as an inalienable and imprescriptible collective domain reserved exclusively for pastoral activities (article 13).

The administrative authorities define which hydraulic infrastructures are defined as pastoral in nature (article 21), and all natural sites of water accumulation are ipso facto considered public and open to all (articles 22–23). Herders may establish wells so as to procure water for themselves and their animals as long as they adhere to the rules and restrictions laid down by the administrative authority as well as concerned pastoralists and agriculturalists (article 24). Such establishment does not, however, provide any form of property rights (ibid.).

In the Pastoral Code, pastoral organizations are defined as groupings of herders who live mainly from their revenues deriving from transhumant animal husbandry (article 30). Such organizations are envisioned to serve as what is termed 'a coordinating structure of local participatory democracy', ensuring the specific interests of herders (article 32). This latter stipulation is of particular interest when it comes to the communal management of pastoral conflicts – a topic that is accorded particular importance in the Pastoral Code (articles 33–44). Disputes concerning access to and use of pastoral resources are to be regulated cordially (*à l'amiable*) between conflicting parties,[7] and only if a resolution is not reached can such be presented in front of a commission of arbitration.

In addition to the above-mentioned codes, juridical arrangements concerning the reform of domain and property laws inform legal approaches to access and rights of use. The rural reform of 1983 marked a drastic reordering of the law regarding property and domains, which was previously in vigour and which largely mirrored occidental laws favouring private property. The main articles of the reform of 1983 stipulate that all land belongs exclusively to the nation and thus every Mauritanian may become proprietor under the condition that he or she conforms to Islamic law (*shari'ah*), thus contributing to the economic and social development of the country (articles 1 and 2).[8] The previously predominant tenure system is abolished by law (article 3), invalidating all property claims not directly attributed to a single person resulting from juridical process (article 4). This reform, then, dismantled the 'tribal' property regime, which was largely collective in nature. This also encompassed wells established by tribal collectives (article 22). In addition, article 38 of the decree explicitly states that persons or collectives who have undertaken the construction of infrastructures – any 'arrangements of nature' – so as to improve the value (*rentabilité*) of a given piece of land, over which they held collective rights before the reform of 1983, hold no supplementary advantage over such benefits than others engaged in pastoral activities in pastoral zones.

Water in pastoral space, then, is formally defined by law as a pastoral resource and an inalienable common good. The laws stipulate that no one can be denied the right to procure water from any water source, private or public, in areas designated as pastoral. The code pastoral recognizes the 'traditional common property regime' for nomads on pastoral lands (articles 9 & 13 in law no. 2000-044). The code, then, legally validates use rights, which represents a dramatic shift away from the previously predominant exclusive ownership rights (Wabnitz 2007: 3). Drafted from recommendations by representatives of the concerned populations of pastoralists and agriculturalists, the 'habitual users' of pastoral space, and building on custom and Islamic law, the Pastoral Code arguably represents an example of adapted, effective legislature, which recognizes the priority of right to mobility (article 10) and access to pastoral resources (article 11), and declaring nomadism as a 'vector of a system of cultural value' (Wabnitz 2007: 3).

So, on paper, there is a wide range of formal laws regulating access to water in the *badia,* but the question remains whether or not these are abided by in reality. Certainly, herders like Médé did not read the many articles discussed above. In the following, I demonstrate how regulation and negotiation of access to water takes place in actual practice at the well of Ain al Argoub.

Figure 11.3 Médé, a herder from the *Hamonat* tribal faction, portrayed as he waits for water at the well *Ain al-Argoub* outside Oualata. Photo by Christian Vium.

A Day at Ain al-Argoub

On this particular day, somewhere between 350 and 400 animals, in six herds, were conglomerating in the *oued*. The herders were drawing water, moving about, attending to the animals, forming groups and discussing. As was generally the case, questions about the nature of pastures, the availability of water at the different wells in the surrounding area, the number of herds and the weather were preponderant, but also concerns over the escalating political instability in neighbouring Northern Mali and rumours of heightened activities of AQIM (al-Qaeda in the Islamic Maghreb) and other nebulous assemblages proliferated (Vium 2013).[9]

At the well itself, two young men drew water using a large tarpaulin bag that held approximately 40 litres of water; it was attached by a long rope to a camel at the other end. A simple wooden spool on a suspended iron bar between two poles held the rope in place above the hole, which had a diameter of nearly a metre. Under the guidance of a third man, the camel pulled up the water and the two men at the well kept the rope in place on the spool and called out to him once the tarpaulin bag had reached the surface, upon which they lifted it off the spool as the camel-driver eased the rope by bringing the camel back towards the well. Water spilled out over the elevated concrete foundation as the men carried the ladle to large metal vessels into which they poured the water, which the animals then drank. They threw the bag back down the hole, repeating the manoeuvre again and again. The sooner they could finish, the sooner they could bring the animals back to pasture. Two other men and a boy were busy arranging the animals in the immediate vicinity of the well, dividing them up into smaller groups, which were then given water from the metal vessels. The boy was moving about swiftly in between the animals, making sure they all were given water. With remarkable speed and focus, the two men arranging the animals were meticulously keeping track of which animals had drunk and how much, maintaining a calculated replacement of those who had quenched their thirst and those who were waiting to do so. Meanwhile, in the vicinity of the well, groups of nomadic herders, also from the Edmaghratt faction of the Hamonat tribe, were preparing two herds of mainly sheep and goats, and two dozen camels, as their turn at the well was nearing. Further away, in the middle of the *oued*, a herder from the venerable Meshrouf tribe was having a loud conversation on a cellular telephone.[10] One of his relatives in the nearby city of Nema who owned herds situated between Nema and Oualata wanted to know about the state of the pastures and how many herds there were in the area around Oualata, so as to decide where and when he should move the herds. Behind this man, on the ridge separating the riverbed from the expanses of the desert, yet another herd of sheep and goats appeared, accompanied by three men. Further away, two different groups identifying themselves as appertaining to the Laghlal tribal confederation were dividing their respective herds into sections, ready to be served at the well one at a time once it was their turn.

Inspecting the activities taking place at the well it appeared that all of Médé's, Islim's and Cher's comments related above were to the point. Indeed, there seemed to be an order in the sense that each time a new group of herders arrived they would orient themselves as to who came immediately before them, figuring out the sequence and then waiting their turn. It was obvious that maintaining order at the well and avoiding conflicts was a collective aspiration. Facilitating the flow of water, procuring water for themselves and their animals, and exchanging crucial information: these were everyday activities fundamental to nomadic pastoral livelihoods.

When Islim and Sidi Ahmed had finished watering their animals and took a rest with Médé and Bona, a younger herder from another Edmaghratt camp some 10 kilometres south-east of Oualata, I joined them and started probing into the issue of why remaining in this area held such importance for them. 'I have always been coming here, but the last three years there has hardly been any water in the wells here in Oualata from April [the early dry season].'[11] Médé fixed his stare, and his disquiet became almost tangible, as he ran his hands over his emaciated face and through his coarse white stubble: 'It is not just the health of the animals we are worried about – it is our own – because there is not even water enough for us to drink.'

I was discouraged at the prospect of hearing more of the familiar lamentations about how hard life was, but fortunately Hama, an old herder camped right outside Oualata, who had been following my work for several days, staying discretely in the background listening to the conversation, wanted it differently: 'You need to understand something about life here. Water is everything; it is the source of life itself.... According to Allah, water belongs to everybody, and you cannot deny someone water. It is the worst disgrace [*haraam*, literally interdicted by Islam]. You just don't do that. Do you understand what I am saying? It is a disgrace; shameful [*fahesha*]'. I silently thanked Hama for providing me with a window onto the moral economy guiding the interactions around water, which had so far remained somewhat elusive to me. In the following section, I propose an elaborated analysis of this conversation and its significance for understanding the socio-political organization of water in the *bâdia*.

Moral and Legal Mechanisms

As we talked, the men illustrated the emplacements of different wells and the location of their camps by drawing in the sand, offering an overview of the topography of the surrounding landscape. They explained how, despite the descending water level, Ain al-Argoub was still the well containing most water in the area of Mantega Rahouwiya (i.e. in a radius of 25 km from the well). Some 80 kilometres south-east, in an area known as Zedék with better pastures, there were deep wells (*bīr*), which enabled permanent access to water. These wells had been established by other collectives of nomadic pastoralists, whom they knew, but had less contact with. I asked them why they had not done as the other nomads Médé had mentioned earlier, and 'moved' their herds to Zedék. Islim was quick to respond:

> Islim: Let me give you an example. If you don't have anything and you ask someone to give you something, he will do so the first and the second time, but the third time he will hesitate. That is how it is. If we show up over there [in Zedék] asking for water at their well and letting our herds graze there, they will understand the first time [season], but if we return the following seasons, they will look down upon us and say we are *toukoussou* ['parasites'].
>
> Christian: What do you mean, '*toukoussou*'? I don't understand that word.
>
> Médé: It is like he said. They will think we are just coming to sponge in their area. Even if the pastures are better there, they are still limited, and they have their animals there.
>
> Christian: What do you mean, sponge? I thought pastures and water were for everybody. That is what you told me before. That's what everybody says. Even the law says it.
>
> Médé: That is true. Yes... but still... Imagine if everybody goes there all of a sudden. It would cause a lot of problems and it would benefit nobody. There would be too many animals and still the same pastures and water. They [the herders already there] would become annoyed. That is what it means, *toukoussou*: someone who has nothing and who comes to demand from others. That is no good. You can't just do as you please.
>
> Christian: So, you can go there, but you don't want to, because they will consider...
>
> Hama interrupted me: We have to stay here, in our area, otherwise they will consider us *tounoussou*, 'confused'. It is like Médé told you.
>
> Christian: Aha! So '*tounoussou*' leads to '*toukoussou*'?

Apparently there was some confusion as to the meaning of the two terms and their relation. *Tounoussou*, the men concurred, literally meant the loss of orientation or being disoriented. This was a word most often used to designated animals that had been separated from the herd and were disoriented and turning around themselves in hunger. Evidently, losing orientation constituted a problem in the *bâdia*, and *tounoussou* seemed to refer not only to literally being unable to navigate the topography, but also to the inability to negotiate the moral economy, which underpinned the socio-political topology. This made sense when coupled with *toukoussou*, which meant something like 'parasite', a term used derogatorily to designate someone who had nothing and would demand pity from others. Being categorized as unable to manage oneself and having to demand assistance from others, knowing that they too were faced with drought and distress, was not desirable. It made sense when Médé said: 'It is a question of solidarity (*assabiyya*). Islam is solidarity'.

The ethnographic account relayed above demands further analytical elaboration, as it provides important insights into the complex conundrum of regulation of access to water and pastures among nomadic pastoralists in a landscape configured by intensified scarcity. As Médé indicated, the prescriptions of Islam play an important role.

The holy Qur'an – the verbatim words of Allah as conveyed to the Prophet Muhammad by the archangel Gabriel (*Jibril*) – along with the teachings and doings of the Prophet Muhammad (known as the *hadith*) proliferate with detailed information and guidelines on sharing and solidarity, which are considered to promote harmony and equilibrium on individual, social and ecological levels (Ansari 1994: 394; al-Munjid 1994: 347; al-Jayyousi 2001: 44; Faruqui 2001). Water holds tremendous importance in Islam and Islamic law (*shari'ah*). In fact the word *shari'ah* originally meant 'the place from which one descends to water' or 'the path to water', and before the term evolved to include the body of laws and rules given by Allah, it comprised a set of rules specifically about water use known as the *shuraat al-maa* (the water laws). In Islam, water is considered a blessing by Allah: a liquid that provides and maintains life, and purifies humanity and the planet as such. It is the source of life, indeed, all life is *made of* water (Qur'an 21:30); it, quite literally, binds together the total ecosystem (Amery 2001: 49). The *hadith*, most often evoked when discussing the notion of sharing, clearly stipulates that Muslims share three 'things' collectively among them: water, pastures and fire (i.e. firewood) (Sunaan Abu-Dawood: 3470).[12] These are considered *mubah* (i.e. beyond individual property law) and, more specifically, water is subject to what is known as 'the right of thirst' (*haq al sharfa*), which establishes the universal right for humans and their animals to quench their thirst. Any Muslim who withholds surplus water from those in need commits a religious sin, and will reputedly be ignored on the Day of Resurrection (Sahih al-Bukhari: 3.838[13]; Caponera 2001: 96).

In the Qur'an, Allah specifies the following to his followers: 'Do not spread corruption (*fassad*) on Earth...' (Qur'an 2:11). *Fassad* can be interpreted as the disorganization of the natural functioning of the world, as exemplified in for example the waste or degradation of natural resources (Tabatabai 1974: 365; al-Jayyousi 2001: 44; Amery 2001: 48). This prescribes the principles of *tatghou* (not to commit excess) such as by wasting or exploiting excessively. *Tatghou* is adhered to vigorously by the nomadic pastoralists inhabiting the *bâdia*. Because the principles of *tatghou* derive directly from divine will, adhering to them becomes a way of leading a pious life (al-Jayyousi 2001: 44). Failure to comply with the will of Allah, such as a violation (*haraam*) of the right to thirst (*haq al sharfa*), compromises aspirations of an afterlife and brings negative repercussions upon the subject. The sharing of water, then, is considered an act of charity according to the *hadith* (Caponera 2001: 95),[14] and charity (*zakaat*), a concrete manifestation of solidarity, is among the most revered virtues in Islam, and one of the five pillars to which any devout Muslim must adhere. Taken together, the fundamental ideological prescriptions described above testify to the importance of moral behaviour as an ordering principle in everyday life. Furthermore they illuminate the logic in Médé's correlation between religion, morals and in particular solidarity (*assabiyya*), and their intricate relation to the question of water and pastures in the *bâdia*. As Hama indicated above, a crucial element organizing life in the *bâdia* is the recognition that one does not deny a person water. Water is life, and denying someone access to water thus represents a severe moral offence, considered *haraam* (an offence against a religious and/or customary interdiction). In other words, there is a clear correlation of morals, honour and solidarity inherent in the everyday procurement water.

Auto-regulation as a Means of Resource Management in a Context of Scarcity

What I want to reiterate from the complex of laws, moral ideologies, religious references and personal narratives presented so far is the fact that they form a plurality. Why was it that Médé and his companions were very reluctant to seek new pastures, given that they were struggling to make ends meet in the Mantega Rahouwiya where water was becoming scarcer? As demonstrated, it was not a question of having rights of access and use or not, it was, rather, a question of solidarity and, ultimately, honour and reputation. Médé and his companions could venture south-east to Zedék to procure water from the well and benefit from the pastures, but this would entail losing status in the face of the inhabitants of the *bâdia*. Rumours would spread that they did not know how to navigate either the drought or the politico-moral codes: that they were *tounoussou* (i.e. disoriented), both literally and figuratively speaking. Consequently, they would be known as *toukoussou* (i.e. parasites) who put increased pressure on the limited resources, to the detriment of the other herders and animals in the area. They would be looked down on, and this would devalue their moral capital and hence their capacity for negotiating other socio-political issues in the future. In so many words, they would lose social capital, and to prevent this from happening they would go to tremendous lengths to avoid having to frequent that particular well. This, I argue, is a pertinent example of how social organization among the nomadic pastoralists of the *bâdia* in south-eastern Mauritania is hinged upon a radical form of solidarity that induces herders like Médé to regulate the appropriation of pastures and water so as not to lose honour – perhaps the most valuable currency in the political economy. Hence, I conjure up the notion of 'moral auto-regulation' as a central mechanism, which ideally serves to ensure the equitable management of scarce and ephemeral resources considered collective property, but is nevertheless imbued with complex systems of regulation. The prefix 'moral' is of particular importance in this regard, as it highlights exactly the moral dimensions of the regulation of access to natural resources, such as water and pastures. The pattern described here may be seen to occur frequently in a great variety of contexts (cf. Ostrom 1990; Ostrom et al. 2001; Widlok and Tadesse 2004; Ostrom and Cole 2012), in which state law operates as the formal legal structure within a dynamic, pluralist system defined by rules determined at the local level. What I want to point to when advancing the notion of 'moral auto-regulation' is the important moral underpinnings of such patterns.

In order to situate the explanations and actions of my interlocutors within the larger societal framework orienting the political economy of nomadic pastoralism, I now turn to an elaboration of the concept of solidarity (*assabiyya*) and advance the position that it is *the* central aspect underlining practical arrangements concerning the regulation of access to water and pastures in the *bâdia*. Alas, to make my argument, I am forced to engage in a brief discussion of tribal organization, 'the great ghost' in ethnographic studies of nomadic pastoral societies.

Abd al-Rahman ibn Muhammad ibn Khaldún (1332–1406), the venerable Arab historian, lawyer, traveller and astute observer of social, political and religious aspects of life in the Maghreb in the Middle Ages, provided a detailed analysis of *assabiyya,* and his revolutionary work, which was founded in a deep knowledge of the Qur'an, the *hadith* literature and *shar'ia,* continue to impact scholarly work in the Middle East. Khaldún believed that 'bedouin' life (i.e. life in the *bâdia,* beyond the confines of cities) was predicated upon closely knit bonds of solidarity among groups considering themselves to be of common descent – in other words tribes (*qabile*), who protected each other and derived nobility and honour from their common affection for and loyalty to their family and group (Khaldún 1958: 262). This solidarity (*assabiyya*), initially based upon agnatic relations (Bonte 2006: 108) constitutes the 'esprit de corps' (group feeling), which binds together the collective (Toupet 1977: 187; Marchesin 1992: 52), ensuring the maintenance of hospitality, while at the same time enabling 'a system of precautions faced with strangers' (Bataillon 1963: 40). In his historical analysis of pre-colonial nomadic organization in Mauritania, Ould Cheikh (1985) similarly argues that *assabiyya,* in Ibn Khaldún's optic, is a form of moral and ideological cement that enables the nomadic population of the desert (*bâdia*) to follow and fight for the path (*al-hudá*) prescribed by Allah (ibid.: 682–83). Furthermore, he argues, *assabiyya* is an element of interposition (*wâzi*), which permits Man to avoid unnecessary manifestations of aggression between people, a capacity he aligns directly with the original meaning of power (*mulk*) (ibid.: 687). Power, to Ibn Khaldún, is always closely connected to the notion of *assabiyya,* which, while originally based on *nasab* or *iltihám* (i.e. tribal consanguinity), is often replaced by the effective institution of affiliation (*walá*), a form of socio-political alliance making (Bonte 2006).[15] *Assabiyya,* then, is the unifying factor of affiliated groups, which fuels the paradoxical process of fission and re-composition commonly termed 'segmentarity' (cf. Evans-Pritchard 1940, 1951; Gellner 1969, 1981; Gellner and Michaud 1972), which predisposes 'the group' or 'tribe' (*qabila*) to pit itself against any exterior force concentrically down to the smallest social unit of the family (Bonte 2006; Cheikh 1985: 703). In discussing the 'ideology of kinship' among the Bedouin of Cyrenaica, Behnke (1980: 184) puts it poignantly: 'Bedouin concepts of kinship are vacuous in that they can be reinterpreted to suit many different situations ... Like money in a market, these concepts are the moral and conceptual currency men trade upon to regulate many different kinds of transactions involving many different kinds of property; the logical structures of the ideas themselves cannot predetermine the way they may be used in a practical context'. And he goes on with even more clarity: 'Men must put forth charters which provide suitable social content and justification for ecologically rational decisions. The inability to erect such a charter spells disaster as surely as does the inability to read correctly the meaning of the natural ecology' (Behnke 1980: 185).

Certainly, the contemporary political landscape of south-eastern Mauritania is governed by a form of acephalous organization that bears some resemblance to the concept of the segmentary lineage (Bonte 2006: 99).[16] But I here limit my focus to a particularity recognized within the notion of *assabiyya,* namely that of reputation (*harîm*), which designates all values – the total integrity – attributed to the individual (Bonte 2006: 102). *Harîm* is what Médé and his companions were primarily concerned with, when they articulated the notions of *tounoussou* and *toukoussou* in our discussion of why they preferred to endure the hardships of life in the Mantéga Rahouwiya as opposed to migrating to Zedék. *Harîm* translates directly as capital in the *bâdia*. It is paramount to the individual's capacity to assert any form of status in society at large, and to any and all negotiations (cf. Behnke 1980: 183). Devaluation of such integrity may, and indeed often does, undermine the position of not only the person, but his entire family. Hence, I dare to propose some sort of ethnographic equation derived from the above explorations, which might serve as an argument concerning the moral auto-regulation of access to water and pastures, i.e. collective properties of the *bâdia*.[17] The equation might look something like this: although pastures are, in principle, recognized as a common or collective good to which each and everyone has inalienable rights of use and access as stipulated in both Islamic law (*shari'ah*) and national legislation, deep-seated moral prescriptions relative to life in the *bâdia* induce people to abstain from freely accessing natural resources. These moral prescriptions, I have argued, are based on the concept of solidarity (*assabiyya*), which is irrevocably connected to the fundamental integrity and reputation (*hárim*) of the moral person.

From the material analysed in this chapter, I have demonstrated how the moral economy informs the regulation of access to water and pastures within a management regime hinged upon notions of collectivity and communality. The nomadic pastoralists resort to a form of moral auto-regulation, which, arguably, represents an ingenious form of social ordering that allows flexible regulation of access to fluctuating and scarce resources, even in times of heightened distress.[18] Having empirically described and discussed activities taking place around the well Ain al-Argoub, contextualized with discussions of contemporary national laws, Islamic law and the central moral mechanisms, which together comprise the water regime in south-eastern Mauritania, I now turn to a concluding anthropological theorization of the well as a particular form of socio-political technology that assembles a bewildering plurality of regulatory mechanisms.

The Well as a Multiple Object

What, in fact, is a well? In the following, I argue that while Ain al-Argoub constitutes a singularity in the topography of south-eastern Mauritania, it is by no means a singular 'object' or 'place' in the social sense. Rather, it makes sense to conceptualize the well as a 'multiple object' (Law 2002: 102), or even a relation, which aggregates a bewildering flow of intensities. In this last section, then, I anthropologically theorize the concept of property as a relation, and build my argument about the well as a 'multiple' and 'fluid' object with reference to a number of discussions from within the field of Science and Technology Studies (STS).[19]

As demonstrated, Ain al-Argoub constitutes a nucleus of the nomadic landscape in south-eastern Mauritania, and during periods of increasing water scarcity, this only becomes more evident. Ain al-Argoub is a point of attachment in a mobile space, with which the nomadic pastoralists identify themselves (Pinchon 1996: 74–75; Thébaud 2002: 85–88; Lechartier 2005: 82–83). As suggested by the observations of Médé and his companions, we may conceive of Ain al-Argoub as a collective symbol of a system of territorial values, in the sense that it materializes and makes visible a set of abstract moral values (cf. Debarbieux 1993: 6; Lechartier 2005: 82). Ain al Argoub is constitutive of and indissociable from the nomadic landscape: it is a centre, which orients 'the social' (cf. Le Roy 1999: 403).[20] Ain al-Argoub, quite literally, assembles a heterogeneous population of nomadic pastoralists who in the process of procuring water also exchange information, knowledge and ideas, and thus (re)produce society. Like any well, Ain al-Argoub is a moral epicentre of the nomadic landscape, in particular in the context of the escalating droughts (Le Roy 1999: 405). Invariably, wells are tied to notions of power, and in the following I explain how this power is implicated within property relations playing out at the Ain al-Argoub.

In south-eastern Mauritania, property (here exemplified by water and pastures) is, I argue, a relational concept that involves a plurality of actors and prescriptions, while enacting 'an economy of sharing' (Thébaud 2002: 221).[21] In the nomadic landscape, this 'economy of sharing' presupposes reciprocity, without which the fluidity of pastoral mobility would be compromised (Behnke 1994: 7). The nomadic pastoralists afford particular attention to the correlated calculation of how many herds are moving where, when and in which areas, and how many resources these areas afford in terms of water and pastures. This is distilled at the well. The term endrodomy, developed by Barral (1974), is instructive here. Deriving from the Greek words *endon* and *dromos*, which signify 'on the interior of' and 'course' or 'trajectory', the term endrodomy is used to designate pastoral terrains or spaces within which the movements of a more or less constant number of herds are effectuated according to a more or less fixed annual cycle (Barral 1974; Thébaud 2002: 232). The regulating mechanism here is the previously discussed principle of *tatghou,* which is actualized to avoid excessive consumption of the natural resources. Hence, within these so-called endrodomic pastoral zones, customary interdictions (*haraam*) are effectuated to enable the collective subsistence of the various user groups. This was what Médé and his companions evoked when they talked about *tounoussou* (disorientation), *toukoussou* ('sponging'), *darje* (honour) and *harím* (personal integrity): moral components entangled in what were essentially matters of cooperation (Ingold 1986: 143).

Hence, the concept of property, and indeed water, is all about relations, and arguably meanings (cf. Henare, Holbraad and Wastell 2007: 3). If we approach the concepts of property and water from the nomadic pastoral point of view, they may indeed dictate the terms of their own analysis (ibid.: 4) So, water and property are imbued with politics and moral reciprocity, and are thus inherently relational concepts. As demonstrated above, property is a man-made institution or social construct that creates and maintains relations between people, which mediate relations to resources (MacPherson 1978: 1; Casimir 1992: 3; Scott 1998: 36; F. and K. Benda-Beckmann and Wiber 2006: 14–15).

As we have seen, focusing on property, and indeed water, entangles one in a history of 'deeply intertwined conceptual discussions, social philosophies and ideological justifications of past, present and future property regimes' (F. and K. Benda-Beckmann and Wiber 2006: 1). With reference to the central case of Médé and his companions presented in this chapter, it is evident how deep-seated norms, values and ideologies correspond to the behaviour involved in accessing and procuring water and pastures at the well of Ain al-Argoub and in the pastoral zone known as the Mantega Rohwiya (cf. Casimir 1992: 6). Property, I have demonstrated, can be understood as 'a cover term that encompasses a wide variety of different arrangements' (F. and K. Benda-Beckmann and Wiber 2006: 15) and, from my descriptions of the 'bundle of rights' (ibid.) enacted or assembled at the well of Ain al-Argoub, it becomes evident that social conditions and practices as well as normative legal frameworks enacted in the regulation of access and use of the water and adjacent pastures are entirely dissociable. Property, then, may be said to be a multifunctional political relation in that it constitutes a system of rights for each person in relation to other persons (MacPherson 1978: 4). What, however, will happen to the analysis if we accept that things (such as a well and the water it contains) may '*consist of* assemblages of social relations, rather than *antedating* those relations?' (Humphrey and Verdery 2004: 7)?

Taking a cue from Marianne de Laet and Annemarie Mol (2000), I propose to investigate Ain al-Argoub as an actor because it *does* all kinds of things (ibid.: 226). Indeed, just like the Zimbabwean bush pump described by de Laet and Mol, Ain al-Argoub both *requires* a community to maintain it, and simultaneously *constitutes* its community. Ain al-Argoub quite literally 'demands' that the community assumes joint ownership and affirms itself *as* a community (ibid.: 245). All of the daily activities taking place around the well, what I call the 'mechanics of the well', quite literally produce the well and enact a particular socio-political process of maintenance, which in significant ways enables the functioning of the pastoral economy while at the same time affirming the ideological and moral foundations of this economy, as manifest in the socio-political mode of organization inherent to nomadic pastoralism. A capitalist analogy could be the U.S. 'Freeway': the objective of it being to ensure a smooth 'unwinding' of traffic and the avoidance of 'constipation'. Indeed, like the other herders, Médé and his friends were obsessed with avoiding constipation at the well, for the simple reason that it could lead to the detriment of their animals and hence their very livelihood. It is tempting to accept de Laet and Mol's idea that the bush pump – in our case the well – is indeed a 'fluid technology' (ibid.: 252). John Law proposes that, when approached from an actor–network theory (ANT) position, objects are 'an effect of stable arrays or networks of relations', which hold together as long as the relations do (Law 2002: 91). Hence, we are directed back to the notion of topology discussed at the opening of this section. The well, I argue, conjugates the regions, networks and indeed fluids (cf. Mol and Law 1994; Law 2002: 92), which compose the nomadic landscape. Law's argument that 'spaces are made with objects' (Law 2002: 96, 102) seems pertinent here. Ain al-Argoub, indeed, is 'enacted in a multi-topological manner' (ibid.: 102) and it is appropriate to conceptualize it as an intersection (ibid.) or 'singularity', aggregating and, more importantly, enacting different spaces, regions, networks, fluids, actors and actants (cf. Hannerz 1997; de Laet and Mol 2000; Mol and Law 2002: 1–22; Law 2004; Latour 2005).

Water binds all of these elements together, and based on the analytical propositions presented in this chapter, this compels me to conclude that Ain al-Argoub is a distinct socio-political technology comparable to a 'valve' in the sense that it enables the regulation of pressure and flows of people, animals, morals, politics and properties.

According to Webster's dictionary (1983), a 'valve' designates 'any device for halting or controlling the flow of a liquid, gas or other material through a passage, pipe, inlet, outlet, etc.', and within anatomy it designates 'a membranous fold or other structure which controls the flow of a fluid, as one which permits blood to flow in one direction only'. There are many reasons why I propose to use this term for the well of Ain al-Argoub. First of all, wells harness a liquid, water, and access to this liquid is a prerequisite for accessing the pastures in the areas surrounding the well. Hence, controlling and accessing the water de facto means controlling and accessing the territory. A valve typically enables regulation of pressure – one can literally turn up or down, open or close. Translated to the socio-political domain, the well, understood as an assemblage consisting of the totality of actors composing it,[22] is *the* central socio-political mechanism, perhaps even 'vernacular institution' with which the flow of people and animals – and indeed political and moral economies – are enacted, manipulated, regulated and ensured. In short, wells such as Ain al-Argoub not only order, but also constitute the nomadic landscape – i.e. nomadic pastoral society, political economy and moral ideology at large. In the context of the increasing scarcity, which presently radicalizes the nomadic landscape of south-eastern Mauritania, wells such as Ain al-Argoub constitute socio-political technologies – valves – serving the purposes of stabilizing the whirlpool of the environment. Hence, they inevitably become centres of heightened socio-political intensity and thus conjugate a veritable complex of trajectories, bundles of rights, moral principles and societal affects. As I have demonstrated with empirical material from south-eastern Mauritania, the well Ain al-Argoub and its content, the water, constitutes relations: fundamental properties of the nomadic landscape of south-eastern Mauritania.

Notes

1. Predominantly Hamonat, Laghlal, Oulad Bellah, Meshrouf and Kounta, the main nomadic pastoral tribal confederations inhabiting the Hodh Ech Chargui region.
2. IRIN 2011; Bauer and Ndiaye 2012; Gamli and Aïnina 2012.
3. Procuring water for the animals is an exclusively male job, undertaken by herders. Procuring water for drinking and cooking is sometimes also undertaken by women.
4. Strategically situated in the dry riverbed (*oued*) at the foot of rocky plateaus, precipitation would run down from the plateau and fill up the riverbed, and thus the well situated in it. Lack of precipitation, however, obviously results in a decrease in the volume of water the well receives. The water level drops, and consequently it takes longer to procure water from the well; and even worse, if subjected to sustained and increased use, it eventually dries out.

5. In the legally binding amendment stipulated in decree no. 2004-024, relative to the Code Pastoral (no. 2000-044), a herder (pasteur) is defined in article 1 as: 'proprietary animal breeder (éleveur propriétaire), transhumant animal breeder (éleveur transhumant), paid animal breeder (éleveur salarié), animal breeder providing services (éleveur prestataire de services), herding animal breeder and commercial animal breeder.
6. Mobility is recognized as a strategy, which permits a sustainable exploitation of pastoral resources and is a 'condition of survival of pastoralists' (article 6, decree no. 2004-024).
7. Article 18 in the accompanying amendments in decree no. 2004-024 stipulates that the administration should favourize the emergence of local conventions (l'émergence des conventions locales) and arrangements in concertation with the concerned groups.
8. This is what is known in Islam as the principle of *Istislah*.
9. See Goïta 2011, Jourde 2011 and Pham 2011 for detailed overviews of the escalating insecurity in the Sahel and the role of AQIM in recent years.
10. Contrary to the rest of the pastoral zone of Mantega Rahowiya, Oulata has an antenna, which provides a telephone signal. The growing number of herders in possession of a cellular telephone often take the opportunity to contact relatives in the cities to receive news.
11. In general, the dry season commences around mid-March and reaches its climax in May–June in south-eastern Mauritania. However, in 2011 and 2012, it was already excessively dry by early May due to the lack of rain in the previous rainy season.
12. The Sunaan Abu-Dawood is a main source for insights into the *hadith*, i.e. the teachings and doings of the prophet Muhammed, collected by the Persian Imam Abu Dawud, who compiled numerous books on the subject in the ninth century AC. The Sunaan Abu-Dawood consists of nearly five thousand collected *hadith*, and is recognized by Sunni Muslims as part of the six canonical *hadith* collections, the Al-Kutub al-Sittah.
13. Like the Sunaan Abu-Dawood mentioned above, the Sahih al-Bukhari constitues one of the most important collections in the Al-Kutub al-Sittah. The Sahih al-Bukhari was collected and compiled by the Persian scholar Muhammed al-Bukhari in the 9th century AC.
14. According to jurisprudence within the malekite tradition of the *Sunni* branch of Islam, which is prevalent in the Islamic Republic of Mauritania, wells destined for the watering of animals cannot in principle be subject to commercialisation (Caponera 2001: 98; Khalil ibn Ishak 1878 article 1220, section 16 & 17; Malik ben Anas 1911: 122; Ali ibn Muhammad 1903–8: 320).
15. As Bonte writes, referring to Ibn Khaldun's principal work, the *Muquaddima*: 'The agnatic definition of the *nasab* gives the illusion of a "natural" formation of the *'assabiyyāt* but it is the result of a local social consensus (*muta'araf*): *nasab* is a matter of imagination, not a reality. Its utility resides in the fact that the social links and sentiments of affiliation that it creates appear as natural (*tabìa*) in the mentality. The "true" role of *nasab* is to classify men, tribes and even the ancestry

of differentiations of human populations. But the "true" foundations of the '*assabiyyât* are not this agnatic descent, they are "kinship links" (*silât al-arhâm*)' (Bonte 2006: 109).
16. Bonte himself explains how his study is historical rather than empirical: 'From the perspective of my analysis of the specific model of the tribe in these Saharan societies, my subject is not an empirical description of present day facts. It is rather the examination of the principles of its tribal model that are invoked to explain the place of the tribe in modern Mauritanian State' (Bonte 2006: 118).
17. This is what ecologist Garrett Hardin (1968), from a rigid and deterministic (neo)Malthusian perspective, termed 'the tragedy of the (unmanaged) commons'. While most certainly instructive, a discussion of this is well beyond the scope of this chapter.
18. Following Elinor Orstrom and other avid and qualified opponents (Ostrom 1990; Ostrom, Gardner and Walker 1994; Dietz, Ostrom and Stern 2003) of Hardin's dated idea of the Tragedy of the Commons (Hardin 1968), I do not see privatization or increased governmental regulation as a solution. In fact, the Mauritanian model presented in the Pastoral Code, discussed earlier in this chapter, appears to be constructive in that it builds explicitly on local pastoral practices, conceptualizations and ideologies regarding communal management.
19. In particular, I engage the work of Annemarie Mol and John Law (1994, 2002), Marianne de Laet and Annemarie Mol (2000), and John Law (2002, 2004).
20. Singularities are attractors for trajectories, and, as de Landa (2002: 26) argues, 'a multiplicity [in this case the nomadic landscape or the drought] is defined by distributions of singularities defining tendencies in a process; and by a series of critical transitions which can take several such distributions embedded within each other and unfold them'. Having worked in Mauritania, Frérot (1995: 4) argues that the territory of the *bâdia* is construed from the traditional anchor points of wells, and animated by linerary as well as conjunctural seasonal movements of concentration and dispersion (i.e. centrifugal and centripetal). See also de Landa 2002: 14, 69, 81; Deleuze and Guattari 2004: 408; Chatêlet 2006; Allen 2011; Harvey 2012; and Lury, Parisi and Terranova 2012 for elaborated discussions on topological analysis.
21. Not surprisingly, conventional 'Western' or 'modern' legislation constitutes a 'deforming prism', which afford us little in the way of analysing a property regime such as the one in rigour in south-eastern Mauritania (Le Roy 1999: 399; Thébaud 2002: 223).
22. Animals, people, land, normative, religious and moral laws, prescriptions and ideologies, relations, alliances, escalating droughts, regional political instabilities and inflating food prices dependent upon a global market economy in crisis, etc.

References

Allen, J. 2011. 'Topological Twists: Power's Shifting Geographies', *Dialogues in Human Geography* 1(3): 283–98.

Amery, H.A. 2001. 'L'Islam et l'environnement', in N.I. Faruqui, A.K. Biswas and M.J. Bino (eds), *La gestion de l'eau selon l'Islam*. Paris: Karthala, pp. 71–82.
Anas, M. ben. 1911. *Le Mouwatta: Livre des ventes*. Vol. 15, translated by F. Pelier. Algiers: A. Jourdan.
Ansari, M.L. 1994. 'Islamic Perspectives on Sustainable Development', *American Journal of Islamic Social Science* 11(3): 394–402.
Austen, R.A. 2010. *Trans-Saharan Africa in World History*. Oxford: Oxford University Press.
Barral, H. 1974. 'Mobilité et cloisonnement chez les éléveurs du nord de la Haute-Volta: les zones dites d'endrodomie pastorale'. *Cahiers Orstom*, Série Sciences Humaines.
Barth, H. 1965. *Travels and Discoveries in North and Central Africa in the Years 1849–1855*. Vol. 3. London: Frank Cass.
Bataillon, C. 1963. *Nomades et Nomadisme au Sahara*. Paris: UNESCO.
Battuta, ibn. 1981. *Al-Rihla*. Translated by J.F.P. Hopkins and Nehemia Levtzion in *Corpus of Early Arabic Sources for West African History*. Cambridge: Cambridge University Press, pp. 281–88.
Bauer, J.-M., and M. Ndiaye. 2012. 'Marchés et réponses à la crise alimentaire', Islamic Republic of Mauritania, United Nations World Food Programme.
Behnke, R. 1980. *The Herders of Cyrenaica: Ecology, Economy, and Kinship among the Bedouin of Eastern Libya*. Chicago: University of Illinois Press.
———. 1994. 'Natural Resource Management in Pastoral Africa', *Development Policy Review* 12: 5–27.
Benda-Beckmann F., K. Benda-Beckmann and M.G. Wiber. 2006. 'The Properties of Property', in F. Benda-Beckmann, K. Benda-Beckmann and M.G. Wiber (eds), *Changing Properties of Property*. New York and Oxford: Berghahn Books, pp. 1–40.
Bonte, P. 2006. 'Individuals, Factions and Tribes among Moorish Societies', in D. Chatty (ed.), *Nomadic Societies in the Middle East and North Africa: Entering the 21st Century*. Leiden: Brill, pp. 98–122.
Bovill, E.W. 1968. *Golden Trade of the Moors*. Oxford: Oxford University Press.
Bruijn, M. de, and H. van Dijk. 1995. *Arid Ways: Cultural Understandings of Insecurity in Fulbe Society, Central Mali*. Amsterdam: Thela Publishers.
Caponera, D.A. 2001. 'La propriété et le transfert de l'eau et des terres dans l'Islam', in N.I. Faruqui, A.K. Biswas and M.J. Bino (eds), *La gestion de l'eau selon l'Islam*. Paris: Karthala, pp. 139–48.
Casimir, M.J. 1992. 'The Dimensions of Territoriality: An Introduction', in M.J. Casimir and A. Rao (eds), *Mobility and Territoriality: Social and Spatial Boundaries among Foragers, Fishers, Pastoralists and Peripatics*. New York: Berg, pp. 1–26.
Chatêlet, G. 2006. 'Interlacing the Singularity: The Diagram and the Metaphor', in S. Duffy (ed.), *Virtual Mathematics: The Logic of Difference*. Manchester: Clinamen Press, pp. 31–45.
Cheikh, A.W.O. 1985. 'Nomadisme, Islam et politique dans la société Maure précoloniale'. Ph.D. thesis. Paris Descartes University.
Cleaveland, T. 2002. *Becoming Walata: A History of Saharan Social Formation and Transformation*. Portsmouth, NH: Heinemann.

Debarbieux, B. 1993. 'Du haut lieu en général et du mont Blanc en particulier', *Espace géographique* 22(1): 5–13.
Deleuze, G., and F. Guattari. (1987) 2004. *A Thousand Plateaus*. London: Continuum.
Dietz, T., E. Ostrom and P.C. Stern. 2003. 'The Struggle to Govern the Commons', *Science* 302: 1907–12.
Evans-Pritchard, E.E. 1940. *The Nuer*. Oxford: Oxford University Press.
———. 1951. *Kinship and Marriage among the Nuer*. Oxford: Clarendon Press.
Faruqui, N.I. 2001. 'Les marchés intersectoriels de l'eau au Moyen-Orient et en Afrique du Nord', in N.I. Faruqui, A.K. Biswas and M.J. Bino (eds), *La gestion de l'eau selon l'Islam*. Paris: Karthala, pp. 163–78.
Frérot, A.-M. 1993. 'Perception de l'Espace en Adrar de Mauritanie'. Ph.D. thesis, University of Provence.
———. 1995. 'Territoires nomades en devenir: Questions à propos de l'urbanisation d'un esâace nomade'. Unpublished paper presented at the conference 'Le territoire, lien ou frontière?', Paris, 2–4 October.
Gamli, A., and M.S. Ould Baba Aïnina. 2012. 'Impact du déficit pluviométrique et de la hausse des prix des produits alimentaires sur la sécurité alimentaire des ménages (Novembre–Décembre 2011)'. Islamic Republic of Mauritania: United Nations World Food Programme.
Gellner, E. 1969. *Saints of the Atlas*. London: Ebenezer Bailey and Son.
———. 1981. *Muslim Society*. Cambridge: Cambridge University Press.
Gellner, E., and C. Michaud (eds) 1972. *Arabs and Berbers: From Tribe to Nation in North Africa*. London: D.C. Heath and Company.
Goïta, M. 2011. 'West Africa's Growing Terrorist Threat: Confronting AQIM's Sahelian Strategy', *Africa Security Brief*, no. 11, February 2011, Washington DC.
Hannerz, U. 1997. 'Fluxus, fronteiras, híbridos: palavras-chave da antropologia transnacional', *Mana* 3(1): 7–39.
Hardin, G. 1968. 'The Tragedy of the Commons', *Science* 162: 1243–48.
Harvey, P. 2012. 'The Topological Quality of Infrastructural Relations: An Ethnographic Approach', *Theory, Culture & Society* 29(4/5): 76–92.
Henare, A., M. Holbraad and S. Wastell. 2007. 'Introduction: Thinking Through Things', in A. Henare, M. Holbraad and S. Wastell (eds), *Thinking Through Things: Theorising Artefacts Ethnographically*. London: Routledge, pp. 1–33.
Humphrey, C., and K. Verdery. 2004. 'Introduction: Raising Questions about Property', in C. Humphrey and K. Verdery (eds), *Property in Question: Value Transformation in the Global Economy*. Oxford: Berg, pp. 1–25.
Khaldún, Abd al-Rahman ibn Muhammad ibn. 1925. *Histoire des Berbères*. Translated by Le Baron de Slane. Paris: Geuthner.
———. 1958. *The Muqadimmah: An Introduction to History*. Translated by Franz Rosenthal. London: Routledge & Kegan Paul Ltd.
Ingold, T. 1986. *The Appropriation of Nature: Essays on Human Ecology and Social Relations*. Manchester: Manchester University Press.
IRIN Humanitarian News and Analysis. 2011. 'SAHEL: Act now to avoid another crisis say aid agencies', 4 December 2011 (http://www.irinnews.org/Report/94466 – accessed 27 February 2012).
al-Jayyousi, O. 2001. 'La gestion de l'eau selon l'Islam et la Déclaration de Dublin',

in N.I. Faruqui, A.K. Biswas and M.J. Bino (eds), *La gestion de l'eau selon l'Islam*. Paris: Karthala, pp. 63–70.

Jourde, C. 2011. 'Décoder les multiples strates de l'insécurité au Sahel: Le cas mauritanien', *Bulletin de la Sécurité Africaine*, Centre d'études Stratégiques de l'Afrique, no. 15 (September): 1–8.

Koechlin, J. 1997. 'Ecological Conditions and Degradation Factors in the Sahel', in C. Raynaut (ed.), *Societies and Nature in the Sahel*. London: Routledge, pp. 12–36.

Laet, M. de, and A. Mol. 2000. 'The Zimbabwe Bush Pump: Mechanics of a Fluid Technology', *Social Studies of Science* 30: 225–63.

Landa, M. de. 2002. *Intensive Science and Virtual Philosophy*. New York: Continuum.

Latour, B. 2005. *Reassembling the Social: An Introduction to Actor-Network-Theory*. New York: Oxford University Press.

Law, J. 2002. 'Objects and Spaces', *Theory, Culture & Society* 19: 91–105.

———. 2004. *After Method: Mess in Social Science Research*. New York: Routledge.

Lechartier, V. 2005. 'L'espace nomade du pouvoir politique en Mauritanie. Des lieux de la bediyya de l'Est à la capitale'. Ph.D. thesis, University of Rouen.

Le Roy, É. 1999. 'A la recherche d'un paradigme perd: le foncier pastoral dans les sociétés sahéliennes', in A. Bourgeot (ed.), *Horizons nomades en Afrique sahélienne*. Paris: Karthala, pp. 397–412.

Lury, C., L. Parisi and T. Terranova. 2012. 'Introduction: The Becoming Topological of Culture', *Theory, Culture & Society* 29(4/5): 3–35.

MacPherson, C.B. 1978. 'The Meaning of Property', in C.B. MacPherson (ed.), *Property: Mainstream and Critical Positions*. Toronto: University of Toronto Press, pp. 1–13.

al-Mahjúbí, Tálib Búbakár, et al. 1927. *Tárikh Waláta*. Ms. KLM 272, in Faculté des Lettres, Université de Muhammad V, Rabat. Translated in Paul Marty: 'Les chroniques de Oualata et de Néma', *Revue des Études Islamiques* 1: 355–575.

Marchesin, P. 1992. *Tribus, ethnies et pouvoir en Mauritanie*. Paris: Karthala.

Marty, P. 1927. 'Les Chroniques de Oualata et de Néma', *Revue des Études Islamiques* 1: 355–575.

Mol, A., and J. Law. 1994. 'Regions, Networks and Fluids: Anaemia and Social Topology', *Social Studies of Science* 24: 641–71.

———. 2002. 'Complexities: An Introduction', in J. Law and A. Mol (eds), *Complexities: Social Studies of Knowledge Practices*. Durham, NC: Duke University Press, pp. 1–22.

al-Munjid. 1994. *Quamous Al Munjid* (dictionnaire de recherche). Beirut: Dar el Machreq.

Nouaceur, Z. 1995. 'Disparités pluviométriques régionales, sécheresse et modification des équilibres de l'environnement mauritanien', *Revue de géographie de Lyon* 70(3/4): 239–45.

Orlove, B., and S.C. Caton. 2010. 'Water Sustainability: Anthropological Approaches and Prospects', *Annual Review of Anthropology* 39: 401–15.

Ostrom, E. 1990. *Governing the Commons: The Evolution of Institutions for Collective Action*. Cambridge: Cambridge University Press.

Ostrom, E., and D. Cole (eds). 2012. *Property in Land and Other Resources*. Cambridge: Lincoln Institute of Land Policy.

Ostrom, E., R. Constanza, B. Low and J. Wilson (eds). 2001. *Institutions, Ecosystems, and Sustainability*. Boca Raton, FL: Lewis Publishers.

Ostrom, E., R. Gardner and J.M. Walker. 1994. *Rules, Games and Common-Pool Resources*. Ann Arbor: The University of Michigan Press.

Pham, J.P. 2011. 'Foreign Influences and Shifting Horizons: The Ongoing Evolution of al-Qaeda in the Islamic Maghreb', *Orbis* 55(2): 240–54.

Pinchon, B. 1996. 'Walata aux marges de la Mauritanie mais au 'centre' d'un système d'échange transfrontalier'. Maîtrise de géographie, University of Rouen.

Raynaut, C. (ed.). 1997. *Sahels. Diversité et dynamiques des relations société-nature*. Paris: Karthala.

Republique Islamique de Mauritanie. 2000. Loi no. 2000-044 portant Code Pastoral en Mauritanie. Nouakchott.

———. 2000. 'Decree No. 2000-089 du 17 July 2000 abrogeant et remplacant le decret No. 90.020 du 31 Janvier 1990 portant application de l'ordonnance 83.127 du 5 Juin 1983 portant reorganisation fonciere et domaniale'. Nouakchott: Journal Officiel de la République Islamique de Mauritanie.

———. 2004. Décret No. 2004-024 portant application de la Loi No. 2000-044 du 26 Juillet 2000 relative au code pastoral. Nouakchott.

———. 2005. Loi No. 2005-030 portant Code de l'eau. Nouakchott.

Scott, J. 1998. *Seeing Like a State*. New Haven, CT: Yale University Press.

Tabatabai, M.H. 1974. *Al-Mizan fi Tafsir al Kor'an* (interprétation modérée du Coran), vol. 19–20. Beirut: Al Alami Library.

Thébaud, B. 2002. *Foncier Pastoral et gestion de l'espace au Sahel*. Paris: Karthala.

Toupet, C. 1977. *La sédentarisation des nomades en Mauritanie centrale sahélienne*. Paris: H. Champion.

———. 1983. 'L'eau et l'espace au Sahel: l'exemple de la Mauritanie', *Revue de Géographie de Lyon* 58(3): 277–85.

———. 1995. 'La crise Sahélienne', *Revue de géographie de Lyon* 70(3/4): 181–86.

Vermeer, D. 1981. 'Collision of Climate, Cattle and Culture in Mauritania during the 1970s', *Geographical Review* 71(3): 281–97.

Vium. C. 2009a. '"Nomad_Scapes": An Ethnographic Account of Contemporary Nomadism in the Islamic Republic of Mauritania'. MA thesis, Department of Anthropology, University of Copenhagen.

———. 2009b. '"Nomad_Scapes": Mobility and Wayfinding as Resilience among Nomadic Pastoralists in the Islamic Republic of Mauritania', in K. Hastrup (ed.), *The Question of Resilience: Local Responses to Climate Change*. Copenhagen: Det Kongelige Danske Videnskabernes Selskab, pp. 178–96.

———. 2013. 'The Phantom Menace: Fear, Rumours, and the Elusive Presence of AQMI in the Islamic Republic of Mauritania', *Strategic Review for Southern Africa*, special issue edited by K. Aning, M. Boås and M. Utas (forthcoming).

Wabnitz, H.W. 2007. 'The Code Pastoral of the Islamic Republic of Mauritania. Return to the Sources: Revival of Traditional Nomad's Rights to Common Property Resources'. Paper presented at the international conference 'Les frontières de la question froncière [At the frontier of land issues]', Montpellier.

Widlok, T., and W.G. Tadesse (eds). 2004. *Property and Equality: Vol. 1. Ritualization, Sharing, Egalitarianism*. Oxford: Berghahn Books.

12

Reflecting Nature

Water Beings in History and Imagination

Veronica Strang

An Aaful Story

One Sunday morn young Lambton went a'fishing in the Wear,
An' catched a fish upon his heuk he thowt leuk't vary queer.
But whatt'n kind ov fish it was young Lambton cuddn't tell,
He waddn't fash[1] te carry'd hyem, so he hoyed[2] it donn a well.

Whisht lads, haad yor gobs,[3] an' aa'll tell ye aall an aaful story,
Whisht lads, haad yor gobs, an' aa'll tel ye 'boot the worm.

This famous Geordie folk song, written in 1867 by C.M. Leumane, but referring to a medieval legend in the north-east of England, tells the 'aaful story' of the Lambton Worm,[4] the water serpent or dragon that a rebellious young nobleman, John Lambton, pulled from the River Wear near Durham while fishing instead of going to church one Sunday. Having cursed the river for failing to yield any fish, he felt a tug on his line, and pulled out the 'queer' black worm. As he could not be bothered to carry it home, he threw it down a well. Later, repenting his sinful ways, he joined the Crusades and became Sir John, a Knight of Rhodes. But while he was in Palestine the worm grew:

Noo Lambton felt inclined to gan an' fight in foreign wars,
He joined a troop ov knights that cared for nowther woonds nor scars.
An' off he went to Palestine, where queer things him befell,
An' varry soon forgat aboot the queer worm i' tha well.
… But the worm got fat an' grewed and grewed, an' grewed an aaful size…

As the serpent grew, local villagers found that the water in the well was poisoned. The creature began preying on local livestock – and worse:

> This fearful worm would often feed on caalves an' lambs and sheep,
> And swally little bairns[5] alive when they laid down to sleep.

The worm returned to live in the river and, following a trail of slime from the well, people saw it curled around a rock. It was now so large that, when it 'craaled aboot' at night, it could 'lap he's tail ten times round Pensha Hill'.

Living 'i' mortal fear', they sent 'news ov this myest aaful worm' to Palestine. To cut a long story short, 'brave and bowld Sir John' returned and, of course, slew the dragon, thus joining the ranks of heroes that stepped forward in the medieval period to rid communities of the marauding serpents reportedly so prolific in Europe at that time.

But why were there so many serpents? Why were they associated with water? And why were they so 'aaful'? Having researched human interactions with water in many parts of the world, I have found representations of water beings to be a valuable imaginative resource for anthropologists, providing a mirror of societies' particular historical and cultural engagements with water and 'nature'. I therefore employ the serpentine story of the Lambton Worm and similar classic tales of

Figure 12.1 The Worm around Penshaw Hill. Drawing by Danny Parkinson.

Figure 12.2 Sir John Lambton slew the worm. Image originally created by John Dickson Batten.

dragon slaying to reflect upon a key turning point in human–environmental relationships. This is the juncture at which European societies, with the coming of Christianity, other major monotheistic religions, and nascent scientism, shifted from the relatively egalitarian bioethical position of 'nature religions', in which the material world was seen as an animate and agentive partner in events, to an engagement in which humanized deities prevailed, and material things and other species were recast as both the objects and subjects of hierarchically superior human dominion. My hydrological narrative is appropriately cyclical: it follows subversive undercurrents through time, and concludes by considering how water beings have resurfaced in contemporary efforts by neo-pagans and environmental groups to critique distanced and exploitative ways of being in the world, and to reconstruct more collaborative, emplaced environmental engagements.

The shift that occurred in relation to water beings in the medieval period allows us to consider the factors that led to these important transitions. Why was it deemed necessary to slay the serpents? Why then? And why in some, but not other, geographic and cultural contexts?

Materializing Water

Water serpent beings were by no means a new phenomenon in the Middle Ages. They had appeared in every cultural and geographical context throughout human history, their form invariably reflecting the fluid properties of water. They were generally serpentine, shining and multi-hued; they lived in or near, or were related in some way to water. There were multiple variations: water beings regularly acquired forms echoing the creatures in their local environments: thus early Egyptian serpents, and those in Australia, often had crocodile-like features; African water beings were described as being like giant boa constrictors; and South American ones were resplendent with colourful feathers. But despite the acquisition of elements of various other species (which, as Gilmore (2003) observes, is intrinsic to the process of making monsters), and important variations in the cultural ideas and practices in which they were located, they invariably retained some formal compositional commonality. Always they reflected, one might say literally embodied, the material properties and behaviours of water: shimmering, glittering and winding through the world; circulating in rainbows between earth and sky; flowing and wriggling across and down into the land. This ubiquity and formal consistency highlights a core principle of cognitive development: humans 'use the world to think', making recurrent imaginative use of its material properties in composing concepts and metaphors (Levi-Strauss 1966; Lakoff and Johnson 1980; Strang 2005b).

Thus water imagery is used cross-culturally to articulate ideas about movement, flow and transformation over time (Strang 2004). Water's essentiality to life has caused all human societies to valorize its generative powers, as well as fearing its potentially destructive forces. For prehistoric societies, whose religious cosmologies often centred on totemic animal beings, there may also have been important associations between serpentine silvery streams of water and the fluid, shining movements of snakes that, like water, also wriggle down into the earth. Thus, in early rock art and material culture, the water beings that manifest the properties and powers of water are often represented as snakes and serpents.

As well as being conceived through cognitive engagement with water's particular material properties, ideas about serpent beings were also carried in the imaginations of the human populations that flowed to all corners of the world. Emerging in different historical and geographic contexts, water beings became, in Australia, the creative Rainbow Serpent from which all life arose; in Africa, the anaconda-like Mami Wata being; in Asia the cloud-born rain-bringing dragons and dragon springs; in India and Nepal, the similarly water-oriented *nāgas*; and in the Pacific, the river guarding *taniwha* and sea-dwelling *marakihau*.

Figure 12.3 Bark painting from western Arnhem Land, Australia. The Rainbow Serpent Ngalyod giving birth to Aboriginal people. Artist, Billinyara Nabegeyo. Image courtesy of Pitt Rivers Museum, Oxford.

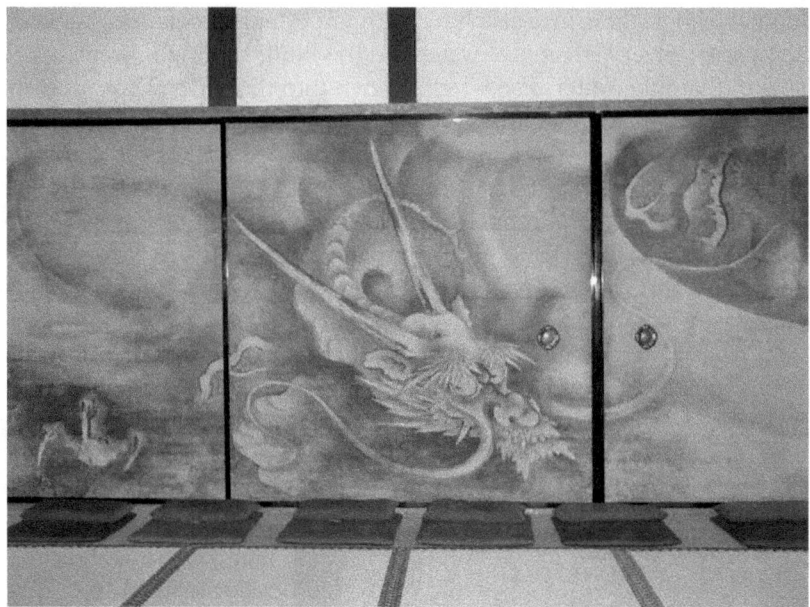

Figure 12.4 Cloud Dragon screen in Kennin-Ji, twelfth-century Zen Temple (Kyoto). Photo by Veronica Strang.

There are numerous examples of early 'snake cults', even in the geographic areas from which Christianity arose. Joines (1968) notes, for example, archaeological evidence of Bronze Age snake worship in Canaan.[6] And there is considerable agreement that the serpents demonized as Christianity gained ascendance had multiple – and more positively regarded – pre-Christian antecedents:

> The Egyptian crowned uraeus on a staff was a common emblem of divine goodness. When the priests of Thebes wished to ascribe the gift of life and the power of healing to the god, they twined the serpent around the trident of Jupiter Ammon. A staff wrapped by a serpent signified the Egyptian god Thoth or the Greek god Hermes Trismegistus, the author of medicine. It was probably Egypt who handed down to Greece the serpent-sceptre, or the caduceus, and the staff of Aesculapius, the god of medicine. The Greek goddess of health, Hygeia, could be represented by a serpent...' (Joines 1974: 86)

Huxley too records that households in ancient Greece typically had a guardian snake that had to be fed with offerings of milk and honey cakes (Huxley 1979: 7).[7] In fact, there seems to have been no pre-agricultural or early agricultural society that did not have sacred serpent beings of one sort or another, and as long as people saw their material environments as being animated and sentient, such beings retained a powerful and central role. This suggests a rather 'organic' relationship between humankind and the material world. Without the objectifying distance provided by scientific deconstruction and technological advancement, there prevailed (as there still does in some hunter–gatherer and small-scale horticultural societies) a more intimate relationship with the material environment, in which the properties and processes of other species and things were recognized as having their own agency.

In early Europe, animated land and waterscapes were inhabited by a range of sentient deities: tree spirits, generalized 'green' powers, and water beings. Because their generative and other powers were respected, these had to be dealt with reciprocally, leading to bioethical positions that, in principle, accommodated their needs as well as those of human beings, focusing on and valorizing the interdependencies between them. Descola and Pálsson (1996) point to the differences between this closely integrated human–environmental relationship and the emergence of dualistic views of nature and culture. While contemporary Western science[8] is underpinned by a vision of all beings – including humans – as part of universal nature (Vivieros de Castro 2004; Latour 2009), religious developments placing humankind in a hierarchically different and superior position sparked a critically alienating process of 'othering' the non-human. This resonates with Ingold's observation that some societies dwell 'in' the sphere of the world rather than taking a more objectifying view of 'the globe' (Ingold 2000). It also highlights the relational implications of 'identifying with' nature in contrast to framing it as 'other' (Strang 2005a).

The fluid relationships between human societies and other species and things are too complex to be visually represented in a comprehensive or indeed comprehensible way, but (with the caveat that these are hugely reductive and unrealistically static) it is possible to offer simple heuristic diagrams highlighting the changes through which, over time, major societies have increasingly dominated material events, prioritized their own needs, and achieved hierarchical distance from the non-human.

It would appear from the archaeological evidence that human–environmental relationships in many small-scale hunter–gatherer or horticultural societies prior to the medieval period were characterized by notions of partnership and parity with the material world and its perceived agency, and by low-key and sustainable resource use.[9] If we also accept as indicative ethnographic accounts of contemporary hunter–gatherer and horticultural societies, this reciprocity with non-human

Figure 12.5 A configuration of early human–environmental relationships.

agency was broadly coherent with relatively simple technologies, and relatively egalitarian social and economic structures: flat gerontocratic forms of governance, some degree of gender equality,[10] and limited common property regimes providing collective ownership and management of land and resources.

In a collaborative relationship between human societies and a 'sentient' material world, hydrolatry, the worship of water and the beings believed to manifest its creative energies, was an obvious outcome. Water beings were seen as both nurturing and authoritative, providing generative power as well as potentially destructive force. Thus in Mesopotamia and across Europe, pre-Christian Canaanite, Celtic, Greek and Roman societies worshipped – and propitiated – river gods and water beings with votive offerings, libations, sacrificial rituals and well-dressings.

Such beliefs and practices continue in societies that have maintained nature religions or elements of these: thus in Aboriginal Australia, key sacred knowledge and ritual focuses on the Rainbow Serpent, which, through a hydrotheological cycle, generates all life and upholds Ancestral Law (Strang 2002, 2009). In India, contemporary ethnography reveals water beings who must be dealt with respectfully if they are not to send punitive floods (Butcher 2013); in Africa they dispense wisdom and, again, punish wrongdoing (Bernard 2013), and in the Pacific, *taniwhas* guard the rivers and cause trouble when angered by developments insensitive to their well-being or that of local *iwis* (tribes) (Strang 2012).

Historically, though, the trajectory of water serpent beings in the Levant and across Europe took a different turn. I suggest that this was related to critical changes in material practices, with the development of irrigation and other forms of technology offering much greater human control over the physical environment. These developments articulated with related transformations in human–environmental relationships and in societies' political arrangements. A brief background sketch of these changes highlights the connections.

New Directions in Water Power

From about 3000 BCE, rather than working with the natural rise and fall of rivers, societies in Mesopotamia developed water wheels, canals, and ways of impounding and directing water. Between 2950 and 2750 BCE, for example, the Sadd El-Kafara 'dam of the Pagans ... sometimes called the oldest dam in the world', was built in Wadi el-Garawi, 18 miles south of Cairo (Biswas 1970: 5).

The development of agriculture also brought related Durkheimian changes in religious forms (Durkheim 1961). The totemic water beings and animal gods of nature religions were replaced by pantheons of human or semi-human deities who, rather than animating local rivers, trees and landscapes, inhabited alternate worlds such as Olympus and Valhalla. With greater investment in crops and infrastructure, land and resources were enclosed both physically and with new, less equal, forms of property. Societies became more hierarchical, and non-human species were defined as 'other', separating previously co-identified human and non-human kinds. In the process, water was redirected into human socio-technical systems as something to be controlled – to be acted *on* rather than acted *with*. These changes brought a new configuration to human relationships with water and the environment.

Representations of water beings altered accordingly. Although the earliest images of water serpent gods, the Egyptian *nommos*, had provided inspiration for multiple cultural manifestations around the world, and early Greek and Roman mythology had framed them in positive terms, there came a point – coinciding with the emergence of cities and their central water supply fountains in Greece c.700–600 BCE – when humanized deities began to compete for power with those in other forms. 'Fountains illustrated then – as they have done throughout the ages – an ideological and cultural notion of the triumph of civilization over nature: water, the giver and taker of life, in the fountain appears at the control of human beings' (Tvedt and Jacobsson 2006: ix). Gilmore observes that 'in the classical Mediterranean world, monsters first appear in literary form in the Homeric legends by 700 BC' (Gilmore 2003: 37). There were some early serpent slayings: for example the triumph of Perseus over the sea monster in the port of Jaffa, and the Herculean slaying of the many headed Hydra at Lerna.

Figure 12.6 A more hierarchical and human-centred configuration of relations with water and 'nature'.

The emergence of major monotheistic religions had an even greater impact. Like the earlier Greek and Roman cosmologies, Christian representations of serpents in the preliminary Biblical texts were laudatory, with Moses' 'bronze serpent' and the fiery Seraphim being depicted positively.[11] But as other writers have observed (Joines 1974; Batto 1992), later texts contained increasingly negative images, culminating in the demonization of the serpent in the Garden of Eden, and the assurance to Christ that 'the dragon shalt thou trample under feet' (King James Bible, Psalm 91:13). Thus Harte describes how baptism came to be linked with 'victory over the old dragon', and notes Psalm 74:13–14 'in which the Lord breaks the heads of the dragons in the waters and crushes Leviathan' (Harte 2011: 7). He suggests that this produced 'a mythical analogue of baptism as dragon-combat' (ibid.: 8), and it is reasonable to suppose that this provided the seedcorn for the myriad dragon-slaying stories – such as the Lambton Worm – that sprang up, like the classical vision of dragons' teeth, as Christianity's battle to subdue the pre-Christian nature religions spread across Europe.

Figure 12.7 Hercules slaying the Lernean hydra, c.525 B.C.E. Collection of the J. Paul Getty Museum, Malibu, California. Digital image courtesy of the Getty Museum's Open Content Program.

The demonization of previously valorized water beings coincided with further technological change in the Middle East and Europe. Urbanization in Greece, as well as initiating new social and material processes, created educated upper classes able to build on the scientific forays initiated by earlier Egyptian elites. This scholarship led to theories about hydrology, and to deconstructions of the material properties of water that were demystifying, opening up divergent notions of nature and culture that proved central to the shaping of contemporary human–environmental relations.

Egyptian and Greek scholarly progress was taken up by the Romans and translated practically into new technology – aqueducts, roads and harbours – which marched with its armies across its empire, and so into Britain. At that time 'Britannia' was still inhabited by Celtic tribes who combined hunting and gathering with low-key agricultural trade and, like the first waves of Roman invaders, worshipped water beings and conducted propitiatory rituals at thousands of sacred water sites across the British landscape.

The Island Hill

Around Durham, there is evidence of human settlement dating back to c.2000 BCE. The Roman legions were strongly resisted, most particularly by the Scots, who continued to harry them and subsequent invaders for centuries, making the north-east one of the most contested regions in Britain. However, the Romans made a stand at Hadrian's Wall and eventually subdued the populations south of it. As Christianity spread through the Roman Empire, Celtic holy wells were renamed after Christian saints who also appropriated their miraculous healing powers.

An important exception was Coventina's Well at Carrawburgh near Hadrian's Wall, and so not far from Durham. This retained its identification with this major pre-Christian water being, the Celtic/Roman 'Queen of the Water Goddesses', whose cult extended across Gaul and into north-west Spain. The spring and well, contained in a cistern in about 130 CE, continued to be a major focus for pilgrims, receiving about sixteen thousand coins and numerous other votive offerings – jewellery, bronze masks, animal figures, etc. (Green 1995; Hingley 2012). However, this propitiation ended in the late fourth century CE, following a stern edict by the Roman emperor Theodosius in 391 that Nicene Christianity was to be the official Roman religion, and pagan practices must cease forthwith. A massive destruction of pagan sites followed, which elevated Theodosius to sainthood. The Church fathers in this period also focused their disapproval on hydrolatry, with Tertullian, for example, stating that water was particularly attractive to demons and the Devil (Oestigaard 2010: 24). The devotees of Coventina therefore hurriedly placed building stones over the well to hide and protect it.

By the early Middle Ages a number of Christian centres had been established in Britain, one of the earliest and most important being the order of monks who came with Saint Aiden to Lindisfarne, often described as the cradle of British Christianity. Their first monastery in 635 CE (supported by King Oswald in nearby Bamburgh), acted as a centre

Figure 12.8 Stone marker from Coventina's Well. Photo by author.

for missionaries keen to convert the pagans of Northumbria to Christianity, and thus to instil its particular beliefs and values. That is not to suggest that there was a sudden shift to environmental 'dominion': indeed, there is evidence that the early Christians expressed concern for the well-being of other species, but even then (as now) this was framed paternally. St Cuthbert provides a well-known example, instituting the first-known bird protection laws to safeguard the friendly eider ducks and other seabirds in the Farne Islands.[12]

Lindisfarne was not safe for humans though: the community suffered a major blow from a Viking attack in 793 CE, and a number of monks were killed. Such depredations were common in Britain's north-east, and it is worth noting that the Vikings, with their serpent-prowed longships, were also regarded as pagans who worshipped these *ormr* or 'worms'. The ferocity of their attacks led the monks to flee the holy island, carrying with them the 'miraculously undecayed' body of St Cuthbert.[13] Their peregrinations in avoiding Viking raiders brought them, eventually, to Durham[14] where they found a readily defensible high peninsula in a loop of the River Wear. Here they built a cathedral, and in doing so laid the foundations for a major religious power base in the region.

The Norman Conquest of 1066 further embedded Christianity in Britain, and the production of the Domesday Book in 1086, under the orders of William the Conqueror, highlights the advancements made by then in subduing the material environment to human needs. It records multiple water mills along every river,[15] and the carving and enclosure of land into tightly managed 'hides' and shires. There was now a sharply hierarchical class system, in which an aristocracy and its manorial holdings shared governance of the hoi polloi and of land and resources with equally powerful religious orders and their great abbeys. This development highlighted the perennial relationship between political power and the ownership of water, although this might not be as inevitably despotic as Wittfogel (1957) claimed.[16] But it appears that the abbeys were frequently the major controllers and suppliers of water to the local peasantry, and their monks were renowned for their expertise in water management (Magnusson 2006).[17]

Water was therefore reconfigured again, becoming the gift of powerful elites and an expression of their political control, and being more closely harnessed to drive new technologies of production. The abbeys were also major centres of scholarship, promoting ideas in which water was represented as the gift of God and – as scientific understandings increased – part of a hydrotheological cycle of water movement according to His plan.

Northumbria had long been central to this scholarship and religious authority, being the home of the Venerable Bede, who, in the late seventh and early eighth century, lived at an abbey in Monkwearmouth which, as its name suggests, lies at the mouth of the River Wear. One of the earliest British scholars, Bede engaged with Greek philosophers in speculating about the sources of the Nile, and helped to lead a transition, during the latter centuries of the first millennium, from looking to the Scriptures for all instruction about 'inexplicable' phenomena to formulating scientific explanations that further crystallized a dualistic view of culture and nature.

Figure 12.9 Illumination from the beginning of St Matthew's Gospel in a Bible bequeathed by William of St Carilef. Image courtesy of Durham Cathedral Library.

Durham itself does not appear in the Domesday Book, as it was administered independently by the Bishop of Durham. St Cuthbert had been granted territory between the Tyne and Wear by King Ecgfrith of Northumbria, and this independence was further reaffirmed by the King of York in the late 800s. Durham was therefore ruled for several hundred years by powerful prince-bishops, who instituted the building of the current cathedral on 'Palace Green' in 1093. Begun under the direction of William of St Carilef (Bishop of Durham 1081–95), this took forty years to complete. A Norman castle was also built on 'the Island Hill' in the eleventh century to provide an outpost of governance and a bulwark against the persistent rebellions in the north. But, far from the southern centres of royal power, in a region recognized by the Normans as a County Palatine, the Durham bishops' authority was said to be equivalent to that of the king, with an independent right to muster armies, hold court, and raise taxes. Crucially, these militaristic holy men were also expected to deal with the troublesome 'worms'.

Slaying the Dragon

The end of the first millennium coincided with a major effort by the Church to achieve ascendancy over the nature religions that continued to flow subversively underground, especially in conquered Celtic nations. This was simultaneously a contest for religious leadership and for political and economic control. It was equally concerned with enforcing the supremacy of culture over nature, being a period in which nature came to be regarded as not only feminine in gender, but also as 'uncivilized' and distasteful. New and punitive forms of asceticism encouraged a horror of 'base nature' and its untrammelled fecundity.

Religions celebrating the generative power of water and nature therefore became even more abhorrent. Water was reclassified: 'good' water arrived via God's beneficence, in timely and sufficient (but not excessive) amounts amenable to human technological management, while the 'primeval' water of nature was recalcitrant and uncontrollable. Holy water was also reframed symbolically as the substance of spiritual being, thus retaining its generative meanings and its long-standing capacities to act as a metaphor of time, connection, wisdom and so on, but this too became a gift from God. Meanwhile, recycling earlier ideas about water's potentially destructive powers, it was felt that water could be polluted by evil, including pagan 'heresy'. All of these negative potentials were represented by the water beings of earlier religions.

Figure 12.10 Russian icon of St George and the dragon, c.1450. Image courtesy of National Museum, Stockholm.

Ideological battles were therefore manifested in contests between the now thoroughly demonized water serpent beings and the Christian male culture heroes whose sacred task it was to subdue them. Medieval Britain was plagued with serpents, most particularly in the areas of highest 'pagan' resistance: in Wales, for example,[18] and in the north-east. Parish churches commonly exhibited 'dragon skins', and there is a plethora of reports of dragons and worms, with several in close proximity to Durham. The tale of the Laidly Worm, like the Lambton Worm, is recounted in ballad form: 'The Laidly Worm of Spindleston Heugh'. Its snake/worm princess (returned to human form by a prince, naturally), appears to be based on an older Nordic saga, 'Hjálmþés saga ok Ölvis'. The Linton Worm, in Roxburghshire near the Scottish Borders, lived in a place still called the Worm's Den. This wyvern[19] was 'in length three Scots yards and bigger than an ordinary man's leg – in form and callour to our common muir edders'[20] (Scott 1815: 6–8). The monster was dispatched by a local hero, (William or John) de Somerville, the Laird of Lariston, and in its dying throes it toppled a nearby mountain, creating an unusual topography of hills consequently named 'wormington'. De Somerville was rewarded with an appointment as Royal Falconer, and became the first Baron of Linton, adopting the wyvern as his heraldic device.

The most important local dragon, however, was the Sockburn Worm, possibly the model for the Lambton story. Sockburn is near Durham, on a peninsula near Darlington. As the most southerly point of the Durham diocese, it was an important site in the Middle Ages: Higbald, Bishop of Lindisfarne, was crowned there in 780 or 781 CE; and Eanwald, Archbishop of York, in 796. The area suffered heavily from Viking raids and there are traces of several Viking settlements in the area. Local historians (e.g. Hutchinson 1823) have speculated that the 'worm' was a name for a particularly savage Viking who made a number of forays into the district.

The medieval Sockburn estate was held by the Conyers family, and it was Sir John Conyers who was said to have slain the marauding dragon.[21] In doing so, he used a falchion, a curved machete-like sword, common in Europe between the eleventh and sixteenth centuries, which could be wielded with one hand like a meat cleaver. The Conyers falchion was subsequently presented to each new Bishop of Durham when he first entered the diocese at a nearby ford or via the Croft-on-Tees bridge, and he was required to swear that he would slay the dragon. The falchion (or probably a later copy)[22] is now held in the Treasury at Durham Cathedral.

Such stories were repeated across Europe. Inspired by legends of St George and St Michael, pestilential dragons were slaughtered by (usually but not invariably male) heroes, many of whom went on to become saints or were otherwise elevated in social rank (Riches 2000). This coincided with an intensely military period in Church history, as Christian leaders struggled to suppress not only the rebellious 'pagans' under their direct governance, but also to fend off competition from the other mon-

Reflecting Nature 265

Figure 12.11 Church carving: crusaders slaying 'infidels', Acca, Israel. Photo by author.

otheistic religious movements and expand their control of other people, land and resources.

Images of dragon slayers were therefore interchangeable with those of saints killing the pagans who, by the late eleventh century, were no longer merely an alternate barbaric religion, but had been redefined as 'heretics'.

Pope Urban II, a committed reformer, made passionate speeches against the evils of paganism. He encouraged a series of Crusades: the 'taking of the cross', in which, incentivized by a promise of remission of sins, cohorts of militia travelled to Palestine to assert the supremacy of the Christian Church over foreign 'infidels'. Home-grown pagan groups also had to be dealt with: there was the *reconquista* in Spain and, in 1209, an Albigensian Crusade was sent to eliminate the 'heretic' Cathars of southern France. Numerous Papal Bulls were issued: in 1184, Lucius III condemned heresy; and in 1198 Innocent III defined it as treason. In 1252, Innocent IV issued an edict that heretics could be burned alive, and this was followed, in twelfth-century France, by the inquisition, guaranteed to terrify the recalcitrant.

The dragon slaying around Durham, a vital centre for evangelical Christianity, can therefore be seen as part of a much larger effort to erase the nature religions regarded as subversive to the normative order defined by the Church. And this order was not purely religious: as noted previously, its ideas, beliefs and values articulated with new social and economic practices, new technologies, and new configurations of people's relationships with water and the non-human world. These relationships were also influenced by the Crusades which, as well as engaging combatively with Levantine cultures, opened up both physical and metaphorical roads to the East and its scholarship. As Riley-Smith (2005) points out, travel to the Kingdom of Jerusalem, and the governance of it, required cultural innovation and encouraged a more cosmopolitan worldview. It exposed Europeans to Islamic and Classical Greek ideas and their sophisticated developments in algebra, architecture, medicine, engineering and science. Such scholarship further deconstructed ideas about sentient land and waterscapes, replacing them with scientific notions of materiality that repositioned nature as being both physically and imaginatively the subject and object of human culture.

For this to succeed, however, the pagan beings manifesting the power of nature had to go, in particular those embodying the most fluid and uncontrollable, the most feminine part of nature. In this context, it makes perfect sense that Sir John Lambton went to Palestine, that he joined 'a troop ov Knights', and that this appears to have been the Knights of St John – the Hospitallers who provided a Christian power base in Jerusalem.[23] This order was served by the Benedictine monks who were to become such a strong presence in Durham.

A historical context also illuminates the other elements of the Lambton story: for example, the representation of the worm as something that emerged from the river because Young Lambton went 'a'fishing' instead of going to church. Its growth in the water of a formerly pagan well nicely expresses a pre-Christian notion of the generative powers of water, but reframes it in 'monstrous' terms. The poisoning of the well represents the pollution of subversive ideas, and the worm's trail of slime reflects the ascetic repugnance for the ambiguity of slime – neither water nor land – which recurs in medieval and subsequent descriptions of underworlds and regions of Hell.[24] Its reported imprint, in the form of the spiral marks still visible on Penshaw Hill,[25] not only recalls the topographical legacy of the Linton Worm, but also carries a faint echo of older origin myths about the creative capacities of water beings to shape the landscape.

In many versions of the story, Sir John is advised by a wise woman that he must kill the worm in the river, so that its severed body parts will be carried away before they can reknit themselves. The idea that snakes and serpents could remake themselves runs through many such legends (for example, that of the Lernean hydra), articulating fears that, though repressed, subversive religions could merely slide underground, like water, to reform and resurface later on. And indeed they did. Although the dragon slayings eased somewhat in the mid twelfth century, as the building of cathedrals and abbeys replaced the Crusades as a way of earning holy 'indulgences', efforts to assert the religious leadership of the Church continued.

In Durham, the castle played a key role in defending its interests, most particularly in the Battle of Neville's Cross in 1346, though by this time the Scots army was no longer pagan, merely resistant to the religious and political rule of the English. But Shakespeare's Henry V tells the Archbishop of Canterbury that the Scots poured southwards 'like a tide into a breach': '[T]he Scot on his unfurnish'd kingdom / Came pouring, like the tide into a breach, / With ample and brim fullness of his force; / Galling the gleaned land with hot essays' (Henry V, Act 1 Scene 3). The invading army almost reached Palace Green, but once again the military advantages of the 'island hill' were demonstrated, and the castle and cathedral remained secure.[26] The Scots king was incarcerated for eleven years, reasserting the power of the prince-bishops.

Further afield, new seafaring vessels and navigational instruments assisted efforts to expand the territories under Christian rule. In the 1400s, Papal Bulls supported missionary conquests of new regions by Portugal and Spain, and in 1521 Leo X issued a statement permitting the use of violence in evangelizing. Christian nations sought to gain control of previously Islamic colonies. Early Muslim states had appeared in the 1300s as beliefs had spread along trade routes, creating enclaves in Java and Sumatra and achieving conversions in Malacca. There were the Mughals in India, the Safavid dynasties in Persia, and the Ottoman Empire in Iraq, Syria and Egypt. And Muslim expansions continued to make ground until the critical Portuguese conquest of Malacca in 1511 (Sutherland 2007).

This was also a period in which scholars such as the Hugonaut Bernard Palissy and – more famously – Leonardo Da Vinci began to articulate scientific ideas about hydrological cycles. Da Vinci's *Treatise on Water* described water as the driving force of nature, presciently drawing connections between the enlivening flow of water in biological, ecological and hydrological systems: 'The same cause which moves the humours in every species of animate bodies against the natural law of gravity also propels the water through the veins of the earth wherein it is enclosed and distributes it through small passages … Where there is life there is heat, and where vital heat is, there is movement of vapour' (Pfister, Savenije and Fenicia 2009).

Religious control within Christian nations also remained critical. In 1484 Innocent VIII condemned 'witchcraft', the change in terminology suggesting that this was now more of an isolated problem rather than the cohesive countermovement implied by 'heresy'. The rise of Protestantism and the Reformation (1517–1648) rejected the 'magical' works of the medieval Catholic Church, including its more instrumental perceptions of holy water (Oestigaard 2010). By 1586, alternate 'magical' beliefs had been further downgraded, with Pope Sixtus V condemning 'judicial astrology' as just 'superstition'. However, even in the late 1700s, a period of major post-medieval scientific advances, 'witch trials' continued in Europe.

But these were mere flashbacks. By this time, enabled by both religious and scientific developments, ideas about human dominion over and distinction from nature were deeply entrenched, and social class systems were similarly well embedded. The previously 'primeval' seas were traversed; 'heathen' peoples were conquered and converted; and their lands and water resources had been made amenable to the great dam building and irrigation projects of the nineteenth century. With the latter came an intensifying effort, which has continued apace, to enclose water resources in increasingly privatized forms of property ownership, thus completing its subjection to human will.

In Durham, the cathedral had ceased to be a Benedictine monastery with the Reformation, but the local powers of the prince-bishops pertained until all such authorities were abolished by the British gov-

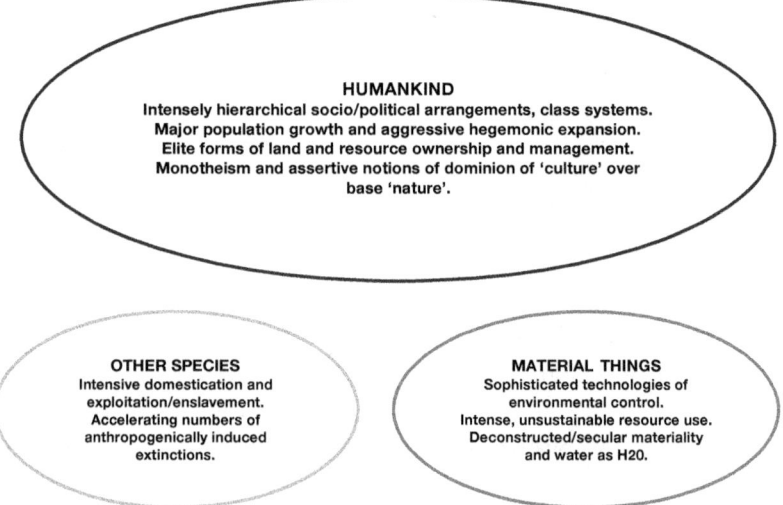

Figure 12.12 A contemporary configuration of human–environmental relations.

Figure 12.13 The Bishop of Durham, Justin Welby, being presented with the Conyers Falchion in 2011. Photo by Keith Blundy | aegiesPR.

ernment in 1836. Even now, the Bishop of Durham is a member of the House of Lords, escorts the sovereign at the coronation and is not merely 'installed' but 'enthroned'.[27] A recent appointee, Justin Welby, observed that: 'To become Bishop of Durham is a huge privilege … It is an ancient diocese, going way back before England itself existed. The heritage is extraordinary; bishops of Durham stand on the shoulders of some of the greatest Christians that Europe has produced, from the 7th century to the 21st' (Durham diocesan web site, accessed 2 June 2011).

In the early 1800s, the falchion waving and promises to slay the dragon were dropped from the rituals accompanying the bishop's arrival in the diocese, but the custom was revived by David Jenkins in 1984. As the Conyers family is no longer in the area, contemporary presentations are usually made by the Mayor of Darlington. In 2011, Justin Welby, received the falchion on the Croft-on-Tees bridge, and was greeted as he crossed the river by a local rector, Adele Martin: 'My Lord Bishop,' she said, 'I here present you with the falchion wherewith the champion Conyers slew the worm, dragon or fiery flying serpent which destroyed men, women and children' (Lloyd 2011; see also Hutchinson 1823).

In 2014, after Justin Welby became the Archbishop of Canterbury, the same ritual greeted the appointment of the new bishop, Paul Butler. Asked what the dragon meant to him, he replied: 'That which we see as evil in our world' (Strang, field notes 2014).

Figure 12.14 The newly appointed Bishop of Durham, Paul Butler, being presented with the falchion in Croft-on-Tees in 2014. Photo by Keith Blundy | aegiesPR.

Figure 12.15 The falchion presented to each new Bishop of Durham. Photo by author.

Conclusion

Today the Lambton Worm is seen as just a fairy tale, a marvellous monster in a popular folk song. The legend is regularly performed by primary school children in venues around Durham, including churches. So why have a ritual in which the new Bishop of Durham swears (or at least implies) that he will slay the dragon? This could be interpreted as an effort to enliven and popularize contemporary church rituals, but perhaps, in a diocese whose motto is 'Helping to grow God's Kingdom in every community', it should be considered seriously as a regular reaffirmation of the dominance of a particular religious perspective.[28]

Given the long history of religious contention in this region, this latter purpose is by no means obsolete. The serpent remains demonically present in Christian religious discourses, as a powerful metaphor of a negative 'other'. These connotations are reflected in multiple secular representations of serpent beings in visual and literary media. The Lambton Worm alone has provided inspiration for numerous artistic efforts, including Bram Stoker's *Lair of the White Worm* (1911), which formed the subject of Ken Russell's film of the same title in 1988. It appears in Ian Watson's fictional novel, *The Fire Worm* (1988); Thomas Pynchon's novel, *Mason and Dixon* (1998); a graphic novel, *Alice in Sutherland,* by Bryan Talbot (2007); and an opera *The Lambton Worm,* composed by Robert Sherlaw (1978). Samuel Taylor Coleridge's poem *Love* (1799) refers to the Sockburn church and the dragon, and there is Andy Goldsworthy's *Lambton Earthworks* sculpture near Chester-le-Street. Perhaps most famously, Lewis Carroll, whose father was the rector in Crofton-Tees, was inspired to invent the Jabberwocky: the 'slithy tove' that 'did gyre and gimble in the wabe':[29]

> And, has thou slain the Jabberwock?
> Come to my arms, my beamish boy!
> O frabjous day! Callooh!
> Callay!' He chortled in his joy. (Carroll 1871)

So, dragon slaying continues in multiple fora, and the persistence of these ritualized re-enactments of the slaughter of the most powerful of the pre-Christian nature beings is telling. Placed in a historical context, they serve as a reminder that water beings are symbols of alternate religious ideas which continue, in the twenty-first century, to valorize subaltern – and subversive – ideas about human relationships with water and with nature.[30]

At his enthronement in the cathedral, following the ritual in Crofton-Tees, Bishop Justin Welby noted that 'the idols of the present age have been toppled and fallen', and he called upon Christians to adopt a 'revolutionary lifestyle'. Their mission, he said, was 'to rekindle the Christian faith in the north-east and reconvert the region' (Tallantire 2012: film).

Meanwhile, founded in 1971, the British Pagan Federation's northeast district holds meetings in Durham and surrounding towns. Its contiguous Cumbrian district website notes that 'religious impulse and fulfilment have often been allied to a sense of closeness to the splendour of nature', and describes 'a flourishing population of adherents to the

Old Religion: Druids, Shamans, Heathens and Wiccans'. The federation says that there are at least fifty thousand and possibly up to two hundred thousand pagans in Britain, and it seeks to support all of them: 'To ensure they have the same rights as the followers of other beliefs and religions. It aims to promote a positive profile for Pagans and Paganism and to provide information on Pagan beliefs to the media, official bodies and the greater community' (Pagan Federation 2013).

The 2011 census for England and Wales records 48,000 people eschewing affiliation to the major monotheisms and noting affiliation to 'other' religions. In a total population of 56.1 million, this represents a rise from 3 to 4 per cent in the last decade. About a quarter of the population now claims to have 'No religion'. Christians still compose 59 per cent of the whole, but in the same period that pagan numbers have grown by 25 per cent, there has been a 13 per cent decline in people defining themselves as Christian (Office for National Statistics 2011).[31]

There is considerable intellectual and moral common ground between neo-pagans and the 'deep green' environmental groups also seeking to challenge humankind's assumed rights of dominion over other species, however purportedly 'benign'. These counter-movements question the model of nature–culture dualism and intentional distance from 'nature' that emerged with greater technological control over the material environment. Both countermovements hope to promote more egalitarian, less anthropocentric bioethical positions in which humankind is socially and morally relocated within ecological systems.

These groups have drawn inspiration from the many indigenous societies around the world whose nature religions are commonly represented as enabling more harmonious and sustainable relationships with their environments. While such representations have undoubtedly been romanticized at times, this should not obscure fundamental differences between contemporary Western, Christian modes of engaging with the material world and those retaining beliefs in non-human sentience and agency. For indigenous communities, environmental groups and neo-pagans, it is not the serpent, but the human–environmental relationships exported by Western societies that is the 'aaful story': a story of excessive impositions on delicate ecosystems; of the overuse of resources; of cumulative environmental damage; and of the enslavement or extinction of other species and less powerful human groups.

It is no coincidence that these contemporary challenges to a normative global order are heavily focused on water. Subaltern concerns have regularly been expressed in (sometimes violent) protests against water appropriation and privatization, and against dams and other diversions of water into human interests at the expense of the non-human

(Strang 2013a). Hydrolatry has also resurfaced, with the reinvention of water rituals and increasing valorization of water's generative power and agency in religion and the arts. For example, in the *Splash!* festival that takes place bi-annually in Australia, on the north Queensland coast, groups from the surrounding water-catchment area bring water from local streams and pour it into a central vessel to celebrate the fluid connections between their communities and their collective connections to the local environment (Strang 2005c). In Britain, well-dressing ceremonies reviving pre-Christian hydrolatry rituals are increasing in popularity. In Durham itself, May Day celebrations – traditionally affirming the spirit and power of nature – remain low key, but a few aficionados gather on Prebends Bridge at dawn, mere steps from the looming towers of the cathedral, to dance and sing above the waters of the Wear.

This serpentine journey suggests that current representational contests are the product of long-term historical flows of ideas, and that ancient dragons continue to animate moral debates about how human societies should conduct themselves in relation to the non-human. While the Lambton Worm may be slain on a regular basis in Durham, Britain has more resistant serpents – for example, the red dragon on the Welsh flag continues to fly over the highest density of pagan groups in Britain. Further afield, indigenous communities, particularly in Australia and New Zealand (but also in the Americas, Africa and parts of Asia), regularly bring their water beings into play in legal and political arena, to promote their own beliefs and values and to critique the ways of life imposed by political and economic colonialism (Strang 2012, 2013b).

To conclude our hydrological cycle, there is also the point at which this story began. The material properties of water continue to flow into the human imagination, carrying ideas about its powers: its capacities to generate life; its potential to carve landscapes and transform itself and other things over time; its ability to subsume events and to disappear. The deep influence of being immersed in these material events is a constant in human lives, continually stimulating, in one cultural form or another, ideas about the agentive powers of water and of nature itself. Ever greater religious and technological hubris on the part of humankind has failed to subsume or completely control these powers; one might say, instead, that it has merely raised the level of the dam.

Notes

1. 'Couldn't be bothered'.
2. 'Threw it down a well'.

3. 'Be quiet lads, shut your mouths...'
4. 'Worm' is an old English term for dragon, relating to the Germanic 'wyrm' and the Old Norse term 'ormr', which as well as describing the leviathans believed by the Vikings to inhabit the deeps, also refers to the serpentine prows of their longships.
5. Children.
6. Joines observes that 'Huxley records that households in ancient Greece typically had a guardian snake that had to be fed with milk and honey cakes (Joines 1974: 7).
7. The notion that marauding dragons could be placated if supplied with milk occurs frequently in medieval stories, and may link with earlier ideas about guardian snakes. These recurrent ideas may also explain the Lambton Worm's predilection for 'milking the coos' at night.
8. Vivieros de Castro (2004) observes that both 'social' and 'natural' science accept an overarching concept of nature (and multiple cultural perspectives), while alternate views, such as those of Amerindians, envisage multiple natures. But in the face of strongly alienating ideas about human difference, even a universalizing concept of nature has not been sufficient to recreate the potential for co-identification – or assumed kinship – with the non-human that was (and in some contexts is still) enabled by totemic belief systems positioning human and non-human beings in reciprocal terms (Strang 2005a).
9. The practices of larger imperial societies in the pre-medieval period were somewhat different, although (as illustrated by the votive offerings at holy wells and by the naming of many rivers for Roman water goddesses) pre-Christian Romans certainly continued to valorize water serpent beings, as did the early Greeks. However, these serpent-oriented religious ideas and practices receded as their societies began to urbanize and develop scientific ideas and new forms of technology.
10. This is a complex issue, and there is insufficient space to explore it here, but if we take as key indicators things such as joint ownership of land and resources and direct participation in religious and political governance, then societies governed by their elders – though they might contain specific gender roles and other forms of inequality – are structurally and thus quite possibly socially more egalitarian than most.
11. In Biblical narratives Moses uses a sacred object, a snake of brass upon a pole (a *Nehushtan*) to cure the Israelites from snakebites (Numbers 21:4–9).
12. Eider ducks are therefore known as 'Cuddy' (Cuthbert's) ducks in the Pitmatic dialect specific to Northumberland and Durham. They are curious birds, seemingly unafraid of humans (Chris Watson, pers. comm.)
13. Archaeologist David Petts notes evidence that some may have remained there, or that the island was not entirely abandoned (pers.comm.).
14. The name is possibly a combination of Dun (the old English for hill) and Holme, an old Norse word for island, attesting to local Viking influences.
15. The Stour, in Dorset, for example, had 66 mills in 70 miles of river.
16. As I have noted elsewhere, while the control of water is fundamentally empowering, much depends on how it is owned: for example, collective forms of water

ownership are closely linked to democratic powers, and may indeed be essential to the maintenance of democracy (Strang 2010).
17. This was drawn upon, for example, in the building of London's 'Great Conduit' in 1237.
18. Although Christianity subsumed paganism in Ireland and Wales (with St Patrick famously driving the snakes out of Ireland in around 432 CE) there was considerable absorption of Celtic religions into Christianity in these areas.
19. 'Wyvern' is a term for dragon coming from Middle English *wyvere* (thirteenth century) via old French *wivre*, originally from the Latin *vipera* (viper) (Hoad 1993: 546). It became a popular heraldic device, most particularly in strongly Celtic areas such as Wales and Wessex (the golden wyvern being the symbol of the ancient kingdom of Wessex). A wyvern usually has two legs, a long serpentine body and a barbed tail, while sea wyverns are typically portrayed with fish tails.
20. 'Sharing form and colour with our adders'.
21. The stone under which the dragon was buried is reportedly still visible.
22. The present falchion is believed to date from the eleventh century.
23. The Hospitallers retained a Christian power base in Jerusalem until Arab military forces regained the area and they had to retreat to Rhodes and then Malta.
24. This antipathy intensified over time, emerging in Bunyan's 'Slough of Despond', in the foul water and mud of Hell in Dante's 'inferno', in Sartre's horror of slime, and in Freud's analysis of the ambiguity of water bodies and fluidity.
25. Archaeological interpretations describe Penshaw Hill as a triple rampart Iron Age fort.
26. Prior Fosser of Durham reported that, before the battle, St Cuthbert had appeared, instructing him to take the corporax cloth that had been found in his coffin in 1104 and carry it to the battlefield: 'Early the following day, the Prior, in obedience to the saint's wishes and accompanied by a number of his monks, took this sacred relic to a site within a few hundred yards of the two opposing armies. There, he and the monks knelt and prayed while the battle raged around them' (Gunn 2013).
27. The most recent incumbent, Justin Welby, was selected in 2012 as the next Archbishop of Canterbury, Britain's most senior Anglican.
28. One might similarly interpret contemporary engagements with Coventina's Well. Now reopened as a 'heritage site', the well attracts visitors who, at times, leave Christian symbols on the altar, though it is unclear whether these are meant as religious challenges or as (rather ambiguous) votive offerings to the Celtic Goddess (Hingley 2012).
29. There is also Terry Gilliam's film, *Jabberwocky* (1977).
30. The most extreme version of this subversion lies in the Satanic Bible, which adopts 'leviathan' directly as a representation of opposition to Christianity. Though not at all representative of the majority of pagan religions, this could be described as being akin to the outliers of religious fanaticism loosely connected with other belief systems.
31. This shift may be due, in part, to strong feminist critiques of a patriarchal Church, encouraging women in search of spiritual expression to revive goddess

cults and join more egalitarian, nature-oriented religious groups (Raphael 1999; Strang 2014).

References

Batto, B. 1992. *Slaying the Dragon: Mythmaking in the Biblical Tradition.* Louisville, KY: Westminster John Knox Press.
Bernard, P. 2013. '"Living Water" in Nguni Healing Traditions, South Africa', in F. Krause and V. Strang (eds), *Living Water: The Powers and Politics of a Vital Substance,* Special Issue, *Worldviews* 17(2): 138–49.
Biswas, A. 1970. *History of Hydrology.* Amsterdam and London: North-Holland Publishing Company.
Butcher, A. 2013. 'Keeping the Faith: Divine Protection and Flood Prevention in Modern Buddhist Ladakh', in F. Krause and V. Strang (eds), *Living Water: The Powers and Politics of a Vital Substance,* Special Issue, *Worldviews* 17(2): 103–14.
Carroll, L. 1871. *Through the Looking-Glass, and What Alice Found There.* Illus. John Tenniel. London: Macmillan.
Coleridge, Samuel Taylor. 1799. *Love,* in Literature Network online. http://www.online-literature.com/coleridge/641/ (accessed 16 January 2013).
Descola, P., and G. Pálsson (eds). 1996. *Nature and Society: Anthropological Perspectives.* London and New York: Routledge.
Durham Diocese. 2011a. 'New Bishop-Designate of Durham Announced'. http://www.durham.anglican.org/news-and-events/news-article.aspx?id=193 (accessed 16 January 2013).
Durham Diocese. 2011b. 'Bishop Justin Enters his Diocese'. http://www.durham.anglican.org/news-and-events/news-article.aspx?id=213 (accessed 16 January 2013).
Durkheim, E. 1961. *The Elementary Forms of the Religious Life.* New York: Collier Books.
Gilmore, D. 2003. *Monsters: Evil Beings, Mythical Beasts, and All Manner of Imaginary Terrors.* Philadelphia: University of Pennsylvania Press.
Green, M. 1995. *Celtic Goddesses: Warriors, Virgins and Mothers.* London: British Museum Press.
Gunn, R. 2013. *The Battle of Neville's Cross.* http://skyelander.orgfree.com/neville.html (accessed 4 January 2013).
Harte, J. 2011. 'Dragons, Saints and Wells', *European Review of History* 18(2): 227–41.
Hingley, R. 2012. *Hadrian's Wall: A Life.* Oxford and New York: Oxford University Press.
Hoad, T. 1993. *English Etymology.* Oxford: Oxford University Press.
Hutchinson, W. 1823. *The History and Antiquities of the County Palatine of Durham.* Durham: G. Walker.
Huxley, F. 1979. *The Dragon: Nature of Spirit, Spirit of Nature.* London: Thames and Hudson.
Ingold, T. 2000. *The Perception of the Environment.* London and New York: Routledge.

Joines, K. 1968. 'The Bronze Serpent in the Israelite Cult', *Journal of Biblical Literature* 87(3): 245–56.

———. 1974. *Serpent Symbolism in the Old Testament: A Linguistic, Archaeological and Literary Study*. Haddonfield, NJ: Haddonfield House.

Lakoff, G., and M. Johnson. 1980. *Metaphors We Live By*. Chicago and London: University of Chicago Press.

Latour, B. 2009. 'Perspectivism: "Type" or "Bomb"?' *Anthropology Today* 25(2): 1–2.

Lévi-Strauss, C. 1966. *The Savage Mind*. Chicago: University of Chicago Press.

Lloyd, C. 2011. 'Bishop Crosses River for Sword that Slew Worm', *The Northern Echo* website, 26 November 2011. http://www.thenorthernecho.co.uk/news/9387015.Bishop_crosses_river_for_sword_that_slew_worm/ (accessed 16 January 2013).

Magnusson, R. 2006. 'Water and Wastes in Medieval London', in T. Tvedt and E. Jakobsson (eds), *A History of Water, Volume 1: Water Control and River Biographies*. London and New York: I.B. Tauris, pp. 299–313.

Oestigaard, T. 2010. 'The Topography of Holy Water in England after the Reformation', in K. Lykke-Syse and T. Oestigaard (eds), *Perceptions of Water in Britain from Early Modern Times to the Present: An Introduction*. Bergen: BRIC Press, pp. 15–34.

Office for National Statistics. 2011. http://www.ons.gov.uk/ons/guide-method/census/2011/index.html

Pagan Federation. 2013. http://paganfed.org/ (accessed 17 January 2013).

Pfister, L., H. Savenije and F. Fenicia. 2009. *Leonardo Da Vinci's Water Theory: On the Origin and Fate of Water*. International Association of Hydrological Sciences. Oxfordshire: IAHS Press.

Pynchon, T. 1998. *Mason and Dixon: A Novel*. London: Vintage.

Raphael, M. 1999. *Introducing Theology: Discourse on the Goddess*. Sheffield: Sheffield Academic Press.

Riches, S. 2000. *St George: Hero, Martyr and Myth*. Stroud: Sutton Publishing.

Riley-Smith, J. 2005. *The Crusades: A Short History*. New Haven, CT: Yale University Press.

Russell, K. (Director) 1988. Film: *The Lair of the White Worm*. Vestron Pictures.

Scott, W. (ed.). 1815. *Memorie of the Somervilles*, Vol. 1. Edinburgh: James Ballantyne and Co.

Sherlaw, R. (composer). 1978. *The Lambton Worm* (opera).

Stoker, B. 1911. *The Lair of the White Worm*. Ireland: William Rider and Son.

Strang, V. 2002. 'Life Down Under: Water and Identity in an Aboriginal Cultural Landscape', *Goldsmiths College Anthropology Research Papers* 7. London: Goldsmiths College.

———. 2004. *The Meaning of Water*. Oxford and New York: Berg.

———. 2005a. 'Knowing Me, Knowing You: Aboriginal and Euro-Australian Concepts of Nature as Self and Other', *Worldviews* 9(1): 25–56.

———. 2005b. 'Common Senses: Water, Sensory Experience and the Generation of Meaning', *Journal of Material Culture* 10(1): 93–121.

———. 2005c. 'Making a Splash!: Water Rituals, Subversion and Environmental Values in Queensland'. Paper presented at Annual Conference of the Association of Social Anthropologists of the UK and the Commonwealth, University of Aberdeen.

———. 2009. 'Water and Indigenous Religion: Aboriginal Australia', in T. Tvedt and T. Oestigaard (eds), *The Idea of Water*. London: I.B. Tauris, pp. 343–77.

———. 2010. 'Fluid Forms: Owning Water in Australia', in V. Strang and M. Busse (eds), *Ownership and Appropriation*, ASA Monograph. Oxford and New York: Berg, pp. 171–95.

———. 2012. 'Representing Water: Visual Anthropology and Divergent Trajectories in Human Environmental Relations', *Anuário Antropológico* 2: 213–42.

———. 2013a. 'Dam Nation: Cubbie Station and the Waters of the Darling', in J. Wagner (ed.), *The Social Life of Water in a Time of Crisis*. Oxford and New York: Berghahn Books, pp. 36–60.

———. 2013b. 'Going Against the Flow: The Biopolitics of Dams and Diversions', in F. Krause and V. Strang (eds), *Living Water: The Powers and Politics of a Vital Substance*, Special Issue, *Worldviews* 17(2): 161–73.

———. 2014. 'Lording It Over The Goddess: Water, Gender and Human–Environmental Relations', *Journal of Feminist Studies in Religion* 30(1): 83–107.

Sutherland, H. 2007. 'Geography as Destiny? The Role of Water in Southeast Asian History', in P. Boomgaard (ed.), *A World of Water: Rain, Rivers and Seas in Southeast Asian Histories*. Leiden: KLTV Press, pp. 27–70.

Talbot, Bryan. 2007. *Alice in Sunderland*. London: Jonathan Cape.

Tallantire, M. 2012. *Film of Bishop Justin's Installation*. Enthronement ceremony 26 November 2011.

Tvedt, T., and E. Jacobsson (eds). 2006. *A History of Water*. London: I.B. Tauris.

Vivieros de Castro, E. 2004. 'Exchanging Perspectives: The Transformation of Objects into Subjects in Amerindian Ontologies', *Common Knowledge* 10(3): 463–84.

Watson, I. 1988. *The Fire Worm*. London: Gollancz.

Wittfogel, K. 1957. *Oriental Despotism: A Comparative Study of Total Power*. New Haven, CT: Yale University Press.

13

The North Water

Life on the Ice Edge
in the High Arctic

Kirsten Hastrup

In this chapter, the North Water is the main character. It is the name of a so-called *polynya*, which is a patch of Arctic sea that is open for most of the year, if sometimes covered by a thin layer of ice in the midst of winter. The word is Russian and immediately suggests that there are more than one polynya in the Arctic seas, where they have formed particularly productive oceanic spaces in terms of primary biomass, crustaceans, fish, and a welter of birds and marine mammals higher up the food chain, all benefiting from the feeding and breathing space offered by the open water. The North Water polynya is situated between northwest Greenland and Ellesmere Land in Canada, where the abundance of game has attracted people to the region since prehistorical times. Even today, there is no way to approach the hunting community in northwest Greenland anthropologically without paying close attention to this natural resource space – by implication also a major social resource. My aim here is to show how the North Water has contributed to the configuration of social life in north-west Greenland. Although my emphasis is on the present community of hunters – increasingly circumscribed by the melting ice in its various forms – we shall also look back to previous times and earlier ethnographies.

Since 2007 I have been conducting a series of successive fieldworks in north-west Greenland, in the region known either as the Thule District or as Avanersuaq – Greenlandic for 'the Big North'. Due to its relative inaccessibility, the region has always been (more or less) isolated from the rest of Greenland, and it still seems a world apart, both from within and from without. While probably one-third of the about seven hundred people living in the district (most of them in the town of Qaanaaq) hail from more southerly parts of Greenland, most still consider themselves to be more or less distinct from the rest of the Greenlandic population, and they speak their own dialect. The former are often passing residents, serving temporarily as administrators, teachers, carpenters, health assistants, or something else, while the latter see themselves as hunters, descending from the old Thule People, identified by that name in the early twentieth century, when they numbered about two hundred and fifty according to contemporary sources (Gilberg 1976). Before that they had first entered into history through the work of John Ross (1819), who had succeeded in crossing the Melville Bay, and to his astonishment met a small group of people north of it. His was a very fleeting encounter, and it was through the extensive visits by Robert Peary, seeking a way to the North Pole from 1891 onwards, that these people were first described in detail (Peary 1898). Peary, too, numbered and named some two hundred and fifty people.

While still geographically apart, people in Avanersuaq are more obviously part of modern Greenland and of the global community now; they are very much part of a wider communicative space than ever before. Yet, the hunters are in many ways still hunters in the old style, using traditional technologies – dogs and sledges, kayaks, harpoons, and other self-made technologies that can easily be repaired with local materials. Modern technologies, such as mobile phones, GPS devices, and radio transmitters are embraced where they make sense. They generally do not when the hunters are on the ice, silently moving towards seals resting by their breathing holes, or approaching walruses lying on the ice edge, or paddling towards a narwhal spotted and pursued by kayak, so as not to scare it off by the noise of an engine.

The Arctic region, as such, is constituted with ice, and the Arctic peoples have been defined by their singularly efficient adaptation to the frosty regions and Arctic seas (Boas 1888; Mauss 1906; Hastrup 2013a, 2013b). Within that constitutive imagery, the ice has been ascribed with a social ontology (Krupnik et al. 2010; Bravo 2010). Having had the privilege of working with a High Arctic community in Greenland over the past years, I must admit to the sociality of the ice. As a hunting community, the Thule people depend totally on the ways and qualities of the ice. As the ice is now shrinking dramatically, the hunters have increasing difficulties in seeing themselves as such – except (soon) in the past tense. Here I shall address the question of how the North Water has configured and still configures social life in the High Arctic region, even if in evermore troubling ways. To prime the canvas, I shall start with some general observations on seawater ethnography.

Seawater Ethnography: Scaling the Social

As is appropriate, let me begin with a bow to one of the founders of Arctic anthropology. On the American side of the Baffin Bay, Franz Boas – later seen as the founder of American cultural anthropology – converted from the natural to the social sciences through his studies of the Arctic Sea. Boas was a student of physics and geography at the University of Kiel, and worked on a dissertation on the understanding of the colour of water (published 1881). Looking back on this work, Boas later wrote:

> In preparing my doctor's thesis I had to use photometric methods to compare intensities of light. This led me to consider the quantitative values of sensations. In the course of my investigation I learned to recognize that there are domains of our experience in which the concepts of quantity, of measures that can be added or subtracted like those with which I was accustomed to operate, are not applicable. (Boas 1938: 201)

The quality of seawater prompted Boas to consider new aspects of sensing and seeing (Stocking 1982: 142), and in many ways this probing became the backbone of his cultural relativist view on the peoples of the North (Helmreich 2011: 134). Before becoming an anthropologist, Boas moved from physics to geography, but after yet another trip to the Arctic, in 1883–84, he moved to anthropology – a relatively new subject at the time. The formative trip went to Baffin Island, where Boas' goal was to 'investigate the influence of environment on people's perceptions and their movements' (Lorini 1998: 1). Here, his interest gradually changed focus. In his own recollection, the experience was a decisive moment in his career: 'A year of life spent as an Eskimo among Eskimos had a profound influence upon the development of my views, not immediately, but because it led me away from my former interests and toward the desire to understand the behaviour of human beings' (Boas 1938: 201).

His was a fieldwork on ice as much as by the seawater; yet even – or maybe particularly – in its frozen form, the sea still shaped local life. In his diaries and letters, mostly addressed to his fiancée, Marie Krackovizer in New York, he wrote about his life with the ice in a forbidding climate. One of his primary wishes was to survey the eastern coast of Baffinland, and to study its impression upon human perception. I shall give you a quote, from 13 December 1883, where a polynya appears in the text. At first only the Eskimos went out hunting, but Boas eventually joined them (the mix of future, present and past tense verbs shows that the entry into the letter-diary was written en route – and could not be sent until later).

> Wilhelm [his valet!] and I will go north tomorrow morning to survey the coast further. We are coming to the water holes, which are kept open by the current and prevent us from going farther. As we were leaving the 3 Eskimos brought our sledge and dogs down the steep ice-foot face. At low tide the face drops steeply about 15', so everything has to be let down on lines.
> The fog hinders us greatly, but we advanced about 4 miles northward. When we came back Ssigna was busy chopping up food for the dogs, i.e. sawing up frozen seal meat, then chopping it into smaller pieces with an axe. Today it is –40° with a strong N wind. Itu and Tome were at the most northerly polynya and brought back 3 seals, whereas Ssigna has none. ...
> You see, Marie, here I am writing the same things on the pages of my journal and to you, since this is the only possibility of getting some information about my daily life to you. The igloo is too cold, so I do not write more than is absolutely necessary and if I wait a few days you will not learn what I am actually doing. So please accept these brief notes with the occasional words addressed specifically to you.
> Now, when we have been in the igloo for about 4 hours, it is warm enough to write something, though it is still not up to the freezing point, yet I feel quite comfortable. Feelings of what is pleasant and unpleasant are really quite relative. At home we would be infinitely sorry for somebody in our situation, yet here we are cheerful and in good spirits. (Franz Boas, 13 December 1883; in Müller-Wille 1998: 151–52)

On the following day, they head further north on a difficult ice foot, where Boas fell into the water, and where they made camp in –38°. 'Ssigna built an igloo and fortunately our meal was ready in 4½ hours' (ibid.: 152). What such passages reveal is the extent to which ethnography in the High North is formatted along with the experiences of cold and ice on the edge of the sea. What is also poignant is the use of the letter-diary addressed to Marie (which could not be sent except after long intervals, when the explorers visited a trading post) as a literary device, by means of which certain dominant figures emerge. Lorini has made the following observations:

> This literary device helped him [Boas] to face a long year in the Arctic among the Eskimo, a world in which water, in its various forms – the ocean, icebergs, rivers, the fog, igloos, etc. – was a metaphor for human struggles. Marie was the absent voice to whom a monologue of geographical, geological, and philosophical speculation was addressed. All Boas' activities, such as rowing Eskimo boats, driving sleds, hunting, eating raw frozen

meat, implied a relationship with water of various kinds ... Water, the most important element in of [sic] material life in the Arctic, provided food for the Eskimo (fish, seals) and for the German scientist who was living with them. (Lorini 1998: 2)

In between, Boas read Kant as an antidote to raw nature, and no doubt this also influenced his thinking about rationality and sensory experience. It has been suggested that for Boas, seawater became a 'theory machine' (Helmreich 2011: 134), and in the following I shall take this further in a sustained attempt at understanding the ways in which the North Water has impinged upon the hunters' lives by the ice edge.

For Boas, we note how his own first hunt at the ice edge made a very strong impression on him. On 14 February 1884, he wrote:

Today I went hunting for the first time, although not with brilliant success since the only [seal] I shot was carried under the ice by the current. I sat there just like the Eskimos at the water's edge behind my ice floe and waited patiently for a head to appear. You can't imagine what an impression it makes, to sit so near the open water at this cold time of the year, and to hear the roaring and rushing again. (Franz Boas 14 February 1884; in Müller-Wille 1998: 181)

While water in its many forms has implicitly shaped the ethnographies of the Arctic, as we understand from the quote above, the sociality of seawater has been understudied in the social sciences, because focus has been on the land, and on nations or villages located on *terra firma*. While this seems natural, the theory machine adopted here is designed at de-naturalizing the landlocked view of the world.

Oceanographers have recently argued that there is an urgent need for 'ocean literacy' by which they call for a deeper and more comprehensive 'understanding of the ocean's influence on you and your influence on the ocean' (Schoedinger et al. 2005: 736). Ocean literacy implies that we understand how the ocean influences weather and climate, how it supports a diversity of life, and how it is inextricably linked to human life. This is a good starting point for seawater ethnography. Boas provided a particular reading of the Arctic Ocean, but once we are alerted to the idea of encompassing the sea into our ethnographies, other examples spring to mind. Together, they enable us to explore the potential of ocean reading more generally, and to see how such reading may operate and produce particular scales of attention (Hastrup 2013d).

A fine example of ocean literacy in the sense I am advocating here (beyond oceanography as such) is found in Fernand Braudel's comprehensive analysis of life and politics around the Mediterranean in the sixteenth century (Braudel 1972). In the preface to this magnificent work Braudel writes:

> No simple biography beginning with date of birth can be written of this sea; no simple narrative of how things happened would be appropriate to its history. The Mediterranean is not even a *single* sea, it is a complex of seas; and these are broken up by islands, interrupted by peninsulas, ringed by intricate coastlines. Its life is linked to the land, its poetry more than half-rural, its sailors may turn peasant with the seasons; it is the sea of vineyards and olive trees just as much as the sea of the long-oared galleys and the roundships of merchants, and its history can be no more separated from the lands surrounding it than the clay can be separated from the hands of the potter who shapes it. (Braudel 1972: 17)

From this recognition of the deep connections between land and sea, peasants and sailors, Braudel moves on to show how the slow rhythm of rising and falling seas infiltrated the political development of the region, and suggests that historical conjunctures are deeply embedded in large-scale natural processes. In the same move, he demonstrates how natural processes had deep historical implications; some will know this from seeing or sensing the many ancient Roman cities along the Mediterranean coasts that are now submerged under water, and accessed only by ocean archaeologists – but sometimes also to be seen from coastal ramparts or piers.

It could be argued that the Mediterranean is a special case, being hemmed in by landforms and coastlines – but then all cases are special, and that is where history proves its mark. Specific studies from many of the major seas and societies of the planet all go to show how the historicity of the ocean stretches to the farthest shores. Thus we know now how Pacific islands emerged or disappeared as centuries passed by, and how they became populated or depopulated by brilliant navigators following the deep human instinct to move (Nunn 2007, 2009); and we know from the Arctic that coastlines have moved up and down, as did human habitation (Gulløv 2004).

Even while living on land, people rarely turn their backs to a nearby sea; rather, they explore and exploit it, cherish and dread it, navigate it and extract its hidden resources for consumption. Fishing is probably as old as humanity itself. Interestingly, fishing and fishermen have often been treated as an anomaly in anthropology, and seen mainly from the shore, as it were. 'The field' itself was defined by the land, and while the fishermen's organization was often studied, the ways in which the sea permeated social life, not only onboard but also on land, was under-explored. In anthropology itself, the sedentary view of society has reigned supreme for a long time; this has marginalized such people as migrants, navigators, and refugees from the proper world, until recently. It is tempting to briefly remind ourselves of the distinction between sedentary and nomadic landscapes, suggested by Deleuze and Guattari. The former rests upon a strong notion of territoriality and parcels out closed spaces to people, while the latter distributes people in an open and indefinite space (Deleuze and Guattari 2004: 420). Along with other social sciences, anthropology has generally sided with the sedentarist view, and resorted to what has been called a methodological nationalism. This is changing along with a less territorial view of the object of the social sciences, coming also with a new awareness of global connection (Hastrup and Olwig 2012).

With respect to ocean ethnographies, a recent example springs to mind, namely Katharina Schneider's (2012) succinct analysis of 'saltwater sociality' in Melanesia. She has studied a community of fishermen islanders living off a larger island, and shown how 'movement' is the predominant mode of objectifying social relations. It seems that they have taken their cue from both past and present movements at sea, from movements between their own tiny island and the main island, and not least from the indeterminate movements of fish, forming the basis of their economy. Schneider suggests that such movements should be seen as objects in their own right; it is not a simple analogy. This installs a certain fluidity into the objects, constantly changing form; as Schneider says:

> [the] definite form of a movement only becomes apparent as a movement is halted (and thus ceases to be a movement, until it starts and changes form again). Movements thus highlight the contingency of outcomes, and pose questions about the relation between single forms and the sequences of forms through which they appear, and that they might hold as a potential. (Schneider 2012: 21)

The crux of the matter, and the force of this example, lie with the ways in which the movable social forms and values, within the saltwater itself, and in exchange systems linking islands with one another and ultimately with the mainland and with the global market, permeate the sense of movable and shifting social relationships.

This substantiates Henri Lefebvre's view about spatial history, implying that space is both where a historical plot unfolds, and simultaneously constituted as a place by the history itself (Lefebvre 1991). The mutuality of space and history suggests that with changing perceptions of the oceanic space, the social relationships emerging from the sea are also changing. While before (to use an imprecise temporal form) fishermen, whalers, pirates and other sailors freely navigated the ocean and drew out natural riches from its depths, their movements were closely related to values on land. Even a brief glance on, for instance, the whalers, exploring and exploiting the Arctic seas in earlier centuries, will show that although they did make up very particular boat-communities – forever remembered in Herbert Melville's famous narrative of Moby Dick, in which he actually referred extensively to the work of the illustrious whaler and innovator William Scoresby who had modernized whaling in the Arctic in the eighteenth (Bravo 2006), adding scientific knowledge to his literary ethnography – it was mainly the European demand for whale oil, to fill the modern street lamps in London, that drove them out. Again, we sense the accordion of possible scalings attached to seawater ethnography. Local and global aspirations are in the same picture, and it is for the analyst to make that clear, in spite of any chosen perspective.

Since Melville's masterpiece saw light, both whaling and sailing have become circumscribed by international regulations, and fishing now is often literally a kind of farming, where hunting has become replaced by harvesting. On the basis of his work on Icelandic fishermen, Gísli Pálsson has suggested that the ocean has been turned into a 'virtual aquarium', pointing to the emergence of ocean management regimes that must be enclosed and partitioned (Pálsson 1998). The sea has become as territorialized as the land, divided by nations and regulated by laws of access and harvesting. This contains a paradox between the essential liquidity of the water itself, including of course its moving inhabitants and the floating fishing vessels, on the one hand, and the essential stability and territoriality related to national thinking on the other. The result is that the once so stable boundary between land and sea sociality is increasingly blurred, such as in the case of salmon and mussel farming (e.g. Lien and Law 2011); yet it is not simply an instance of extending sedentarist views to the sea, but also of incorporating the sea into the society in new ways. Sea farming not only creates new economic niches, but also contributes to a social reshaping of the relationship between nature and society, and to a dissolving of the opposition between land and water. Thus it actually adds momentum to the development of seawater ethnography.

To close this section on seawater ethnography, I simply want to stress that the sea scales social communities in multiple ways, supported by distinct perspectives that are far from fixed and certainly closely tied up with particular interests. This will be further substantiated when we move on now to north-west Greenland, where the community subsists mainly on access to marine mammals, not least by the semi-permanent edge between the ice and the sea at the North Water – an increasingly volatile part of the fabric of sociality.

The North Water Vernacular

Once we dive into a particular sea, be it Arctic or Mediterranean, and whether bounded by ice, land or imaginative boundaries, ocean reading becomes a matter of understanding a particular vernacular. Even though the North Water is one of several polynyas in the Arctic seas, it is still a very particular one when it comes to biological, and I would argue, social productivity. Polynyas allow for rapid growth of phytoplankton and become biological hotspots, sometimes seen as 'oases' in the sea (Thomsen 2000). Once the sea opens up, the water becomes warmer from the penetrating sun, the ice-algae bloom, and the production of zooplankton and benthic invertebrates – various organisms residing in the sediment at the bottom, including different species of crustaceans – takes off. From here the food chain moves upwards, through smaller and larger fish, and to marine mammals and seabirds feeding off the various smaller organisms. It is a complex system in which a number of lesser processes must not go wrong, lest the entire food chain breaks asunder. Natural scientists have documented the processes meticulously and shown how the openings and closures of the ice have major repercussions in the entire biotope on the edge, including seals, whales, walruses and polar bears – being the most cherished game of the hunters in Avanersuaq. Adding to the effect of the relative thickness of the ice is both the snow cover and the sea currents. Fascinating though the entanglement of these processes is, I cannot go deeper into it here, but simply note that the defining feature of the Arctic ecosystem for the past five million years has been the sea ice, including the permanent cap of multi-year ice on the Polar Sea, extending and retracting seasonally and over years. The sea ice has structured the Arctic ecosystems, and the polynyas have always been 'areas of high productivity where large numbers of marine birds and mammals congregate to feed' (Meier et al. 2012: 32).

Interestingly, most depictions of biological sea-ice communities do not have humans in the picture. In some cases people are simply added on, as consumers of the 'sea-ice system services', such as in the recent AMAP report. The changing sea ice alters its possible services (Meier et al. 2012: 52ff). While not wrong, the idea of sea-ice system services reflects a troubled notion of ecosystem services, which is at base a model for valuing natural processes in social (economic) terms, and which has remarkably little to add to an understanding of the natural/social entanglements in the Arctic (or elsewhere). We need a new degree of seawater literacy to unpack the implications of ecosystemic changes, in which the place of humans is acknowledged. People in the High Arctic might barely have survived were it not for the North Water being an almost self-refilling larder of meat and birds; in their turn, the hunters contributed to the balance (or imbalance) of the seawater resources.

As a permanent or recurring polynya, unlike some of the smaller occasional openings occurring closer to the shores – such as the ones observed by Boas along the coast of Baffinland – people could depend upon the regular ones, even if both kinds of openings were always susceptible to winds, sea currents and tides, not all of which could be predicted (Meier et al. 2012). At some points in time, whalers and explorers tolled heavily upon whales and walrus in particular, and with the slow reproduction of these species, the stable resource turned into a more liquid one.

Archaeologists have shown beyond doubt how in prehistoric times Greenland was populated from North America through several distinct waves of immigration across the narrow strait separating the lands (Gulløv 2004). Not only was it possible to walk over the sea ice between them, it was also possible to live fairly well from the riches of the polynya, in addition to which tidal cracks around stranded icebergs would also allow for seals, walruses and birds (Vibe 1950: 16). Polar bears that live from sea mammals also gain from such openings (Sørensen 2010: 33–34). Such observations testify both to the known prehistorical immigration route from North America to Greenland over the fast ice in Nares Strait, and to the expediency of open water for life on the edge of the world – in the classical Thule beyond the horizon (Hastrup 2007).

The North Water has fed the northernmost peoples on the globe, the people of the Thule District in Greenland, for thousands of years. It has served as an invaluable resource space for tiny groups of people who migrated from the northern coasts of Canada and into Greenland, and constituting diverse prehistoric Eskimo cultures that spread further south, settled and (later) disappeared, to be replaced by new people, new (prehistoric) cultures. In the nineteenth century, European whalers, who named the polynya, delighted in its reaches, whenever they could get so far north. Small wonder that a dominant figure in the oral tradition was the Mother of the Sea, who was in charge of the sea animals and the one to discharge them to the humans – the stories of whom were highly susceptible to local conditions and to particular hunting interests, including those of foreign whalers (Sonne 1990).

When, in 1903, the Danish polar traveller and recorder of Eskimo life, Knud Rasmussen, first came to the Thule District (only named so a little later, when he established the first trade station, and hence colonial presence in the NW region, in 1910), one of his feats was to document the last immigration into Greenland, having taken place in the 1860s (or possibly the 1880s) and led by the legendary Quillarssuaq. Rasmussen cites a man, Merqusaq, who was one of the few people from the 'great journey' left in Thule. The man tells Rasmussen how on the other side (in North America) many Eskimos lived, and that some thirty-eight people on ten sledges had been driven by curiosity (and Quillarssuaq's vision) to search for their rumoured kinsmen further east (in Greenland). The migrants were not lacking food, because the coasts were open and the game abundant. After two winters, five sledges turned back while five continued, urged on by Quillarssuaq who said that they were soon to reach the new land.

> Late in the spring we came to a place where the sea narrowed to a small channel. (before this we had crossed two very broad inlets of fjords). Here Qitdlarssuaq pitched camp and conjured spirits. His soul took an air-flight over the sea, while his body lay lifeless behind. When the incantation was over, he announced that it was here we were to cross the sea. On the other side we should meet with people. And all obeyed him, for they knew that he understood the hidden things.
> So we crossed the sea, which was frozen over, and camped on the opposite coast. There we found houses, human habitations, but no people. They had left the place. But we understood then that we had very little farther to go before meeting with people, and great joy filled us all; our veneration for the man who for years had led us towards the distant goal knew no bounds ... This was Etâ.
> While we were there, there was a cry one day of 'Sledges! sledges!' And we saw two sledges approaching, sledges from a strange people. And they saw us and drove up to us.
> They were people of the tribe [for whom] we had been looking for so long. The one man was called Arrutsak, the other Agîna, and their home was a place called Pitoravik, not far from where we were encamped. We shouted aloud with joy; for now we had found new country and new people. (Rasmussen 1908: 30–31)

This was the last time people migrated from North America to Greenland across the Nares Strait; the newcomers allegedly taught the people on the side of Etah (Etâ) a lot of things that they had never known, or had forgotten, or could no longer manufacture due to lack of the material needed, not least wood. 'And we taught them to build kayaks, and to hunt from kayaks. Before that they had only hunted on the ice, and had been obliged during the spring to catch as many seals, walruses, and narwhals as they would want for the summer, when the ice had gone'

(Rasmussen 1908: 32). Again, it was the polynya that had saved them and allowed them to survive under very severe ice conditions, because it allowed for ice edge hunting – and now with new kayaks, apparently a forgotten technology.

All available historical sources and archaeological finds testify to the significance of the polynyas as baselines in Inuit life and migration patterns in the High Arctic. Given the great variability in weather and winds that always characterize the Arctic, the recurrent polynyas played a major formative role in the making of society, because they were reasonably predictable (Sørensen 2012). It appears that the North Water was a reliable provider of food and, by implication, tent covers for summer dwellings, bedding, clothing, straps, and fodder for dogs. It made more or less permanent dwellings or at least recurrent returns to particular places possible in a nomadic landscape, where the social morphology was deeply marked by seasonality (Mauss 1906). Evidently, when climate and the ways of water change, social resilience is affected (Hastrup 2009a).

An important side effect of open waters and sea currents is the transportation of driftwood, the complexities of which are worth a note; as a trans-local resource it depends on natural transport by sea currents. Its value as a resource for the Arctic peoples not only depends on its origin, and hence the time spent in transport, but also very much on its kind – different species would soak up different amounts of water and would keep afloat for longer or shorter periods – and the degree of damage it has suffered in water and ice (Alix 2005). Even in the treeless expanses of the Arctic, wood was an essential resource, and we know for instance that the Yupiit of Alaska sang and danced for the return of driftwood in the spring as they did for salmon (Fienup-Riordan 1996: 153). The wood was used for utensils, house construction, tent poles, sledges and firewood. Knowledge of driftwood locations was as highly regarded as knowledge of good fishing grounds (Alix 2005: 84). Such knowledge depended on a degree of predictability, which again was a function of particular driftwood cycles, some of them very impressive.

When people migrated, which was an integral part of their survival (as noted already by Boas in 1888), part of the adaptation to new places was to locate stranding points for driftwood. Around the Baffin Bay, being at the tail end of cycles that originated both in North America and in Siberia, the transport time was long, and for the driftwood to survive as useable wood it had to be encapsulated in ice for the better part of the time, so as not to be destroyed by the water. Even so, the logs came in smaller fragments, and had lost most of their flexibility (Grønnow 1996; Alix 2005: 85). The archaeological record documents that driftwood in this region was not used for house construction, but for artefacts and tent poles (Mathiassen 1927: 128; Alix 2005: 85). What is more, the driftwood locations were unpredictable, not least because the ice would pack up for extensive periods of time. This was evident also in the materiality of their life. When John Ross met this group of Eskimos in 1818, he not only gave the first historical account of this people, 'believing themselves alone in the universe' (Ross 1819), he also brought one of their sledges back to British Museum, where it still testifies to the ingenuity of the people who, in lack of wood, replaced it with whalebones, ivory and hide. Even this had apparently become impossible a little later, because the pack ice also complicated access to whales.

When Mauss wrote about the Eskimos in the Thule District in 1906, he noted their extreme poverty. Summarizing the situation of these people on the basis of the works by Ross, Astrup and Rasmussen, Mauss concluded that the Eskimos at Smith Sound (as they were called until 1910) were in a miserable state; and he continues:

> The expansion of inland ice and the persistence of drifting ice throughout most of the year not only put an end to the arrival of driftwood but obstructed large whales, and made it impossible to hunt whales, walruses and seals in open waters. The bow, the kayak, the *umiak* [the women's boat] and most of the sleds disappeared because of a lack of wood. These unfortunate Eskimo were reduced to such circumstances that they retained merely the memory of their former technology. (Mauss 1979: 42–43)

Again, we note how the power of the ice, and the concomitant effect of limited access to open waters (and driftwood), circumscribes social life in the Thule District. The noticeable decline in living conditions, and the inability to renew the essential parts of the material culture, was not only a matter of limited game but very much of the near absence of wood for extended periods of time. With the advent of the (Danish) Thule Trading Station in 1910, the miserable (material) conditions were gradually lifted. Sledges and kayaks were restored, and they still play a central role in the hunting activities of the north.

Ocean Literacy under Threat

The noticeable changes in the sea ice that are now taking place are generally, so far at least, viewed as threats to life in the High Arctic. A major issue are the changes in the size and rhythm of the polynyas (ACIA 3: 66, 68; ACIA 12: 662). In Avanersuaq, the polar bear hunts take place mainly in April, along the northern edge of the North Water (Rosing-

Asvid 2002: 20). With the new openings of the ice, it is very difficult to get to this place from Qaanaaq. The sea ice will not carry the sledges so far, and the land route is next to impossible. Meanwhile, the polar bears are also left with fewer and more fragile platforms of sea ice from where to hunt for seals and fish. Thus they move on land, and every year now they show up quite close to the settlements and to people. Here they will often be shot as a measure of self-defence; otherwise strict quotas have been introduced in the region (Born 2005; Born et al. 2011).

The fragility of the ice platform, and the inaccessibility of old haunts has also severely affected the walrus hunt – a matter of pride and a token of abundance – which is further circumscribed by strict quotas, due to the limited stock. Walrus in particular suffer from changes in the benthic communities, but also from the fact that they are forced up onto land, where the young are more vulnerable, not least to hungry polar bears. Narwhal has always been the summer crop in the region. They are first taken by the ice edge, and later, when summer allows for a couple of months of open water, in the fjord. Recently, the catch has become difficult; the whales are confused by the new sea currents (the hunters say), and scared by the thunderous calving of the glaciers. Apparently, all the mammals are coming out of step with the surroundings, as is the rest of the sea-ice community at the upper end of the food chain. Adding to this are new political winds and geopolitical realities.

These winds blow a lot of vessels surveying marine resources into the Baffin Bay. It has recently been suggested, on the basis of careful observation and analysis, that the extensive seismic activity in the region may in fact have disturbed the narwhals (Heide-Jørgensen et al. 2013). The hunters I have talked to are in no doubt about something going wrong; they refer to the winter of 2009/10 as a major source of general uncertainty. Twice during the winter, they experienced *sassat* in the fjord. This refers to an entrapment of whales closed in by the ice and drowned. The hunters are concerned and so are biologists, who have established some correlation between seismic activity in Baffin Bay and the three most recent entrapment incidents in the general region, where a total of more than one thousand whales perished, including the two instances of *sassat* close to Qaanaaq just mentioned. The biologists write:

> Persistent disturbance of narwhals (and other acoustically sensitive Arctic species) could disrupt important behavior, cause the animals to abandon important summering areas, and change their migration patterns. As they leave their summering grounds, narwhals are generally heading towards winter feeding grounds, and disturbance could cause them either to return and risk ice entrapment or to move to areas that are sub-optimal for feeding. Considering that narwhals already appear to be approaching their physiological capacity and may have little flexibility to adjust their swimming and

diving behavior ... it seems critical that the whales are not disturbed to such an extent that their basic annual cycle is disrupted. (Heide-Jørgensen et al. 2013: 53)

The implications of the disrupted movement cycle of the narwhals in and around the North Water, are of course not only biological but also intrinsically social, the narwhal being the main (and almost only) cash crop for the hunters, who are suffering the consequences of submarine explorations.

Adding to the seismic noise, which is but one factor in the confusion among the sea animals, is an increasing number of minor earthquakes taking place in Greenland, where the thinning of the ice cap and the rising temperatures affect the rock bottom; these also create noise and increase the velocity of the glaciers. When these break off into the sea in unprecedented masses, it again affects the salinity of the water and the sub-surface soundscape. In short, the current changes in climate deeply affect the compound qualities of the resource space – which is rather different from a particular place or territory, as discussed above.

While, certainly, the North Water *centres* social life in the Thule region, and has done so for millennia, the *territory* in the Deleuzian sense has always been relatively unmarked. In the polar North the Inuit migrated, moved apart, regrouped, and exchanged news and kinsfolk as a matter of course. This in itself makes a huge difference from living within more confined spaces, where territory is closely related to boundaries, property rights, and other well-defined social relationships (Hastrup 2009b). Even though today most people of Avanersuaq live in the town of Qaanaaq, the North Water is still their main source of game, and as the hunters move about in pursuit of game wherever it takes them, they spend a lot of time at the ice edge – even though it is neither fixed nor stable. Their room for manoeuvring is shrinking, not only because of the melting ice, however, but also due to the international race towards the Polar Sea, precipitating new territorial interests. Somewhat paradoxically, with the opening of the ice, new boundaries are invented.

The opening means a revival of the old dream of a reliable North West Passage that would cut down transport time between East and West considerably; as ever, an open sea potentially forges new connections. Yet in the process, the dream of fossil fuel on the bottom of the Arctic seas has changed the context of the international Law of the Sea (UNCLOS), reshaping territorial interests in the process – quite apart from the territorial interests of narwhals and other species. It raises a rather fundamental question of how anybody can lay claim to own fluid forms (Strang 2011). The notion of the virtual aquarium has transformed into a notion of virtual territories, measured out as real.

While people in Qaanaaq may eventually profit from the increasing intensity of passage, and possibly find new avenues for making a living, they will also have to live with an ocean of disappearing game. Even if it is not actually disappearing or dying out, the hunt becomes circumscribed by international quotas, enforced to protect the individual (animal) species. Hunting may soon be a feature of the past. Already now, the hunters are all too aware that the intensifying traffic in the region, which includes large tourist cruise ships, severely affects the animal resources – and amplifies the effects of the breakdown of the age-old exchange between the deep sea, ice, animals and people of the North Water.

With this, we can also begin to see how far human and animal life are still infiltrated in one another and venture a more general statement about the co-constitution of species, which is one of the prominent questions on the edge of anthropology (Hastrup 2013a). Clearly, the primal domestication of animals contributed to the shaping of human society, as did the invention of agriculture in the Neolithic period. This is so much taken for granted that we have almost overlooked the fact that it signals a co-constitution of humans and animals, and of humans and grain. Multiple ethnographies of cattle breeders, herders and farmers have been written that implicitly testify to this fact, however the focus has remained on the singular human species and its immense powers of invention. A new multispecies ethnography has already been heralded (Kirksey and Helmreich 2010), and a notion of companion species has been suggested, positing animals as significant others (Haraway 2003, 2008). Animals, including sea mammals, are part of a shared social space, configuring a particular seawater sociality.

With the case of the North Water in mind, I would argue that within the bounds of social life, humans have endless, actual or potential, companion species, creating multiple – possible – social forms. This forces anthropology to rethink the fluid boundaries of its object. This is stressed also by new anthropological studies of microbial seas (Helmreich 2009), where oceanographers and biologists are currently discovering new oceanic realities and a new future for the system of scientific knowledge.

Closing the Argument: Water as Theory Machine

The historical and social implications of living on the edge between ice and sea are immense; there is no way in which we can deal with water as an abstraction (cf. Linton 2010). Life by the North Water makes a clear-cut case of the co-constitution of water and society, and the pervasive fluidity of the environment – stretching in all directions in time and space, undermining and/or creating territoriality in social practice. These years the water is opening up at increasing speed, the ice edge is becoming increasingly fragile, and the entire biotope is changing. The new race for the Polar Sea and its presumed riches in the form of oil runs right through the North Water and disturbs both animals and hunters, as do the new submarine currents. Focusing on the North Water itself has enabled us to see how it not only infiltrates people's lives and movements but also to scale it. By being in itself a fluid form, the North Water highlights the temporariness of social forms in the High Arctic and shows how in general it is impossible to think of an environment as external to the social. Nature is part of the infrastructure, one might say (cf. Carse 2012).

The general message is that water, including the North Water, is a powerful resource, not only for survival and production, but also for the configuring of particular social forms and social values. It has a profound existential meaning (Strang 2005); in addition to the existential meaning for humans, suggested by Strang, I would argue that a careful reading of the North Water (and other seas) shows the entangled socialities of all the different species, who are part of each other's resource space – crustaceans, fish, whales, walrus and humans. Ocean literacy opens up for a new way of understanding the complex co-constitution and mutuality of the species.

Seawater connects and disconnects, and when it freezes it may open up or close down particular passages or routes for people, animals, driftwood, tankers and other vessels. The vernacular of the North Water thus leads us back to the necessity of cultivating a new degree of ocean literacy. Helmreich has even suggested that we see current global trends in terms of a pervasive 'oceanization', already infiltrating our vocabularies (Helmreich 2011: 137), in some ways echoing Bauman's suggestion that our times are liquid. Water's imprint is everywhere – material, political and bio-political (Bauman 2007; cf. Bakker 2012).

I would argue (along with others) that the form of water we know as ice, but which is known by many more terms in the Arctic (see Krupnik et al. 2010), confirms this. Elsewhere, I have argued that ice may be seen as an argument (Hastrup 2013c). It is an argument that precipitates a particular story along, such as the story of changing life conditions around the North Water. It propels openings and closures alike – spatially, temporally, socially and theoretically. As Helmreich suggests in *Alien Ocean* (2009), once we enter into deep waters, we are bound to work athwart theory; in his case it implied reading anthropological and oceanic materials and theories through each other (Helmreich 2009: 23). 'Working athwart theory, I not only cross-wire ethnographic and marine microbiological theories (of, e.g., space, place and community) but also claim that such transverse, oblique, operations can produce compelling renderings of a real world' (ibid.).

As a theory machine, water thus fosters a new kind of interdisciplinarity, which likewise works athwart specialisms in Strathern's terms (Strathern 2005: 127). It involves an ability to consciously mix different kinds of knowledge, and assess and compare their epistemological claims. In fact, the fluid environments, which spring forth once we allow them to do so, demand to be taken seriously beyond established categories. The good news is that precisely because anthropologists are used to operating in between different epistemological modes, this kind of interdisciplinarity looks very much as a well-known method of lateral thinking – with water.

References

ACIA. 2005. *Arctic Climate Impact Assessment*. Cambridge: Cambridge University Press.

Alix C. 2005. 'Deciphering the Impact of Change on the Driftwood Cycle: Contribution to the Study of Human Use of Wood in the Arctic', *Global and Planetary Change* 47: 83–98.

AMAP. 2012. 'Snow, Water, Ice and Permafrost in the Arctic (SWIPA): Climate Change and the Cryosphere'. Oslo: Arctic Monitoring and Assessment Programme.

Bakker, K. 2012. 'Water: Political, Biopolitical, Material', *Social Studies of Science* 42(4): 616–23.

Bauman, Z. 2007. *Liquid Times: Living in an Age of Uncertainty*. Cambridge: Polity Press.

Boas, F. (1888) 1964. *The Central Eskimo*. Lincoln, NE and London: The University of Nebraska Press.

———. 1938. 'An Anthropologist's Credo', *Nation* 147(6): 201–4.

Born, E.W. 2005. *An Assessment of the Effects of Hunting and Climate on Walruses in Greenland*. Oslo: Natural History Museum, University of Oslo.

Born, E.W., et al. 2011. 'Polar Bears in Northwest Greenland. An Interview Survey about the Catch and the Climate'. Copenhagen: Museum Tusculanum Press (MoG).

Braudel, F. 1972. *The Mediterranean, and the Mediterranean World in the Age of Philip II* (translated by S. Reynolds). London: Collins.

Bravo, M.T. 2006. 'Geographies of Exploration and Improvement: William Scoresby and Arctic Whaling, 1782–1828', *Journal of Historical Geography* 32: 512–38.

———. 2010. 'Epilogue: The Humanism of Sea Ice', in I. Krupnik et al., *SIKU: Knowing Our Ice. Documenting Inuit Sea-Ice Knowledge and Use*. New York: Springer, pp. 445–52.

Carse, A. 2012. 'Nature as Infrastructure: Making and Managing the Panama Canal Watershed', *Social Studies of Science* 42(4): 539–63.
Deleuze, G., and F. Guattari. 2004. *A Thousand Plateaus: Capitalism and Schizophrenia* (transl. by Brian Massumi). London and New York: Continuum.
Fienup-Riordan, A. 1996. *The Living Tradition of Yup'ik Masks: Agayuliyararput, Our Way of Making Prayer.* Seattle: University of Washington Press.
Gilberg, R. 1976. *The Polar Eskimo Population, Thule District, North Greenland.* Copenhagen: Nyt Nordisk Forlag Arnold Busck (Meddelelser om Grønland, 203/3).
Grønnow, B. 1996. 'Driftwood and Saqqaaq Culture Woodworking in West Greenland', in B. Jacobsen, C. Andreasen and J. Rygaard (eds), *Cultural and Social Research in Greenland, 96/96: Essays in Honour of Robert Petersen.* Nuuk: Ilisimatusarfik/ Atuakkiorfik, pp. 73–89.
Gulløv, H.C. 2004 ed. *Grønlands Forhistorie.* Copenhagen: Gyldendal.
Haraway, D. 2003. *A Companion Species Manifesto: Dogs, People, and Significant Otherness.* Chicago: Prickly Paradigm.
———. 2008. *When Species Meet.* Minneapolis: University of Minnesota Press.
Hastrup, K. 2009a. 'Waterworlds: Framing the Question of Social Resilience', in K. Hastrup (ed.), *The Question of Resilience: Social Responses to Climate Change.* Copenhagen: The Royal Danish Academy of Sciences and Letters, pp. 11–30.
———. 2009b. 'The Nomadic Landscape. People in a Changing Arctic Environment'. *Danish Journal of Geography* 109 (2): 181-189.
———. 2013a. 'Introduction: Anthropology on the Edge', in K. Hastrup (ed.), *Anthropology and Nature.* London and New York: Routledge, pp. 1–26.
———. 2013b. 'Of Maps and Men: Making Places and People in the Arctic', in K. Hastrup (ed.), *Anthropology and Nature.* London and New York: Routledge, pp. 211–32.
———. 2013c. 'The Ice as Argument', *Cambridge Anthropology* 31(1): 52–68.
———. 2013d. 'Scales of Attention in Fieldwork: Global Connections and Local Concerns in the Arctic', *Ethnography* 14(2): 145–64.
Hastrup K., and K.F. Olwig (eds). 2012. *Climate Change and Human Mobility: Global Challenges to the Social Sciences.* Cambridge: Cambridge University Press.
Heide-Jørgensen, M.P., et al. 2013. 'Narwhals and Seismic Exploration: Is Seismic Noise Increasing the Risk of Ice Entrapments?' *Biological Conservation* 158: 50–54.
Helmreich, S. 2009. *Alien Ocean: Anthropological Voyages in Microbial Seas.* Berkeley: University of California Press.
———. 2011. 'Nature/Culture/Seawater', *American Anthropologist* 113(1): 132–44.
Kirksey, S.E., and S. Helmreich. 2010. 'The Emergence of Multispecies Ethnography', *Cultural Anthropology* 25(4): 545–76.
Krupnik, I., et al. 2010. *SIKU: Knowing Our Ice. Documenting Inuit Sea-Ice Knowledge and Use.* New York: Springer.
Lefebvre, L. 1991. *The Production of Space* (translated by D. Nicholson-Smith). Oxford: Blackwell.
Lien, M.E., and J. Law. 2011. '"Emergent Aliens": On Salmon, Nature, and Their Enactment', *Ethnos* 76(1): 65–87.
Linton, J. 2010. *What is Water? The History of a Modern Abstraction.* Vancouver and Toronto: University of British Columbia Press.

Lorini, A. 1998. 'The Cultural Wilderness of Canadian Water in the Ethnography of Franz Boas', *Cromohs* 3: 1–7.

Mathiassen, T. 1927. 'Archaeology of the Central Eskimos II: The Thule Culture and its Position within the Eskimo Culture'. Report of the Fifth Thule Expedition 1921–24, 4(2). Copenhagen: Gyldendal.

Mauss, M. (1906) 1979. *Seasonal Variations of the Eskimo: A Study in Social Morphology* (with H. Beuchat; trans. J.J. Fox). London: Routledge and Kegan Paul.

Meier, W.N., et al. 2011. 'Sea Ice', in AMAP 2012. *Snow, Water, Ice and Permafrost in the Arctic (SWIPA): Climate Change and the Cryosphere*. Oslo: Arctic Monitoring and Assessment Programme (AMAP), Chapter 9 (9.1–9.87).

Müller-Wille, L. (ed.). 1998. *Franz Boas among the Inuit of Baffin Island, 1883–84: Journals and Letters*, edited and introduced by Ludger Müller-Wille; translated by William Barr. Toronto: University of Toronto Press.

Nunn, P.D. 2007. *Climate, Environment and Society in the Pacific during the Last Millennium*. Amsterdam: Elsevier.

———. 2009. *Vanished Islands and Hidden Continents of the Pacific*. Honolulu: University of Hawai'i Press.

Pálsson, G. 1998. 'The Virtual Aquarium: Commodity Fiction and Cod Fishing', *Ecological Economics* 24: 275–88.

Peary, R. E. 1898. *Northward over the "Great Ice". A Narrative of Life and Work along the Shores and upon the Interior Ice-cap of Northern Greenland in the Years 1886 and 1891-1897*. London: Methuen & Co.

Rasmussen, K. 1908. *The People of the Polar North. A Record* (Compiled from the Danish Originals and edited by G. Herring). London: Kegan Paul, Trench, Trübner & Co. Ltd.

Rosing-Asvid, Q. 2002. *The Polar Bear Hunt in Greenland*. Nuuk: Greenland Institute of Natural Resources. Technical Report No. 45.

Ross, J. 1819. *Voyage of Discovery, made under the orders of Admiralty, in his Majesty's ships Isabelle and Alexander, for the Purpose of Exploring Baffin's Bay, and inquiring into the probability of a North-West Passage*. London: John Murray.

Schneider, K. 2012. *Saltwater Sociality: A Melanesian Island Ethnography*. Oxford: Berghahn Books.

Schoedinger, S., et al. 2005. 'Ocean Literary through Science Standards'. *Oceans*, Proceedings of the MTS/IEE, Vol. 1: 736–40

Sonne, B. 1990. *The Acculturative Role of Sea Woman: Early Contact Relations between Inuit and Whites as Revealed in the Origin Myth of Sea Woman*. Copenhagen: Meddelelser om Grønland, Man & Society, vol. 13.

Sørensen, M. 2010. *The Archaeology of Old Nuulliit. Eigil Knuth's Investigations in the Thule Region, North Greenland, 1952–1990*. Copenhagen: Museum Tusculanum Press (Monographs on Greenland, vol. 349).

———. 2012. 'Inuit and Climate Change in Prehistoric Eastern Arctic: A Perspective from Greenland', in K. Hastrup and K.F. Olwig (eds), *Climate Change and Human Mobility: Global Challenges to the Social Sciences*. Cambridge: Cambridge University Press, pp. 35–57.

Stocking, G.W. (1968) 1982. 'From Physics to Ethnology', in *Race, Culture and Evolution: Essays in the History of Anthropology* (with a new Preface). Chicago: University of Chicago Press, pp. 133–60.
Strang, V. 2005. 'Common Senses: Water, Sensory Experiences and the Generation of Meaning', *Journal of Material Culture* 10(1): 92–120.
Strang, V., and M. Busse (eds). 2011. *Ownership and Appropriation*. Oxford: Berg Publishers.
Strathern, M. 2005. 'Anthropology and Interdisciplinarity', *Arts and Humanities in Higher Education* 4: 125–35.
Thomsen, H.A. 2000. 'Polynier – "Oaser" i Højarktis', in B.H. Jakobsen et al. (eds), *Topografisk Atlas Grønland*. Copenhagen: Det Kongelige Danske Geografiske Selskab & Kort og Matrikelstyrelsen, pp. 94–97.
Vibe, C. 1950. *The Marine Mammals and the Marine Fauna in the Thule District (Northwest Greenland) with Observations on Ice Conditions in 1939–41*. Copenhagen: Meddelelser om Grønland, vol. 150.

NOTES ON CONTRIBUTORS

Astrid Oberborbeck Andersen has a Ph.D. in anthropology from the University of Copenhagen, and was affiliated with the research project 'Waterworlds', exploring how water is enacted in multiple ways along the urban waterscape in Arequipa in arid southern Peru. Andersen is currently a postdoc at the Department of Anthropology, University of Copenhagen.

Brian Dowd-Uribe is assistant professor in the International Studies Department, University of San Francisco. Formerly he was a postdoctoral research scientist at Columbia University, and then assistant professor at the University for Peace. He conducts applied interdisciplinary research at the nexus of food, water and agricultural policy in Burkina Faso and Costa Rica.

Frida Hastrup is associate professor at the Saxo Institute, Ethnology Section, University of Copenhagen. Hastrup was a postdoc in the research project 'Waterworlds', and has conducted fieldwork in coastal south India; her publications on this include a monograph entitled *Weathering the World: Recovery in the Wake of the Tsunami in a Tamil Fishing Village* (Berghahn Books 2011). Currently, she is the research leader of a collaborative research project on natural resources, focusing on how these travel, are valuated and quantified through diverse practices.

Kirsten Hastrup is professor of anthropology at the University of Copenhagen. She received an ERC Advanced Grant for the collaborative research project 'Waterworlds' (2009–2014). She has worked intensively with the entwinement of the long-term natural and social histories in

Iceland, from the Medieval Warm Period, through the Little Ice Age, and up until the present; this work has been published by Oxford University Press in three monographs. In more recent years, she has worked with a hunting community in High Arctic Greenland, facing unpredictable environmental changes.

Richard D.G. Irvine is a lecturer in Social Anthropology at the University of Cambridge, with an interest in the moral and temporal dimensions of environmental change. His current ethnographic and historical research takes as its focus a particular British landscape, the East Anglian fenlands. He explores how wetland is enclosed as a resource and examines the politics surrounding the kind of resource that it becomes. He is currently research coordinator for the AHRC funded project "Pathways to understanding the changing climate: time and place in cultural learning about the environment".

Mette Fog Olwig is assistant professor in international development studies at Roskilde University. She did her Ph.D. in geography while affiliated with the research project 'Waterworlds', focusing on floods in Ghana. Her research applies a multi-sited, multi-level perspective on the social dimensions of climate change and development.

Ben Orlove is professor of anthropology at Columbia University, New York, and co-director of the Center for Research on Environmental Decisions at the Earth Institute of Columbia University. He has published widely on environmental issues; among them are *Lines in the Water: Nature and Culture at Lake Titacaca* (2002); *Weather, Culture and Climate* (co-edited with Sara Strauss, 2003); and *Darkening Peaks: Glacier Retreat, Science and Society* (co-edited with E. Wiegandt and B.H. Luckman, 2008).

Mattias Borg Rasmussen was a Ph.D. within the research project 'Waterworlds'. Based on long-term fieldwork in highland Peru, he has explored questions of environmental change, local resource governance and state–citizen relations in poor peasant communities. He is currently an assistant professor at the University of Copenhagen.

Laura Vang Rasmussen has a Ph.D. in geography, and is currently (2015) a postdoc at the School of Natural Resources and Environment, University of Michigan. Her research focused on land use changes in the Sahelian drylands of Africa.

Anette Reenberg is professor emeritus of geography at the University of Copenhagen. She has been involved in the Waterworlds project as a senior researcher, primarily engaged with the dryland pillar of the project. She has almost thirty years of field experience in human–environmental interactions in the Sahelian region of West Africa, notably in Burkina Faso and Niger. Lately, she has led a project involving African colleagues about the triple exposure of land use systems to globalization, climate variations and population pressure, which complement her work in Waterworlds (see www.lasyresahel.ku.dk).

Maria Louise Bønnelykke Robertson holds a Ph.D. from the University of Copenhagen, and was affiliated with the research project 'Waterworlds'. She is an environmental anthropologist with a multidisciplinary profile and extensive fieldwork experience from Kiribati in the Central Pacific, and she has collaborated with engineers, natural scientists and designers in solving problems in the private and the public sectors.

Carla Roncoli is a Senior Research Scientist in the Department of Anthropology and Associate Director of the Master's in Development Practice at Emory University. For the last 20 years, she has worked with interdisciplinary research programs exploring the intersections of climate, environment, agriculture, and livelihoods in Africa. She has published extensively in scholarly journals and advised development agencies on climate risk management.

Cecilie Rubow is associate professor at the Department of Anthropology, University of Copenhagen. As a senior researcher at the research centre 'Waterworlds' she has focused on social and metaphysical aspects of environmental change in coastal areas of the Cook Islands. In particular, she has been working with questions of climate projections, changing sea levels and cyclones in the nexus between climate sciences, governmental agencies, various types of expert knowledge, and local residents on the main island Rarotonga.

Astrid Bredholt Stensrud has a Ph.D. in social anthropology from the University of Oslo. Stensrud has done extensive fieldwork in the southern Peruvian Andes and was a postdoc in the research project 'From Ice to Stone', affiliated with Waterworlds, at the Department of Anthropology, University of Copenhagen. Stensrud is currently a postdoc at the Department of Social Anthropology, University of Oslo, as part of the ERC-funded research project 'Overheating: The Three Crises of Globalization'.

Veronica Strang is professor of anthropology, and executive director of the Institute of Advanced Study at the University of Durham, UK. Her books include *The Meaning of Water* (2004), *Gardening the World: agency, identity and the ownership of water* (2009) and *Water: culture and nature* (2015). Her work is interdisciplinary: as well as conducting ethnographic fieldwork in Australia, the UK and New Zealand, she has worked collaboratively with philosophers (in a project 'Thinking With Water'), and with archaeologists, cognitive scientists and psychologists on materiality and meaning. She is currently drawing on history, archaeology, ethnography and theology in an internationally comparative project examining religious cosmologies, water beings, and the long-term development of diverse human-environmental trajectories.

Christian Vium was a Ph.D. within the 'Waterworlds' research project, working on water scarcity in the Islamic Republic of Mauritania. Vium is currently a postdoc at the University of Aarhus, within the project 'Camera as Cultural Critique'. Photography and film are integral parts of Vium's methodological and analytical approach.

INDEX

adaptation, 94, 117–18, 121, 123, 198, 200, 280, 290
adaptive strategies, 189
Adger, W. Neil, 111, 112
agricultural encroachment, 194
agriculture, 32–34, 41, 54–60, 88, 116, 146, 152, 167, 190, 193, 195–99, 206, 255, 294
agroforestry products, 195
aid, 55–56, 111, 120, 124, 130
Andes, 17, 75, 203
Anthropocene, 1–3, 7, 12–13
anticipation, 3, 83, 211, 214
apocalypse, 107
arable farming, 24, 32–35, 37–38
Arctic ecosystem, 287
Arequipa, 76, 162
Asian tsunami, 5, 129, 134
Assabiyya, 222, 232–36
atoll, 18, 141–55
Avanersuaq, 279–80, 291

Badia, 228–36
Banfora, 54–67, 73
Bateson, Gregory, 15
Bauman, Zygmunt, 5–6, 13, 80, 295
Bay of Bengal, 18, 129, 135
Boas, Franz, 281–83,
boreholes, 193–94

Braudel, Fernand, 283–84
bridging effects, 121
bureaucracy, 132, 139
Burkina Faso, 17, 46, 110, 189

carnival, 162–81
Charney hypothesis, 113, 117
Chicago School, 165
christianity, 104, 214, 249–65, 275
citizenship, 17, 70–72, 134, 137, 210
CLE. *See* Comités Locaux de l'Eau
climate change, 68, 76, 80–81, 83, 89, 94, 97, 105–7, 111–25, 157–58, 162, 186, 211–16
climate change narratives, 18, 121–4
climate forecasts, 46, 69
climate variability, 115–16, 187, 198
collective property, 222–25, 234
colonialism, 14, 29, 273
Comités Locaux de l'Eau, 52
common property, 228
Comoé River, 52–64
Compaoré, Blaise, 51
complexity, 65, 104, 177, 180, 198
conservation, 33–37, 40–41, 137
context, the construction of, 213
controversy, 142–48
Crapanzano, Vincent, 101–2
crisis discourse, 111, 122–24

crisis narrative, 122–24
critical description, 7, 12
crop yield, 151
cultural norms, 190

damming, 36, 60
dam-building, 48
Das, Veena, 5
decentralization, 46
decreasing yield, 155
deforestation, 112, 118–20, 123
desertification, 113
development intervention, 123–24
development sector, 111, 116, 125
Diffa province, 195
disaster, 4, 5, 7, 119–22, 134, 191–92, 214, 226, 235
discourse analysis, 111
dragon, 247–76 (*See also* serpent, water being)
drainage, 24–39, 189
driftwood, 290, 291, 295
drought, 18, 79, 110–23, 152–54, 184–99, 221–37

ecological crisis, 1, 105
ecosystem services, 287
eco-theology, 105
enactment, 138, 147–59, 169–70, 175–76
engineers, 25, 33, 76, 146–52, 168, 174, 177, 203, 215
entitlements, 17, 46
environment, 77, 81–83, 86–89, 94–101, 104–5, 123, 295–96
environmental challenges, 9
environmental ethics, 94, 107
environmental management, 118, 123
environmental narratives, 34, 111, 121, 125
equity, 50–51, 186, 208, 210
ethnographic moment, 3
European expansion, 14
evaporation, 57, 146–47, 188, 199

famine, 47, 48, 113–14, 152

farming, 24, 35, 38, 76, 123, 185–86, 286
fauna, 32, 40
Ferguson, James, 112, 124
Ferlo region, 193–94
fishermen, 131
flood, flooding, 27, 116–17, 120
fluidity, 20, 76
fossil water, 188
fresh water, 6, 18, 50, 146–49, 191
futures, 204, 216

Gell, Alfred, 206, 216
Ghana, 49, 73, 110–24
Ghyben-Herzberg Lens, 144
glaciers, 4, 75–88, 168, 204–9, 292–93
Global South, 122–23, 186
global warming, 4, 75–81, 94, 106–7, 123, 168, 204
governance, 17, 18, 46–51, 64–72, 133, 139, 162, 170–74, 186, 204, 216, 254, 260
governmental organizations (GOs), 117
Greenland, 279–80, 288
groundwater, 18, 19, 23, 141, 184
groundwater recharge, 197

Haddon, Alfred C., 8–10, 14–16
Hardin, Garrett, 122, 242
health, 26, 51, 149, 198, 230, 252, 280
Helmreich, Stefan, 7, 13, 141, 295
holy wells, 258
human agency, 204
human-environmental relations, 164, 249, 253–57, 268, 272
Hurricane Katrina, 5
hybrid forums, 149–50
Hydra, 256, 267
hydro-climatic variability, 184
hydrological cycle, 75
hydrology, 6, 167, 171, 197, 257

Ibn Khaldún, 234–35
illness, 81–82
imaginary, 5, 101, 214

immanent transcendence, 94, 100–102
infrastructure, 11, 145, 154, 168–81, 209, 226–27, 295
Ingold, Tim, 101–2, 175, 178, 206–7, 253
Integrated Water Resources Management (IWRM), 48–52
interdisciplinarity, 296
interdisciplinary encounters, 7, 12, 17, 18
International Commission on Large Dams, 49
irrigated agriculture, 196
irrigation, 7, 19, 48–49, 54, 56, 59, 76–78, 163, 168, 170, 178, 193, 203, 255, 268
Islamic law, 227–28, 232, 236

Jørgensen, Dorthe, 102

Kafondo, Michel, 51
Karfiguela, 55–72
Kern, Stephen, 4
Kiribati, 141

land degradation, 105, 112–14, 123
land use, 36, 56, 115, 145, 185, 192, 195, 198
land use changes, 115
landowners, 25, 37–38, 145, 150–56, 209
landscape, 23, 55, 76, 93–94, 101–107, 165–66, 206–14, 221, 285
Latour, Bruno, 85, 149, 151
Leach, Melissa and Robin Mearns, 111–12, 121
Lefebvre, Henri, 285
legitimacy, 149, 176, 208, 210
Leviathan, 256, 274–75
liquid fear, 5–6
liquid worlds, 3, 6, 17
Little Ice Age, 10, 11
Locke, John, 29, 39–40

MacDougall, W., 8
Mami Water being, 251

mapping, 18, 76, 162
maps, 27, 28, 164
material properties, 19, 31, 250–51, 257, 273
materiality, 7, 18, 76, 164, 168–69, 178, 207, 216, 266, 291
Mauritania, 194, 219
Mauss, Marcel, 291
measurement, 47, 77, 84–85, 142, 153, 174, 196
Medieval Warm Period, 10–11
Mediterranean, the, 256, 283–84
Melville, Herbert, 286
modernity, 5, 14, 16
Møhl, Perle, 165
Mol, Annemarie, 138, 143, 239, 242
monotheism, 268, 272
monsters, 250, 256
mountains, 82, 86, 88, 101
multiplicity, 76, 142–43, 180
multispecies ethnography, 294
Munn, Nancy, 207
Myers, C. S., 8

narrative disconnect, 112
narwhal hunt, 292–93
National Trust, 34, 37–39
natron excavation, 195
nature religions, 249, 254–72
nature, 99–100
Neo-Malthusian narratives, 112, 121
Neo-Malthusian environmentalism, 121
NGOs, 51, 53, 113, 117, 121–24, 129, 170, 212
Niger River, 52
nomads, 221, 228
nomadic landscape, 221–22
nomadic pastoralists, 223, 230–32
nomadism, 228
non-human agents, 12, 180
non-human beings, 76, 89, 273
non-human life, 7, 10, 255
non-humans, 12–13, 89, 145, 165, 253
North Water vernacular, 287–95
North West Passage, 293
Nunn, Patrick, 10, 99

Index

oasis, 195
ocean literacy, 283, 291, 295
ontological practice, 82
other-than-human beings, 18, 86, 88
Oualata, 219–30
Oudalan province, 114, 189

Pacific Basin, 11
Pacific Ocean, 10–11, 18, 93, 141
paganism, 265, 272, 275
Pandian, Anand, 137
pastoral mobility, 193, 226, 237
pastoral production, 189, 194
peat, 23–27, 31–32, 40
Peru, 18, 19, 75, 162, 203
plant growth, 188
plantations, 14, 27, 54, 58, 67
polar bear hunt, 291–92
Polynya, 279–95
precipitation, 18, 23, 59, 62, 77–80, 84, 113–15, 144, 174, 187, 193, 211, 219
private property, 29, 227
property, 226, 235–38
property laws, 227
property regime, 223, 227–28, 238, 254
property rights, 19, 48, 227, 293

Quillarssuaq, 289

rain, 17, 18, 75, 110, 170, 184, 205, 225
rainbow serpents, 251, 254
rainfall, 52, 59, 68, 110, 146, 153, 174, 187
rainstorm, 191
rainwater, 145, 168, 189
Ramadan, 69
Rasmussen, Knud, 288–89
Recuay, 203–16
relational worlds, 88
religion, 94–107, 233, 249–72
resonance, 206
resource mismanagement, 110–11, 120–21

rhythms, 206–7
rice, 46, 53, 55, 191, 199
Rio Conference on Environment and Development, 50
rising sea levels, 41, 106
ritual, 75, 86–88, 254
Rivers, W. H., 8–9, 16
Roe, Emery, 112, 124–25
Ross, John, 280, 291
Royal Society for the Protection of Birds, 36

Sahara, 221
Sahel, 19, 58, 68, 110, 184, 220
saltwater sociality, 10, 285
Sankara, Thomas, 51
scaling, 20, 76, 85, 281, 286, 295
scenarios, 83, 112, 125, 214
Schneider, Katharina, 10, 285
Science and technology Studies, 46, 138, 143, 148, 165, 237
sea-ice community, 287, 292
seasonality, 18, 75–76, 211, 216, 290
seasons, 75, 206, 216
seawater, 86, 146
seawater ethnography, 281
seawater literacy, 288
seawater sociality, 294
seismic noise, 293
Seligman, C. G., 8
Sen, Amartya, 47
serpent, 19, 247 (*see also* dragon, water being)
South East India, 129s
springs, 82, 86
Strang, Veronica, 6, 19, 87, 142, 150, 166
Strathern, Marilyn, 139, 296
STS, *See* Science and Technology Studies
sugar, 33, 46, 54, 66, 195
sustainable yield, 146

Tamil Nadu, 129
Tamil Nadu government, 131, 134
Taniwha, 251, 254

Tarawa, 141
taskscape, 206
Taylor, Charles, 5
temporality, 206, 213
temporalizing practices, 210–16
territory/territoriality/territorialisation, 285, 293
Thule, 279–96
Thule District, 279–96
Thule trading station, 289, 291
time-map, 207, 215–16
timing, 84–85, 211, 225
Titanic, 3–5
Todas, the, 16
Torres Strait Expedition, 8–9, 16
toukoussou, 231–38
traditional knowledge, 190, 198
transpiration, 146
Tsing, Anna, 7, 12, 137
Turnbull, David, 14–15, 165

unbounded socialities, 12, 17, 19
uncertainties, 2, 5, 80, 89, 94, 147
UNCLOS, 293
Upper Comoé, 46, 53

valuing water, 47, 163, 186
vandalism, 144
violence, 5, 67–68, 267
virtual aquarium, 286, 293
Volta River, 52
vulnerability, 187, 192

waiting, 211, 224
walrus hunt, 292

waste, 29, 31–40
water availability, 168–74, 188, 198, 210–16
water beings, 247 (*see also* dragon, serpent)
water budget, 147
water legislation, 145, 171
water literacy, 19, 185
water management, 46, 51, 142, 162, 204, 222, 226
water regime, 48, 22, 226–28
water reserve, 144, 150, 156
water scarcity, 50, 68, 162, 176, 184, 198, 210, 221–23, 237
water sustainability, 186, 198–99
water table, 38, 144, 151, 188, 195–97
water use strategies, 185–86, 199
water, potable, 144, 150, 168–76
water–agriculture nexus, 198
waterscape, 18, 23, 164, 182, 253, 266
weather, 13, 68, 75, 77, 117, 134, 186, 204–6, 211, 283, 290
wells, 19, 145, 155, 189, 194–97, 219–40, 258
West Africa, 18, 46, 110, 188
whalers, 286, 288,
Whatmore, Sarah, 11
wind, 24, 38, 79, 89, 95, 131–39, 204–6, 282, 288, 290
World Commission on Dams, 50
worlding, 3, 6
world-making practices, 139
worm, 19, 247

www.ingramcontent.com/pod-product-compliance
Lightning Source LLC
Chambersburg PA
CBHW070910030426
42336CB00014BA/2349